T0336709

Technology as a Tool for Diversity Leadership:

Implementation and Future Implications

Joél Lewis
University of South Alabama, USA

André Green
University of South Alabama, USA

Daniel Surry
University of South Alabama, USA

Information Science
REFERENCE

Managing Director:	Lindsay Johnston
Editorial Director:	Joel Gamon
Book Production Manager:	Jennifer Yoder
Publishing Systems Analyst:	Adrienne Freeland
Development Editor:	Myla Merkel
Assistant Acquisitions Editor:	Kayla Wolfe
Typesetter:	Deanna Jo Zombro
Cover Design:	Jason Mull

Published in the United States of America by
Information Science Reference (an imprint of IGI Global)
701 E. Chocolate Avenue
Hershey PA 17033
Tel: 717-533-8845
Fax: 717-533-8661
E-mail: cust@igi-global.com
Web site: http://www.igi-global.com

Library of Congress Cataloging-in-Publication Data

Technology as a tool for diversity leadership : implementation and future implications / Joel P. Lewis, Andre M. Green, and Daniel W. Surry, editors.
     p. cm.
 Includes bibliographical references and index.
 Summary: "This book focuses on the technological connection between diversity leadership and the focus on inclusivity, evolvement and communication to meet the needs of multicultural environments"-- Provided by publisher.
  ISBN 978-1-4666-2668-3 (hardcover) -- ISBN 978-1-4666-2699-7 (ebook) -- ISBN 978-1-4666-2730-7 (print & perpetual access) 1. Diversity in the workplace--Management. 2. Leadership. 3. Technological innovations. I. Lewis, Joel P., 1975- II. Green, Andre M., 1973- III. Surry, Daniel W., 1962-
  HF5549.5.M5T43 2013
  658.3008--dc23
                              2012033553

British Cataloguing in Publication Data
A Cataloguing in Publication record for this book is available from the British Library.

All work contributed to this book is new, previously-unpublished material. The views expressed in this book are those of the authors, but not necessarily of the publisher.

Table of Contents

Section 1
Introduction to Diversity Leadership

Section 2
Diversity Leadership and Technology

Section 3
Design of Diversity Leadership

Detailed Table of Contents

Section 1
Introduction to Diversity Leadership

This introductory chapter covers the need for professionals in all sectors to embrace and adopt diversity leadership practices. This imperative outlook on how we use technology to connect, communicate, solve problems, and educate is explored in order to provide an overview of diversity leadership. It also addresses the main ideas of the chapters in the book.

Diversity is a critical component in sustaining vibrant complex adaptive organizations. This chapter introduces the key conceptual elements of complex adaptive systems, shows how essential diversity is to organizations that thrive in states of change, and concludes showing relational network research identifying how to lead networks in the knowledge era.

Technology has made communication more straightforward, trouble-free, and efficient. Masses or specifically targeted groups can be easily identified, targeted, and reached. This chapter explains how leaders in higher education and business have incorporated technology to communicate with diverse leadership groups.

Section 2
Diversity Leadership and Technology

Chapter 4

Porche Millington, North Carolina A&T State University, USA
Lemuria Carter, North Carolina A&T State University, USA

The purpose of this chapter is to assess the current state of the digital divide in the United States. The digital divide refers to the distinction between the information haves and have-nots, the gap between the computer literate and the computer illiterate. This chapter discusses the substantial percentage of the population that lacks the skills necessary to effectively interact online.

Chapter 5

Anna C. McFadden, University of Alabama, USA
Juanita F. McMath, University of Alabama, USA
Michelle Hale, University of Alabama, USA
Barrie Jo Price, University of Alabama, USA

This chapter includes data and issues related to technology access and variables for how technology is used in any leadership setting. The features related to leadership in unique, geo-political environments are exacerbated by technology access and use. This chapter broadly describes technology access and use in a global context, emphasizing research data and examples from academic sources and popular press.

Chapter 6

Dorothy Guy Bonvillain, Love-Based Leadership Consultants, USA
David R. Faulkner, Defense Equal Opportunity Management Institute, USA
William Gary McGuire, Defense Equal Opportunity Management Institute, USA

This chapter addresses the linkage between diversity technologies and performance in educational, medical, business, and military organizations. It emphasizes the need for diversity characteristics, competencies, and technologies to be filtered through formal instructional systems, design processes, and evaluation procedures in order to help stakeholders identify strengths and weaknesses within the organization regardless of the type of organization. This chapter shows how this linkage can be supported and measured with structured programs that currently exist.

Chapter 7

Alvin J. Williams, University of South Alabama, USA

This chapter addresses the expansive role of technology in strengthening the viability of minority-owned firms. Given the competitive global business climate, it is imperative that diverse suppliers of products and services embrace a plethora of technology-based tools to have access. The chapter offers guidance on how both diverse buyers and sellers can use technology to improve their global position in competitive markets.

Section 3
Design of Diversity Leadership

Chapter 8

David R. Faulkner, Defense Equal Opportunity Management Institute, USA

This chapter focuses primarily on how diversity programs in the Government and Military intersect, how some instructional design process(es) may be implemented to ensure that the essence of diversity is projected into the programs, and how to improve programs to ensure diversity training is impacting organizations.

Chapter 9

Kizzy M. Parks, K. Parks Consulting, Inc., USA

Felicia O. Mokuolu, Florida Institute of Technology, USA

Daniel P. McDonald, Defense Equal Opportunity Management Institute, USA

A diverse workforce is equipped with unique capabilities, talents, knowledge, and skills that can be utilized to accomplish organizational goals. In order to capitalize on these diverse skills, organizations must foster an inclusive work environment that values, integrates, and embraces individual differences, as well as similarities. This chapter focuses on diversity metrics, which correctly gauge the progress of diversity and inclusion programs.

Chapter 10

Mike A. Guest, Defense Equal Opportunity Management Institute, USA

Elizabeth Culhane, Defense Equal Opportunity Management Institute, USA

Daniel P. McDonald, Defense Equal Opportunity Management Institute, USA

This chapter reviews emerging trends in technology that have implications for diversity management. Social networking and simulation technologies will be discussed with specific examples of recent and ongoing research and development projects applicable to diversity management.

Chapter 11

Stacey C. Nickson, Auburn University, USA

Carol M. Archer, University of Houston, USA

S. Raj Chaudhury, Auburn University, USA

Culture Bump theory and process, a cross-cultural communication tool developed by Dr. Carol Archer almost 30 years ago, has been used to train corporate, educational, government, and other leaders from over a dozen countries. This chapter offers the meta-theory of Cross Cultural Emotional Intelligence that allows this computer-based activity to effectively foster communication between diverse individuals, addressing differences that include culture, gender, soci-economic, age, and ethnicity, among others.

The effectiveness of any diversity program is determined by the leaders and managers in organizations, including educational, medical, business, government, and the military. This chapter covers how the effectiveness of such programs must be linked with technology tools that can guide leaders through successful organizational programs. It also emphasizes that once the effectiveness levels are defined and classified into levels of performance (as well as behavior), leaders and managers can create operational plans of action and milestones as well as actionable strategies to implement and sustain diversity programs.

Chapter 13

Leaders must find means of understanding the interactions of religious/Humanist attributes with other diversity attributes, both visible and invisible. This chapter focuses on how technology—specifically the use of an anonymous survey instrument—becomes a critical component in gathering religious diversity data and exploring the effects this diversity may have on operations and development of organizational strategic and long-term goals.

Section 4
Diversity Leadership in Education

Chapter 14

The lack of certified science teachers is a major cause of poor achievement and low expectations for high-risk students. This problem is greatly exacerbated in both rural and urban areas because schools in these locales are most likely to serve disadvantaged children and to have teachers who are teaching out of field. This chapter addresses perhaps the most critical characteristic for Pathway to Science, mentoring of these newly minted teachers. It gives an overview of an approach that ensures that new teachers will provide effective instruction in their classrooms and are set on a pathway to becoming career teachers.

Chapter 15

This chapter details how technology may be implemented and utilized in K-12 and post-secondary classrooms as a resource for inviting two-way communication between American students, educators, students, and educators from other countries. This chapter also covers potential expectations and outcomes from such a teaching tool.

Mark Mouck, American Cooperative School of Tunis, Tunisia

This chapter is an exploration of Langer's Envisioning Literature: Literary Understanding and Literature Instruction in the context of the 21st century. It provides research-based examples of skills and lessons that teachers can use to develop well-informed global citizens off-line as well as on. This chapter explores the social-construction of knowledge in the classroom and online to prepare them to be participants in the social construction of knowledge in the Information Age.

Peter M. Eley, Fayetteville State University, USA

This chapter utilizes technology as a leadership tool in the mathematics classroom by leading the way to student motivation for learning. In this chapter, the historical progression of technology and how it has changed teaching pedagogy in mathematics education adds to the discussion around the teacher being more of a facilitator of learning and students developing their own ideas and constructs through exploration using technology.

Andrea M. Kent, University of South Alabama, USA

It is strong leadership at the classroom level that makes a difference with colleagues and students, regardless of ethnicity, gender, or social class, and can ultimately impact an entire school culture. This chapter integrates these core characteristics in an effort to guide the understanding of the necessity of developing teacher leaders to meet the challenges inherent in 21st century schools and classrooms.

Catherine L. Packer-Williams, Jefferson Davis Community College, USA
Kathy M. Evans, University of South Carolina, USA

The purpose of this chapter is to review the need for diversity leadership in higher education, explore the challenges of diversity leaders, specify the need for mentorship in diversity leadership, and offer recommendations on how to incorporate technology as tool for mentorship in diversity leadership in higher education.

The chapter examines the connection between the diversity of community college students and community college administrators. It includes strategies that can be used to increase diversity in community college leadership, with an emphasis on the role that technology can play in promoting diversity leadership.

Preface

We live in an increasingly diverse world. Organizations in every area, including K-12 schools, higher education, health care, the military, banking, government, telecommunications, and manufacturing, are continually being impacted by the challenges and opportunities presented by diverse groups of students, customers, and workers. In order to overcome the challenges and maximize the opportunities presented by our diverse world, organizations have to develop leaders who are not only knowledgeable about their own business or industry, but are also culturally aware and technologically sophisticated.

The editors' purpose in developing this book was to provide an opportunity for leading researchers and practitioners in the area of diversity leadership to explore the complex interactions between technology, diversity, leadership, and organizational development. At the beginning of this process, we hoped we would be able to present an inclusive, compelling, current, and broad group of perspectives related to the topic of diversity leadership. In looking now at the final collection of chapters in the book, we are very impressed with the breadth of viewpoints presented, the quality of the discussions, the range of backgrounds of the authors, and the timeliness of both the technologies and theories presented.

The chapters in this book provide an interesting overview of technology's role in promoting diversity leadership in organizations. Each of the chapters provides a current and thoughtful discussion related to the implementation of diversity leadership into an organization. Taken as a whole, the chapters present a comprehensive knowledge base that researchers, practitioners, managers, and others can use to understand and facilitate diversity leadership through technology.

The first chapter, by two of the editors, is an introductory chapter to diversity leadership principles, barriers, and implications. This chapter also includes a model for implementation of diversity leadership. Chapter 2, by Kowch, describes a crisis in leadership, discusses evolving perspectives of leadership thought, and proposes that we begin to think about organizations as complex ecosystems. The chapter highlights the importance of diversity within organizations. The next chapter, by Sanders and Cain, takes up the crucial issue of how technology can be used to facilitate effective communication between diverse groups within an organization. Their chapter includes a thoughtful discussion of the positive and potentially negative aspects of using technology for communication.

The fourth chapter, by Millington and Carter, describes the digital divide and discusses four types of barriers that limit access to the internet and other powerful technologies. The focus of the chapter is on one type of access barrier, psychological access. Prospect theory is presented as a valuable tool that practitioners can employ to address psychological access barriers and, as a result, close the gap in technology use. Chapter 5, by McFadden, McMath, Hale, and Price, explores how technology is changing leadership in political, economic, and educational contexts. Of particular note in this chapter, is the discussion of how emerging technologies are altering the types of interactions between leaders and their followers. The chapter also includes interesting discussions of how technology is changing the time and place elements of leadership and the roles of the individual and the group.

In Chapter 6, Bonvillain explores the different types of "personality shapes" within an organization and the importance of having a variety of shapes represented on a team. The chapter also includes a discussion of the "Cultural DNA" of an organization. The seventh chapter of the book, by Williams, moves the focus away from educational settings and provides a discussion of the important topic of supplier diversity. The chapter begins with an overview of supplier diversity, discusses minority firm ownership, and discusses the role technology plays in enhancing supplier diversity.

In Chapter 8, Faulkner presents 8 keys to the design and development of effective diversity instruction. He emphasizes the importance of analysis and evaluation to the instructional design process. Chapter 9, by Parks, Mokuolo, and McDonald, presents a useful framework for measuring the effectiveness of diversity and inclusion programs. In the book's tenth chapter, Guest, Culhane, and McDonald present a definition of diversity management, discuss emerging technology-based tools for supporting diversity management, describe current issues, problems, and controversies in the field, and present an interesting set of recommendations that could benefit diversity management programs. Chapter 11, by Nickson, Archer, and Chaudhury, focuses on an innovative approach for enhancing cross cultural communication and developing diversity leadership. The twelfth chapter, by McGuire, emphasizes the crucial role that leadership plays in effective diversity management in organizations. The chapter looks at various aspects of diversity management in different types of organizations including the military, education, medicine, and business. Chapter 13, by Hunter and Smith, offers a compelling discussion of religious diversity and technology. Their chapter presents the results of a survey of religious beliefs given to active-duty military personnel and provides recommendations for how military leaders might use information about religious identification to improve the performance of their organizations.

In Chapter 14, Green, an editor of the book, describes the role of diversity leadership in preparing new science teachers by mentoring. This chapter explores the development of community with use of technology. The next chapter, by Ferguson Martin, proposes that technology can be an important tool for K-12 educators to elevate the status of students from traditionally marginalized groups. The chapter includes a fascinating case study of how one teacher used technology to address issues related to diversity and cultural differences. Chapter 16, by Mouck, presents a thoughtful discussion of the literary classroom as an active community and the challenges and opportunities for collaboration provided by Web 2.0 technologies. Mouck also includes a series of recommendations for teachers hoping to create a collaborative student-centered classroom on the Internet.

In Chapter 17, Eley explores a number of task and technology tools that can be used to enhance student motivation in mathematics instruction. The next chapter, by Kent, describes the concept of teacher leaders, explores the role of teacher leaders in school reform and creating diversified learning communities, and discusses the significant part technology plays in teacher leadership. Chapter 19, by Packer-Williams and Evans, describes the importance of mentoring in developing diversity leadership in higher education and discusses how technology can play a key role in the mentoring process. The book's final chapter, by Sterling and Williams, examines the connection between the diversity of community college student and community college administrators.

The main themes that run throughout this book are the importance of diversity to the success and growth of an organization, the vital role that technology plays in fostering diversity, and the need to develop and nurture leaders who understand the complex interactions between diverse groups of people and emerging technological tools. We hope the readers of this book will reflect on these main themes and look for opportunities, both large and small, to take on leadership roles, promote diversity, improve their technological competencies, and change their own organizations, and our society as a whole, for the better.

Joél Lewis
University of South Alabama, USA

André Green
University of South Alabama, USA

Daniel W. Surry
University of South Alabama, USA

Acknowledgment

At its inception, this book was derived out of a gap in the literature on diversity leadership, particularly how technology brings us together to be more inclusive in leadership. We knew that we would have to solicit a special group of professionals who were practicing diversity leadership. This group is few and far between; however, an outstanding group of authors were eager to write about how they exemplify diversity leadership in different contexts.

We would like to express our sincere gratitude to the chapter authors for their contribution to this book and for sharing their perspectives on diversity leadership. Without their variety of experiences and depth of knowledge, we would not have reached our goal to span several sectors of society and to provide examples and practical solutions. We would also like to thank the editorial board and reviewers. These talented experts and practitioners gave their valuable time and effort to make this book a success, and for that we are extremely grateful. We would like to thank all the diversity leadership professionals, from outside consultants to leaders within, who facilitate the development of diversity leadership organizations. Lastly, we would like to thank our families, especially Bevley Green, Melinda Surry, Robert F. Lewis Sr., and Paulette Lewis. With the contributions of our colleagues, collaboration with other professionals, and support of our families, this edited book further expands the literature on the discipline of diversity leadership.

Joél P. Lewis
University of South Alabama, USA

André M. Green
University of South Alabama, USA

Daniel W. Surry
University of South Alabama, USA

Section 1
Introduction to Diversity Leadership

Chapter 1
Diversity Leadership:
A Necessity for the Future

Joél P. Lewis
University of South Alabama, USA

Daniel W. Surry
University of South Alabama, USA

WHAT IS DIVERSITY LEADERSHIP?

When mentioning the title of this book, people often ask, "What is diversity leadership?" One basic response is "Leading with diversity as the center principle." It normally takes a few examples and further explanation for people to understand it. Considering that diversity leadership is a relatively new term, defining it is necessary to increase its acceptance as a discipline and to foster its increased application in organizations. Diversity leadership is not a new concept to the many professionals who practice it, however some professionals are implementing diversity leadership but not label-ing their work as such. Using the term diversity leadership is essential to its development as a practice and to the establishment of its foundation in research. There is a need for an increase in research on both leadership and diversity in theoretical and methodological approaches to leadership (Lumby & Coleman, 2010). Organizations that have diversity leadership at the core of their values are evident by their ability to innovate valuing different perspectives and to reflect the communities they serve.

This is not the first time a former component of leadership has moved to the forefront to become a type of leadership. Servant Leadership is an excellent example of how a type of leadership is based on a former component of leadership.

DOI: 10.4018/978-1-4666-2668-3.ch001

Robert Greenleaf envisioned leadership based on being a servant to those you lead (Greenleaf, 1998). This concept has been well received and is practiced widely in all sectors of society. Very similarly, diversity leadership is based on developing values, strategic plans, and engagement based on diversity. There is vast amount of literature and research in both leadership and diversity but research that combines both is difficult to find (Lumby & Coleman, 2010). Diversity and inclusion should be emphasized in leadership theories (Chin, 2010). Due to the lack of emphasis of diversity in leadership, there is plethora of work to be done on diversity leadership in terms of theory, research, and practice.

Diversity and Leadership

Diversity and leadership separately are not new concepts, however changing populations, advances in technology, developing theoretical perspectives, and the need for 21st century collaborations have led to the emergence of this type of leadership. Looking at these concepts separately is one way to approach defining diversity leadership as a discipline. Diversity is often narrowed down to ethnicity and race. However, the Diversity Dictionary defines diversity as "A situation that includes representation of multiple (ideally all groups) within a prescribed environment..." Within the context of this book, diversity refers to the wide range differences within any population (Lumby & Coleman, 2010). There are many perspectives of leadership that have been used for decades. Stoghill's (1950) perspective is that "Leadership must be viewed from standpoint of influence on organizational activity, rather than on group members" (p. 3). Ulrich and Smallwood (2012) assert that "Leadership occurs when the organization builds a cadre of future leaders who have the capacity to shape an organization's culture and create patterns of success" (p. 9). When referring to leadership in this book, our thinking will be in line with Rost (1991) who wrote "Leadership is an influence relationship among leaders and followers who intend real changes that reflect their mutual purposes" (p. 6).

Diversity Leadership

According to the Military Leadership Diversity Commission (2010), "Diversity leadership addresses how leaders at all rank and organizational levels shape the impact of diversity dynamics..." (p. 1). Specifically, diversity leadership is comprised of the ways in which people and groups relate to one another and how leadership decisions are made at the center of the differences, similarities, and problems among groups (Lim, Cho, & Curry, 2008). Aguirre and Martinez (2006) describe diversity leadership as a way to strengthen organizational policies and practice in order to center diversity at the foundation of an organization's culture. Although Lewin (1944), mentions a contradiction about the source of leadership because some believe that leaders are born while others believe that individuals should be trained to be leaders. We assert that diversity leaders are not born, they are created through life experiences and increased cultural competencies through training.

Diversity leadership is an important emerging discipline defined by the combination of diversity principles and leadership competencies within an organization. The key to the combination between diversity and leadership is the desire to connect employees, clients, students, co-workers, customers, organizations, and communities to each other in ways that ensure productive actions that lead to desired outcomes in all sectors of our society. Centering on inclusivity, involvement, and communication, these connections via technology are essential to meet the needs of multicultural environments. Its importance is further emphasized by the increasing number of diversity leadership academies, programs, and workshops available for professionals to increase the competencies in diversity leadership.

According to Robinson (2001), Director of the Office of Civil Rights for the U.S. Department of State, five key conditions have to exist in order for diversity leadership to be in action. The first condition is that diversity leadership has to be visible. Strategies to achieve visibility may include statements in a mission statement, evidence in policies, resource allocation, and enculturation. There may be a few challenges to visibility from an organizational point of view. This topic is not always popular and is sometimes uncomfortable for some people. If not consistent, spurts of visibility can diminish the impact of diversity leadership. For example, if the only instance that diversity is mentioned is to satisfy governmental, accreditation, or regulating purposes, there is most likely not a commitment from the top of the organization.

The second condition of diversity leadership is specificity. Details in addressing the current condition, the optimal condition, and the performance gap encompass the framework in which these details can be identified. Determining the actual current status of an organization's diversity leadership indicates a willingness to identify weaknesses and address those weaknesses through new opportunities. These details also depend on the first condition: Visibility.

The third condition of diversity leadership is making it personal. This condition indicates that leaders need a personal story to relate to in order to be an effective diversity leader. This condition also indicates that leaders should make sure that individuals know diversity leadership principles and are evaluated on them regularly. This level of commitment requires establishing criteria related to diversity leaderships as well as specific outcomes expected from the inputs and actions invested.

The fourth condition of diversity leadership is persistence. A consistent theme throughout an organization presented to employees, clients, and consumers is necessary in order for everyone to be aware of this principle. There are many organizations that create logos, themes, slogans, and other marketing strategies to inform people on their principles. This condition requires frequent reinforcement in order to be fully implemented.

Lastly, and what some would say most importantly, the fifth condition of diversity leadership is that it must be intentional. If change is desired, leaders have to make intentional efforts to lead others with diversity as the central means of progress and productivity. If people in positions of leadership are not deliberate in the actions related to their leadership style, the type of leadership, and or the core principles of leadership, the culture will not exhibit the outcomes of diversity leadership.

According to Carr-Ruffino (1996), the criteria for organization's position on diversity is tolerance for ambiguity, demand for conformity, value placed on diversity, cultural fit, and acculturation. If an organization uses these criteria to evaluate its approach to diversity, it may reveal obvious strengths and unforeseen weaknesses. The connection between diversity and increased performance is not automatic. It requires diversity-conscious leadership (Military Leadership Diversity Commission, 2010a). In some organizations, all administrators may not be convinced on the concept of diversity leadership. It may require support for its need and benefits.

WHY DIVERSITY LEADERSHIP?

Essential actions for the future include aligning with the needs of increasingly diverse environments (Aguirre & Martinez, 2006). According to the Pew Research Center's Pew Demographic and Social Projection Report, "If current trends continue, the population of the United States will rise to 438 million in 2050, from 296 million in 2005, and 82% of the increase will be due to immigrants arriving from 2005 to 2050 and their U.S. born descendants…" (p. 1). This report also projects that "The nation's elderly population will more than double in size from 2005 through 2050" (Taylor & Cohn, 2012, p. 1).

In various population projection reports, you will find that the population will increase; the percentage of people of color will increase; and in some regions, life expectancy will increase. This truly depicts a different picture of the make-up of business, customers, services, philanthropy, and government. In order to meet the changes in current and future population changes and considering these projections, diversity leadership strategies are essential to organizations that are striving to create and implement a cultural proficiency model (Aguirre & Martinez, 2006). Organization-wide practice of diversity leadership requires a top down approach of inclusion. The case for diversity leadership can be difficult in organizations that lack vested interest in leading with outreach rather than inclusion. In a post election interview on CNN, Newt Gingrich, former speaker of the U.S. House of Representatives, made an analogy on the difference between outreach and inclusion. "Outreach is when five white guys have a meeting and call you. Inclusion is when you're in the meeting, which inherently changes the whole tenor of the meeting" (Gingrich, 2012, p. 1). The administration must desire to have all voices present to increase the likelihood decisions represent and consider the entire community. When the perspectives of different groups are valued, the environment is on its way to a diversity leadership culture and moving toward being an inclusive organization.

DIVERSITY LEADERSHIP CULTURE: BARRIERS AND STRATEGIES

Developing Culture

The culture of diversity leadership is one of complexity and unity. You might ask how culture can be complex and unified, simultaneously. According to Connerley and Pedersen (2005), the complexity of a culture is difficult to address. It requires various approaches. We function in many cultures in our everyday lives, some more complex than others. These cultures vary in norms, practices, groups, language, and other aspects. There are several approaches to developing a diversity leadership culture within an organization. These approaches include research on diversity leadership, potential resistance from the dominant group, establishing commitment, and the overall perception of diversity by individuals.

The lack of research on diversity leadership is evident by the lack of resources, tools, books, and peer-reviewed studies available for organizations to effectively promote and apply diversity leadership. There is a vast amount research on diversity and leadership within many disciplines. Research that links the two, however, is minimal (Lumby & Coleman, 2010). According to Dreachslin (2008), if an organization is looking to assist its stakeholders to reach their full potential, effective diversity leadership must be in place. This is one of the main reasons that this book and the development of other resources are the important to preparing to meet current and future needs.

There are different types of resistance that may develop in the creation and implementation of a diversity leadership agenda. Resistance may stem from several sources: a dominate group, traditionally underrepresented groups, and conflict between traditionally underrepresented groups (Kezar, 2008). Typically, a dominate group may predict that change would have a negative impact on their status in the organization as it relates to authority, voice, comfort, and rank. Resistance from the underrepresented group may be as a result of process, lack of commitment from the top, lack of policy changes, and overall dissatisfaction with progress of lack thereof. The conflict that can develop between dominant and underrepresented groups can have a devastating impact on moral, interpersonal relationships, and overall productivity. When these types of resistance arise in an organization as a result of implementation of a diversity leadership agenda, Kezar (2008) suggests the following strategies: use data to neutralize, take a pulse of the environment, and develop a coalition.

For an organization to see "real and measurable improvement in diversity," Robinson (2011) states, "individual commitment of the leaders is absolutely essential" (p. 8). In a current study of presidents of small colleges and universities, our preliminary data suggests the college presidents who had impactful diverse experiences were more likely to have not only inclusive but also aggressive diversity efforts. This is further echoed by the results of the Insight to Diversity December 2012 Issue in which includes the top diversity colleges and universities that have not only addressed underrepresented groups but have implemented policy, training, and infrastructure that reflect a campus DNA centered on diversity and inclusion (Rainy, 2012).

The perception that diversity is a problem as opposed to a desirable aspect of an organization can be impactful on the culture (Aguirre & Martinez, 2006). This negative perspective is a root cause of the stagnation in the development of a diversity leadership agenda. "Most businesses, however, are not doing enough to connect to the emerging markets or to their diverse employees. Thus, they stand the significant chance of stagnation or reduced profitability, and the opportunity costs of poor diversity recruitment, performance, and retention" (Graham, 2011, p. 1).

Unnecessary limitations have been placed on the role of diversity within organizations. Asking questions and evaluating leadership are a few approaches to identifying the source of those limitations. To determine if diversity is limited in an organization a few questions can be posed. These questions may include: What does the organization's mission state about the diversity? Are diversity initiatives implemented? Who can lead from within? Does the organizational culture show how diversity can benefit everyone?

Another way that diversity can be limited is by considering diversity as only a component of leadership. In this approach to leadership, upper level administrators are responsible for the facilitation of diversity and representation among groups does not necessarily play an important role in decision-making and operations. Addressing diversity in this manner can have a negative impact on the bottom line as well as on the development of progressive communities.

Barriers

When trying to understand the complexity of culture, exploration of individual bias, experiences, and values are good starting points. For example, if an employee in an organization has accepted the concept of sameness, this can be a challenge for promoting diversity (Aguirre & Martinez, 2006). The effort required from the administration to address bias requires a true commitment to not only accept differences among those inside the organization, but to promote inclusion among stakeholders. An intentional effort to promote diversity leadership can produce an analysis of the alignment of the organization with the diverse environment in which it serves (Aguirre & Martinez, 2006). According to Kezar (2008), we can promote diversity leadership by acknowledging possible barriers such as cultural baggage, creating a diversity agenda, and developing cultural competencies.

Individuals within a culture represent an amalgamation of experiences, some positive and some negative. These experiences create baggage. Baggage in this context refers to allowing previous experiences to impact future interactions and decisions negatively. In order for a leader to function as a diversity leader, the leader must "acknowledge their cultural baggage" (Kezar, 2008).

Another barrier to developing a culture of diversity leadership is to not address diversity directly as a core approach to leadership. It can come from the positions of authority or it can emerge from employees who are invested in the progress of the organization (Kezar, 2008). Many of us have experienced situations in learning and work environments that have addressed diversity as a sidebar conversation or merely as a necessity for a report. These approaches can sometimes lead to decreased productivity and conflict sourced in diversity issues such as lack of sensitivity in communication or the development of policies that marginalize certain groups (Kezar, 2008).

The lack of cultural competence can also be considered a barrier to the implementation of diversity leadership. Dreachslin and Hobby (2008) advocate that cultural competence should be enabled, cultivated, and reinforced. This requires a substantial investment on the part of decision makers and administrators. Training, accountability, and equity management are methods used to advance the cultural competency of individuals within an organization. In a study of college presidents, Kezar (2008), found that use of various strategies helped the administrators implement diversity agendas. These various strategies included developing coalitions, analyzing the pulse regularly, anticipating resistance, using data to neutralize, showcasing success, and capitalizing on controversy. These strategies and others help identify diversity leadership in action.

Strategies

In an effort to identify ways that environments could move toward a diversity leadership approach, Kezar (2008) identified the following strategies: developing allies, mediation, persuasion, and bargaining and negotiation. Developing allies involves engaging different groups in the culture and leadership. This in turn creates a power group of people supportive of creating an inclusive culture. If the top administration is not implementing diversity leadership, Kezar also suggests familiarizing the authoritative figures with the need for leadership with diversity at the forefront.

The skill of persuasion is particularly important in promoting diversity in an organization (Kezar, 2008). Due to the sometimes unpopular sentiment on diversity, persuasion is critical to the application and acceptance of diversity leadership. Developing a platform for success stories and experts can communicate the benefits of diversity. Stories create a personal connection between the experience of the storyteller and disengagement of the audience. Experts can provide the opportunity for enlightenment on cultural competencies and an outside perspective. The Triple A Model of Diversity Leadership addresses how these barriers can be met by three processes integrated by technology.

MODEL OF DIVERSITY LEADERSHIP

As technology brings people together, faster than ever before, there is an ever-pressing need for individuals and organizations to not only accept but embrace the uniqueness in others and to find innovative ways to reach high levels of performance together. It is important to explore the theoretical framework, application, and research of diversity leadership in multiple organizational settings. This will result in a unique and important addition to the literature and lay the foundation for diversity leadership to be a vital tool for organizational development.

The Triple A Model of Diversity Leadership supports the assertion that leadership should model practices that represent justice and fairness within the community and value each stakeholder's perspective (Aguirre & Martinez, 2006). Utilizing this inclusion approach to engage individuals is an essential underpinning of diversity leadership. The strategies emphasized in this model involve the use of technology as a tool to apply the principles of diversity leadership by way of analysis, access, and application. The following description includes how these processes can be used to elevate an organization's diversity leadership. First, the process of analysis is used to determine the status of equity and inclusion in an organization. Second, the process access centers on input and opportunity. Lastly, the process of application addresses the development of values and strategies. Combined, the use of technology to execute these processes represents a model that empowers organizations to progress to diversity leadership culture (see Figure 1).

Figure 1. The Triple A model of diversity leadership

ANALYSIS OF EQUITY AND INCLUSION

The process of analysis is critical in determining the status and starting point of an organization regarding diversity leadership. The components of this analysis can include, but are not limited to, the causes of the current status, cultures involved, and the competencies of diversity leadership. With technology as the tool, these components can be analyzed utilizing the following matrix across individuals, departments and the entire organization (see Table 1).

Causes represent the history and possible barriers that can be identified at the beginning of the analysis process. These data infer the root causes of the current status of the type of leadership implemented and the lack of diversity leadership evident in the policies, procedures, and values of the organization. Technology can be used to

Table 1. Diversity leadership analysis matrix

Level	Causes	Culture	Competencies
Individual			
Department			
Organization			

gather information to compare and contrast data across levels, as well as to explore existing data.

Does the culture reflect diversity leadership at all levels? Are there elements in the culture that are impede diversity leadership? Do the policies and procedures reflect diversity leadership values? As mentioned earlier in the chapter, culture is extremely important in the implementation of a diversity leadership agenda. The analysis of culture will require a desire to see the reflection of the interaction between policy, individuals, customer/clients, and services. Knowing the intricacies of a culture may require change. Therefore, many organizations refrain from conducting these analyses because they do not want to put for the effort to set new policies, implement new training, nor create an inclusive infrastructure. This analysis can be in the form of a climate questionnaire, demographic information on populations inside and outside of the organization.

How culturally competent are the individuals in the organization? Do they have the necessary skills to practice diversity leadership and transfer competencies from the training context to the performance context? Are individuals, departments, or the organization as a whole, equip to meet the needs of global citizens? Diversity leadership competencies can cover objectives related to age, race, ethnicity, sexual orientation, and ability level, etc. Technology can be used to deliver training by way of a corporate university, online modules, self-paced instruction, instructor-led workshops, on-the-job training, or some combination of any training medium. Based on the issues within each organization, the competencies should be prioritized. Assessment methods could include role-play, quizzes, essays, and or on-the-job performance.

Overall, the Diversity Leadership Analysis Matrix is a useful tool for organizations to begin to assess the status of diversity leadership across levels and to identify possible opportunities for growth and application of diversity leadership principles.

ACCESS OF INPUT AND OPPORTUNITIES

Access is an essential component of the Triple A Diversity Leadership Model. Access to existing data, knowledge management, professional development, and decision making within an organization are just a few examples of how access can be used to promote diversity leadership. Depending on the organization, the collection of data over the years can be used to identify trends, impact of external events, and possible opportunities for growth. Technology allows for increased access to people, resources, and knowledge management. Providing professional development for all individuals especially in areas of skill development and diversity, allows for them to contribute more to the organization as well as increase the return on investment.

Current messaging, interpersonal communication, organizational communication structures as well as policies, procedures and actions reflect the access individuals have to provide input within an organization to the administration. If there are not communication channels for individuals from top to bottom, access is limited. Collaboration and cooperation between all levels of command are an indication of the level of which diversity leadership is being implemented. This suggests that the results of diversity leadership include higher level of cooperation and exchange of information, which can result in changes in the organizational cultures of diverse environments (Aguirre & Martinez, 2006). This increases the value of individuals to the organization and the emphasis on the value of human capital. According to Darden (2003), Senior Vice-President, U.S. Operations, United Parcel Service, one approach to linking workforce initiatives and shareholder value is to assess a company's human capital strategy, of which diversity leadership is essential.

Opportunity to contribute is essential to the development of a diversity leadership agenda. The potential of each individual to contribute to the organization must be considered if optimal performance is desired. Access to mentorships, workshops, interdisciplinary collaborations, appropriate tools, productive evaluations, decision-making, and visioning may provide potential avenues for promotion from within, increased retention, and maximum return on investment.

APPLICATION OF VALUES AND STRATEGIES

Application refers to the practice of diversity leadership. Once an organization has utilized technology to conduct an analysis and provide access to all, application of the vision of diversity leadership must come to fruition. Diversity leadership has to be intentional and planned. Therefore, the application component of diversity leadership is strategic and deliberate on the part of upper management or administration in order to provide a path forward for all those involved. According to Graham (2011), "As we compete globally and are increasingly competitive in all industries, business, and international commerce become less concerned about race, creed, or gender. Diversity has become a permanent business characteristic with significant economic impact" (p. 1).

The Triple A Model of Diversity Leadership encompasses process that can be used by any organization to become a diversity leader. So what are the characteristics of a diversity leadership organization? According to Carl Darden, (2003), diversity leadership leads to competitive market leadership by increasing retention and attracting investors. Underrepresented groups not only have a voice but an equal playing field is available for all who want to work hard and pursue opportunities within the organization. With the use of technology, analysis, access, and application can lead to a culture of inclusiveness and a diversity leadership organization prepared to meet the challenges of the future.

With leaders encountering tough decision-making, conflict resolution, and changing demographics, diversity leadership can assist organizations that struggle to increase individual and organizational performance. Developing partnerships, collaborations, and learning communities for the 21st Century, diversity leadership must be included in the strategic plan. As we strengthen ethical foundations to connect with individuals and other organizations, legislative requirements and international factors have a role in our growth and approach in moving into the future. These and other factors support the idea that this field of research has substantial opportunity to link diversity and leadership to further build on diversity leadership as a discipline for growth in applications, research, program development, needs assessment, evaluation, and culture.

REFERENCES

Aguirre, A., Martinez, R. O., & Association for the Study of Higher Education. (2006). *Diversity leadership in higher education*. San Francisco, CA: Jossey-Bass.

Carr-Ruffino, N. (1996). *Managing diversity: People skills for a multicultural workplace*. Cincinnati, OH: International Thompson.

Chin, J. L. (2010). Introduction to the special issue on leadership and diversity. *The American Psychologist, 65*(3), 150–156. doi:10.1037/a0018716

Connerly, M. L., & Pedersen, P. B. (2005). *Leadership in a diverse and multicultural environment*. Thousand Oaks, CA: Sage Publications.

Darden, C. (2003). *Delivering on diversity: A walk in the other guy's shoes*. Retrieved from http://www.ohio.edu/orgs/one/dd.html

Gingrich, N. (2012). *Interview*. Retrieved from http://www.mediaite.com/tv/gingrich-contrasts-inclusion-and-outreach-outreach-is-when-5-white-guys-have-a-meeting-and-call-you/

Graham, S. (2011). *A diversity leadership program*. Retrieved from http://www.stedmangraham.com/

Greenleaf, R. (1998). *The power of servant leadership*. San Francisco, CA: Berrett-Kohler Publishers, Inc.

Kezar, A. (2008). Understanding leadership strategies for addressing the politics of diversity. *The Journal of Higher Education, 79*(4), 406–441. doi:10.1353/jhe.0.0009

Lewin, K. (1944). A research approach to leadership problems. *The Journal of Applied Psychology, 17*(7), 392–398.

Lumby, J., & Coleman, M. (2007). *Leadership and diversity: Challenging theory and practice in education*. London, UK: Sage Publications, Ltd.

Military Leadership Diversity Commission. (2010). *Business-case arguments for diversity and diversity programs and their impact in the workplace*. Retrieved from http://diversity.defense.gov/Resources/Commission/docs/Issue%20Papers/Paper%2014%20%20Business%20Case%20Arguments%20for%20Diversity%20and%20Programs.pdf

Rainey, M. (2012). The first annual higher education excellence in diversity award. *Insight into Diversity*. Retrieved from http://www.insightintodiversity.com/aarjobs/index.php?option=com_content&view=article&id=39:virginia-state-university&catid=20:aar-closer-look

Robinson, J. M. (2011). Leadership makes the difference for EEO and diversity effectiveness. *State Magazine*. Retrieved from http://digitaledition.state.gov/publication/index.php?i=57364&m=&l=&p=11&pre=&ver=swf

Rost, J. C. (1991). *Leadership for the twenty-first century*. New York, NY: Praeger.

Stogdill, R. M. (1950). Leadership, membership, and organization. *Psychological Bulletin*, *47*(1), 1–14. doi:10.1037/h0053857

Taylor, P., & Cohn, D. (2012). A milestone en route to a majority minority nation. *Report of Pew Social & Demographic Trends*. Retrieved from http://www.pewsocialtrends.org/2012/11/07/a-milestone-en-route-to-a-majority-minority-nation/

Ulrich, D., & Smallwood, N. (2012). What is Leadership? In Mobley, W. H., Wang, Y., & Li, M. (Eds.), *Advances in Global Leadership* (pp. 9–36). London, UK: Emerald Group Publishing Limited. doi:10.1108/S1535-1203(2012)0000007005

United Nations. (2004). *Report of United Nations populations division*. Retrieved from http://www.un.org/esa/population/publications/longrange2/WorldPop2300final.pdf

Chapter 2
Towards Leading Diverse, Smarter and More Adaptable Organizations that Learn

Eugene G. Kowch
University of Calgary, Canada

ABSTRACT

Leadership is in crisis. Technology has enabled our complex and interconnected world, making it much easier for organizations and entire ecosystems to collaborate—quickly—while older mindsets based on the organization as a machine model are proving to be grossly inadequate. Simultaneously, we have failed to predict and to understand, for example, the cascading financial system failures that threaten lives, institutions, and nations. This chapter takes a complexity thinking perspective to carefully examine specialization, diversity, and organizational change in new ways so that we can extend our leadership thinking about the adaptability of our organizations. Because diversity is a critical condition for complex organizational change, the authors explore diversity from two disciplinary perspectives. First, they take a learning science (education) perspective to find that leaders should consider organizations as emergent collectives that are able to learn and to become capable of "learning ahead" in turbulent contexts. The authors then explore, from an organizational science perspective, how diversity exists as an essential condition for identifying differences and novelties as seeds for innovations (changes) made possible only by collective work attracted to these novelties. Finally, the author presents a framework for understanding and leading and knowing the potentials of diverse, smarter, more adaptive complex organizational ecosystems.

DOI: 10.4018/978-1-4666-2668-3.ch002

If change is inevitable but unpredictable, then the best tactic for survival is to act in ways that retain the most diversity; then, when circumstances do change, there will be a chance that a new set of genes, a species, or a society will be able to continue under the new conditions. Diversity confers resilience, adaptability, and the capacity for regeneration (Suzuki &McConnell, 1997, p. 162).

1. A CRISIS IN LEADERSHIP

In 1996 Peter Drucker crystallized his life's research in *The Leader of the Future* to predict an emerging "knowledge era" where organization leaders and followers need to be *smarter* and much more *nimble* to lead knowledge era work. History is proving Drucker right. By 2011, leaders everywhere are facing pressure to "know better" and to "better guide" our more technologically interconnected and constantly changing organizations in the knowledge era (Fullan, 2002). However, leading *smarter* (more intelligent) and *adaptable* organizations well in persistently unsteady-state conditions is a task beyond the grasp of many leader-practitioners and researchers. In 2011, the world witnessed The Arab Spring, civil unrest across Greece, the global 'Occupy Movement' and profound new tremors across the European Union (2011). These are macroexamples of both rational and irrational, and yet highly interconnected economic, political, and cultural systems coexisting as an undeniable backdrop for public leadership thought today. It is nearly impossible to reduce such a complex backdrop to merely "leadership" or "management" objects anymore, yet many leaders try to make those pieces "manageable" by attempting to reduce organizations to working "pieces." That is a serious delimitation for today's leadership thinkers while the public once again wonders why leaders and scholars cannot avoid all manner of repeating and cascading system failures impacting millions of lives (Marion & Uhl-Bein, 2001; Goldstein, 2010). The day of the

Great Lone Leader is gone. In this technological age leaders can no longer simply parse our work to generate organization structure, to set values or to focus on human relations organizations, for example. Leaders need to learn *with and across our* organizations to generate the very possibility for our organizations to adapt in a new age (Schlechty, 2009).

Leaders struggle to understand the "whole system" perspectives. We also struggled to understand and react to cascading economic system growth from 2001 to 2008 in both the developed and developing world (OECD, 2010). For example, we failed to predict the cascade of North American banking failures and subsequent European sovereign debt crises. History teaches us that these patterns of growth and collapses have happened many times before (Reinhart & Rogoff, 2009), but in the 21st century, we have clearly been unable to develop ways to predict these major events. Our perceptual narrowing occurs when we reduce the concept of leadership into structural functionalism—this is akin to planning this year's annual picnic just as we did last year but without accessing current weather information, food preference changes or changes in the picnickers themselves. Most academics and public sector and government leaders, particularly education system leaders—have similarly failed rather miserably to predict or to learn in concert with our emerging, unstable, connected worlds of economics, cultures, finances, politics, and ideals since the economic crisis of 2008. We seem overwhelmed. Complexity theorists warn us that prediction may, in fact be impossible when we realize that everything is always in flux—so the ability to adapt and to learn (the subject of this chapter) may be much more important to leaders of technologically engaged, changing organizations (Cilliers, 1998; Capra, 2002). Perhaps our collective ability to adapt and to learn as leaders in unsteady states is too constrained by a proliferation of specializations among us while our individual ideas, approaches, and tactics lack a certain degree of diversity or "difference" that is so necessary for people to co-create or to learn in many of these situations (Rorty, 1989). Does this sound familiar to you? Are we overspecialized for the times? Are we underspecialized? Leadership scholars today all gesture to important "change" features and to what complexity theorists see as "preconditions" for organizational adaptability in complex systems. Changing organizations in general are told to embody a necessary degree of tension, difference, and heterogeneity that will allow us, as Einstein warned, to think differently than the ways that got us to where we are today. In this chapter, we focus on two such features of organizations (1) *leader and follower abilities to learn* about the changing context of the organization (Schlechty, 2009; Marion & Uhl-Bein, 2001; Davis, Sumara, & Kapler, 2008) and (2) the *capability of leaders and followers to adapt* (Bertalanffy, 1969; Goldstein, Hazy, & Lichtenstein, 2010; Kowch, 2007). If, as leaders, we accept that things are in constant flux and that things are all interconnected to each other, we must also consider that the very *possibility* for some sort of purposeful adaptability at the organization level will depend on a concept that includes the ironies and tensions found between difference, specialization, redundancy, and other features of the modern organization.

Meanwhile, billions of lives in many nations are pushed and pulled every day by global leaders doing their best to respond to many change forces with the aid of modern communications and digital learning technologies that allow people to connect quickly and powerfully over space and time. Too familiar with bureaucratic and hierarchical realities in organization life that were common before such ubiquitous connective technologies, leaders today feel pressure from the new, incredible connectivities offered and they must learn to lead within these complex systems, not just to "manage" parts of the organization (Oblensky, 2010). Tied together both tightly and loosely by communication networks the leaders of today's organizations

have responded to a public and employee demands for less rigid organization models. One response is to connect to "fads" of the day, thereby clinging to convenient metaphors and models like "distributed leadership" most recently indicating once again that we are indeed aware of the new relational context of our organizations (Forno & Merlone, 2007). Sadly, as we explore in the brief history of leadership thought summarized in the next section, the "network metaphor" is widely used as a descriptor of what "could be" but when we review organization change data showing what most organization networks actually do, we find that almost no one actually studies networks and relation patterns in education (or any) organizations (Kowch, 2009) beyond simplistic 'social' network study. Convenient metaphors are not enough. As leaders in these technology-involved ecosystems we are, indeed, failing to "walk the talk" reflected by our new language about agility, transformation, and change particularly in the public sector where organizations still exist as very bureaucratic organizations (Mclellan, 2010), and this author's 20 years of research and experience leading large organizations is testament to an emerging language about change creating a vast shadow over the important work to realize organization change:

The financial industry had always been intended to be something of an unseen backroom support for the broader economy…yet in the years leading up to the crisis the financial sector itself became the front room (Sorkin, 2009, p. 538).

Embedded in this quote is subtle evidence of a predominant old-world view of organizing as a set of stable structures divided by partitions where we sort and promote different and specialized functions or work done by people. The idea that industry or any organization can be sorted into "back rooms and front rooms" within structures (houses) is indicative of this *piecemeal* mindset problem where we sort and partition complex industries and entire sectors in our minds. Worse, within that "building" we imagine sub-structures where very specific visible and hidden specialized activities occur as separate from the rest of the world. Fixated on "the building," we lose sight of the neighbors, who comes and goes from our building, and indeed the fact that we share parts of it, lose parts of it and exist in a neighborhood, city, region and nation. This causes tremendous oversimplification.

Leaders know that there is a lot more to an organization than structure, nested structures or even a set of cultures, just as we know that there is a lot more to organizing than mere human relations, culture or shared values often studied in a piecemeal fashion as completely separate "models" describing how people get things done. Piecemeal thinking and overspecialization is prohibiting a comprehensive understanding of our complex, constantly changing organizations today. So it is easy to see why *we face an imperative to blend information and educational technology disciplines for new leadership thinking* (Kowch, 2009) as we unpack the implicit, uncritical ideas and metaphors for 'structure' to understand the very potentials of our new organizations to adapt as mixes of diverse, specialized (but not too specialized) ideas, people, contexts and issues. For nearly 15 years, this author's research has found that these implicit, uncritical ways of knowing organizations guide everything we do as leaders—and we need to face that limitation to move forward. We can begin by exploring a few of the very features that empower complex systems (not fixed structures) to adapt via a mixture of *diversity*, *specialization*, and *redundancy*, as we do later in this chapter. As leaders, we must accept these newer approaches to *discovering adaptability* because earlier structural models incorrectly assume machine-like connections between people and "functions" existing within implicitly steady states among those heavily partitioned structures of the mind (you cannot actually "see" a department, for example). We cling to these mindsets

so uncritically but in reality, every atom of every artifact in all the structures are in states of flux ranging from static (dead) to wildly (surprisingly) chaotic (Cilliers, 1998).

It is imperative that new scholars and leaders build up our interdisciplinary knowledge of leading to better learn and to lead better in the knowledge era (Thompson-Klien, 2010). We *can* understand organizations less intuitively, and more as a context for patterns of work that occur as a bricolage of both *learning* and *adapting* efforts done between and among people in "near chaotic" relational networks. Information-age work framed by a new information technology design mindset is no longer work done by specialized labor from partitions or cubicles—it is the work done by co-creators who emerge from across "organizations" seeking innovation, change, and new mental models for a new era (Miller & Page, 2007). Leadership literature, especially in the public education sector stacks high with commentary on *distributed* leading and *transformation* while in the next second a writer or reader can gaze across any office situation to find powerful, entrenched bureaucracies that *look, act and feel nothing like what is read or written.* These tensions must be better understood. Are we becoming too similar to one another as leaders or scholars in this field? Are idea fads and consulting 'gold rushes' sapping the potential of our organizations to adapt and respond to our changing challenges head-on? Are we losing our own scholarly diversity to wave of popular, metaphor-laden overspecialization within our ranks as 'fads' make our ways of knowing leadership seem (wrongly) homogenous "Fall of the Faculty" (Ginsberg, 2011)? To understand diversity today, we need to understand our *academic and practice contexts better.*

More robust concepts are emerging from new research to help us understand leading complex change in the knowledge era organizational ecosystems. Today, leaders and followers are re-imagining the ubiquitous "cubicle" metaphor more as a leaf in a forest that is part of the interdependent work we do with each other in more open, connected "space." We also need to know more about the entire organization ecosystem to really understand the qualities, contexts and common patterns work (not just social contacts) that comprise such complex (eco)systems (Castells, 2004; Fisher, 2009). In the future, your job as a leader will no longer be limited to care for the leaf, the tree or for the forest in pieces—your job will be to learn, to change and recognize special work done within and around that diverse forest as both process and product, as both means and ends in states of constant flux (Rorty, 1989). Similarly, we will need to expand the space of the possible in our leadership thinking domains and to *diversify our very perceptions of the "organization"* well beyond a set of nested structures where specialized work occurs in linear box or "organization flow-chart" patterns. Far too much research is showing that the constant explosion of jargon underpinning convenient industries selling "transformational leadership" mantra is being understood as temporary 'trends' and as 'means' to ends (Kowch, 2007, 2008).

Old ideas die hard. We often notice new students to our advanced leadership classes that can quickly recognize and critique the latest technology and leadership 'fads' or *'trends'* with precision and acuity. However because they most often understand *organizations* mostly as structures in steady conditions, these future leaders interpret 'fads' or diverse change features, especially *technological* change as one big set of constant change pieces. They often write of these as pieces in a steady "change rhetoric" happening 'outside' the organization—almost like cloudy weather—until we, as (great) leaders 'adopt' them or close our windows.

This author recently waited in a traffic jam across from a beautifully renovated large two-story home (circa 1890) in metropolitan Calgary. He noticed a plethora of new, high-tech windows, roof skylights and top-quality landscaping additions enhancing this completely renovated archi-

tecture. Since the renovation was done around 2000, a group of five twenty-story plus condo towers emerged on *all* sides of this home. This is a perfect example of what happens when change leaders (at the home) engage the kind of thinking we explored in the previous section. That thinking leads precisely to a "successful" home renovation project (change) by change leaders not ignoring, but rather 'compartmentalizing' the possibility of unconventional building (and zoning) changes in the environment. If the change leaders had been old-style leadership specialists, it is easy to imagine what their language would have been at the post-renovation house-warming party:

By the end of the renovation, our "blue-sky" planning considered internal and external features to the property, some which we adopted and some we did not. Some, like what happens beyond the structure property line are beyond our control anyway, for we hear that some building may occur in the area. This too may pass - people are always building. Looking at the changes to the house we imagined, our renovation was: "distributed," planned, designed and built collaboratively among highly effective and efficient, specialized architects and contractors; community focused and open; maintaining craftsmen architecture and the architectural diversity of the neighborhood; cost effective; customer centred; sustainable; value-driven and evidence-based. The transformation is green and ecosystem-friendly too, for the house and garden will be bathed with natural light.

In 2012, sunlight never lands on this property. The front porch light burns brightly at noon. There are indications of large tree and plant removals. One of the neighboring towers just changed ownership while a weathered Realtor sign rises from the home's front lawn. If we could hear the voice of the specialists and condo builders we would likely hear different prose describing the impact of this house transformation, reflecting differently upon "change leader" abilities to lead and to adapt. In

2012, leaders of our large, indebted public systems can no longer afford such less complex, closed-system thinking. Neither can private corporations, cities, governments, nations or our natural ecologies stand the pressure of piecemeal systems thinking where everyone does their specialty on a closed set. We are simply *far* more interconnected than we think we are in a diverse, technological age (Barabasi, 2003; Baker, 2008).

We must re-conceptualize change, leadership and organizations to become better leaders now by evolving our leadership knowledge for a new context (Levin & Fullan, 2008).

A company is not a living machine...its people get better by learning, evolution, and flexible adaptation (Capra, 2002, p. 114).

Other chapters in this book offer more specific explorations of specific kinds of diversity including social, psychological, and cultural diversity that leaders must consider better to lead in a technological age. In this chapter, we consider rather that the presence of (many kinds) of diversity is an important precondition to leading any kind of systemic or complex (organization wide) change, and we explore the conditions under which a varying mix of diversity and redundancy allow us to achieve the start-point for change, as leaders.

This kind of thinking has existed for years in business (Goldstein, et al., 2010) and information technology sectors (Miller & Page, 2007) while and very little of it is going on in education but for in curriculum study (Davis & Sumara, 2008). By contrast, almost no complexity-thinking research is published in the education subfields such as technology or education leadership. Yet the discipline of education is the academic "home" of this author who studies relational structures for learning and leading in any organization context.

First, we need to understand the context of leadership and organization thinking that got us only so far, as we do in the next section of this chapter. Then we can explore what complex organizations are and how important diversity is to the ecosystem's very potentials for change (real change and adaptation is very unlikely without a mix of *diversity* and *redundancy* in ecosystems).

2. SHIFTS IN LEADERSHIP THOUGHT: AN EVOLUTION FROM CLOSED TO "WHOLE SYSTEM" THINKING

Only leaders who are equipped to handle a complex, rapidly changing environment can implement the reforms that lead to sustained improvement (Fullan, 2002; Levin & Fullan, 2008).

Complexity thinking often prompts researchers to think with "a *trans-disciplinary* research attitude" (Sumara, Davis, & Kapler, 2008, p. 111). This interdisciplinary work shares leadership perspectives on diversity from two sister-disciplines across the humanities; (1) *organization science* (business/economics and organization theory and practice) and (2) the *learning sciences* (education leadership and learning theory and practice). Together these lenses offer rare and penetrating glimpses into complex system organization and leadership conditions and qualities such as diversity, specialization and redundancy. Before we outline how important specialization and diversity are for leading the networked organization of the future, we should first examine the constantly shifting terrain of leadership theory (or thought).

Next, A quick examination of sweeping changes in leadership thinking over the last century offers readers an important backdrop for leaders who need to evolve a space for 21st century thinking about: (1) varying degrees of *specialization*, inclusive of; (2) a mix of *diversity*, duplication (*redundancy*) with; (3) the *ability of people networks* to (4) organize their interests and *work together* as critical foundations for leading change across complex organizations.

2.1. The Evolution of Leadership Thinking: From Scientific Management to Complexity Theory

A brief account of leadership theory over time allows us to better understand two important points before we delve into leading diversity in an organization that 'learns' to adapt: (1) *complexity thinking* may be a 'tipping point' in the development of leadership theory and that (2) *diversity*, as a feature of specialization is critical to new understandings about leading complex and emerging (transforming) systems. For most of our historical leadership theory, we have modeled or theorized the organization as existing in "steady state" or stable realities, not as "far-from-equilibrium" states that characterize today's technologically engaged organizations- where *technology can be the single largest disruptive change catalyst in complex organizations* (Goldstein, Hazy, & Lichtenstein, 2010; Christensen, Horn, & Johnson, 2008).

A problem of incoherence: Leadership models have evolved over time as scholars and practitioners responses to the inadequacies found in the preceding models (Hallinger, 2002; Willower & Forsythe, 1999). Today, stakeholders and leaders alike complain that our current leadership models still fail to describe true leadership in our world and that there is little connection between leadership rhetoric and the leadership needs in organizations. This has been going on for too long, but there are good reasons for it.

Contemporary thinking about *leadership*, which is a term that is somewhat ironically impossible to define from the literature (Hargreaves, 2010), has evolved from centuries of reductionist, cause-effect, linear explanations of physical and social phenomena about people and organizations. More recently we have shifted to thinking *in toto* about organizations, work, partnering and people engaged via technology as a more organic, nonlinear way of knowing where uncertainty and unpredictability can be accounted (Goldstein, 2010; Schlechty, 2009; Marion & Uhl-Bein,

2001). This overall movement has been possible because faster computers, large datasets, analytics and evidence-based decision making allow us to witness more of a whole-system gaze and an ecological mindset—a mindset that we could not possibly have attempted in earlier sort-and-study time periods (Schwandt & Szabla, 2007; Kowch, 2009), though not all leaders are sufficiently technologically oriented to make use of such tools and ideas (Cuban, 2011). The following brief review of leadership thought over the last few decades offers solid grounds for this author's subsequent argument that leadership theory has transformed to a point where we must can consider complex organizational change as completely dependent upon the existence of two important features of specialization—diversity and redundancy.

- **1900 to 1950:** Organizational theorists Schwandt and Szabla (2007) point out that scientific management in the early 20th century tried to accurately portray work-life cause-effect relations between workers and efficiency by assuming that all organizations exist in a state of equilibrium. By 1945, leaders began to think about system and human relationships as features that could be "managed" to maintain equilibrium through a mix social choices and problem-solving interventions. To use an anthill metaphor, in this period we studied the contingent behaviors of the ants amidst the interventions of the (great) ant-leader.

- **1950-1960:** At the dawn of the information processing age, educational administration scholars understood leaders as top-down actors in hierarchies. We focused on specialized, highly trained people with roles performing specific functions within relatively isolated bureaucratic institutions (Griffiths, 1964). Leaders set out goals and provided interventions to achieve specially prescribed outcomes in times when people counted as parts in a set of *work trans-*

actions within machine-like organizing processes. As a response to interventions that had not worked, open and closed systems thinking arrived, shifting us toward a slightly subjective or 'it depends' stance, and systems thinkers emerged to ponder the functions and variations in information processes. Leaders focused on internal organization processes before the 1970s, where leader behavior and models of internal and external system transactions emerged. Alas, leader *results* often did not match their intentions in the transactions era and since. Using our anthill metaphor again, in this era we studied the inputs and outputs and what ants did to each another, as well as the structure of the hill as it may have shaped their work.

- **1960-1970:** The *social systems approach* followed in the 1960s to focus on leader *transactions* based on general systems theory. Here, the focus of the leader was remained on the inputs, outputs, work flows and rules for doing things (actions) according to (work) functions while also considering the importance of socialization processes (Evers & Lakomski, 1996). Still mechanistic in nature, leading work was thought about as an activity not done alone but within social system processes as well (Schwandt & Szabla, 2007). Thinking about values began to emerge as socialization over older structural ideas caused tensions for 'more social' leaders. Revisiting the anthill metaphor, here we studied the causes and effects of social discourse among teams of ants and individuals, with leadership focusing on developing power and shared norms among as part of ant leadership socialization. The diversity inherent to socializing differing people and units led to unexpected outcomes and a strong critique of the social systems approach, particularly as television and mass communication connected diverse

people and settings. Tending the ant society in all its complexity was found to consume infeasible amounts of leader time, requiring further leader specialization.

- **1970-1990:** By the 1980s, North American populations objected to leaders that were found spending far too much time on ever-changing "machine maintenance" management activities resulting from the social systems approach. Cries for "*critical social theory*" rose where leaders aimed to integrate socialization and more value based principles for leading organization socialization (Bates, 1982; Greenfield, 1984). Simultaneously, the introduction of values as post –rational ways of knowing emerged so that individual and social norms without "ends" in mind framed a fresh approach to leading organizations. Leadership theory exploded, but overall student learning achievement in education systems was not found to improve, despite these more holistic trends in leading. During the 1970s, 80s, and 90s most contemporary research then shifted again from social transaction studies to *instructional leadership and school effectiveness* movements (Blasé & Blasé, 1996). These approaches slowed when evidence of bureaucratic leader "management" duties were found to conflict too often with more broad "leadership" goals that, overall resulted again in very little system performance improvement (in education, student achievement) gains (Hargreaves & Fink, 2006). Here we studied ant leader's value and how ant leaders offered followers a shared sense of emancipation at work. In the education discipline we studied the effectiveness of ant leader policy and organization (especially planning) to improve system outputs (learning). We studied the ant social machine, values and student learning as the 'customer' moved to the center of the organization in terms of interest (actual results were mixed).

- **1990-2000:** In the 1990s, *more holistic, transformational models* emerged describing leaders who aroused human potential, satisfied higher needs, and elevated communal work aimed at higher commitments and performances (Leithwood, et al., 2005; Sergiovanni, 1989). This led to a predominantly, leader-centered egoist ideology among *effective practitioners*, a problem that is oddly reminiscent to the "great man" (sic) trait theory limitations of the 1940s. When we realized this shortcoming, we extended social and structural thinking to imagine and study decentralized and distributing leadership work as a more inclusive, shared concept (Gronn, 2002). At the same time, the more traditional power-based cause/effect models for structuring human relations were found to fall well short as descriptive models for most 21st century era schools and global education systems (Mitchell & Sackney, 2011). In this era, we studied the queen ant types in the context of dominant social, political and change "forces" acting on organizations to explain and craft interventions. We modeled and designed operational and social systems to harmonize better so that the ant (worker) society could transform its own systems (even perhaps to move to a new hill) through the simultaneous empowerment of leaders, followers and public pressure. The "gold rush" of organizational transformation consulting and rhetoric proliferated—but research showed little evidence of the ideas impacting education system learning achievements (Leithwood & Jantzi, 2005; Kowch, 2009).

- **2000+:** In the 21st century, *distributed leadership* models emerged, bearing more *relational* system features to focus more the best practices of leaders and followers who share the work of guiding large, bureaucratic systems with the overarching ethos of 'letting go' of their power within far more integrated, intuitive decision making collectives (Gronn, 2002; Harris, 2008), yet very few leadership scholars actually studied the networks, preferring to use the convenient metaphors instead. By 2012, distributed leadership has yet to gain empirical or research evidence base proving the ideas. A nagging problem, so far, is that these theorists *seldom explore the structural and dynamic features* of 'distributed organizations' specifically, so they don't help leaders to understand the idea beyond a general understanding of it as another form of delegation (Harris, 2008). By 2011 the distributed leadership is losing popularity among scholars and practitioners because even this holistic, more integrated organization approaches still appears to be "piecemeal" in terms of really integrating and designing *total* systemic change inclusive of most dynamics within changing institutions (Reigeluth & Duffy, 2008; Gronn, 2002). Somewhere in between distributed leadership thought and complexity thinking are the many micro and meso level *communities of practice* theories and other professional development leadership models that promoting social interaction within the profession (DuFour & Eaker, 2005), but these models also fall short of reality as "…easy concepts that were seldom realized in terms of [actual] leadership communities" (Levin & Fullan, 2008; Kowch, 2007).

So today in leadership theory we espouse that the "ants": (1) really do share their work; (2) communicate with technology and data continuously; (3) are heavily connected to the collective work they do and to one another; (4) share values; and that (5) (cultural) diversity among the ant hill population is absolutely necessary for socialization. In this era, ants seem to talk a lot about socialization and culture mainly to please leaders who tend to share or express sharing more of the work during more collective transformation efforts.

2.2. A Shift to Complexity Thinking?

Organizations are complex systems (Uhl-Bein, et al., 2007). How do we understand a complex system (organization) as something with the potential for adaptation/change? With new knowledge that complex systems can be understood as patterns of relations organized according to certain rules applying to unsteady state conditions, leadership researchers are thinking about complexity approaches to understanding organization at the same time as learning system researchers focused on engaging learners in completely new ways (Uhl-Bein, et al., 2007; Davis, 2005). Complexity thinking works to understand *learning* systems (Doll, 2010; Davis, Sumara, & Kapler, 2008) and organizations (Goldstein, et al., 2010), and that is important because *learning* and *adaptability* are connected ideas here, when and if the right amount of diversity exists in the system. Connected here is the concept of *diversity* in the natural world as it informs our way of knowing organizations of people when we lead systemic change (Hargreaves & Fink, 2006). As complexity thinkers, we respect advice from Darwin that "*groups of the best need not be the best groups*" (Page, 2007, p. 671), and that diversity matters in complex systems, ecosystems, and organizations. This idea will be evolved in the next sections of this chapter.

It is a parallel 'ant hill' perspective of agents (people), actions and conditions for collaborative work that is informing this newer perception of diversity for organization leaders. Today, more interdisciplinary research from business, IT and organization theory fields informs the Humanities so we can see new patterns, features and principles for collective work (Thompson-Klien, 2010). Combined with policy and social network relation mapping, we understand much more about actual networks of people and organizations working together, turning complex system analytics into much less of a metaphor to offer deeper understanding about of collective work potentials, individual

and institutional dynamics, relation types, patterns and ideology in constantly changing environments (Kowch, 2003, 2007, 2009). Here we study how ants learn by understanding what's happening around the ant hill and inside of it in concert with knowledge about influence and social relations, patterns of relations, degrees of specialization and degrees of specialization and diversity among ants. We see as well the supra-systems or weather (politics, history, economics) in the ecosystem by remembering that the hill is always changing with these interdependent features. This marks a *definitive change* in the way education system scholars and most scholars conceptualize change leadership (also known as emergence) when entire organizations are concerned.

The real voyage of discovery consists not in seeking new lands but seeing with new eyes (Proust, 1899).

2.3. Shifts in the Way Leaders Think About Change

It is important to realize that *technology is the single largest amplifier or feature in accelerating change across complex organizations*. Reigeluth (1991) merged technology and learning design thinking with systemic change theory to suggest a necessary paradigm shift as a pre-condition for systemic change in education systems of any scale by noting the *critical importance of technology for learning* in the modern context. In 1995, change theorist Everett Rogers offered a view of organization change as dependent upon an S-curve innovation adoption process in business. The idea evolved to incorporate the concept of constant change in *Disrupting Class* (Christensen, Horn, & Johnson, 2008). Christensen used education as an example where technology-led education system replacements will likely be enacted by new governance and learner choices for better education via distance learning. His work supports the ideas of education change theorists who also claim that when most participants in an ecosystem find a better alternative or product than what is offered by failing (public) systems, alternative organizations emerge that can totally change the competition overnight (Fullan, 2002; Hargreaves & Fink, 2006). These shifts mark a change from classical functionalist thinking to post structural, complex perspectives about change in organizations.

Ecosystems are more open to change than we have thought, and they are inherently unstable. More recent research includes the idea that organizations are not in steady, rather they are in constant flux with an incredible number of relational factors influencing one another—just like in every living ecosystem (Davis & Sumara, 2006; Oblensky, 2010; Fullan, 2002; Hargreaves & Fink, 2006). In the 1980s-1990s, systems theorists Bertalanffy and Simon translated information system logic to social systems. Systemic change and complexity (emergence) theorists work today with network theory to understand "the expanding space of the possible" (Hazy, 2008), and they consider too how educational technology and leadership thinking must combine to prepare leaders for these new contexts (Kowch, 2009).

Next, we explore how organizations are complex, emerging (changing) ecosystems that are very, very dependent on a mix of diversity, redundancy and interest organization capabilities to change (emerge) and adapt (learn).

3. FRAMING ORGANIZATIONS AS EMERGENT COMPLEX ECOSYSTEMS

Business schools have treated organizations as if they were machines that could be analyzed, dissected, and broken into parts. According to that myth, if you fix the parts, then reassemble and lubricate, you'll get the whole system up and running. But this exactly the wrong way to approach a complex problem... it misses the fact that under the right conditions a complex system can adapt,

whereas a piece of machinery cannot... an aircraft cannot reconfigure itself but an organization can (Goldstein, et al., 2010, p. 3).

3.1. Emergence

In social contexts, invention and innovation arise in much the same way, through a process of emergence. In complex systems that learn, diversity is a critical condition for the emergence of innovation and learning in organizations (Davis & Sumara, 2006), as discussed in the coming sections. However first we must recognize that emergence is not merely a technical term for any old kind of organizational change. Rather, it refers to levels of change that are deeply rooted in the organization where significant characteristics in the environments increase "the contours of the possible" for change itself (Davis & Sumara, 2006). This is a difficult concept for us when we realizes that in a state of constant flux we need a way to understand factors that influence the possibility for change (diversity) and the characteristics of levels of change/emergence (Goldstein, 2010). An example works best:

When carbon, oxygen, and hydrogen atoms bond in a certain way to form sugar, the resulting compound has a sweet taste that is not in any of the separate atoms themselves (Capra, 2002).

Sweetness is a feature that *emerges* from complexity in Capra's example. It is more than the sum of its 'parts.' The same is true for organizations. Emergence is not a synonym for transformation. *Emergence* is complexity science's term for the creation of organizational processes, structures, and practices that add greater functionality and adaptability in the face of an increasingly turbulent environment. So given that emergence is a phase of change in complex systems, and that diversity and redundancy create the potential for emergence (via learning among people), we need to understand a some of the features of complex systems or ecosystems that we will call complex organizations.

3.2. Complex Systems

Complex systems cannot be reduced to their parts because "they are always caught up with other systems in a dance of change" (Davis, Sumara, & Kapler, 2008). Complex systems are more spontaneous, unpredictable, irreducible, contextual and adaptive. Complex and complicated systems are often confused and that confusion represents our paradigm shift. Table 1 illustrates the distinctly different features of complicated and complex systems:

Cilliers (1998) identified ten characteristics of complex systems: (1) big, with many agents; (2) actors change one another over time; (3) all elements interact with others. Some redundancy; (4) relations are nonlinear; (5) short range network connections; (6) positive and negative feedback looks regulate activity; (7) open systems; (8) state of disequilibrium; (9) Context, history and time matter; (10) each element is ignorant of the entire system. Characteristics 2 and 3 [actors *change each other* over time via interaction and *all elements interact with each other* and (8) state of

Table 1. Complicated vs. complex systems (source: Davis, Sumara, & Kapler, 2008, p. 77)

Complicated (Mechanical/Functional)	Complex (Learning or Organizing)
Physics (Newton)	Biology (Darwin)
Machine metaphors	Ecosystem metaphors
Linear imagery	Cyclical, recursive imagery
Input/output flows	Feedback loops/regulation
Efficiency-oriented	Sufficiency-oriented
Goal-oriented	Growth-minded
Reducible to parts	Incompressible (fractal)

disequilibrium] matter most toward our understanding about why *diversity* and *learning* lead to *adaptable* and *smarter* complex organizations (McKelvey & Lichtenstein, 2007).

3.3. Can Organizations be Framed as Ecosystems?

Yes. The Greek word *"eco"* means "household" or "community, so the term "ecology" refers to a particular kind of community. Examples from the biology disciplines include coastal bays, rain forests and such as nested systems just as organizations have units, task forces and subgroups (Marion & Uhl-Bein, 2001). Both biologists and complexity researchers agree that a thriving ecology is a set of nested subsystems embedded in a community of resonant interactions with each other and their shared environments. A vibrant ecology is always changing in many, many ways so it is considered to be an *emerging* complex system. Few scholars study organizational emergence today but those who do find that diversity is critical to emergent learning and emergent adaptive organizations (Goldstein, et al., 2010; Oblensky, 2010). *Organization ecosystems* have the same basic features of *complex* systems, summarized as: (1) diversity (across the networks); (2) Experiments (with novelty emerging from diversity); (3) Intricate networks connecting nested subsystems to one another; (4) Innovation conferring new functionalities and adaptability (to jolts); (5) Critical periods of instability. Yes, organizations can be framed well as ecosystems. We have learned that organizations are complex emergent ecosystems that are depending on some specific conditions for their chances to emerge and to adapt. Next, we explore that complex systems do exhibit intelligence and that complex systems with people (organizations) can adapt effectively via collaborative learning (see Table 2).

Table 2. An example of simple "intelligence" in complex natural organizations

Computer science complexity thinkers discovered (simple) basic rules that individual fish, birds and bees follow to organize their movements in large swarms so that they change speed and direction with terrific speed without crashing into each another (Partridge et al., 1980). These simple rules are used for all computer game animations today where many bodies travel in "swarms." (Organization theorists muse that if employees could do this, organizations would be more adaptable).

The rules are simple:
1. **Avoidance & separation** (avoid bumping into the being ahead, behind, above and below you.
2. **Alignment** (move in the direction that those closest to you are heading).
3. **Cohesion & Attraction** (move toward the position of those closest to you).

So swarms are intelligent. They can also learn and adapt together. Scientists have modeled this behavior as well to analyze traffic, human crowds and to set up Google searchers on the Internet. The basic principles of pattern recognition and collective movement hold up pretty well.

3.4. Emergent Intelligence: Can Ecosystems "Think and Learn" (Adapt)?

The only stable ecosystems in existence are dead systems (Waldrop, 1992). Living systems are in constant flux (Waldrop, 1992; Capra, 2002). It follows that: (1) an organization cannot be dead; (2) organizations are in constant stages of flux, called emergence; and that (3) existing organizations are complex systems. Some complexity researchers find that emergence (system wide change) across an organization is guided (or enabled) by a simple set of innovation rules dependent on diversity in the system (Goldstein, et al., 2010). So what is the cause of organization emergence? For parsimony

and before we explore *organization emergence*, we should offer a simple example of complex emergent "intelligence" or "smartness" from nature.

Basic rules *do* apply within unsteady state and seemingly chaotic complex systems. These are not chaotic, free-for-all or unbound systems at all, yet they do flourish as open systems. By discovering the rules, researchers can understand cause/effect relationships (Partridge, et al., 1980; Barabasi, 2010) (see Table 3).

Have you ever wondered how swarms of bees fly to a patch of blooms with such speed and accuracy, without each bee crashing into one another or getting lost? The answer is a far less 'managed' process than you might expect (Fisher, 2009). In fact, similar complex rules/thinking underpins the way Google searches, smartphone tower and face recognition technology function. Social science researchers use these principles to describe and analyze large political, social (Scott, 2000) and influence networks (Kowch, 2003).

How a bee swarms organizes their collective work has been described by digital photo technology and it has been successfully simulated since by using Partridge's (simple) rules. Applying those rules gave Martin Lindauer the first understanding of how bees organize their *emergent intelligence*. Lindauer discovered that a few leading and faster 'streaker' bees possessing a clear idea of the location of the target take

Table 3. The conditions for complex adaptation

While people are far more evolved than bees of course, we can use a bee swarm example to realize that while complex fish swarms use rules to act collectively, bee swarms can make decisions collectively (as can groups of people).

This means that complex systems (organizations) can learn and adapt (become smarter) using similar principles.

While complex organizations can adapt via collaborative, networked learning, certain conditions must exist for that complex organization to have a chance to adapt.

Those conditions are: *specialization, diversity, redundancy and the ability to organize interests* as networks.

flight first, followed immediately by hundreds of worker bees. Guidance is achieved by a cascade effect in which uninformed individuals (with no idea where they are going) align their directions and speed with those of their neighbors. Even if only *a few of the bees* know their way Partridge's three rule (avoidance, alignment and cohesion/attraction), the whole swarm moves in the direction of the 'streaker' bees. The purposeful movement of bee swarms, in other words, is an example of a very simple form of complex "intelligence" that arises from simple local interactions. Beyond the scope of this chapter, similar principles are used by organization researchers to map and interpret the emergence of influence and interest organization relationships across organizations (Kowch, 2003, 2007). Yes, complex can organizations think (and learn). As leaders, it is out challenge in the 21st century to understand the conditions necessary for system intelligence as a thoughtful mix of diversity and redundancy within our envelopes of 'specialization,' so that people and organizations (complex systems) can learn well.

If a system has intelligence and if it is complex, it can learn and it can adapt. However, what does diversity have to do with that? Answer: Without diversity, the organization cannot change, as we explore next.

4. DIVERSITY AS A CONDITION FOR ORGANIZATION EMERGENCE: IT IS ALL ABOUT POTENTIAL

While demonstrating a primitive form of network intelligence, the bee swarm example did not demonstrate the importance of diversity in a complex, emergent (changing) organization. Researchers have found that diversity is a critical attribute for any complex organization to change completely (transform). In this chapter we have foreshadowed that two fields of study can overlap to offer a powerful framework for understanding the *critical importance of diversity* to complex organizations: (1) diversity offers an organization its very *potential* for "*learning* its way ahead" (smarter emergence) in unsteady states (via learning/knowledge building) and; (2) diversity offers an organization its very *potential* for *novelty* and subsequent innovations (organization science/innovation) that attract people toward change.

A bee swarm with emergent intelligence capability can become 'smarter' and adaptable. First, we must imagine bees swarming in an unpredictable context—say when a road is constructed across the bee flight path. To survive, a swarm must be able to adapt so it can make honey another day. Fort his learning to occur, Davis (2006) says that diversity must be present as a potential for the swarm to learn and to adapt its organizing abilities. For example, to be robust (live) our 'streaker' bees would need to have learned, over time, flight-path-avoidance techniques for intrusions for that system to be "smarter" or more intelligent. That knowledge building (potential) depends on some *differences* among the challenged streaker bees—specifically on their degree of specialization, which is created by the tension between the diversity among the streakers and their redundancy in the system. The same is true for groups of people with differences among them—alternative perspectives, representations and interpretations for example add potential for a complex group of intelligent people to do better on a problem, collectively for as Page finds in his social simulations "diversity trumps ability" when it comes to innovative problem solving (2007). Therefore, *diversity found across the organization offers the potential for complex groups to do better work*. Next, we explore the potential for an organization's "smarter emergence" from a complex systems learning perspective, finally outlining how features of complex systems offer such organizations the chance for system wide change (emergence). Here, we explore a shape of the possible.

4.1. "Smarter Emergence": Diversity and Redundancy as Conditions for System Intelligence Rethinking Specialization

Every organization is emerging at some rate in order to exist. Learning science researchers have discovered that the very potential for system emergence is critically dependent on three learning system conditions: (1) *specialization*; (2) *network learning*; and (3) *enablers and regulation* (Davis & Sumara, 2006). Conditions 2 and 3 are more related to the qualities or dynamics of an emerging system, so they are beyond the scope of this chapter. However, *specialization* contains the key to understanding diversity and its importance for an organization to even have a fair chance at emerging as a network of complex goings-on.

- **Specialization:** Necessary tensions (Kuhn, 1977; Rorty, 1989) exist in all ecosystems, and do specializations among people. There is a need for both differences and similarities in complex systems because unsteady states *demand* different contributions (diversity) in different system contexts (Waldrop, 1992; Cilliers, 1998). As well, a degree of commonality and duplication among the subsystems so that they can "stand in" and share meaning with each another, should one fail (redundancy) is also necessary for a complex system. Thus, diversity is one of two elements comprising an organization's *degree of specialization*. If a system is overspecialized, it has little chance to perform let alone change (imagine a hospital with 100% of its staff being cardiologists). Specialization is the single most important condition in terms of learning system affordances that offer organizations a chance (potentials) for (good) systemic tensions to exist between (a) *diversity* and (b) *redundancy* in the learning project as "energy for emergence." Diversity and

redundancy are *complementary*, not opposing features of specialization that "define the range and contours of possible responses" in a learning context (Davis & Sumara, 2006, p. 137).

- ○ **Diversity in complex learning systems**: According to Davis and Sumara (2006), the development of systemic intelligence depends critically upon diversity among its participants (agents, actors, learners, or nodes, however defined). Indeed, the robust intelligence of a complex organization depends on levels diversity found among and between collaborating participants as a source of (more) possible responses to emergent circumstances. Some of the *diversity attributes* found in people and complex system organizations (and subsystem units) that learn are:
  - ▪ **Contextual:** history, experience, skill, knowledge, values, and ideologies
  - ▪ **Difference:** among participants, creating a source and range of possible responses to emergent learning circumstances or knowing. The possibility for novelty in learning/knowledge building.
- ○ **Redundancy in learning systems**: Redundancy means that the other guy has just enough of what you have to both communicate and work with you and to possible do the tasks you do, in some measure. It does NOT mean wasteful duplication. In ecosystems, *redundancy plays two roles* in emergence. First, redundancy: (1) *makes working together* possible through (knowledge and same-knowledge of) shared texts, language, experience, and responsibilities, and (2) second,

redundancy *makes systems more robust* because people or subsystems are capable of "standing in" for one another over time, or for "filling in" the gaps in each other's knowledge or capabilities. While duplication is a problem in efficiency management, redundancy in ecological, computing and complexity science means there are "backup" elements in dynamic systems that can co-compensate. This is particularly handy for systems that acknowledge that they exist in our commonly far-from-equilibrium ecosystems.

Figure 1 demonstrates the complementary roles of redundancy and diversity as catalysts for emerging learning systems.

4.2. A Framework for Leading Smarter, Adaptive Organizations: Knowing Your Organization's Capacity for Emergence

(The right mix of diversity, redundancy and the capacity of organizational networks to organize interests in far-from-equilibrium contexts).

We have examined that specialization (redundancy and diversity) in an organization is about the intensity of collective participant experience realized as a mix of *diverse* characters and *redundant* features among the network participants. Overspecialized work networks (the wrong mix) are much less likely to organize interests well as high capacity interest organization network (Kowch, 2003). By mapping these high and low diversity and redundancy features in a learning system, we realize that inflexible systems have

Figure 1. Diversity and redundancy as affordances for learning system emergence (Davis & Sumara, 2008)

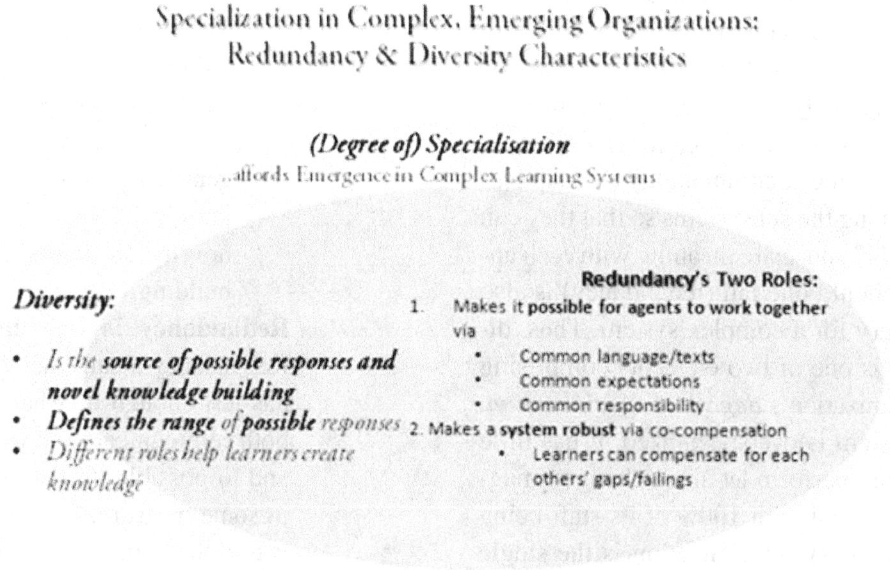

Specialization in Complex, Emerging Organizations:
Redundancy & Diversity Characteristics

(Degree of) Specialisation
...affords Emergence in Complex Learning Systems

Diversity:

- *Is the source of possible responses and novel knowledge building*
- *Defines the range of possible responses*
- *Different roles help learners create knowledge*

Redundancy's Two Roles:

1. Makes it possible for agents to work together via
   - Common language/texts
   - Common expectations
   - Common responsibility
2. Makes a system robust via co-compensation
   - Learners can compensate for each others' gaps/failings

minimum redundancy and a high degree of specialization, where adaptable systems have a high level of redundancy and a low level of specialization. Organizations with the highest potential to emerge really are capable of systemic intelligence (Davis & Sumara, 2006) or "smartness" thoughtful, collective acts of emergence shaped by diversity.

Getting work done together in a complex organization (that learns) means also having the *capacity to make decisions or to organize interests* not as a hierarchical structures per se, rather *as learning networks* embedded with the right mixes of diversity and redundancy among people.

Only a handful of education leadership scholars closely examine complex organization relational networks beyond the use of such a "convenient" metaphor, as we have said. However, empirical studies are emerging to describe and analyze the ability, type and potential of relational (leader networks) (Kowch, 2003, 2005, 2007, 2009). By adding the dimension of interest organization capacity for our working networks (Figure 3), we can characterize emergent learning system potentials for emergence with their potential to get work done. In sum, we can plot the mixture of diversity, redundancy, and network capabilities to get work done in one context for the first time.

Kowch (2003) demonstrated that the complex emergence of ideas and policy networks across large institutions and political ecologies across entire states could be defined, interpreted and predicted using network and policy theory to identify six characteristics of high capacity networks (Kowch, 2005, 2007, 2009):

1. A clear *concept of role* in collective work.
2. A supporting *value system*.
3. A unique, *professional ethos* in the field.
4. A capability to *generate information* internally.
5. A capability to maintain *cohesion*.
6. A capability to *organize and manage complex tasks*, leading toward the creation of a response.
7. A capability to *rise above self interest*.

In the knowledge era, much has been written about networked, transforming organizations Modern technologies allow us to describe and interpret patterns within, among and between vastly complicated, organized collective work/ within relational, networked ecosystems (Castells, 2004; Kowch, 2009). Yet most leaders focus on power, pyramid structures or culture to understand our collective work in organizations, of which most are deeply embedded with old and neo-bureaucracies (Clegg, Harris, and Hopfl, 2011). Table 3 is a useful new framework for leaders to understand this important interplay between diversity and redundancy in complex learning systems.

Thus, Figure 2 offers framework for characterizing previously inconceivably complicated system or organizations that learn. Unlike previous thinking, this framework recognizes that the organization and its networks exist in unsteady states as an interconnected collection diverse and redundant people with a range of abilities to organize interests and to spark innovation across a range of diversity and redundancy characteristics.

By analyzing these features with an eye to mapping out just how likely certain mixes of these features indicate an entire organization's potential to emerge, we can identify high, medium and low potentials for emergence (Figure 3). This is a framework for helping leaders to understand if your complex organization is mostly comprised of show horses, racehorses, bureaucratic horses, or workhorses, independently of the state of emergence or the volatility in your contingent ecosystems.

4.3. "Adaptive Emergence": Diversity as a Seed for Novelty and a Source for Adaptability

Complexity researchers studying both organizations and learning both agree that diversity is a critical factor enabling (and constraining) the emergence of complex organizations. A slight difference is that organization scholars are shifting toward the concept of "ecologies of innovation"

Figure 2. The characteristics of complex adapting organizations that learn (source: Davis & Sumara, 2006, 2008)

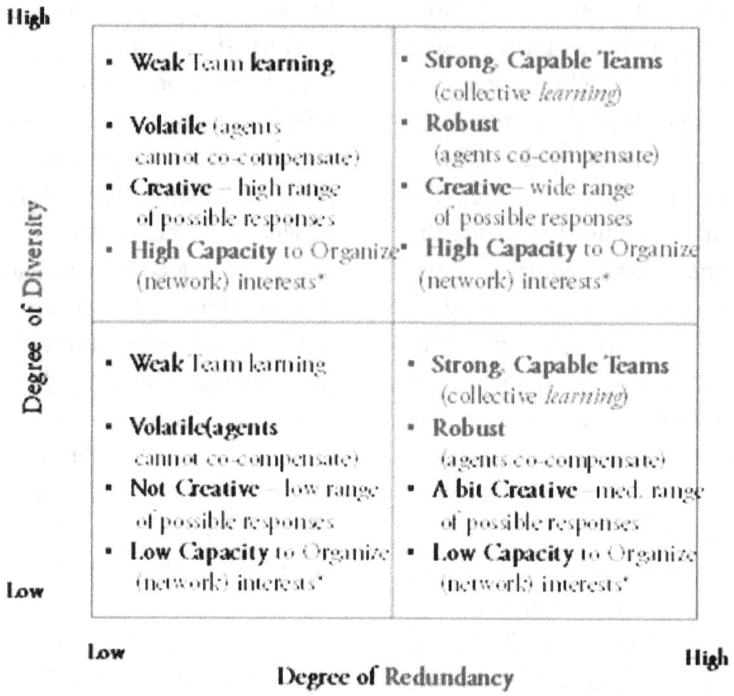

High

• **Weak** Team **learning**	• **Strong, Capable Teams** (collective *learning*)
• **Volatile** (agents cannot co-compensate)	• **Robust** (agents co-compensate)
• **Creative** – high range of possible responses	• **Creative** – wide range of possible responses
• **High Capacity** to Organize (network) interests*	• **High Capacity** to Organize (network) interests*
• **Weak** Team **learning**	• **Strong, Capable Teams** (collective *learning*)
• **Volatile** (agents cannot co-compensate)	• **Robust** (agents co-compensate)
• **Not Creative** – low range of possible responses	• **A bit Creative** – med. range of possible responses
• **Low Capacity** to Organize (network) interests*	• **Low Capacity** to Organize (network) interests*

Degree of Diversity

Low

Low   High

Degree of Redundancy

Figure 3. Complex organization emergence potentials (source: Davis & Sumara, 2006; Kowch, 2003)

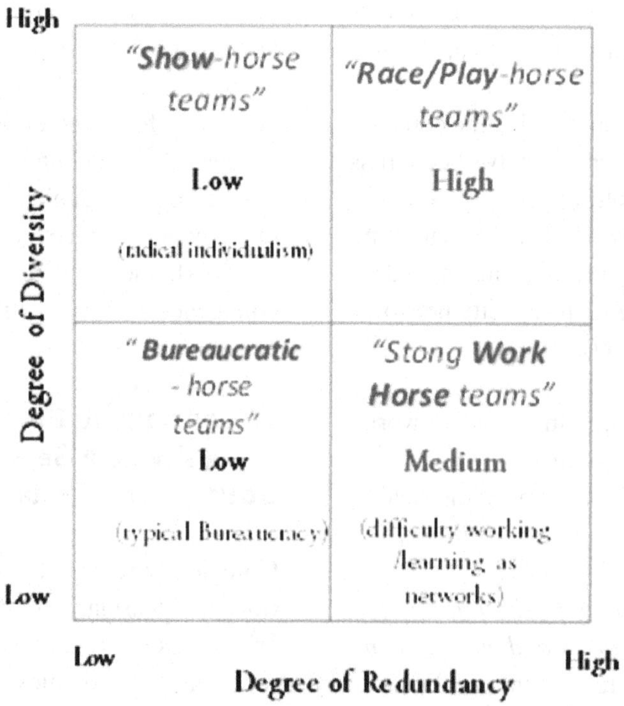

High

"**Show**-horse teams"	"*Race/Play-horse teams*"
Low	**High**
(radical individualism)	
"*Bureaucratic - horse teams*"	"*Stong **Work Horse** teams*"
Low	**Medium**
(typical Bureaucracy)	(difficulty working /learning as networks)

Degree of Diversity

Low

Low   High

Degree of Redundancy

recently, taking a perspective that organization emergence, one possible can occur through the creation of *innovation* ecologies in the context of the organization (Goldstein, et al., 2010, p. 8). Ecologies of innovation are, not surprisingly a consolidation of some of the complex ecosystems explored earlier (Cilliers, 1998; Davis, Sumara, & Kapler, 2009) but exhibit the following 5 features:

1. These *are systems of difference* where micro level *diversity* supplies the ecology with seeds of novelty
2. *Experiments* in the system move parts of the system away from normal routines, resulting in *novelties* that move the system to new opportunities (sometimes)
3. Intricate *networks connect to interdependent subsystems*
4. *Innovations* conferring new functionalities that enhance adaptability to unexpected changes or "jolts" from the environment. A 21st century leader competency will be the ability to recognize, amplify, and nurture networks where novelties and tension are directly associated in firms (Johnson, et al., 2011).
5. *Critical periods of instability* exist that allow for substantial transformations of behaviors and dynamics. A 21st century leader competency will be to lead and recognize these periods of instability along with the phases of emergence (change).

Organization theorists focus on diversity in terms of *systems of difference* some, but more recently more exclusively on *diversity as the source of adaptability* in the emerging organization.

Differences in intentions and perspectives are the fuel for complexity...for the generation of information that is central to novelty creation... [And from novelty creation follows experimentation, amplification and innovation emergence] (Goldstein, et al., p. 84).

4.2.1. Systems of Difference

Difference in organizations is a seed for novelty, which is the spark to the kindling for experimenting new things. Difference is energy in an emerging system. Linking closely to biodiversity research, organization theorists say that a prime feature of innovation ecosystems is *difference* among system elements or 'agents' as a precondition to stability. This came from biodiversity research showing that populations oscillate (a lot) when there was little difference between species in an ecosystem (Elton, 1955).

Organization thinkers understand emergence is not a continuous arc, but that emergent systems occur in a certain order with distinct features: (1) disequilibrium, (2) amplification, (3) recombination, and (4) feedback and stability. Difference and diversity happen both before stage 1, and during "disequilibrium." As meaning emerges through differences in member's backgrounds skills, opinions and perspectives these differences help drive emergence as people search to find meaning in between and within the "noise" or "gaps" between expected information and the perceived meaning of actual circumstances (information sciences). Patterns in this discourse emerge whereby the *strength of weak ties and relations* (network theory) and other analytics help researchers understand which differences matter to what sorts of relational patterns, and how issues emerge as catalysts for collective work in unsteady contexts (Kowch, 2003; Scott, 2000). A main task for future leaders will be unearthing differences in the agents and patterns of organization as conditions for system emergence. Contemporary organizational theorists also posit that *diversity, not just difference* is a more important feature in leading ecologies of innovation (Goldstein, et al., 2010).

4.3. Diversity as the Seeds of Novelty: The Sources of Adaptability

A lot of emerging goes on before a novelty in an organization fits within an adaptable organization. In ecology research, the greater the diversity within a system, especially at the micro levels of individual differences and group-level heterogeneity, the *higher the potential exists that these differences* can be amplified into real innovations (Bradbury, et al., 1996; Forno & Merlone, 2007). A particular form of diversity at the micro level is suggested as a place for leaders to focus when nurturing novelty.

Micro (human, person) level diversity is the seed for novelty, and it is possible only if there is freedom to depart from what is expected. Organizational theorists point to *technology* as the best example one of the most significant system novelty or "discontinuity" so important in the initial stages of emergence (disequilibrium) in complex organizations (Hazy, 2009). They use technology examples to explain how diversity is the source of adaptability, and how leaders must step back and promote the tensions between expected performance and actual performance, letting novelty attract enough interest to be tested in the organization. They find that when *novelty or a small variation* is expressed through a small discontinuity in technology, it becomes an attractor for experimentation an ever-faster emerging organization (disequilibrium phase). Once the novelty is adopted or receives "attraction," the system develops beyond the "amplification" stage via the subsequent tensions created in the amplification and recombination stages of emergence. People coalesce around new ways of doing. This results in greater levels of adaptability from the system. Since emergence pushes beyond the specific context in which it appears, what actually emerges (patterns, items, or ideas) is not known beforehand, and is accordingly outside the control of any "leader."

Goldstein et al. (2010) offer one example of micro diversity in unsteady conditions. When Netflix began in 1998, DVD players were rare, and this organization was in the business of renting DVDs by mail at a time when few DVD players could be found in homes. So Netflix teams looked outside the firm (across semipermeable organizational boundaries) into their wider ecosystem to partner with DVD makers and to offer free DVDs to DVD machine buyers, generating a potential customer list for DVD rentals. When Amazon.com began shipping DVDs soon after, Netflix again worked with the ecosystem to learn and to partner with Amazon to advertise Netflix products online. It strengthened its relations in the movie distribution ecosystem, which helped them enormously when they partnered again to ship their movies online. This diversity of thinking and adaptability demonstrates the Netflix organization's adaptable, robust (sustainable) emergence during terrific change contexts both *outside* and *inside* the firm. "structure." As we learned from Section 2.0 in this chapter, that feature of "outside looking" emergence (and perhaps inside *learning*) marks a profound difference between complex adaptive systems/diversity thinking and even the most current "distributed learning" and 'transformation theory' underpinning leadership thinking today. Much more research needs to be done on the topic of diversity as a seed for novelty and emergence patterns. This research is still too abstract, and needs to be taken up in the study of emerging organization more globally. One of the original thinkers on micro diversity offers sound advice for leaders and scholars in this emerging research area:

Even though one cannot understand what exactly creates the micro-diversity underlying a system, it can be established that all the underlying phe-

nomena obey the same kind of behavior—that of evolving complex systems. By allowing ourselves to be "evolvers" and by exploring our own diversity, a richer set of possibilities are created on which the collective system can thrive (Allen, et al., 2010).

5. CONCLUSION

Cascading financial failures and inevitable resource shortages in the public are indeed changing the personal, social, economic, and political landscapes in our world. As a response and for new leaders, this chapter traced organization and leadership history to suggest evolution in our way of thinking about organizations as complex systems. Instead of denying the tremendous connectivity that modern technologies afford us today, we discovered that the seeds of emergence in tomorrow's organizations arise from knowing a mix of diversity and redundancy better within our organizational ecosystems, not from organization charts. We explored that system intelligence or "smartness" is possible, and includes leader and system learning potentials made available only by leaders knowing the diversity and redundancy in organization networks. To increase the chance that we will lead more adaptable organizations against the backdrop of constant change, we can consider the differences and novelties arising from system "noise" as seeds for new experiments that change the very purpose of organizations emerging in stages. In preparing this chapter, the author also realized a serious need for more focused research on diversity in leadership contexts.

The complex ecosystem (leadership) study area is populated by very few interdisciplinary researchers integrating technology, administration, and policy and organization theory. This is unbelievable when we know that technology and innovation not only drive organization emergence, but often create instability in the ecosystems engaging modern large organizations. Overall, complexity thinking about leading education systems is 20 years behind that of our colleagues in other disciplines, yet we uniquely understand learning as a function of adaptability. We should catch up sooner to prepare Ducker's new generation of leaders to lead adaptable organizations with the potential to avoid so many cascading system failures in our emerging knowledge era.

Anything less will result in more skylights among taller towers amidst increasing public displeasure with our approach to leadership today.

REFERENCES

Allen, P., Strathern, M., & Varga, L. (2010). Complexity: The evolution of identity and diversity. *Complexity, Difference and Identity. Issues in Business Ethics*, *26*(2), 41–60. doi:10.1007/978-90-481-9187-1_3

Baker, S. (2008). *The numerati*. New York, NY: Houghton Mifflin Harcourt.

Barabasi, A. (2003). *Linked: How everything is connected to everything else and what it means*. New York, NY: Plume Publishing.

Barabasi, A. (2010). *Bursts: The hidden pattern behind everything we do*. New York, NY: Dutton. doi:10.1063/1.3431332

Bates, R. J. (1982). Towards critical practice of educational administration. *Studies in Educational Administration*, *27*, 1–21.

Blase, J., & Blase, J. (1996). Micro-political strategies used by administrators and teachers in instructional conferences. *The Alberta Journal of Educational Research*, *42*, 345–360.

Capra, F. (2002). *The hidden connections: A science for sustainable living*. New York, NY: HarperCollins.

Christensen, C., Horn, M., & Johnson, W. (2008). *Disrupting class*. New York, NY: McGraw Hill.

Cilliers, P. (1998). *Complexity and postmodernism: Understanding complex systems*. New York, NY: Routledge.

Clegg, S., Harris, M., & Hopfl, H. (2011). *Managing modernity*. Oxford, UK: Oxford University Press.

Cuban, L. (2011). Teacher, superintendent, scholar: The gift of multiple careers. *Leaders in Educational Studies*, *3*, 45–54. doi:10.1007/978-94-6091-755-4_5

Davis, B. (2005). Teacher as consciousness of the collective. *Complicity: An International Journal of Complexity and Education*, *2*(1), 86–88.

Davis, B., & Sumara, D. (2006). *Complexity and education*. New York, NY: Lawrence Erlbaum.

Davis, B., Sumara, D., & Kapler, R. (2008). *Engaging minds* (2nd ed.). New York, NY: Routledge.

Drucker, P. (1996). *The leader of the future*. San Francisco, CA: Jossey-Bass.

DuFour, R., & Eaker, R. (2005). *On common grounds*. Bloomington, IL: Solution Tree.

Evers, C., & Lakomski, G. (Eds.). (1996). *Exploring educational administration: Coherentist applications and critical debates*. New York, NY: Pergamon.

Forno, A., & Merlone, U. (2007). The emergence of effective leaders: An experimental approach and computational approach. In Hazy, J., Goldstein, J., & Lichtenstein, B. (Eds.), *Complex Systems Leadership Theory* (pp. 205–227). Mansfield, MA: ISCE Publishing.

Fullan, M. (2002, May). The change. *Educational Leadership*, 16–20.

Ginsberg, B. (2011). *The fall of the faculty*. Oxford, UK: Oxford University Press.

Goldstein, J. (2007). A new model for emergence and its leadership implications. In Hazy, J., Goldstein, J., & Lichtenstein, B. (Eds.), *Complex Systems Leadership Theory* (pp. 62–91). Mansfield, MA: ISCE Publishing.

Goldstein, J., Hazy, J. K., & Lichtenstein, B. B. (2010). *Complexity and the nexus of leadership: Leveraging nonlinear science to create ecologies of innovation*. New York, NY: Palgrave Macmillan.

Granovetter, M. (1973). The strength of weak ties. *American Journal of Sociology*, *6*, 1360–1380. doi:10.1086/225469

Greenfield, T. (1984). The decline and fall of science in educational administration. *Interchange*, *17*, 57–80. doi:10.1007/BF01807469

Griffiths, D. E. (1964). The nature and meaning of theory. In Griffiths, D. E. (Ed.), *Behavioral Science and Educational Administration*. Chicago, IL: University of Chicago Press.

Gronn, P. (2002). Distributed leadership. In Leithwood, K., & Hallinger, P. (Eds.), *Second International Handbook of Educational Leadership Administration* (pp. 653–697). Boston, MA: Kluwer. doi:10.1007/978-94-010-0375-9_23

Hallinger, P. (Ed.). (2002). *Second international handbook of educational leadership and administration*. London, UK: Kluwer.

Hargreaves, A., & Fink, D. (2006). *Sustainable leadership*. San Francisco, CA: Jossey-Bass.

Harris, A. (2008). *Distributed school leadership*. London, UK: Routledge.

Hazy, K. (2007). *Complex systems leadership theory*. Mansfield, MA: ISCE Publishing.

Johnson, L., Smith, R., Willis, H., Levine, A., & Haywood, K. (2011). *The 2011 horizon report*. Austin, TX: The New Media Consortium.

Kowch, E. (2005). The knowledge network: A fundamentally new (relational) approach to knowledge management & the study of dependent organizations. *Journal of Knowledge Management Practice, 6*, 13–37.

Kowch, E. (2007). *Alberta central server/thin client shared services: System leadership study 2.* Edmonton, Canada: Alberta Education Publication.

Kowch, E. (2009). New capabilities for cyber charter school leadership: An emerging imperative for integrating educational technology and educational leadership knowledge. *TechTrends, 53*(1), 40–49.

Kowch, E. G. (2003). *Policy networks and policy communities in three western Canadian universities and two provinces: A neo-institutional approach to a pan-institutional issue.* (Unpublished Doctoral Dissertation). University of Saskatchewan. Saskatoon, Canada.

Kowch, E. G. (2008). *Characteristics of high capacity, semi-autonomous teams – Are you ready for this?* Paper presented at the meeting of the Association of Education Communications and Technology Annual Conference. Orlando, FL.

Kuhn, T. S. (1977). *The essential tension.* Chicago, IL: University of Chicago Press.

Leithwood, K., & Jantzi, D. (2005). A review of transformational school leadership research: 1996-2005. *Leadership and Policy in Schools, 4*(3), 177–199. doi:10.1080/15700760500244769

Levin, B., & Fullan, M. (2008). Learning about system renewal. *Educational Management and Leadership, 36*, 289–304. doi:10.1177/1741143207087778

Marion, R., & Uhl-Bien, M. (2001). Leadership in complex organizations. *The Leadership Quarterly, 12*(4), 381–556. doi:10.1016/S1048-9843(01)00092-3

McClellan, J. L. (2010). Leadership and complexity: Implications for practiced within the advisement leadership bodies at colleges and universities. *Complicity: An International Journal of Complexity and Education, 7*, 32–51.

McKelvey, B., & Lichtenstein, B. (2007). Leadership in the four stages of emergence. In Hazy, J., Goldstein, J., & Lichtenstein, B. (Eds.), *Complex Systems Leadership Theory.* Mansfield, MA: ISCE Publishing.

Miller, J. H., & Page, S. E. (2007). *Complex adaptive systems.* Princeton, NJ: Princeton University Press.

Mitchell, C., & Sackney, L. (2011). *Profound improvement* (2nd ed.). New York, NY: Routledge.

Oblensky, N. (2010). *Complex adaptive leadership: Embracing paradox and uncertainty.* Burlington, VT: MPG Books.

OECD. (2010). *Economic outlook interim projections.* Paris, France: OECD.

Page, S. (2007). *The difference: How the power of diversity creates better groups, firms, schools and societies.* Princeton, NJ: Princeton University Press.

Partridge, B., Pitcher, P., Cullen, J., & Wilson, J. (1980). The three dimensional structure of fish schools. *Behavioral Ecology and Sociobiology, 6*(4), 277–288. doi:10.1007/BF00292770

Reigeluth, C., & Duffy, F. (2008, May). The AECT futureminds initiative: Transforming America's school systems. *Educational Technology.*

Reigeluth, C. M., & Garfinkle, R. J. (1994). Envisioning a new system of education. In Reigeluth, C. M., & Garfinkle, R. J. (Eds.), *Systemic Change in Education.* Englewood Cliffs, NJ: Educational Technology Publications.

Reinhart, W., & Rogoff, J. K. (2009). *This time is different: Eight centuries of financial folly.* Princeton, NJ: Princeton University Press.

Rogers, E. M. (1995). *Diffusions of innovations.* New York, NY: Collier Macmillan.

Rorty, R. (1989). *Contingency, irony and solidarity.* Cambridge, UK: Cambridge University Press. doi:10.1017/CBO9780511804397

Schlechty, P. (2009). *Leading for learning.* San Francisco, CA: Jossey-Bass. doi:10.1002/9781118269497

Schwandt, D. R., & Szabla, D. (2007). Systems leadership: Co evolution or mutual evolution towards complexity? In Hazy, J., Goldstein, J., & Lichtenstein, B. (Eds.), *Complex Systems Leadership Theory* (pp. 35–59). Mansfield, MA: ISCE Publishing.

Scott, J. (2000). *Social network analysis: A handbook.* London, UK: Sage.

Sergiovanni, T. (1989). The leadership needed for quality schooling. In Sergiovanni, T., & Moore, J. (Eds.), *Schooling for Tomorrow.* Boston, MA: Allyn and Bacon.

Sorkin, A. R. (2009). *Too big to fail.* New York, NY: Penguin Group.

Suzuki, D., & McConnell, A. (1997). *The sacred balance: Rediscovering our place in nature.* Vancouver, Canada: Greystone Books.

Thompson-Klein, J. (2010). *Creating interdisciplinary campus cultures: A model for strength and sustainability.* San Francisco, CA: Jossey-Bass.

Uhl-Bein, M., Marion, R., & McElvey, B. (2007). Complexity leadership theory: Shifting leadership from the industrial age to the knowledge era. *The Leadership Quarterly*, *18*(4), 298–318. doi:10.1016/j.leaqua.2007.04.002

von Bertalanffy, L. (1969). *General system theory.* New York, NY: George Braziller.

Waldrop, M. (1992). *Complexity.* New York, NY: Simon and Schuster.

Willower, D. J., & Forsythe, B. (1999). A brief history of scholarship on educational administration. In Murphy, J., & Louis, K. (Eds.), *Handbook of Research on Educational Administration* (pp. 1–25). San Francisco, CA: Jossey-Bass.

Wilson, T. (2004). *Strangers to ourselves.* Boston, MA: Harvard University Press.

Chapter 3
Utilizing Technology to Communicate with Diverse Groups

Patricia F. Sanders
University of North Alabama, USA

Butler Cain
West Texas A&M University, USA

ABSTRACT

The concept of diversity has become an issue at the forefront of discussions in all sectors of society. This includes the business centers and their workplaces, higher education, and non-profit institutions. As the world becomes more and more ethnically diverse, methods of communication also become even more relevant, critical even. One way in which organizations are finding it easier to engage with those within their walls and get their ideas across to one another is through technology and the availability of social media. Digital tools such as Facebook, Twitter, email, YouTube, smart phones, virtual conferencing, Skype, and an indispensible amount of downloadable software applications, have paved the way for easier communication and the ability to reach not only diverse groups but in a varied number of ways. Over the past couple of decades, the ability to communicate has rapidly transitioned away from traditional modes of communication in the vein of land-based telephone lines, written letters, and verbal communication. This chapter focuses on how two major areas of society communicate with their diverse constituencies utilizing these sundry technologies. Specifically, it examines successful strategies higher education and businesses employ to disseminate information to diverse groups.

DOI: 10.4018/978-1-4666-2668-3.ch003

INTRODUCTION

The concept of diversity has become an issue at the forefront of discussions in all sectors of society. This includes the business center and their workplaces and higher education. As the world becomes more and more diverse, methods of communication also become even more relevant, critical even. One way in which organizations are finding it easier to engage with those within their walls and get their ideas across to one another is through technology and the availability of social media.

Digital tools such as Facebook, Twitter, email, YouTube, smart phones, tablets, virtual conferencing, Skype, laptops and an indispensible amount of downloadable software applications, have paved the way for easier communication and the ability to reach not only diverse groups but in a varied number of ways. Over the past couple of decades, the ability to communicate has rapidly transitioned away from traditional modes of communication in the vein of land-based telephone lines, written letters, and verbal communication.

This chapter specifically examines how some business owners and administrators within higher education use technology to implement and practice their goals to reach diverse constituents within their organizations. The emergence of digital technology and social media and its influences on organizational communication has grown and continues to flourish.

Two major areas of society, communicate with their diverse constituency utilizing sundry digital and electronic technologies. Specifically, there is the examination of successful strategies higher education and businesses employ to disseminate information. Logically, each of these entities shares common groups with which they communicate at regular intervals such as media and employees. However, each also has unique characteristics within them as well. Higher education institutions have a constant need to communicate with students, staff and faculty whereas businesses must communicate with clients or customers and employees. Nonetheless, both are using social media and other modes of technology to communicate with these groups.

Therefore, the questions of *what*, *why* and *how* business and higher education institutions are communicating in relationship to maintaining, training and embracing diversity need to be analyzed in order to provide suggestions for others to successfully implement similar strategies in their organizations. They also explain the tools they are using, positive and negative consequences of digital technology and social media and ways in which technology can be improved upon.

LITERATURE REVIEW

The term "diversity," as it is used within the context of higher education, has been defined in numerous ways. However, Owen (2009) identified two common meanings for this concept. The first simply involves valuing differences, while the second reflects the concern of "making the academy inclusive and equitable" (p. 187). Institutions of higher education have spent the past few decades increasingly focused on improving both of these interpretations and ensuring that diversity is reflected throughout campus. According to the *ASHE Higher Education Report* (2006), "the transformation of higher education needed to include diversity as a core value if it was to increase the capacity of colleges and universities to prosper and keep pace with changes in the environment" (p. 37).

One of these changes is America's increasing racial diversity, and colleges and universities are uniquely positioned to provide leadership on this matter. Gurin, Day, Hurtado, and Gurin (2002) noted that many students who arrive on college campuses have lived their entire lives in segregated communities. Therefore, "colleges that diversify their student bodies and institute policies that foster genuine interaction across race and ethnicity provide the first opportunity for many students to learn from peers with different cultures, values, and experiences" (p. 336). However, interaction must be more than simple contact if individuals are to learn anything from each other. It must include learning about differences in backgrounds, experiences, and perspectives in an intimate and personal way (Gurin, Day, Hurtado, & Gurin, 2002). Though it would be expected that administrators within higher education would have had greater exposure to people of different racial and ethnic backgrounds than students, the same concept for successful interaction still applies.

According to Williams and Wade-Golden (2008), change and diversity are going to be permanent characteristics of higher education in the twenty-first century, but it is not simply because diversity is morally right.

Diversity efforts are important because they are fundamental to quality and excellence in the world in which we live today. Moreover, diversity is more than a black-and-white binary; it now includes race, ethnicity, gender, sexual orientation, ability, nationality, religion, and a host of other dimensions (p. B44).

Some universities and colleges have sought to address this need by hiring "chief diversity officers," individuals whose sole responsibility is to examine, and improve upon, issues affecting ethnic minorities. However, Williams and Wade-Golden (2008) suggest such officers will succeed only in environments that are conducive to increasing diversity, equity, and inclusion. "Without supportive campus leaders, institutional readiness for change, and a commitment to long-term, systemic efforts and financial investments, the work of a chief diversity officer can have only limited impact" (p. B44). Therefore, diversity within higher education is not something that can be relegated solely to the efforts of one individual. To be successful, diversity initiatives must have the full support—and understanding—of university

administrators. Hurtado, Milem, Clayton-Pedersen, and Allen (1998) suggested that one way to improve this would be to increase the number of previously excluded and underrepresented racial/ethnic minorities within a university's administration. A "greater appreciation for the multiple voices/perspectives of diversity" are necessary to "mobilize the values of equity and inclusion that diversity initiatives encourage" (Oliha & Collier, 2010, p. 62).

However, Hurtado, Milem, Clayton-Pedersen, and Allen (1999) also recognized that campuses are complex social systems that are defined and influenced by bureaucratic procedures, structural arrangements, personal relationships, and institutional goals, values, and traditions. Such institutions are slow to adapt, so "the success of efforts to achieve institutional change will rely on leadership, firm commitment, adequate resources, collaboration, monitoring, and long-range planning" (p. 70). Cook (2008) echoed this sentiment when he urged college and university presidents to "realize that their role in this process is absolutely pivotal and that they must be both forward-thinking and aggressive in advancing their diversity goals" (p. 6).

If an institution's leadership does not make diversity a priority and support it with genuine passion and significant resources and recognition, if diversity efforts take a back seat to projects that promise more immediate or more tangible results, the effort starts out hobbled and may never gain its footing…. It is important to create a campus climate in which every member of the community feels invested in the effort's success, so that the challenges revealed become something for the community as a whole to meet, just as the successes become a cause for the community to celebrate (pp. 6-7).

Though specifically addressed to university presidents, Kezar (2007) suggested three phases of leadership strategies that are equally applicable to university administrators with an interest in improving diversity. Phase One involves creating and articulating a vision, increasing motivation for the vision and developing infrastructure to support the vision (p. 423). Phase Two requires revitalizing the agenda, broadening its ownership, and moving from rhetoric about diversity to taking action (p. 427). The third phase involves deeply engraining diversity into the campus culture so that it manifests itself in individuals' assumptions (p. 431). However, successfully implementing diversity initiatives is a complex task and is "much more than a simple response or adaptation to demographic representation—it is about the intergroup dynamics that characterize colleges and universities in both structure and culture" (ASHE, 2006).

The pursuit of diversity in the business sector is equally complex. A senior vice president at a U.S. cable network said her industry's challenge with diversity is to actually understand what it means. "When you ask people to define diversity they get a deer-in-the-headlights look, but then everyone has a different answer," she said (Miller, 2008, p. 19). According to Miller (2008), that is why diversity training plays a key role in establishing a workplace where differences are respected and valued. Communication is also important, as Irizarry and Gallant (2006) noted in a study of health care workers. In this report, a large majority of health care managers supported engaging in more discussion forums regarding diversity management in order to improve communicative understanding among all parties (p. 47).

Having a thorough understanding of how a particular organization influences itself is another key factor in diversity management. Glastra, Meerman, Schedler, and de Vries (2000) argued diversity management efforts "should have an informed idea of how the structural arrangements, the cultural patterns, the core business, the external relations and the strategic mission of a given organization" shape it (p. 709). That must be combined with "adequate policies in the fields

of education, labour [sic] market and the struggle against discrimination" in cooperation with "partners in governmental and political institutions" (p. 714). Muse (2009), in an appeal to the advertising industry, also urged a proactive approach when focusing on diversity in the workplace.

Most of you guys who run ad agencies don't live among the average, multicultural consumer. You live largely isolated from people of color. And you bring that isolationism to work every day. Spend more time out of the executive dining room and more time at the deli counter looking, feeling, and, yes, smelling some of the customers that help pay for those million-dollar cribs on the hill (p. 8).

Marie Hollein, president and CEO of Financial Executives International, described the case for initiating diversity programs and inclusion initiatives as "a no-brainer" (Hollein, 2011). "If our companies don't enact better and more effective diversity initiatives, they're going to be left behind. U.S. demographics are changing dramatically with each passing decade" (p. 6). Siegel (2006) notes that the global economy and a changing labor force have made attention to diversity issues a practical necessity in the business sector. Diversity is important because

it allows the penetration of multicultural consumer markets, helps companies establish relationships with business partners and governments in the international arena, is a source of innovation, and has been shown to result in notable performance advantages such as the enhanced creativity of work teams (p. 471).

However, just as the literature suggests with higher education, diversity cannot be implemented successfully in a top-down approach. A successful diversity initiative must be owned by everyone, not just members of senior management and the human resources department (MMR, 2011, p. 24).

ISSUES

Diversity is not always easily defined or comfortably embraced by all organizations. It is oftentimes seen as a political hotbed. As for higher education and efforts to address issues related to diversity, Kezar (2008) noted "little research has examined how leaders address these complicated political situations that arise on campuses across the country" (p. 406). This suggests that while the ability to discuss, embrace and take action on increasing diverse constituencies amongst faculty, staff and students, more still needs to be done; not only from a normal day-to-day basis but along a line of formal investigations as well.

College campuses and business environments face the same challenges as other communal groups in other areas who are oftentimes brought together, not necessarily by choice but through compulsory circumstances. Those suggested situations include work, community settings, sports arenas, religious gatherings, and others.

SOLUTIONS AND RECOMMENDATIONS

Many areas of business and higher education already incorporate the use of technology into their day-to-day operations. Technology has such a prevalent presence in society, naturally it has disseminated into both aforementioned areas. It is, therefore, especially imperative that each area of higher education and business organizations successfully use technology to reach diverse groups with which they interact on a frequent or daily basis. Technology is ubiquitous in that it allows various groups to be communicated with in large or personalized groups.

Communities of people who need to be reached with certain communiqués can be contacted by creating "communities." These communities can be as diverse or targeted as needed when attempting to reach leaders or potential leaders on a college campus or within a business, regardless of its size. Huffaker (2010) discusses online communities and influence leadership has in such groups.

The members of these online groups create and share information at an unprecedented level, resulting in millions of messages, photos, or videos, but more importantly opinions, ideas, and a finger on the pulse of the needs and beliefs of the massive audience that makes up the Internet (p. 593).

These online communities can allow for sharing of resources, common interests or activities (Huffaker, 2010, p. 593). Colleges and businesses can easily identify these groups, establish them and then communicate directly through technology. Lin and Ha (2009) posited courseware Blackboard is instrumental to many higher educational institutions that adopt computer information technologies to facilitate communication within their constituents (p. 564). Even though systems such as Blackboard and Angel Learning (angellearning.com) are used for instruction and information sharing concerning academics, it can also be utilized for specific and diverse groups of students. Lin and Ha (2009) stated that Blackboard is not only useful as a teaching resource but is also "a comprehensive computer-mediated information system that can be used for information search, teaching, providing and receiving services from the university, and community communications (p. 566).

In the business realm, diverse groups are seen as becoming more and more varied as well, which means that technology's role grows increasingly more important in the communications process.

As organizations increasingly operate in a multinational and multicultural context, understanding how diversity in the composition of organizational groups affects outcomes such as satisfaction, creativity, and turnover will be of increasing importance. For example, as organizations globalize their operations, it is likely that the frequency with which employees will interact with people from different countries will increase (Milliken & Martins, 1996, p. 402).

Therefore, there are various ways in which institutions of higher learning and businesses, regardless of size, can utilize technology when communicating with leaders within their diverse groups. Interviews conducted with principal persons in the realm of higher education and businesses, focused on technology's use to communicate with students, faculty and staff, customers and employees.

HIGHER EDUCATION, BUSINESS PROFILES, AND DEFINING DIVERSITY

Dr. Wade Shaffer is the associate provost of West Texas A&M University in Canyon, Texas. It is a public institution and a member of the Texas A&M University System. Shaffer, a 48-year-old white male, defines diversity as "more than simply race and ethnicity. It also has to do with socio-economic background. It has to do with previous experience at college, i.e. is it a first generation student or not. And it has to do with diversity of opinions, diversity of political perspectives" (W. Shaffer, personal communication, December 14, 2011). One of WTAMU's primary diversity pushes is to become a recognized Hispanic-Serving Institution (HIS). That requires 25 percent of the student population to self identify their ethnicity as Hispanic. Right now, WTAMU is at 19.6 percent, but according to Shaffer, each of the last two years the incoming freshman class has been 25 percent Hispanic. He said the increase reflects a conscious decision on the university's part to focus on recruiting not only a diverse student body but a diverse staff and faculty, as well.

Concerning business organizations, three different businesses shared their ideas on how they define diversity and how they communicate with customers or employees. Case in point, Sandra

Nickel, a 68-year-old white female, is a Broker and Owner of Hat Team REALTORS; a small real estate firm in Montgomery, Alabama. She has an extremely diverse staff, even though there are only six employees in the firm. The company employs two Caucasian women, three Caucasian men, and one African American man. Nickel noted, "Among the six of us there are four straight people and two gay people. In addition, our ages range from a low of 30 to the high sixties. We pretty much cover the waterfront" (S. Nickel, personal communication, November 1, 2011). Nickel stated she embraces diversity, which she defines as:

Old, young, black white, rich poor, gay straight, male female just a whole plethora. Interestingly just this past September our chamber just sponsored a diversity summit and race was only mentioned in passing. The whole thrust of the conference was on generational differences. So diversity to me is any two people who are not the same, which is practically all of us (personal communication).

Nickel is considered a "Rainmaker" within her organization, a term she said evolved from the legal profession that describes the person whose primary job it is to bring in business. In her words, "not necessarily work the business, but generate the business. In a nutshell, my job is to make the phone ring and the doors open" (S. Nickel, personal communication, November 1, 2011). She agreed that the term diversity also includes differences based on race, gender, sexual orientation, nationality, and religion. "Right, all of those feed in to make us a rich soup or stew, personalities and attitudes" (S. Nickel, personal communication, November 1, 2011). In order to continue further the idea that diversity is important, Nickel said her intent is to hire a middle-aged African American female to help round out her team of workers. Such efforts within organizations help to cultivate diverse leaders within their ranks and to achieve future goals and benchmarks in order to diversify their environments.

Tomi Selby is President of Information Transport Solutions, a relatively medium-sized technology firm located in Wetumpka, Alabama. She is a 46-year-old white female who employs 140 people. Of that number, 103 are men and 37 are women. Within that number, African Americans represent 20.4 percent of those employed by her company. Selby defines diversity as "a combination of racial, age, educational, and socioeconomic differences. Diversity allows us to leverage different frames of reference in developing innovative solutions" (T. Selby, personal communication, October 31, 2011).

A much larger company, Alabama Power with corporate headquarters in Birmingham, Alabama, is a public utility that provides power to 54 counties and 1.4 million customers in the state. Corporate communications representative Isaac Pigott sees diversity in a variety of ways. First, he sees diversity as "being inclusive of backgrounds and opinions. Not everyone is going to have the same approach and not everybody's going to have the same perspective" (I. Pigott, personal communication, December 13, 2011). He began using digital technology as a mass communications tool while working with the nonprofit American Red Cross before joining Alabama Power. He found digital tools were an easy and inexpensive way to communicate with large groups of people in a much quicker fashion.

The American Red Cross needed an outlet to be able to publish information to our stakeholders and potential clients. I found during a number of circumstances during crises and disasters, these tools for a nonprofit budget were a no-brainer. They were easy, free and ubiquitous. They gave us an opportunity to reach a lot of people without delay of media filters (personal communication).

Though different in size, all three companies have to deal with diverse constituencies and find efficient ways in which to communicate with them. In addition, technology appears to be the one perfect fit for all of them. Each tailors the technology to fit their individual needs.

TECHNOLOGY TOOLS AND COMMUNICATION USE

In the realm of higher education, Shaffer says new and existing technology plays a vital role in communicating with WTAMU's diverse campus groups. He uses the Internet, e-mail, his smart phone, the online class management system Angel—even Facebook—on a daily basis. He describes them as vital to his role as associate provost.

So much information is being passed electronically now, and so often decisions have to be made very quickly that the old method of writing out a memo or calling everybody together in the same physical space to discuss it at the same time would really hinder the effectiveness of my job. I might have a different answer if I were purely in a faculty role, but in the role that I'm in now, I would see it as essential to conducting the day-to-day, the work that we do in the provost's office (personal communication).

Shaffer prefers to use a combination of electronic communication that includes e-mail and text messages. He said e-mail offers two primary advantages. First of all, it has become such an ingrained part of workflow that people often stop whatever they are doing to respond to an e-mail. "And so you get quicker responses when you might need them, which helps in decision making" (W. Shaffer, personal communication, December 14, 2011). Another advantage e-mail offers is that it leaves an electronic trail.

Many, many times we've had discussions or we've had, sometimes, even arguments that can be resolved by going and finding an old e-mail and saying "Well, here's what the policy states" or "Here's what you told me to do" or "Here's the decision that was made about this." And so the ability to store essentially limitless number of e-mails, organize them, [and] search through them quickly to retrieve other information cuts down on the time that I spend filing, the time that I spend locating information, the time that I spend resolving problems (personal communication).

To avoid becoming irrelevant, Shaffer said WTAMU began experimenting with Facebook to reach out to and maintain contact with incoming students. When new students arrive for summer orientation, they are placed in Facebook groups. Student peer leaders then contact them throughout the summer to help strengthen students' new ties with the university.

And we've seen a buy in much quicker of the students to the community when they're in this social network setting, and it also signals to them that we're aware of these tools, that we know how to use these tools and we know this is where they live and where they're comfortable. It beats the heck out of sending them letters in the mail or even e-mails that they increasingly don't respond to (personal communication).

Each of the businesses profiled here uses a variety of digital and electronic tools for communication. In addition, each technology can be adapted to fulfill the need to reach out to clients and others. First, Nickel uses her Blackberry smart phone on a day-to-day basis, carries a digital camera with her wherever she goes and keeps a Flip Camera readily available. In addition, she has a laptop, on which she sends and receives between 500 and a thousand emails per day. It is simpler and easier for her to reach diverse groups of clients, staff, and various organizations.

A goodly amount of the communication is with my team members, test clients and current prospects. Industry information comes to me from other agents in market places and my national organization and various organizations in which I participate. And I have myself involved in at least ten civic groups and volunteer groups (personal communication).

Technology has similar uses in a mid-sized firm, Information Transport Solutions. However, the basis for using it appears to be the same. Selby utilizes technology such as email, video conferencing, Web-X, training, text messaging, and Moodle as methods of communicating with employees within her company. Based on its website, Moodle.org is "an Open Source Course Management System (CMS), also known as a Learning Management System (LMS) or a Virtual Learning Environment (VLE)."

Selby's company and its employees rely heavily on technology. She sees technology as a primary focus when it comes to communicating with employees and employees communicating with each other.

Using technology is the core element to our success. The advancement of technology has helped to enhance the ways and effectiveness in which we communicate with each other. One way technology has advanced communication is through the consumerization [sic] of electronic communication devices and the growth of broadband networks (personal communication).

Selby supplies her employees with a variety of digital resources in order to make their jobs easier, cell phones, iPads, eBooks, and laptops. With seventy-five percent of her business being education-based, Selby strongly supports utilizing use of technology to conduct day-to-day operations and complete personal tasks.

These devices have helped to make communication more accessible and convenient. Technology also allows us to keep up with the ever-increasing speed of our customers and balance the demands of our personal lives (T. Selby, personal communication, October 31, 2011).

Working with a much larger organization of 6,500 employees company-wide at Alabama Power, Pigott uses a Windows smart phone to make daily updates concerning his company. He monitors their external website for any mentions of the company's name and quickly responds. "So if we get a mention that flags up or someone mentions Alabama Power directly, I'll get some type alert or notification, and I can go in and see what it's about" (I. Pigott, personal communication, December 13, 2011). His digital arsenal also includes a personal iPad, and a company-issued personal computer. His company also has a corporate Twitter feed and an external website. News releases are distributed, for the most part, electronically via email.

POSITIVES AND NEGATIVES OF TECHNOLOGY AND COMMUNICATION

Technology is a fast solution in many ways to identifying problems or issues within groups, finding ways to address those problems and provide a quick way to offer numerous suggestions for resolving them. Conversely, though, some find there are also negatives to using technology when communicating.

West Texas A&M University Associate Provost Dr. Wade Shaffer is concerned that one of the positive things about e-mail is also one of its potential negative aspects.

I know that I stop almost anything I'm doing to respond to an e-mail. So I'm privileging one form of communication over another. So we now have an expectation of an immediate response. We now have an expectation that we will get to this immediately instead of being more purposeful about how we plan our day or about how we utilize our time and our resources (personal communication).

Isaac Pigott, with public utility Alabama Power, also contends that technology oftentimes is not used in the most efficient way by a number of companies and organizations, including his

own. From his perspective, the use of technology is "legacy driven" (personal communication). In other words, he asserts most companies use technology in a way that it was originally used and always has been used rather than making attempts to rethink their use and apply it in a better way. For example, Pigott believes there is an over reliance on use of e-mail as well.

We send an email because it's urgent for us to get that off our to-do list. I just remembered something I was supposed to tell Bill. I've got to jump on it right now. I've got to email Bill so that it's off of my brain. But unfortunately, it is now a series of interruptions for Bill whether it's important to him at that moment or not (personal communication).

Pigott feels companies would do a much better job of utilizing technology by embracing newer tools on the market that can communicate items that are important to the sender but not necessarily to the recipient at the moment. What are those tools: corporate wikis and Yammer. Yammer. com describes its software as a solution "that lets employees share and connect with coworkers in a private, secure enterprise social network." Pigott uses Yammer to reach certain groups of people with information that is pertinent to them and their job but does not result in over-sharing with people who may not need the information at the moment.

Nickel, too, supports the concept that, as is common with all changes within the workplace when employing technology, there are positive and negative qualities. She stated it does save time in not having to go to individual employees or clients. "It has simplified our work and eliminated a lot of running around. It has made us much more productive" (personal communication). On the other hand, she says, "I think that we have lost a good bit of the personal touch. That's the dark cloud" (personal communication, November 1, 2011).

Pigott sees it as a valuable tool has to be used correctly.

What we've done, and I say we, America, is created a communications culture where we're constantly interrupting each other. Because you have to go out of your way to say I'm going to turn my email off or my smart phone off but now it's sort of defeating the purpose for being available for really important things (personal communication).

Selby sees using technology as critical to success and competitiveness. In addition, she believes it makes her employees more content with their work. "Customers and employees today are tech-savvy; using technology to communicate creates happier employees, families and customers" (T. Selby, personal communication, October 31, 2011).

Social media and networking as with a large percentage of people in the United States, has found its way into daily use by businesses and higher education. Nickel states she uses Facebook almost daily in connection with her small real estate company. She has both a personal page and a business fan page. She also utilizes Twitter and YouTube for business purposes. Linked-In is used for networking purposes.

Pigott and Nickel also addressed the well-documented existence of a digital divide whereby some people do not have access to digital technology. In addition, both believe smart phone technology is doing and will do a great deal to dissipate or erode the divide. Pigott argues even if people do not have a personal computer and Internet access in their homes, they more than likely would have a smart phone and an inexpensive data plan for it. Nickel believes the same. Smart phone technology has opened access to a number of people who otherwise would not have a way to communicate digitally. She believes texting will play a heavy hand in providing those groups with Internet access. Selby, in the meantime, feels the way to target and reach more diverse groups is to increase their access to the technology.

In all three instances, regardless of whether it is a small, mid-sized or a large company, all participants use smart phones, computers, and social networking to connect with groups of all types within and outside of their organizations.

TRAINING AND IMPROVEMENTS FOR USING TECHNOLOGY

While technology is infiltrating businesses and higher education organizations incrementally, how do leaders keep up with the fast-paced changes that occur? Training is believed to be a major factor. While Pigott attends training seminars for digital technology, he also conducts training sessions. Selby believes there is always room for improvement as well. She maintains there should be more training for online work, Web-X, and video conferencing. Nickel recently accepted a proposal for a social media [training] program, which she says will help her make the best use of social media and to market her business. In addition, while she has not attended any conferences devoted entirely to technology training, she would attend a workshop if it centered on hands-on application.

UTILIZING TECHNOLOGY FOR COMMUNICATION IN THE FUTURE

Moving ahead and finding better ways to incorporate technology into a variety of communication techniques is definitely on the radar of those involved in working with diverse constituencies. Forward thinking is at the forefront of the minds of administrators at WTAMU. Planning and purposeful use of new technology will be especially important in the future because Shaffer said he believes modern society is on the verge of another communications revolution. He is concerned that those who are currently in positions of authority at universities are from an older generation and "tend to not fully embrace that new technology" (personal communication). He said there are still many campus processes that need to be digitized and streamlined to take advantage of the new ways in which students interact with the university.

And if we're not careful, we're going to become increasingly irrelevant to our students, who inhabit entirely that world. I worry sometimes that we haven't embraced that technology to its fullest potential in order to remain connected to our students in that way (personal communication).

Continuing, Shaffer said the university is using new communication technology to correspond with students in another personal way, as well. In 2011, the university purchased ten thousand greeting cards from an electronic card company and began sending electronic birthday cards to every student who came through the university's Student Success Center.

And we're able to track how many students ... open their birthday cards. And right now we're at 65 percent. That was an insignificant amount of money for us to send a digital birthday card to every student saying we know it's your birthday, we wish you a happy birthday, we're thinking of you. And again, it's in electronic format, which they're comfortable with (personal communication).

Even though he said universities have not been "nearly as adept as the private sector in terms of embracing and using [new media technology] its potential," the current efforts being undertaken at West Texas A&M University are "baby steps" in the right direction (personal communication).

As mentioned beforehand by Isaac Pigott with Alabama Power, I've long stated that social media can be this huge time sink. But if you use it properly, you use it to cultivate the network that makes you smarter. And if you think about it, [in an exaggerated way] we've got ten thousand people following Kim Kardashian and thirteen million are following Lady Gaga. People are choosing to

use these tools to make them smarter about things that don't matter (personal communication).

However, he argues technology can be used effectively and efficiently to increase knowledge and improve communication.

But, if you use them to manage the relationships you already have, build a network of people who will let you know about things that you wouldn't have known otherwise, or you didn't even know to ask about, and then you take those same tools and use them internally, you can create a culture of incredible business intelligence. Where people are in the know about things that are going on. When things begin to develop elsewhere they are plugged in and we can minimize mistakes and alter course more quickly. You end up with a more nimble and flexible organization using those tools (personal communication).

Selby, President of Information Transport Solutions, a technology-based firm in the small town in Alabama is of the opinion that technology is the future and that all groups of people must be prepared and attuned to working "in a technology-rich, information-based society. We absolutely must integrate technology into instruction in K-12 and higher education in the United States in order to be competitive" (S. Nickel, personal communication, November 1, 2011).

Three companies and a higher education administrator have offered suggestions for many ways in which technology has adversely affected and positively impacted their organizations. Each of them will continue to look for ways to use it to benefit their communication efforts with their constituents.

Sandra Nickel summed up the way in which communication with diverse groups can work.

Find out what kind of technology and communication works for your intended recipient of your contact and communication and behave in that way. And I think an increasing number every day are going to opt for digital of one kind or another, either through social media, email or texting or whatever the next great thing in that milieu. I don't think it will ever go away. I think it'll be different and better. But never gone (personal communication).

Technology is here to stay. It will continue to grow and have a stronger presence in not only people's personal lives but in such areas as business and higher education.

REFERENCES

ASHE. (2006). Diversity, leadership, and organizational culture in higher education. *ASHE Higher Education Report, 32*(3), 23–45.

Cook, R. J. (2008). Embracing diversity at Allegheny College: Signs of success at a residential college of the liberal arts and sciences. *Journal of Diversity in Higher Education, 1*(1), 1–7. doi:10.1037/1938-8926.1.1.1

Glastra, F., Meerman, M., Schedler, P., & de Vries, S. (2000). Broadening the scope of diversity management. *Industrial Relations, 55*(4), 698–721.

Gurin, P., Day, E. L., Hurtado, S., & Gurin, G. (2002). Diversity and higher education: Theory and impact on educational outcomes. *Harvard Educational Review, 72*(3), 330–366.

Hollein, M. N. (2011). Making the business case for diversity. *Financial Executive, 27*(5), 6.

Huffaker, D. (2010). Dimensions of leadership and social influence in online communities. *Human Communication Research, 36*, 593–617. doi:10.1111/j.1468-2958.2010.01390.x

Hurtado, S., Milem, J., Clayton-Pedersen, A., & Allen, W. (1998). Enhancing campus climates for racial/ethnic diversity: Educational policy and practice. *The Review of Higher Education, 21*(3), 279–302. doi:10.1353/rhe.1998.0003

Hurtado, S., Milem, J., Clayton-Pedersen, A., & Allen, W. (1999). Enacting diverse learning environments: Improving the climate for racial/ethnic diversity in higher education. *ASHE-ERIC Higher Education Report, 26*(8).

Irizarry, C., & Gallant, L. (2006). Managing diversity: Interpretation and enactment in a healthcare setting. *Qualitative Research Reports in Communication, 7*(1), 43–50. doi:10.1080/17459430600964901

Kezar, A. (2008). Understanding leadership strategies for addressing the politics of diversity. *The Journal of Higher Education, 79*(4), 406–441. doi:10.1353/jhe.0.0009

Kezar, A. J. (2007). Tools for a time and place: Phased leadership strategies to institutionalize a diversity agenda. *The Review of Higher Education, 30*(4), 413–439. doi:10.1353/rhe.2007.0025

Lin, C., & Ha, L. (2009). Subcultures and use of communication information technology in higher education institutions. *The Journal of Higher Education, 80*(5), 564–590. doi:10.1353/jhe.0.0064

Miller, S. (2008, September 15). Workforce diversity. *Broadcasting & Cable*, 19-20.

MMR. (2011). How to advance women, build diversity and grow your business. *MMR, 24*.

Moodle.org. (2011). *Website*. Retrieved November 1, 2011 from http://www.moodle.org

Muse, J. (2009). How to win the diversity battle. *Advertising Age, 80*(7), 8.

Oliha, H., & Collier, M. J. (2010). Bridging divergent diversity standpoints & ideologies: Organizational initiatives and trainings. *The International Journal of Diversity in Organisations. Communities and Nations, 10*(4), 61–73.

Owen, D. S. (2009). Privileged social identities and diversity leadership in higher education. *The Review of Higher Education, 32*(2), 185–207. doi:10.1353/rhe.0.0048

Siegel, D. J. (2006). Organizational response to the demand and expectation for diversity. *Higher Education, 52*(3), 465–486. doi:10.1007/s10734-006-0001-x

Williams, D. A., & Wade-Golden, K. C. (2008). The complex mandate of a chief diversity officer. *The Chronicle of Higher Education, 55*(5), B44.

Yammer.com. (2011). *Website.* Retrieved December 13, 2011 from https://www.yammer.com/

Section 2
Diversity Leadership and Technology

Chapter 4

Using Prospect Theory to Explore the Digital Divide

Porche Millington
North Carolina A&T State University, USA

Lemuria Carter
North Carolina A&T State University, USA

ABSTRACT

The growing popularity of Internet-based technology in both the public and private sector has led to a disparity known as the digital divide. The digital divide is described as the gap between those who have access to the Internet and other Internet-based technologies and those who do not (Wattal, Hong, Mandviwalla, & Jain, 2011). J. van Dijk (1999) outlines the digital divide as four types of access barriers: material, psychological, skills, and usage. This chapter reviews the four types of access divides and uses prospect theory as a means to highlight the impact of computer anxiety and computer self-efficacy on psychological access. Suggestions for future research are provided.

INTRODUCTION

In the 1990s, the term "digital divide" began to appear in reports and academic journals (van Dijk, 2006). Before the use of this term many scholars referred to the concept of access disparity as an information inequality or an information gap (van Dijk, 2006). The U.S. Department of Commerce's National Telecommunications and Information Administration is the first to use digital divide in an official publication (NTIA, 2000). Larry Irving,

former Assistant Secretary for Communication and Information for the U.S. Department of Commerce, states that the emerging digital economy is a major driver in the nation's economic well-being and "one of America's leading economic and civil rights issues" (NTIA, 2000, p. 2).

As of May 2010, six in ten American adults go online wirelessly using a laptop or cell phone, slightly up from five in ten American adults in 2009 (Smith, 2010). The statistics have improved; however, the data still shows great disparities between socioeconomic groups. Approximately 94% of households with an income of more than

DOI: 10.4018/978-1-4666-2668-3.ch004

$100,000 had access to broadband in 2009 while only 36% of households with an income of less than $25,000 had broadband connection (U.S. Census Bureau, 2010). Reports show that education plays a role in creating the digital divide as well. Approximately 84% of households with at least one college degree have broadband and just over 28% of households without even a high school diploma are connected (U.S. Census Bureau, 2010). The gaps are beginning to close but researchers question if it is closing fast enough (van Dijk & Hacker, 2000; Fontenay & Beltran, 2008). Recent discussions show that although the increase in Internet access is steadily growing, the United States' wealthy urban and suburban areas have access to high-speed Internet within their households (Crawford, 2011). This is a problem that directly affects lower-income and minority Americans. According to the Department of Commerce (NTIA, 2011b), 4 out of every 10 households with an annual household income of 25,000 or less have Internet access at home. In comparison to the 93% of households with higher incomes, low-income households' growth in access lags tremendously.

Existing literature frequently analyzes this gap in terms of individual demographic factors while ignoring the impact of social class (Wattal, Hong, Mandviwalla, & Jain, 2011). Despite government intervention through a variety of programs, the digital divide remains problematic (Leigh & Atkinson, 2001; NTIA, 2011a). Other factors that cause the disparity are geographic regions (Crang, Crosbie, & Graham, 2006). More recently, funding for increasing broadband connections in rural areas are beginning to pay off, leaving 51% of rural households with broadband connection just slightly lower than the 66% of urban households with broadband connection (U.S. Census Bureau, 2010).

The purpose of this chapter is to review existing literature and present recommendations for future research on the digital divide. Some enthusiasts proclaim that a shrink in the digital divide will be the key to reducing socioeconomic inequality because of the Internet's potential to lower barriers to information, which may cause people of all backgrounds to improve their human capital and in turn increase their opportunities (Hargittai, 2003). This chapter reviews the four types of access divides: material access, psychological access, skills access and usage access. In particular, the chapter presents prospect theory as a means to highlight the impact of computer anxiety and computer self-efficacy on psychological access.

BACKGROUND LITERATURE

The definition of the digital divide varies. According to Gunkel (2003) the term digital divide is "deeply ambiguous." The most common definition of the digital divide is "the gap between people with effective access to digital Information and Communications Technology (ICT), and those with very limited to no access to ICT" (Wattal, et al., 2011, p. 3). Hargittai (2003) labels those with effective access to ICT as the "haves" and those with limited to no access to ICT as the "have-nots."

One challenge in exploring the digital divide and information inequality is developing a multifaceted concept that thoroughly measures this disparity (Barzilai-Nahon, Gomez, & Ambikar, 2008). Measurements of the digital divide often use simple or single factor metrics that do not illustrate the whole picture (Barzilai-Nahon, et al., 2008; Korupp & Szydlik, 2005; van Dijk, 2006; van Dijk & Hacker, 2000). For this reason, the simplistic approach continues to be criticized (Barzilai-Nahon, 2006; Gurstein, 2003; Yu, 2001).

UNDERSTANDING THE DIGITAL DIVIDE

According to J. van Dijk (1999) the digital divide refers to four barriers to technological access:

1. **Material Access:** Little to no access to computers and network connections.
2. **Psychological Access:** Low digital experience caused by lack of interest, computer fear, and unattractiveness of the new technology.
3. **Skills Access:** A lack of digital skills caused by cumbersome technology and inadequate education.
4. **Usage Access:** A lack of significant usage opportunities within the home or workplace.

According to J. van Dijk (2006), access problems gradually shift from material access and psychological access to skills access and usage access. The shift in access results in a larger usage gap where the population is split into those who gain significant benefits from technological advancements and those who only use technology for basic applications (van Dijk & Hacker, 2000).

Material Access

Digital divide research began with the observation and collection of the amount and classification of people who have access to both a computer and network connection (van Dijk, 2006). The largest portion of digital divide research devotes much of its inquiries on simply accounting for users in particular demographics. Research that covers the amount and grouping of Internet-based technology users has a technological orientation (van Dijk, 2006). Much of this research focuses mainly on material access; it offers suggestions on how to improve the disadvantaged population's access to computers and the Internet.

The most common categories explored in this portion of research include income, age, sex, education, geographic location and ethnicity (Dewan & Riggins, 2005). The first five American National Telecommunications and Information Administration (NTIA) reports (NTIA, 1995, 1998, 1999, 2000, 2002) are the most thorough surveys in that period. The poorest households, incomes of less than $10,000, in central cities followed by rural households are number one and two on the disadvantaged list (NTIA, 1995). The implications for the NTIA (1995) report includes efficiently targeting the disadvantaged groups and improving their access to computers and the Internet by building community centers.

Studies focusing on geographical locations and network connection show how rural locations impact material access (Graham, 2002; Hsieh, Rai, & Keil, 2008; Kvasny & Keil, 2006; Lentz & Oden, 2001; Selwyn, 2003). Lentz and Oden (2001) analyze technology access in the Mississippi Delta region to better understand the impact of poor rural areas on technology diffusion. The study shows a combination of absent telecommunication manufacturing and service firms with low levels of connectivity cause a daunting material access problem for the region (Lentz & Oden, 2001). Lentz and Oden (2001) suggest that rural businesses, governments and non-profit institutions begin to close the material access gap by gaining access to an advance telecommunications infrastructure. Graham (2002) explores the unevenness of ICT development in geographical locations. Results show that new community centers equipped with computers and network connections begin to create traction in providing the geographical disadvantaged access to ICT (Graham, 2002). Graham (2002) calls for practitioners and policymakers to incorporate ICT with local, urban, national and international growth. Both studies (Graham, 2002; Lentz & Oden, 2001) conclude that the cost of network connections in poorly connected areas are high. This leaves low-income, rural communities with inferior, costly services (Graham, 2002; Lentz & Oden, 2001).

Psychological Access

J. van Dijk (1999) defines the psychological access divide as a low digital experience caused by a lack of interest, computer fear or undesirable new technology. One primary social explanation is the idea that the Internet does not appeal to those with low income or low education (Katz & Rice, 2002). Recent research suggests that the most pronounced factor of psychological access is computer anxiety or phobia (van Dijk, 2006). Computer anxiety is an overwhelming feeling of stress, discomfort and fear when faced with interacting with a computer (Brosnan, 1998).

Surveys exploring the fear of computers or technophobia, a fear of technology in general, find startling results. Approximately 30% of new American Internet users report that they are moderately to highly technophobic (UCLA, 2003). The "mental barrier" is commonly thought to only affect old people (van Dijk & Hacker, 2000). However, the "mental barrier" affects other groups of people like housewives and illiterates (van Dijk & Hacker, 2000). An American survey (NTIA, 2000) states the four main reasons for refusing to use computers and the Internet include no significant usage opportunities, little or no time, rejection of the technology or fear of the unknown. According to He and Freeman (2010), computer knowledge and computer anxiety are both factors of computer self-efficacy. He and Freeman (2010) call for more empirical research to test the "generalizability of [their] findings" (p. 239).

Skills Access

The skills access divide refers to people who have inadequate knowledge to operate technology and to manage hardware and software (van Dijk & Hacker, 2000). J. van Dijk (1999) is one of the first studies to analyze the skill level of users. J. van Dijk explored the variety of skill sets and the general level of skill for each age group. Steyaert (2000) introduces the concept of digital skills. The most basic are instrumental skills. Instrumental skills refers to one's ability to work with hardware and software (Steyaert, 2000). Steyaert (2000) posits that there is a difference between instrumental skills and strategic skills. Steyaert (2000) defines strategic skills as the ability to utilize computers

and Internet access for a particular purpose or goal, which is why this particular skill set is the hardest to master.

Additional studies focused on the relationship of digital skills and task completion. Hargittai (2003, 2002) replicated skill tests to find the average time it took to complete certain tasks. Hargittai (2002) found a disparity with the time it takes to complete a simple online task—seniors take between 7 and 14 minutes to search a term while others take only a few seconds. The general impression from surveys and tests measuring skill level is that the gap in skills widen between those with high and low educational levels as well as between those who are considered to be young and senior citizens (van Dijk, 2006). Hargittai (2002) find that having a higher level of traditional literacy impacts the possibility of having a higher level of digital information skills.

Usage Access

Utilizing ICT is the final stage as well as the ultimate goal of complete access (van Dijk, 2006). There are a variety of usage access barriers that affect ICT access. J. van Dijk (2006) describes four elements to measure the extent of usage as usage time, diversity of usage, creative use and use of broadband and narrowband. The average American spends more than 60 hours a month online which equates to about 30 days a year (Nielsen Company, 2008). Social networking accounts for 22% of the time and about 42% is spent viewing content (Nielsen Company, 2008). The percentage of American adults who use the Internet at least once a day is 55% (Zickuhr, 2010). Of those American adults about 45% use the Internet to send or read emails while only 5% of American adults use the Internet to buy a product or to play online games (Zickuhr, 2010).

Different categories of users prefer different types of applications. They also spend different amounts of time on the Internet. Lenhart et al. (2003) posit a correlation between usage applications and the demographic characteristics of users. Several studies find that users interact with the Internet for a variety of reasons and services (Agarwal, Animesh, & Prasad, 2009; Crang, et al., 2006; Segev & Ahituv, 2010). Segev and Ahituv (2010) posit that in English-speaking and Western countries the most popular searches are entertainment related. Germany, Russia and Ireland have greater diversity of search terms where the most popular searches are sociopolitical related. Agarwal, Animesh, and Prasad (2009) discover local patterns of usage and social influence on the diversity of usage in the U.S. In poor urban areas, the users predominantly use computers and Internet connection to complete simple tasks (e.g. sending emails) (Crang, et al., 2006).

Prospect Theory

Decision making theories may be a useful tool for explaining the diverse access divides. There are numerous decision making theories in the literature (Kahneman & Tversky, 1979; Kuhberger & Tanner, 2010; Tversky & Kahneman, 1992). Two popular decision making theories are Prospect Theory and Expected Utility Theory (Brown, 1996; Kahneman & Tversky, 1979). According to Kahneman and Tversky (1979) prospect theory directly addresses how choices are evaluated during the decision making process. In particular, it evaluates how individuals make decisions in risky situations.

According to the information systems literature, perceived risk is defined as the user's subjective expectation of suffering a loss in pursuit of a desired outcome (Warkentin, et al., 2002). Perceived risk is composed of behavioral and environmental uncertainty. Behavioral uncertainty exists because online service providers may behave in an opportunistic manner by taking advantage of the impersonal nature of the electronic environment, while environmental uncertainty arises due to the unpredictable nature of Internet-based technology that is beyond the control of the consumer

(Pavlou, 2003). In light of the risk associated with electronic services, we posit that prospect theory would be an appropriate theory to apply to our exploration of the digital divide.

Below is the simplest form of prospect theory:

$$w(p_i)v(x_i)=w(p_1)v(x_1)+w(p_2)v(x_2)+...+U=\sum_{i=1}^{n} w(p_n)v(x_n)$$

According to Kahneman and Tversky (1979), *x1*, *x2,* and *xn* are potential positive or negative outcomes; *p1*, *p2,* and *pn* are the respective probabilities of the positive or negative outcomes; *w* is the probability weighting function. The variable *v* is the value function which is derived from risky choices (Kahneman & Tversky, 1979).

Prospect theory is grounded in the expected utility theory and psychophysical models (Kahneman & Tversky, 1979). Expected utility theory is also a descriptive model of decision making in risky situations; however, it fails to predict outcomes in many scenarios including those without monetary worth and those with individual choice (Brown, 1996). Kahneman and Tversky (1979) apply psychophysical principles to explore judgment and decision making to show that normative theories need to be abandoned altogether. Normative theories describe what ought to be and are usually hard to prove or disprove (Schiffer, 2002). However, the digital divide is measurable which is shown by the numerous statistics on usage and access.

In this chapter, we explore prospect theory instead of expected utility theory because it is better suited for complex decisions (Brown, 1996; Kahneman & Tversky, 1979). According to Brown (1996, p. 19), utility is "understood to exist independent of probability" in classical decision models (p. 19). Those who try to apply classical decision models to difficult or personal scenarios face the obstacle of placing an objective value on an outcome (Brown, 1996). The obstacle of placing an objective value on an outcome makes it hard to assess utility and implications for everyday behavior (Brown, 1996). Because it is difficult for people to assess utilities, Kahneman and Tversky (1979) develop an alternative model with a much stronger foundation in psychological theory and experimentation. Kahneman and Tversky (1979) state that prospect theory is designed to explain an overall common pattern of choice. Prospect theory is used in the following section to explain the decisions of individuals with psychological barriers as well as future research directions.

BRIDGING THE DIGITAL DIVIDE

Prospect theory has been used by numerous researchers (Bromiley, 2010; Gaziolglu & Caliskan, 2011; Kuhberger & Tanner, 2010; Viswanath, Venkatesh, & Goyal, 2010) in diverse contexts, including gambling (Rachlin, 1990), financial investments (Barberis, Huang, & Santos, 2001; Hens & Vlcek, 2011), international relations (Levy, 1997), and human behavior (Tuggle, Sirmon, Reutzel, & Bierman, 2010). However, to-date, few researchers have used it to explore the digital divide. Due to its ability to explain decision making in diverse situations and to accurately assign value to both losses and gains, the authors recommend it as a useful tool for explaining a complex socio-economic phenomenon like the digital divide (Abdellaoui, Bleichrodt, & L'Haridon, 2008).

Other similar areas of research such as technology adoption and consumer choice use decision making theories to explain and measure data (Putler, 1992; Thaler, 1980; Viswanath, Venkatesh, & Goyal, 2010). According to Venkatesh and Goyal (2010) information systems adoption research uses the Expectation-Disconfirmation Theory (EDT) to explain how and why user reactions to ICT change over time. This research provides valuable insight into the phenomenon of technology adoption (Viswanath, Venkatesh, & Goyal, 2010). Similar to EDT use in technology

adoption research, prospect theory use in digital divide research can offer a fresh and innovative view of ICT inequality.

Although social and economic literature have pointed out several potential answers to bridging the digital divide, the most popular solutions address material access (van Dijk, 2006). Because of this trend additional research is needed on the other types of access: psychological access, skills access and usage access. We posit that prospect theory is a good lens through which to view psychological access.

Prospect Theory and Psychological Access

As aforementioned, psychological access refers to a lack of digital experience caused by a lack of interest, computer anxiety, and unattractiveness of new technology (van Dijk, 2006). Initially, computer anxiety was thought to only affect the elderly but research suggests it affects a variety of demographics (Fuller, Vician, & Brown, 2006; Thatcher & Perrewe, 2002; van Dijk, 2006). The level of one's technological knowledge and computer self-efficacy is usually correlated with gender, age, race, and socioeconomic status (Jones, Johnson-Yale, Millermaier, & Perez, 2009).

Studies have found gender differences in computer anxiety and self-efficacy (Cooper, 2006). According to Pinkard (2005), women are less likely to take computer classes and to graduate with IT degrees. The distinct differences between genders could cause social and economic disparities. A higher level of computer anxiety is seen to be a factor that deters women from using as well as pursuing careers in technology (Cooper, 2006). Both recent and decade-old studies found differences in Internet access and use across racial lines (Jones, et al., 2009). In the late 1990s, Hoffman and Novak (1998) findings showed a visible gap in Internet access and higher levels of computer anxiety between Caucasian and African American students. About 73 percent of Caucasian students were more likely to have Internet connection in the home and lower levels of computer anxiety than African American students (Hoffman & Novak, 1998). A more recent study found differences in race and socioeconomic status. Asian and Latino students were less likely to trust Internet sites than Caucasian (Norum & Weagley, 2006). Students with parents in higher income brackets were more likely to trust Internet sites than students with parents in middle and low income brackets (Norum & Weagley, 2006).

Computer anxiety is defined as the feeling of uneasiness, apprehension or fear about current or future use of computers (Fuller, et al., 2006). Research suggests that computer anxiety has an important correlation to computer self-efficacy (Fuller, et al., 2006; Thatcher & Perrewe, 2002; Venkatesh & Davis, 2000). Computer Self-Efficacy (CSE) refers to an individual's judgment of his capabilities to use computers and complete goals. According to Venkatesh and Davis (2000) individuals with high CSE have a tendency to form positive perceptions of Internet-based technologies. Both CSE and computer anxiety mediate the effect of computer experience (Jashapara & Tai, 2011).

A critical issue from a practitioner perspective is the ability to prepare the current and new generations for the digital-age (Fonseca, 2010). Transitioning from the industrial age into the digital era calls for major cultural, political, and educational transformations (Fonseca, 2010). Although several researcher have addressed the digital divide from different perspectives (Agarwal, et al., 2009; Barzilai-Nahon, et al., 2008; Belanger & Carter, 2009; Dewan & Riggins, 2005; Hsieh, et al., 2008; Jung, Qui, & Kim, 2001; Katz & Rice, 2002; Peng, 2010; Robinson, Dimaggio, & Hargittai, 2003; Vehovar, Sicherl, Husing, & Dolnicar, 2006), researchers have not thoroughly addressed the psychological barriers that impact the digital divide (van Dijk, 2006). Prior research shows that the benefits of IT investments are often hindered due to users' unwillingness to use the available systems and the same can be said about computer and Internet use (Devaraj & Kohli, 2003; Venkatesh & Davis, 2000). Practitioners can use data about computer anxiety and cyber phobia to understand ways to develop user-friendly technology.

A common theme in prospect theory research is that most decision making requires one to make a choice without the advance knowledge of all consequences (Trepel, Fox, & Poldrack, 2005). Those with a "mental barrier" or phobia concerning the use of Internet-based technologies find that they are also unable to state the negative consequences of using the technology that causes them to experience such anxiety (Chua, Chen, & Wong, 1999). Prospect theory can also address the best way to compel individuals with computer anxiety to seek help and solutions to lessen the apprehension of using a computer.

In the light of the need for more research on the digital divide and the influence of computer anxiety and computer self-efficacy on psychological access, this chapter presents several directions for future research. Given prospect theory's ability to measure both gains and losses, we recommend using prospect theory based research questions that highlight the impact of psychological access on computer and broadband usage. Table 1 shows future research questions related to both computer anxiety and computer self-efficacy.

FUTURE RESEARCH DIRECTIONS

Based on the literature, there are numerous opportunities for future research on the digital divide. Future research should empirically test the role of prospect theory on the digital divide, in general, and psychological access in particular. Trepel et al. (2005) suggest that prospect theory should be the focus of studies dealing with decision making in the context of normative models. Using prospect theory could lead to a fuller understanding of the cognitive neuroscience of decision making

Table 1. Research questions

Computer Anxiety	Computer Self-Efficacy
1. Does gender, education, or age moderate the relationship between computer anxiety and one's attitude towards the Internet and Internet-based technologies? 2. What factors impact computer anxiety? How can prospect theory be used to assign weighted value to each factor? 3. How does computer anxiety affect technological progress in society? 4. How can prospect theory help behaviorist understand computer anxiety and uncertainty towards Internet-based technology? 5. What types of programs should be implemented to decrease computer anxiety?	1. What is the relationship between time spent on the Internet and computer self-efficacy? 2. How does computer phobia impact computer self-efficacy? 3. What is the level of computer self-efficacy among those who have extreme computer phobia? 4. Can prospect theory help explain the negative/positive outcomes of having low/high computer self-efficacy? 5. What types of training are most effective to increase computer self-efficacy?

(Trepel, et al., 2005). A better understanding of decision-making can help researchers explain and measure the complex factor of human choice, which goes beyond finite resources like income. Future research should also use other theories like rational choice theory or utility theory to better understand the three less explored types of access.

Future research should answer J. van Dijk (2006) calls for more longitudinal studies that follow a variety of demographic groups. J. van Dijk (2006) states one myth of the digital divide is that people are either in or out, included or excluded. However, surveys reveal that the population of Internet users is ever shifting (Lenhart, et al., 2003). Therefore, research analyzing usage diversity could help us understand those who are not classified as included or excluded. Social media can be used to reach members of the digital divide because users possess diverse demographic characteristics.

According to Cooper (2006), girls and women have expressed a higher level of computer anxiety and more negative attitudes toward computers than boys and men in the past two decades. This could explain the low representation of female leaders in ICT based careers. In a society where employers emphasize ICT skills, women and other minority groups are underrepresented. The gap in minority groups' work participation requires attention. Developing ways to shrink access barriers could in turn help minority groups who are most affected by the digital divide. Minority groups often face additional barriers to organizational advancement

than non-minority groups. Major barriers can include a lack of mentors, the lack of exposure to the technology sector and a lack of ICT skill sets. A low self-efficacy could hinder an individual's goal to advance and take part in leadership roles.

In addition to future research on ICT and the digital divide, there are also numerous opportunities for future research on leadership and diversity. A leader influences individuals' growth and achievement. Leadership, especially diversity leadership, is important for organizational performance and organizational culture. More minorities in leadership positions can have a positive effect on organizational capability. According to Acar (2010), diverse leadership facilitates employees' ability to recognize different perspectives. Increasing mentor programs for minority groups within the technology sector could develop great leaders and facilitate creativity within the industry. Future research should explore how ICT skills and psychological barriers affect minority groups' inclusion in ICT careers including leadership roles.

Widespread citizen access to broadband access is just one of the answers to bridging the digital divide. Major investments should be made to generate more innovative learning to enhance the skills of citizens using Internet-based technologies. Future research should also explore the learning needs of unlikely users. Armed with a better understanding of learning approaches, practitioners can develop plans to infiltrate communities with high populations of unlikely users.

LIMITATIONS

There are limitations associated with using prospect theory. Although prospect theory can be used to explain well-defined problems, it only allows for one outcome. Hence, this theory is not suited to assess all four access barriers. Its use is appropriate in this chapter since we explore one barrier—psychological access barrier—in detail. We posit that this theory can be a useful tool for exploring each barrier in depth. Future studies that wish to examine multiple barriers should employ a different theoretical foundation. In addition, in this study, we present a conceptual framework that examines the role of computer self-efficacy and computer anxiety on psychological access, future research should conduct a qualitative or quantitative study to empirically validate our propositions.

CONCLUSION

The digital divide is a challenge with immense social, economic and technological implications. Fonseca (2010, p. 29) states that "digital technologies can and should be powerful accelerators of social change and economic growth" (p. 29). Digital technology has the potential to transform modern society (Fonseca, 2010). The role of these innovations however, will continuously depend on the users' ability to adapt and navigate them in order to gain its full benefits.

This chapter responds to a call for additional research on the diverse types of digital divides. It is an initial step toward an enhanced understanding of one of the multiple elements of the digital divide and its impact on society. It uses prospect theory to highlight the impact of computer anxiety on the psychological usage aspect of the digital divide. The chapter shows possible connections from the digital divide to other decision-making theories. It also highlights the need for more research on the various components of the digital divide.

REFERENCES

Abdellaoui, M., Bleichrodt, H., & L'Haridon, O. (2008). A tractable method to measure utility and loss aversion under prospect theory. *Journal of Risk and Uncertainty, 36*(3), 245–266. doi:10.1007/s11166-008-9039-8

Acar, F. P. (2010). Analyzing the effects of diversity perceptions and shared leadershiop on emotional conflict: A dyanmic approach. *International Journal of Human Resource Management, 21*(10), 1733–1753. doi:10.1080/09585192.2010.500492

Agarwal, R., Animesh, A., & Prasad, K. (2009). Social interactions and the "digital divide": Explaining variations in Internet use. *Information Systems Research, 20*(2), 277–294. doi:10.1287/isre.1080.0194

Barberis, N., Huang, M., & Santos, T. (2001). Prospect theory and asset prices. *The Quarterly Journal of Economics, 116*(1), 1–53. doi:10.1162/003355301556310

Barzilai-Nahon, K. (2006). Gaps and bits: Conceptualizing measurement for digital divides. *The Information Society, 22*(5), 269–278. doi:10.1080/01972240600903953

Barzilai-Nahon, K., Gomez, R., & Ambikar, R. (2008). Conceptualizing a contextual measurement for digital divides: Using an intergrated narrative. In Ferro, E., Dwivedi, Y. K., & Williams, R. G. (Eds.), *Overcoming Digital Divides: Constructing an Equitable and Competitive Information Society*. Seattle, WA: University of Washington.

Belanger, F., & Carter, L. (2009). The Impact on the digital divide on e-government use. *Communications of the ACM, 52*(4), 132–135. doi:10.1145/1498765.1498801

Bromiley, P. (2010). Looking at prospect theory. *Strategic Management Journal, 31*(12), 1357–1370. doi:10.1002/smj.885

Brosnan, M. J. (1998). The impact of computer anxiety and self-efficacy upon performance. *Journal of Computer Assisted Learning, 14*, 223–234. doi:10.1046/j.1365-2729.1998.143059.x

Brown, T. (1996). Prospect theory. In Kiel, L. D., & Elliott, E. (Eds.), *Chaos Theory in the Social Sciences* (pp. 15–44). Ann Arbor, MI: University of Michigan Press.

Chua, S. L., Chen, D.-T., & Wong, A. F. L. (1999). Computer anxiety and its correlates: a meta-analysis. *Computers in Human Behavior, 15*(5), 609–623. doi:10.1016/S0747-5632(99)00039-4

Cooper, J. J. (2006). The digital divide: The special case of gender. *Journal of Computer Assisted Learning, 22*(5), 320–334. doi:10.1111/j.1365-2729.2006.00185.x

Crang, M., Crosbie, T., & Graham, S. (2006). Variable geometries of connection: Urban digital divides and the uses of information technology. *Urban Studies (Edinburgh, Scotland), 43*(13), 2551–2570. doi:10.1080/00420980600970664

Devaraj, S., & Kohli, R. (2003). Performance impacts of information technology: Is actual usage the missing link. *Management Science, 49*(3), 273–289. doi:10.1287/mnsc.49.3.273.12736

Dewan, S., & Riggins, F. J. (2005). The digital divide: Current and future research directions. *Journal of the Association for Information Systems, 6*(12), 298–337.

Fonseca, C. (2010). The digital divide and the cognitive divide: Reflections on the challenge of human development in the digital age. *Information Technologies & International Development, 6*, 25–30.

Fuller, R. M., Vician, C., & Brown, S. A. (2006). E-learning and individual characteristics: The role of computer anxiety and communication apprehension. *Journal of Computer Information Systems, 46*(4), 103–115.

Gaziolglu, S., & Caliskan, N. (2011). Cummulative prospect theory challenges traditional expected utility theory. *Applied Financial Economics, 21*(21), 1581–1586. doi:10.1080/09603107.2011.583393

Graham, S. (2002). Bridging urban digital divides? Urban polarisation and information and communications technologies (ICTs). *Urban Studies (Edinburgh, Scotland), 39*(1), 33–56. doi:10.1080/00420980220099050

Gunkel, D. (2003). Second thoughts: Toward a critique of the digital divide. *New Media & Society, 5*(4), 499–522. doi:10.1177/146144480354003

Gurstein, M. (2003). Effective use: A community informatics strategy beyond the digital divide. *First Monday, 8*(12).

Hargittai, E. (2002). The second-level digital divide: Differences in people's online skills. *First Monday, 7*(4), 1–20.

Hargittai, E. (2003). The digital divide and what to do about it. In *New Economy Handbook* (pp. 821–839). New York, NY: Elsevier Science.

He, J., & Freeman, L. A. (2010). Understanding the formation of general computer self-efficacy. *Communications of AIS, 26*(12), 225–244.

Hens, T., & Vlcek, M. (2011). Does prospect theory explain the dispostion effect? *Journal of Behavioral Finance, 12*(3), 141–157. doi:10.1080/15427560.2011.601976

Hoffman, D. L., & Novak, T. P. (Producer). (1998). *Bridging the digital divide: The impact of race on computer access and internet use*. Retrieved from elab.vanderbilt.edu

Hsieh, J. J. P.-A., Rai, A., & Keil, M. (2008). Understanding digital inequality: Comparing continued use behavioral models of the soci-economically advantaged and disadvantaged. *Management Information Systems Quarterly, 32*(1), 97–126.

Jashapara, A., & Tai, W.-C. (2011). Knowledge mobilization through e-learning systems: Understanding the mediating roles of self-efficacy and anxiety on perceptions of ease of use. *Information Systems Management*, *28*(1), 71–83. doi:10.1080/10580530.2011.536115

Jones, S., Johnson-Yale, C., Millermaier, S., & Perez, F. (2009). U.S. college students' Internet use: Race, gender and digital divides. *Journal of Computer-Mediated Communication*, *14*(2), 244–264. doi:10.1111/j.1083-6101.2009.01439.x

Jung, J. Y., Qui, J. L., & Kim, Y. C. (2001). Internet connectedness and inequality. *Communication Research*, *28*(4), 507–535. doi:10.1177/009365001028004006

Kahneman, D., & Tversky, A. (1979). Prospect theory: An analysis of decision under risk. *Econometrica*, *47*(2), 263–291. doi:10.2307/1914185

Katz, J. E., & Rice, R. E. (2002). *Social consequences of Internet use, access, involvement and interaction*. Cambridge, MA: MIT Press.

Korupp, S. E., & Szydlik, M. (2005). Causes and trends of the digital divide. *European Sociological Review*, *21*(4), 409–422. doi:10.1093/esr/jci030

Kuhberger, A., & Tanner, C. (2010). Risky choice framing: Task versions and a comparison of prospect theory and fuzzy-trace theory. *Journal of Behavioral Decision Making*, *23*(3), 314–329. doi:10.1002/bdm.656

Kvasny, L., & Keil, M. (2006). The challenges of redressing the digital divide: A tale of two U.S. cities. *Information Systems Journal*, *16*, 23–53. doi:10.1111/j.1365-2575.2006.00207.x

Leigh, A., & Atkinson, R. D. (2001). *Clear thinking on the digital divide*. New York, NY: Progressive Policy Institute.

Lenhart, A., Horrigan, J., Rainie, L., Allen, K., Boyce, A., & Madden, M. (2003). *The ever-shifting internet population: A new look at internet access and the digital divide*. Washington, DC: Pew Internet and American Life Project.

Lentz, B., & Oden, M. (2001). Digital divide or digital opportunity in the Mississippi delta region of the US. *Telecommunications Policy*, *25*(5), 291–313. doi:10.1016/S0308-5961(01)00006-4

Levy, J. S. (1997). Prospect theory, rational choice, and international relations. *International Studies Quarterly*, *41*(1), 87–112. doi:10.1111/0020-8833.00034

Nielsen Company. (2008). *Three screen report: Television, internet and mobile usage in the U.S.* New York, NY: The Nielsen Company.

Norum, P. S., & Weagley, R. O. (2006). College students, internet use, and protection from online identity theft. *Journal of Educational Technology Systems*, *35*, 45–59. doi:10.2190/VL64-1N22-J537-R368

NTIA. (1995). *Falling through the net: A survey of the "have nots" in rural and urban America*. Retrieved from http://www.ntia.doc.gov/ntiahome

NTIA. (1998). *Falling through the net II: New data on the digital divide*. Retrieved from http://www.ntia.doc.gov.ntiahome

NTIA. (1999). *Falling through the net: Defining the digital divide*. Retrieved from http://www.ntia.doc.gov/ntiahome

NTIA. (2000). *Falling through the net: Toward digital inclusion*. Retrieved from http://www.ntia.doc.gov/ntiahome

NTIA. (2002). *A nation online: How Americans are expanding their use of the internet*. Retrieved from http://www.ntia.doc.gov/ntiahome

NTIA. (2011a). *Broadband adoption report.* Retrieved from http://www.ntia.doc.gov/report/2011/exploring-digital-nation-computer-and-internet-use-home

NTIA. (2011b). *New commerce department report shows broadband adoption rises but digital divide Persists.* Retrieved from http://www.ntia.doc.gov

Peng, G. (2010). Critical mass, diffusion channels and digital divide. *Journal of Computer Information Systems, 50*(3), 63–71.

Pinkard, N. (2005). How the perceived masculinity and/or femininity of software applications influences students' software preferences. *Journal of Educational Computing Research, 32*, 57–78. doi:10.2190/3LEE-MLCE-NK0Y-RUEP

Putler, D. S. (1992). Incorporating reference price effects into a theory of consumer choice. *Marketing Science, 11*(3), 287–309. doi:10.1287/mksc.11.3.287

Rachlin, H. (1990). Why do people gamble and keep gambling despite heavy losses. *Psychological Science, 1*(5), 294–297. doi:10.1111/j.1467-9280.1990.tb00220.x

Robinson, J. P., Dimaggio, P., & Hargittai, E. (2003). New social survey perspectives on the digital divide. *IT & Society, 1*(5), 1–22.

Schiffer, S. (2002). A normative theory of meaning. *Philosophy and Phenomenological Research, 65*(1), 186–192. doi:10.1111/j.1933-1592.2002.tb00194.x

Segev, E., & Ahituv, N. (2010). Popular searches in Google and Yahoo!: A "digital divide" in information uses? *The Information Society, 26*, 17–37. doi:10.1080/01972240903423477

Selwyn, N. (2003). ICT access for all? Access and use of pubic ICT sites in the UK. *Communicatio Socialis, 6*(3), 350–375.

Smith, A. (2010). *Mobile access 2010.* Washington, DC: Pew Internet & American Life Project.

Steyaert, J. (2000). *Digital skills: Literacy in the information society.* The Hague, The Netherlands: Rathenau Instituut.

Thaler, R. (1980). Toward a positive theory of consumer choice. *Journal of Economic Behavior & Organization, 1*(1), 39–60. doi:10.1016/0167-2681(80)90051-7

Thatcher, J. B., & Perrewe, P. L. (2002). An empirical examination of individual traits as antecedents to computer anxiety and computer self-efficacy. *Management Information Systems Quarterly, 26*(4), 381–396. doi:10.2307/4132314

Trepel, C., Fox, C. R., & Poldrack, R. A. (2005). Prospect theory on the brain? Toward a cognitive neuroscience of decision under risk. *Brain Research. Cognitive Brain Research, 23*(1), 34–50. doi:10.1016/j.cogbrainres.2005.01.016

Tuggle, C. S., Sirmon, D. G., Reutzel, C., & Bierman, L. (2010). Commanding board of director attention: Investigating how organizational performance and CEO duality affect board members' attention to monitoring. *Strategic Management Journal, 31*, 946–968.

Tversky, A., & Kahneman, D. (1992). Advances in prospect theory: Cumulative representation of uncertainty. *Journal of Risk and Uncertainty, 5*, 297–323. doi:10.1007/BF00122574

UCLA. (2003). *The UCLA internet report: Surveying the digital future, year three.* Los Angeles, CA: University of California.

U.S. Census Bureau. (2010). *U.S. census bureau, current population survey: Computer and internet use.* Washington, DC: U.S. Department of Commerce.

van Dijk, J. (1999). *The network society, social aspects of new media.* Thousand Oaks, CA: Sage.

van Dijk, J. (2006). Digital divide research, achievements and shortcomings. *Poetics, 34,* 221–235. doi:10.1016/j.poetic.2006.05.004

van Dijk, J., & Hacker, K. (2000). *The digital divide as a complex and dynamic phenomenon.* Paper presented at the International Communication Association. Acapulco, Mexico.

Vehovar, V., Sicherl, P., Husing, T., & Dolnicar, V. (2006). Methodological challenges of digital divide measurements. *The Information Society, 22,* 279–290. doi:10.1080/01972240600904076

Venkatesh, V., & Davis, F. D. (2000). A theoretical extension of the technology acceptance model: Four longitudinal field studies. *Management Science, 46,* 186–204. doi:10.1287/mnsc.46.2.186.11926

Venkatesh, V., & Goyal, S. (2010). Expectation disconfirmation and technology adoption: Polynomial modeling and response surface analysis. *Management Information Systems Quarterly, 34*(2), 281–303.

Wattal, S., Hong, Y., Mandviwalla, M., & Jain, A. (2011). *Technology diffusion in the society: Analyzing digital divide in the context of social class.* Paper presented at the Hawaii International Conference on System Sciences. Maui, HI.

Yu, P. (2001). Bridging the digital divide: Equality in the information age. *Cardoza & Entertainment, 20*(1), 1–52.

Zickuhr, K. (2010). [*Major trends in online activities.* Washington, DC: Pew Internet & American Life Project.]. *Generations (San Francisco, Calif.),* 2010.

KEY TERMS AND DEFINITIONS

Computer Anxiety: A feeling of uneasiness, apprehension, or fear about current or future use of computers.

Computer Self-Efficacy: Refers to an individual's judgment of his capabilities to use computers and complete goals.

Digital Divide: Refers to the disparity between those who have access to the Internet and those who do not.

Expected Utility Theory: A way of defining preferences and decision-making power pertaining to uncertain outcomes.

Internet-Based Technology: Refers to the communications infrastructure of the Internet.

Material Access Divide: Little to no access to computers and/or network connections.

Prospect Theory: A decision-making theory that describes alternatives with uncertain outcomes.

Psychological Access Divide: Low digital experience caused by lack of interest, computer fear, and unattractiveness of the new technology.

Skills Access Divide: Lack of digital skills caused by cumbersome technology and inadequate education.

Usage Access Divide: Lack of significant usage opportunities within the home, workplace or community.

Chapter 5
Factors in Fluidity of Leadership in Emerging Contexts:
Technology Access and Use

Anna C. McFadden
University of Alabama, USA

Michelle Hale
University of Alabama, USA

Juanita F. McMath
University of Alabama, USA

Barrie Jo Price
University of Alabama, USA

ABSTRACT

Using the definition of Hesselbein, Goldsmith, and Beckhard (1996), leaders are defined as those with followers and who garner influence with and among those followers. Mobile technologies, social media, and other computer-mediated communication tools have changed how those followers are connected to leaders and organizations as well as how influence can be exerted by the followers themselves. Leadership in political, economic, and educational contexts is examined through examples taken from research and current events. Three common themes emerged within each of the leadership sectors examined: time and place, the role of the individual vs. the group, and interactivity. These themes are explored through a framework of questions and leadership actions.

INTRODUCTION

In the foreword of Drucker Foundation's *The Leader of the Future: New Visions, Strategies, and Practices for the Next Era* (Hesselbein, Goldsmith, & Beckhard, 1996), a leader is defined as someone who has followers. Leaders have to have influence over or with individuals and within or among groups in order to have followers. Some readers may argue that this is definition is too narrow because it fails to speak to character or purpose of leadership. The relationship between followers and influence are key to leadership in a multicultural world in which technology is the conduit for information and is at the core of the discussion in this chapter.

DOI: 10.4018/978-1-4666-2668-3.ch005

How individuals and organizations get and use information, either as leaders or as followers, feature prominently in this examination of leadership. Since the publication by the Drucker Foundation of that seminal work on leadership, much has happened in terms of technology, and, as a result, in terms of leadership. The process of reaching and creating followers certainly now reflects emerging technologies such as those of social networking. The creation of influence has been changed, too, as a result of the changing technologies. Who has influence and how it is measured has changed drastically. Leaders who understand that technology has produced broader audiences, consisting of self-selecting individuals are the leaders who have used the technology successfully, whether for the larger good or personal enhancement. Either way, leaders create and, in some ways, manage followers by managing the technology, thus creating and using influence among those followers. Followers also have some sense of self-direction in their choices and, as followers, have technological means for influencing leaders, also as a result of technological changes. This chapter explores how leaders can use technology to create influence and, thus, inspire followers in the fields of politics, economics, and education while acknowledging that the unique interactive nature of today's technology empowers followers with influence in ways not possible in previous decades. Some of the resultant issues are identified in the emergence of leadership and the role of leaders in managing interactive organizations in a multinational, multicultural context. Leadership must be considered in terms of the factors of time and place, individuals vs. groups, and interactivity in determining leaders and followers.

BACKGROUND

Retired General Collin Powell, United States Army, was interviewed by Piers Morgan on CNN (November 10, 2011) and, among other topics, he discussed the difficulties experienced by today's leaders in reaching *compromise* on any issue. He described how, with access to media, extremists at either end of the spectrum can become immediately engaged in the situation whereas in the past, leaders had a chance to work together quietly and privately to reach common ground before experiencing broad involvement of others. Leaders' efforts today are under constant exposure to scrutiny and discussion by anyone with access to the information through the technologies available. Leaders today sometimes have to weigh and perhaps defend decisions before those decisions are even fully developed. The multitude of voices entering any decision-making process has changed the process of leadership as well as its timing. There is no longer time for that leadership and its decisions to emerge, considered and mature. The other side of this issue is the transparency being imposed on decision-making events and the policy makers because of the potential interactivity resulting from both leaders and followers having access to information.

Successful leaders now realize that these broader audiences, official or otherwise, impact how they function as leaders. Followers also realize their power, implicit or explicit, in influencing the decision-making process. Clearly, there are both positive and negative implications of open access to information by masses of individuals and groups. It is this balance of broad exposure to the widest range of audiences ever encountered by leaders as well as transparency with the need for measured, considered decision making that is at the heart of this chapter. The reader is reminded that the definition of leader used in this chapter is an individual with followers as a result of influence garnered.

Among factors contributing to the shortened time frame for the emergence of leadership decisions include the presence within an organization or culture of the *digital natives* (Prensky, 2001a, 2001b). Palfrey and Gasser (2008) provide insights into this unique generation in *Born Digital*, from

The Digital Natives Project of The Berkman Center for Internet and Society at Harvard University and The Research Center for Information Law at the University of Gallen. Digital natives are described in research reports and popular press articles as having a distinct array of characteristics as a group or generation (Digital Youth Network, 2012; Edutopia, 2012; Prensky, 2001b; Szekely & Nagy, 2011; Hargittai, 2010), including the desire for empowerment, engagement with information, self-directed learning, and creativity. These characteristics, when coupled with their use of communication technologies, create in them an expectation of participation and immediacy; this same expectancy of immediacy permeates much of modern life and colors leadership, impacting what is expected of leaders and how followers respond.

Communications technologies play a key role in changing leadership functions and timetables as well as location. Just as place has diminished in importance as a result of asynchronous tools, time has an altered role in decision making processes. While the expectation of immediacy and the need for access to information at an ever growing rate of speed create a sense of 'now' in decision-making, the process of decision making can take on a 24/7 nature. Asynchronous tools make it possible for teams to work together but not at the same time or same place. Changes in time and place make the process of how decisions are made within an organization almost as important as the outcomes of those decisions. Participation may no longer be limited to a specific group within the organization (i.e. all employees are asked for suggestions on quality improvement not just the quality department) or even to only internal participants (i.e. customer satisfaction surveys and online exit interviews are common).

Historically access to information might be limited by geography (place). Previously there were parts of the world without telephones or television which now have access to smartphones and Twitter. Some countries controlled all of the news channels (newspapers, radio, television) and even limited travel outside of the country, and in doing so, controlled the information flow within their borders. Now, blogs and Facebook manage to serve as conduits, even if illegally, so location is no longer the sole indicator of access.

In certain times in world history, only wealthy individuals owned books because of the time involved in creating them; they were a symbol of wealth. Umberto Eco's *The Name of the Rose* (1980) eloquently described the time when books were copied by hand; now documents are available almost instantly via cloud computing tools such as a wiki and ebooks. Even in open cultures, television, radio and newspapers traditionally had editors and editorial boards who took the time to filter the news as well as to control its timetable for distribution, but today blogs and Twitter, among other tools, are unfiltered and immediate avenues for information. The Web is dynamic, open, sometimes characterized by conversation, community, commons and collaboration (Levine, 2006; Birbeck, 2005); Flickr, MySpace, Facebook, and blogging redefine the avenues by which information can be immediately distributed, filtered only by the people posting and allowing immediate interaction by followers-viewers from anywhere (Lankes, 2006). Mass communications have become operationalized as individualized communications with individuals in almost all locations and stations in life *gaining and expecting immediate access to information*, legally or otherwise, regardless of time or space. Speeches are on YouTube.com. Policy manuals are on public wikis, and SKYPE™ (VoIP) discussions are uploaded as podcasts, making the possible audiences almost unpredictable, time of viewing unpredictable, and place irrelevant, giving access to information by followers in any location with access the Internet.

Access to Information

It is important to explore the current status of broadband access and mobility in tools, followed by a brief exploration of the policies associated with determining who has access to avenues for information and how that information is managed. Understanding what kind of information and technical access is available to individuals and organizations sets the stage for more in-depth review of the multicultural, multinational implications for leadership.

The spread of broadband throughout the world has resulted in next-generation connectivity typified by increased speeds and the sense that connectivity is ubiquitous, part of the landscape of modern life (Berkman Center, 2010). Open access policies are emerging in varying degrees in almost all developing Internet-accessed environments, though the rate of development may be slower in some countries. Even so, access to broadband is rapidly expanding around the world (Wallsten, 2009; Eurostat Society, 2012). Mobile technologies are also emerging as a force in organizational leadership. Smartphones may be the key to access because they are more affordable than a laptop and are portable (Nagel, 2011). They are used to access information as well as posting information to Twitter, blogs, etc. using access to networking and computing power.

With the onset of technology, particularly mobile technologies, many politicians and others thought Internet access would erode divisions between socio-economic positions, creating greater opportunities without barriers. Though much progress has been made globally, divisions are still observed along some familiar demographics: economic, social, cultural and cognitive (Notten, Peter, Kraaykamp, & Valkenburg, 2008). Research shows an increase in the United States in access in minority and low-income homes, but gap differences still exist related to income and race, with higher income and greater levels of education correlating positively with greater levels of access (Warschauer & Matuchniak, 2010). There is a relationship between a country's wealth/educational expansion and Internet access at home (Notten, et al., 2008). However, mobile tools, such as the Smartphone, have bridged gaps

previously created by geography, politics, and economics (Shin, Shin, Choo, & Beam, 2011). However, the increased access to smartphones is still framed by factors such as income and race. Though research continues to reveal differences in Internet access based on economic and educational levels, there are efforts in the United States (Stelter, 2011) and other countries to increase access for lower income and/or geographically isolated areas (Berkman Center, 2012). Leadership is changing as a result of the increased access to broadband coupled with the burgeoning use of individually controlled, personal tools such as social media to instigate and/or document events.

World events have driven increased access to the Internet and therefore information in one form or another, as was made obvious by the events of *the Arab Spring*. The Arab Spring began with a wave of demonstrations and protests in Egypt, spreading through other Arab countries in the spring of 2011. The political, economic, and social implications of those protests were astounding and are still being revealed and documented as shown in the research by Mansour (2012). Mansour's work examines the role of Social Networking Sites (SNSs) in the January 25th 2011 revolution in Egypt. The research confirmed that SNSs anchored the Arab Spring events through their use as a source of non-governmental information and a means of informing internal and external audiences of events as they played out in Egypt and spread to other countries.

For the purpose of this chapter, the focus is on the role technology played in those events, such as described by Mansour and also found in the research of Benmamoun, Kalliny, and Cropf (2012) and their work on virtual public spheres for access. Prior to the Arab Spring, some leaders might have dismissed the societal implications of personal access applications such as Facebook or Twitter as merely entertainment or some kind of self-serving promotion. However, with the Arab Spring events revealed, these tools represent a shift in their use, with a growing role in society beyond entertainment. For example, Andy Carvin, Senior Strategist at National Public Radio (NPR), demonstrated through his own Twitter account that it is possible to provide accurate and complete news coverage of important events. His Twitter coverage of the demonstrations in the Arab spring superseded the coverage of mainstream news sources (Schillinger, 2011). As Schillinger said in describing Carvin's work, "…social media is more about narratives than isolated content" (p. 5).

As Mansour (2012) and Benmamoun et al. (2012) report, social media played a particularly important role in the Arab spring events, a position supported by these data (Taylor, 2011):

- The rate of tweets about the Egyptian government and political change increased ten-fold in the week before the resignation of then-President Hosni Mubarak.
- The opposition increased the content on Facebook, video sites, blogs, and other such social media sites, resulting in increase of widespread audiences.
- The day Ben Ali resigned in Tunisia, blog postings assessing his leadership were up 40% over the previous month.

A confluence of events, including increased access to broadband, has resulted in important changes in almost all organizations, especially those in politics, business, and education. Technical access and tools, coupled with changing abilities and expectations of individuals, produced a fluid and unexplored context for leadership. Leadership requires an examination of both the technical and social factors surrounding leadership. This chapter is devoted to explaining how access to information and its use by multicultural, diverse individuals inform the type of leader and leadership functions required by today's rapidly changing organizational landscape. The consequences of the emergence of technologically empowered followers and leaders are explored in terms of time and space, individuals vs. groups, and interactivity.

SHIFTS IN SELECTED FACTORS INFLUENCING LEADERSHIP IN POLITICAL, ECONOMIC, AND EDUCATIONAL ORGANIZATIONS

There are multiple factors influencing today's leadership, but the ones on which this narrative is focused include how technology changes have altered the relationship of time and space to leadership, the role of the individual vs. groups in decision making, and the nature and amount of interactivity possible within constituencies. These factors are manifested in slightly different ways within each leadership situation, but there are some common themes that will be explored later in the chapter. First, a discussion of leadership in politics, business, and education is in order to illustrate some of the shifts in processes and outcomes resulting from technology as well as to reveal some of the questions they produce for leaders.

Leadership in Political Contexts

The issues of technology access and use in political contexts relate to how technology is being used for information gathering and sharing (i.e. how followers and leaders are created or evolve). Internet sharing results in organizing others for a like cause, with the possible outcome being a demand for change. Leaders must be aware of how more open access to information is leading to not only transparency but also greater citizen action (Relly, 2011). The new media now available are being used in ways that were initially not intended; users have found unique ways of utilizing social media. The impact of communicating and organizing is far reaching and with this comes global scrutiny and accountability.

Obstacles encountered by today's political leaders may be related to policy. For example, in China the Internet is censored, Google products are filtered, and Facebook, Twitter and YouTube are blocked (LaFraniere & Barboza, 2011), yet information continues to flow in and out of these countries through individual use of personal technologies circumventing those policies. Australia has proposed voluntary Internet censorship limiting some 500 websites, prior to a reintroduction of mandatory Internet filter for child-abuse sites (Dudley-Nicholson, 2011). In the UK, allegations of surveillance of Smartphone use, including the ability to disconnect phone access services and interrupt text messages of items deemed dangerous communications after recent civil unrest, are being investigated (Whittaker, 2011). The interpretation of what is and is not appropriate is determined by the respective governments, though leaders recognize that followers often find technological ways to circumvent these limitations, making policy irrelevant or disconnected from reality. Mital, Israel, and Agarwal (2010) report on information exchanges and disclosure in social networking websites, including how this use of technology impacts the role of trust in communication of information, a direct impact on leadership actions and interactions.

Regardless of policies or access, examples exist to illustrate the impact of technology on the political processes: *crowd sourcing*, *tweeting on Twitter*, and *the use of mobile devices*, particularly smartphones. Crowd sourcing is the use of social media for communicating with or organizing people across boundaries—political, geographical, and cultural. The results are diverse opinions, thoughts and findings that are cross cultural, drawing the masses in civic and/or personal engagement. Political divisions are being voiced through social media and the outcomes, in many instances, result in political and social change (Kelleher, Whalley, & Helkkula, 2011). Crowd sourcing featured prominently in Tunisia in the organization of political protests associated with the Arab Spring. Twitter and Facebook were used to organize participants (Nelson, 2010). Organizations of people demanding change spread from Tunisia to Egypt and across the Middle East. Prior to the Arab Spring, crowd sourcing in the Philip-

pines resulted in over 1 million people gathering in Manila to protest the government's decision to suppress key information from the impeachment trial of the president (Sherky, 2011). Approximately 7 million text messages were sent and as a result of the citizens' actions, evidence was not suppressed and the president was removed. Crowd sourcing is also used in pro-active activities across organizations and between citizens. Currently, protests for change are seen in the United States with the Occupy Wall Street movement, spreading from New York across the country (Millership, 2011). People are not only organizing within their political or geographical boundaries, but they are using social media to share how to organize (Millership, 2011). This networking is another example of the global reach of social media. Even if each person speaks a different language, translations are available through technology, so common language is no longer a barrier.

Governmental agencies use Twitter to inform constituencies, giving and receiving information. For example, the Texas legislature used social networking to open the discussion on a bill on payday lending (Hamilton, 2011). The process gave the representatives information on what the people thought of the bill as well as suggestions for crafting a better bill. In this way, technology conveys opportunities for leaders to engage followers thus garnering influence, while, at the same time, giving followers an opportunity to influence the decisions of leaders (Berkovich, 2011). Such examples typify the interactive nature of technology in political contexts. For some politicians, monitoring Twitter postings for trends and Tweeting may replace polling in the traditional sense.

Twitter is also being used to inform citizens during a state of emergency, tweeting to say where resources can be found or where to report for help. The University of Alabama Faculty tweeted to locate students, inform students and others (with smartphones) of shelters, food, and where to go for assistance after the April 27th tornado in 2011 when there was no other form of communication beyond Twitter; at the same time, students and faculty members tweeted about needs, locations of help, and updates on individuals and situations. The two-way communications, though asynchronous, enhanced governmental and university leadership's role in the Alabama recovery, while engaging and empowering individuals worldwide to become part of the process as well. How leadership reacts in a time of crisis has to be couched in terms of the use of computer-mediated communication technologies. The difference between the situation following the Alabama tornadoes in 2011 and the period following Hurricane Katrina in New Orleans in 2005 was marked, in some small part, by the availability of social media tools such as Twitter. In Mexico City, citizens used social media to spread the news of dead bodies and a gunman at an intersection, helping others avoid a dangerous situation (Cave, 2011).

In addition to crowd sourcing and Twitter, political leaders must acknowledge the role of mobile technologies. Smartphones have created a new, affordable way of access that is also more portable and immediate (Hertz, 2011). With this immediacy, leaders have to make adjustments to their approach to the audience in order to survive in the political arena (Surin, 2010). For example, social media tools are filling a news gap, and Twitter is more trusted than local news in Mexico City (Cave, 2011). The reporter can be the person holding the smartphone, creating the blog or YouTube video or Twitter (Surin, 2010). The follower can become the leader or the leader can influence the follower, depending on the use of the technology, particularly the mobile technologies.

This use of technology for collective knowledge speaks to time and space issues as well as individual vs group means in traditional reporting in the emerging political environment. Technological access can *form* and *inform* followers and show transparency in the process (not anonymous); it also gives the politicians a forum for information gathering from the citizens, leading to greater participation in the political process (Hamilton,

2011; Smith, 2010). The interactive nature of the technologies, allowing two-way communication unlike any other news or communication means, ultimately informs how political leaders function and even who those leaders are. There are critical questions resulting from this shift in communications (Korstanje, 2011). Korstanje's work with leadership in disaster situations related to swine flu raised questions about whether or not news should be edited or transmitted in rough form during such uncertain times. The debate described in Korstanje's work relates to non-edited news, its potential impact on society, and the implications for freedom of the press if monitored or controlled.

Drucker and Gumpert (2007) made a sound case that the transparency possible as a result of communication technologies is a two-sided concept associated with openness but also with opportunity for observation previously not experienced by leaders such as politicians. Thus, current research may be said to raise more questions than to provide answers. The questions to which today's leaders must seek answers include these: What is the role of the individual in political decision-making? How does the technology change the time and place for leadership in political contexts? What constitutes political communities?

Leadership in Economic Contexts

Technology is a vital component in economic, social, and technological progress, and it is critical for the sustainability of economies all over the world (Daniels, 2005; Adegbuyi & Uhomoibhi, 2008; Wang &Hong, 2009). The merger of computers and telecommunications and their incorporation of microelectronics began redefining organizations in the 1960s, and the collective impact of these micro-level changes resulted in a shift to a new structure that was variously described as an "information," "knowledge," "networked," "services," or "post-industrial" economy. This information revolution marked an economic change on par with the industrial revolution in the form of fundamental macroeconomic changes such as increased productivity and new business models. For example, corporate competition became global, outsourcing labor internationally became commonplace, and longstanding barriers to free trade and capital mobility came under scrutiny (Libecap, 2011).

Today the economy is undergoing yet another major shift in composition and focus. There are still global economies emerging (Girod & Bellin, 2011), and these are still impacted by the disparities in telecommunications networks and services between rich and poor countries, apparent in the last decades of the 20th Century (Drake, 2000). However, technology, broadband access, and individual, mobile access tools, have changed that status quo in small but important ways. While the divide still exists to varying degrees, its impact on economic development is less defined by traditional economics than by those revolving around Internet broadband and access by individuals and small groups (Chakravarthy & Coughlan, 2011). Micro-loans coupled with individual technologies using global infrastructures have, in some ways, circumvented the need for the establishment of large, corporate structures and their traditional hierarchical Information Technology (IT) structures.

Efforts such as those of Nobel Prize Winner, Muhammad Yunus, and The Yunus Centre emphasize new economic models including the use of technology to develop small-scale, individually managed economic activities (Yunus Centre, 2012). This shift fits with an economy emerging as more individually driven in many ways. Pink (2011) suggests a change in focus for large corporate organizations from the shareholder to the customer. He says organizational leaders need to focus on the customer as an individual and as a critical group, a recommendation consistent with economic changes in focus. Instead of thinking of the organization as an entity itself, responsible only to shareholders, he advocates focusing on individuals as customers. This fits with a shift to a focus on individuals empowered by tools and

demonstrating creativity, whether as creators of businesses or as customers. While large-scale, mass-marketing promotions still exist in traditional media forms, there are also parallel efforts directed at individuals through the use of social media and other individually-controlled technologies. For example, individual reviews of products online are important factors in purchasing decisions, second only to word-of-mouth recommendations (Johnson, 2008). At the same time, consumers can complain or compliment a product and instead of only reaching the complaint department of the company, literally millions of readers (and potential customers) may be influenced by such statements from one consumer. All of this speaks to the growing economic power of individuals as small business generators, employees, and consumers.

Leaders in today's business environment in large corporate environments have to adjust to the fact that information formerly restricted to upper levels within an organization may now be widely distributed, legally or otherwise. Information sometimes now moves unilaterally without the traditional channels of hierarchy. There is wide scrutiny of the corporate actions, with criticism and input coming more and more from the individual level, such as from the consumer. Blogs, wikis, YouTube, and other forms of social media are used by employees, customers, business wonks, and individuals inside and outside the organization, with audiences well beyond the official ranks of the organization. While corporate moguls such as Steve Jobs managed to keep most information restricted to company personnel or an inner circle, there is still always the possibility of a 'leak' (i.e. Wikileaks). Just being aware of the potential for mass distribution, intended or otherwise, changes the leadership structure within an organization and changes how information is handled.

Responding to these broader audiences, with their greater diversity, becomes a challenge that sometimes require the leader and organization to resort to using these same individually driven avenues and incorporating them into the business processes. For example, companies use a myriad of consumer or client polls or surveys via Facebook or Twitter to constantly interact with employees or customers for new ideas. Leaders have changed the timelines for responses to customers and clients, acknowledging the 24/7 model for most businesses today. Quick Response (QR) tags are used to quickly direct individual smartphone users to the company's website, to feedback locations and to rewards such as printable coupons. Through these technologies, followers are being included in the planning, evaluation, and design processes, and products of the company but on a much shorter timetable than in traditional marketing study groups and without regard to place. For example, a company might have a QR tag that takes smartphone users directly to a special website for a contest on designing the new container for an adult beverage. Clicking on the link enters the individual user in a contest for a free vacation while collecting the customer's idea for the container. Thus companies have access to crowd sourcing in that, via the contest site, individual participants form a critical mass for research and development ideas, all free, except for the price of the award vacation.

Individuals responsible for small companies, agencies, and non-profits also find that these technologies available to them via mobile devices empower them to reach out to more diverse groups (Kuflik, 2011). International development for economic purposes and also for social progress are impacted by technology, changing the way these organizations do 'business' (Tyler & Pillers, 2011). Social media accomplished via mobile devices contribute to the empowerment of individuals served by these groups as well as allowing informal and formal input from a wide range of experts. The interactive nature of the mobile technologies and the low-level technical expertise required to participate via these technologies have significant implications for non-profit groups and other development organizations.

Because of the technology, groups have power in developing and managing economic activities. Non-profit groups find that they can engage artisans in global marketing and for-profit groups can market to international audiences from anywhere, even single-vendor enterprises, using tools such as Twitter. This means that leaders of small or single-vendor operations can, if knowledgeable about the diversity of their audiences, appeal to potential users/clients/customers who in previous times would have been well beyond their budget and therefore their reach.

As mentioned earlier, the presence of digital natives in the workforce creates different situations for leaders than encountered in employment of earlier generations. The need for engagement (involvement) can be seen in the way in which work groups are structured for and by digital natives: flextime, work-from-home, computer-mediated communications (Price, 2008). As described by Price, the difference between *going to work* and *doing work* is implicit in the expectations of the economic models of today, especially as they relate to digital youth. Work becomes disassociated with time or place. Workers may reside on two different continents while their team leader (i.e. supervisor in previous workplace models) lives on yet a third continent. The ability of these workers to *work together but apart* is central to the emerging economies built on access to broadband and individual access tools. The future of work is significantly tied to changes in the composition of the workforce and the use of technology by the population of citizens and workers (Pew Internet and American Life Project, 2012). The challenge for leaders is captured in this statement: "Organizations must build expertise and establish a common skill set that supports the (organization's) goals" (Henschen, Stodder, Crosman, Mcciellan, Mcwhorter, & Patterson, 2007, p. 2). As organizations change to reflect the goals of distributed work and less hierarchical workplace structures, leaders must change (Garrity, 2010).

Changes in social behavior as a result of technological changes directly impact the workplace and the management of work (Time Magazine, 2010). More women will be in the workplace, more flexible schedules will be required, and perks expected by workers will include time for family. Workforces will include older workers who are not ready to retire, as well as the younger, digital generation, presenting its own set of challenges for managers. The newer employees will expect more input (digital youth), and at the same time, they will consider exploring flatter management structures with less traditional hierarchy. Changes resulting from the technology embedded in society have implications for businesses and how they are managed, including how to manage digital natives armed with mobile technologies that define 'the workplace' as wherever they are (Price, 2008).

The changes in society are reflected in the technologies of this decade. Facebook is only about ten years old. Twitter began in 2006. LinkedIn was founded in 2002. All of these developments have occurred since the turn of this century. While there may be international differences, soon many or most workers will have similar experiences and expectations. Workers in an industry in one country can use Twitter or LinkedIn to compare wages, work environment, and leadership models with workers on the other side of the world. In the end, business leaders have to look at the diversity in the audiences they reach, the employees they hire, and the products or services they offer and consider the tools for interacting with them, producing important questions that need answers: How does technology change the time and place of *work?* How are individuals melded into a customer or employee base or community? How does technology impact process and outcomes for this organization?

Leadership in Educational Contexts

Education today is a global endeavor. Geographical boundaries which once existed have been virtually erased since technology allows global communication in ways which could have only been imagined even a decade ago. In addition, education is no longer limited to a particular time and place; like the concepts of work or political constituency, teaching and learning have changed as a result of multiple forces, including technology access and use. While there are still brick and mortar schools, the idea that teaching and learning occur only in a classroom in a school building at a prescribed time is as outdated as the idea of a *job description* for today's autonomous worker. Work no longer requires all workers to be in the same place at the same time: *doing work* vs. *going to work* (Price, 2008). Teaching and learning are no longer confined by the traditional view of 'school.' Creativity, self-direction, engagement and empowerment are as critical as factors in teaching and learning as they are in defining work or marshalling political followers; when those characteristics are coupled with individual technology tools such as smartphones, iPads™, netbooks, and broadband access anywhere in the school and community, teaching and learning become more defined by outcomes than by process. Time and space become less relevant; individuals become more prominent than groups. Interactivity takes on new meaning.

Technology has changed where, when and how education takes place, thus changing the role of teacher to one more related to managing learning opportunities than to *presenting* as in the traditional lecture (Drumheller & Lawler, 2011). Some classrooms are flipped, meaning much of what was presented in traditional group-instruction formats is now captured with technology for individual access (Vajoczki, Watt, Marquis, Liao, & Vine, 2011; McFadden, 2008); examples include podcasts, using PowerPoints with Voice-Over created by Camtasia™ or JING™ and mini-demonstrations captured with teachers' desktop Webcams and uploaded to Google Sites™ or the school's Moodle server. These products can be integrated within the class (Yang, Chen, & Jeng,

2010), but they can also be assigned outside class time as homework, leaving more time during the class period for Socratic discussions and *what if* questions and conversations, represented by the upper levels of Bloom's Taxonomy (1956) or Revised Bloom's Taxonomy (Anderson & Krathwohl, 2001). While flipping the classroom is still open to debate, leaders are recognizing the potential of changing this paradigm, given personal ownership of mobile technologies observed in today's school students.

An educational leader's charge is to harness the power which technology affords to empower the students, regardless of age, culture, or geographic location and try to meld that individualized opportunity with what has been, primarily, a group culture. The near ubiquity of the Internet makes vast opportunities for collaborative learning and team building within learning communities, regardless of time or place, but what constitutes these learning communities and how they are managed becomes an issue. The challenges of the educational leader include conveying these changes to educators, particularly in terms of the differences created in outcomes and processes, the role of the individual in learning, and how to manage the interactivity available. Like politicians and business leaders, educational leaders have to examine time and place as factors in creating communities, whether of workers, supporters, educators, and students. Humans learn from one another through communication, and technology is causing a pedagogical shift in how this is accomplished (Tamin, Bernard, Borokhovski, Abrami, & Schmid, 2011). It is necessary to determine how best to integrate this natural tendency for learning in a community with the use of individually managed technologies.

Computer-Supported Collaborative Learning (CSCL) focuses on employing the benefits of collaborative learning via Internet-enabled computers, tablets, and smartphones. In fact, communications have progressed and smart, handheld devices have emerged so quickly that the

necessity of the traditional computer's "support" is almost arguable. The end-goal is to make use of the power of technology based on reliable and ubiquitous computing environments to facilitate and support learning in all communities. The outcome is establishment of a supportive environment for learning with no regard for time or place, and the process is interactive, driven in part by followers (students, parents, and teachers). Just as politicians and business leaders are collecting information from followers, teachers must begin to learn to find those larger narratives as described earlier by Schillinger (2011) within individual expressions from Twitter and other sources from parents and students.

An important factor of computer-supported collaborative learning is the recognition of the importance of socialization to learning and the significance of that socialization to developing higher order thinking skills. Today's knowledge economy requires a much-advanced set of cognitive and analytical skills. Therefore, group socialization, discussion, and collaboration play an ever-significant role in defining pedagogical end-goals (Fischer, Rhode, & Wulf, 2007; Yang, Chen, & Jeng, 2010). The higher-order cognitive and problem solving skills require the analysis of processes within complex contexts, rather than just end products resultant from a teacher-centered classroom. The benefits received illustrate the shift towards technological environments that promote authentic group learning and an increasing role for all technological components that form a global network (Carroll & Bishop, 2005). Diverse audiences learning via their own individual mobile devices, perhaps in their own space and time, require a different mixture of lesson planning and teaching skills to implement student collaboration, consideration of multiple perspectives, and self-directed learning (McFadden, 2007), thus changing the traditional nature of professional development, evaluation and observation of results.

Computer-supported collaborative learning is often less than successful due to a lack of, or poorly timed, communications among and between students and instructor. Sometimes the impact of these problems of communications between teacher and student are exacerbated by the availability of mobile devices for communication and the nature of the digital youth; the tools are there but unused by uninformed educators. Communication is often not properly built into the learning plan, being left to serendipity. Teachers are not accustomed to thinking of teaching and learning as a 24/7 interactive activity. Rarely is there professional development on how to manage email communications, other than to present the rules that protect the school. Managing email as virtual office hours, for example, can make important differences in the attitudes of the teacher and the students or parents, yet this may not be part of teacher training. Leaders in these environments have to assume responsibility for changing the view of education to reflect something more akin to Boyer's Basic School (Boyer, 1995) or the view of schooling extending beyond the classroom walls and the school day because of the technologies available to both student and teacher. That is a major shift in the conceptualization of education. Time and space may be diminished as factors; the focus may shift from group to individuals. Influence as a result of interactivity may not be obvious.

Another challenge for educational leaders is getting the educational organization to acknowledge that a vital factor to the success of the tasks within the learning plan is the student's perceived authenticity of them. Today's students are motivated by engagement with the information, empowerment, and self-direction of their own learning, and, of course, creativity in the learning process. Students have access to astounding resources via the Internet and expect what they do in class to incorporate those resources. Students are less likely than ever to be content to sit and listen to a teacher *describing* a volcano, even with presentation slides outlining the lecture. This cannot compare in engagement or creativity to students using their own net books or smartphones to visit

The National Geographic's Volcano site where they can watch live video of actual volcanoes, chart changes in the lava flow in real time, and even ask questions, perhaps live, of a volcanologist. Students expect to be asked to deliver more in the way of assessments than a quiz built on the lowest levels of Bloom's Taxonomy. Straight information recall is no longer acceptable, either to teacher or to students; they have the tools to answer the "what if" questions associated with true learning.

The design of a lesson must be flexible to allow for adjustments for the students' existing background, knowledge and experiences (Young, 2008). To some degree, this means making adjustments with regard to direction from the students themselves (Walters, 2009). Carroll's Mastery Learning (Carroll, 1963) is a pedagogical model from the 1970s that now, with individual technologies available to students, can be brought to fruition if teachers are willing to allow the technologies into the classroom. Students can have standardized outcomes but engage in individually designed learning activities (i.e. read a lecture, listen to a lecture as a podcast, watch a video of the lecture, engage in a scavenger hunt to locate the information, etc.) using their individual tools (smartphone, netbook, iPad™, etc.). Educational leaders have to examine how the organization can embed this individualized design with individual tools into a traditionally group-oriented, teacher-directed environment. Marsh and Ketterer (2006) make the case for reconceptualizing intimacy and distance in learning, something even more important in light of today's mobile technologies.

The newest laptops and tablets are relatively small and lightweight. Their mobility allows students to maintain a higher comfort level simply due to being able to access the Internet from any number of places. Comfortable surroundings combined with the small size of a laptop, tablet or smartphone equate to relaxed, receptive, and more productive students and teachers (Rajala, 2003). One of the issues resulting from this shift is that traditional spaces associated with teaching and learning no longer seems consistent with this new mobility. Wireless access has added to this mobility in learning. Physical space, accommodations such as security for individually owned equipment that is highly portable, and policies appropriate for individualized, mobile learning within and out of school are issues that leaders have to address. In the final analysis, the issues of time and space become paramount for educational leaders. When and where do teaching and learning occur? How does the organization plan for learning communities to evolve? What roles do individuals play in their own learning? How does technology impact school's processes and outcomes?

Framework for Developing Answers

The examination of some of the shifting factors within the three contexts for leadership (political, economic, and educational) produced leadership questions to guide the reader to the next level of understanding the fluid nature of leading in today's culture. The very fluidity of those factors makes it difficult to provide answers that stand up to the test of time in the face of emerging technologies, cultural shifts, and changing expectations. To only answer these questions for the moment does not make sense; the shelf life of specific information is limited. Instead, it is more useful to provide a framework for organizing and analyzing information related to the questions. The specific questions are repeated below:

- **Political Context**: What is the role of the individual in political decision-making? How does the technology change the time and place for leadership? What constitutes political communities?
- **Economic Context**: How does technology change the time and place of *work?* How are individuals melded into a customer or employee base or community? How does

technology impact process and outcomes for this organization?
- **Educational Context**: When and where do teaching and learning occur? How does the organization plan for learning communities to evolve? What roles do individuals play in their own learning? How does technology impact school's processes and outcomes?

These questions can best be examined through a framework focused on these factors, all influenced by technology access: *changes in time and place*, *the role of the individual vs. the group*, and *interactivity*.

Time and Place

If the reader accepts the original definition of leadership as one who has followers and influence, then the role time and place in securing and managing those followers have to be addressed. Time is shortened due to constant scrutiny by wider audiences, with faster results expected from actions. Leaders know that the time between action and reaction is shortened now by widespread access to information as a result of technology. The time for interaction with followers is no longer dictated by the leader's schedule; followers can be contacted or observed anytime if asynchronous means are used (i.e. Twitter). The other side of that is that followers expect access to be available anytime, meaning leaders and their organizations have to be prepared to accept and respond to followers on a 24/7 model, including education. Political groups and schools, like businesses, have to be organized in some fashion to acknowledge the need for followers to have access, irrespective of time. Parents are no longer satisfied with calling the school office between 8am and 3:30pm in order to get information. Voters want to be able to post their thoughts on an issue immediately after seeing it discussed on the evening news. Managing time as a shifting factor means using asynchronous tools and restructuring human resources needed to support a 24/7 access plan. Tactics might include staggering office support, using online support to answer questions all hours, realigning secretarial help from 8-5 models to management of email queries and Twitter postings, and employing planning strategies that allow both synchronous and asynchronous input. Parents who work can contribute to the Community Guidebook if it is on a wiki. Volunteers who have small children can edit and post on Twitter for a non-profit group or political group from home for the organization, while the children nap.

Place, too, becomes secondary to purpose. Leaders ask, "Do all of these people really have to be in the same room in order to have this conversation?" Teachers can meet via SKYPE™ from their own homes at a time of their choosing to discuss the upcoming accreditation visit, thus not disrupting their travel arrangements after school and allowing them to work from home. Political headquarters may be some distance from the residences of volunteers; why not use SKYPE™ for them to sit in on the meeting, saving the gas for driving or time for commuting to the meeting? Instead of asking if someone can come to a meeting, ask if that person has time to meet. Contributions to group work could be conducted on a wiki, with each person's contribution actually observable and measurable; no longer would people come to meetings to sit and fail to be engaged. Even in education, educators should ask questions about whether or not the student has to actually be in the classroom in order to learn a particular concept. Tradition may dictate that learners have to come to a centralized location (school) and that the teacher has to be present in order for teaching and learning to occur. But now learners have books and more, plus they have tools of their own for accessing information and creating new knowledge, available to them outside of school. Students can access the information on their own time, leaving Face-to-Face time (F2F) time for the most interactive parts of the teaching-learning

process, and even those can be accomplished via computer-mediated technologies (Price, 2008).

In the end, the means by which followers interact with the organization and by which influence is created must be planned and conducted in such a way that time and place do not limit that interaction. Time and place cannot be left to chance or designed for the convenience of the organization and its leaders. Followers, such as students, parents, volunteers, customers, clients, vendors, and any others engaged in interaction with the organization, have to be considered in decisions. Even consideration has to be given to those followers whose input is not sought per se. *Every action in the organization should be examined within a framework of time and place.*

- Each function should be reviewed to see if it is absolutely necessary that it be synchronous; could asynchronous tools be used?
- Make changes in the organizational structure to accommodate asynchronous activities that recognize the diminished role of time and place in work.
- Look for other process or outcomes measures consistent with the avenues available for participation via technology. For example, attendance is not an appropriate singular measure of participation.

The Role of the Individual vs. the Group

Much has been made historically about the group, whether that means customers, students, employees or others; research often reported on group results, educational planning was about what the group would do, and politicians sought groups for support. Individual communication technology tools changed all of that. Individuals now have power as a voice through blogs, Twitter, Facebook and other such tools, but many organizations still are organized for relationships with groups. Slowly businesses are acknowledging the voice of the individual through opportunities for feedback, customer reviews, and 1:1 customer support. Organizations are beginning to seek input from individuals as feedback loops on their Web pages, through online surveys connected to purchases, and even using individual connections to create crowd sourcing opportunities. Still much needs to be done in most organizations to acknowledge that individuals with mobile technologies and Internet access have tremendous power and influence in their own right.

Sometimes followers actually become leaders as a result of that influence. Personal blogs become professional avenues: The Pioneer Woman Blog (thepioneerwoman.com, Ree Drummond) or the movie Julie and Julia (www.julieandjulia. com). The followers develop their own influence and followers, changing their role completely, all without organizational structure. Individuals can post on YouTube, Twitter, post on Facebook and even create Google Sites about a trend, an observation, an event, or just an opinion and, in doing so, create momentum in one direction or another. Organizations and their leaders should examine their management to see if there are opportunities to maximize this individual power or, at the least, to make sure the organization is acknowledging this power, not ignoring it. Advisory boards can be as diverse as the followers within the organization, no longer limited by time and space or the need to belong to a particular group. Bloggers become recognized for their blogs and sometimes become mainstream-referenced sources for information. Organizations need to look for opportunities to allow individuals to add to the value of organization in this way.

In educational organizations, an examination is in order for how planning structures can be focused on individual activities. Planning documents need to focus on what individual students are doing or might do as opposed to group planning. Schools with so-called 1:1 computer programs should reconceptualize these initiatives as *engaged learning initiatives,* which is a better

and more accurate characterization. Individual students become engaged with the content, with the teacher supporting those activities. In terms of communications, educators must embrace computer-mediated technologies as important means of sharing information, not merely youth-driven tools focused solely on entertainment. To discount the power of Twitter as a means of communicating with students and vehicle for observation of their interests and needs is to miss a powerful opportunity to interact individually. To walk away from the communication technologies used in social media is the same as to walk away from a student wanting to ask a question or share a concern. It is an opportunity missed with potentially life-long consequences for the student. It also represents a missed opportunity for the teacher to sample the narrative of that individual.

Remember the recommendation by Daniel Pink (2011) cited earlier in which he suggests that corporations focus less on shareholders and more on individual customers. That same focus on the individual within all organizations now takes on more than rhetoric because of the individual's use of his/her own technology. Detractors may say that there is so much information generated by individuals that it is impossible to incorporate their feedback and/or questions into organizational planning efficiently. However, a return to the comment by Schillinger (2011) concerning Andy Carvin's reporting on the Arab Spring with a Twitter account is in order. Schillinger correctly commented on how social media should be seen as a narrative, not individual, iconoclastic comments. Organizational leaders can aggregate individual comments and questions into a meaningful narrative, useful to them in guiding their organizations. Strategies to refocus on the individual vs. the group might include:

- Examine all data collection activities in the organization to see if all potential stakeholders are allowed ways to provide comments, feedback, and to ask questions.

- Determine how the organization can monitor and study individual comments related to the functioning of the organization or its products and processes.
- Review the mission of the organization to see if it is consistent with today's individual access to information. Determine whether or not there are sufficient formal reviews of those data on a regular basis.

Interactivity

At the basis of leadership in the changing environments of today's organizations is interactivity. Organizations and their leaders have to interact with followers, whether they are considered students, voters, or employees. In addition, followers interact with each other, forming loosely structured groups. Followers also interact with their OWN followers, thus becoming leaders in this fluid world mediated by individual technologies. The interactive nature of information creation and dissemination is potentially a little like the children's game of Gossip. In that game, everyone sits in a circle and the one at the head of the circle whispers a statement in the ear of the next person, who then turns to repeat it to the next person in the circle. And so it continues around the circle. Finally, the person at the end of the circle repeats what was repeated. The final statement is compared with what the first person said to begin the game; sometimes it is very accurate and other times there is little or no relationship between the original statement and the final one. The same potential for both accurate and inaccurate communications as seen in the game of Gossip exist in the interactivity of individualized, mobile communications. Accuracy may not equate to the speed of those communications, but the frequency of interactions is not diminished even when fraught with possible miscommunications. This downside is part of the immediacy and engagement in interactivity, especially when there are no traditional filters or checking agencies. Attitudes are changed

or cemented through rapid interactions at many levels, well beyond any official outlet. Stars post updates on their martial situations on Twitter. Political candidates confirm or deny rumors on Twitter. Teachers announce quizzes on Twitter. Individuals launch personal attacks against foes. Lovers exchange intimate endearments. Like any vehicle for information, there is the potential for use and abuse.

The exchange of information, taking place at rates and through easily accessible media, is a part of today's world. To lament the abuses and to regale listeners with the evils is unproductive for a leader. Instead interactivity should become a focus for additional study and analysis, framed by the needs of the organization. For example, if a service organization offers customer services in a particular segment of the economy, then what is said ABOUT and TO the organization is important. Observing Facebook postings, tweets, and blog postings from customers and others provides important data. If a school is discussed in a negative way on a teachers' blog or a school review Web site, instead of railing against those postings, leaders have to examine them and determine what course of action is needed to counter or address the postings. Proactive organizations marshal data to support their own Web presence, filling the voids with accurate and relevant information, so searches produce positive results. In this way, organizations are interacting with the information itself instead of the individuals.

As the above discussions illustrates, interactivity with individuals and with Web-based tools combines to create a Web presence. It is that Web presence that represents the actual entity. Individuals have a Web presence, meaning what is found in a search, what virtual depictions exist and what means are used for access. So do organizations. Interactivity includes how virtual data connects to present an image of the organization. There are employee comments, official websites, and a myriad of references, all interacting to create a Web presence. Or worse yet, there is NO Web presence. No Web presence means there is no interactivity. It is like being invisible. While some may wish to stay below the radar, so to speak, it results in a loss of opportunity for interactivity. There is no opportunity to provide or collect information. There is no means for customers or other stakeholders to interact via social media. If the organization only provides static information, even on the Web, the lack of interactivity is a disadvantage. Leaders must have information from which to determine the most appropriate actions. Traditional one-way communications may convey the image desired by the organization, but it gives no opportunity to collect information from the followers, thus omitting a valuable avenue for input and feedback.

Capitalizing on the vast opportunities for interactivity means creating a dynamic organization, rich with vehicles for interaction among all stakeholders and others. Interaction has to be viewed as adding value to the organization, so it is included in planning and management activities, not left to chance. Leaders may:

- Conduct an information flow to determine precise what avenues can be exploited as interactive channels for collecting information within and about the organization.
- Develop an actual plan for ways in which interaction can be incorporated into all aspects of the organization. For example, schools' technology audits include interactivity as a component. Business organizations create an information flow plan that has information flowing in and out of the organization. Political groups examine avenues used by their group and by their followers to convey or challenge points then make those avenues permanent activities.
- Encourage all leaders in the organization to become aware of and use social media for interactivity.
- Make interactivity part of the organizational mission and strategic plan.

FUTURE RESEARCH DIRECTIONS

When examining the three leadership sectors (political, economic, and educational), there is important information in terms of the factors identified in this chapter: time and place, the role of the individual vs. the group, and interactivity. There is also information on digital youth, the workers of today and the future. Even in this brief treatment, the intersection of these factors and the population is obvious and can be implied from existing research. However, future research needs to be conducted on collateral issues.

- **Trust:** Increasing the role and, therefore, the power of the individual in business, politics, and education, along with the increasing interactivity, the issue of trust has to be examined. While increasing the individual's role as follower and, perhaps, leader, exerting influence through both roles, trust has to be presumed but it is unclear how this trust is manifested. Blogging on a subject for long periods of time does not speak directly to trust, though, for the present, longevity and consistency seem to speak to trust in some sectors. Bloggers are increasingly quoted, for example, as primary sources on various topics. Researchers need to determine what conveys *trust* in communications that do not always benefit from the availability of visual cues and proximity.
- **Authenticity:** Researchers will need to examine how, in this future powered by individual interaction and influence, authenticity is defined and identified. Fake websites will be posted. Fraudulent Twitter accounts will spread misinformation. How will individuals and organizations identify authentic sources, given that many of the intermediate filters will no longer exist? Organizations and individuals will need some kind of standard or designation (Seal

of Approval) and/or perhaps some kind of template or training to identify sources. Whether this is a code or standard or a matter of education, the matter of authenticity lies at the heart of what worries many about the interactive nature of the Internet and presents one of the biggest challenges for leaders.

- **Privacy:** In this chapter, interactivity and emphasis on the individual have been common themes. Leaders have been urged to pursue these as values and also as tools for leadership. However, it is important to acknowledge that with these tools comes responsibility for how data collected are handled. Codes of behavior have been legislated but the results are still mixed as to the ability of those codes to protect. Future researchers need to investigate where the line resides between collecting and sharing information and violating privacy.

CONCLUSION

As defined in this chapter, a leader is someone who has followers and leaders have influence among those followers. At the same time, because of today's computer-mediated communication technologies including mobile devices, followers also have influence, sometimes creating change in the leaders and the decisions they make. This chapter explores the two-way interactivity between leaders and followers as well as among groups of followers, examining the implications in three sectors of leadership: political, economic, and education. Scenarios were from business, politics, and education, illustrating within each sector, how leadership must be based on information provided to and from followers. Leaders and followers potentially have access to almost immediate information and the ability to share that information widely and without editorial filters. In examining the implications of this ability to share informa-

tion, especially through computer-mediated tools, three themes were selected for examination across the leadership sectors: *time and place*, *the role of the individual vs. the group*, and *interactivity*.

The three factors were examined through examples and the resulting questions arising from leaders within the sectors. A framework was provided for organizational review, addressing each of the three themes with potential actions cited. Individual empowerment, accompanied by opportunities for expression, has become part of the landscape of leading an organization. Time and place, the role of the individual vs. the group, and interactivity all contribute to the dynamic contexts of leadership, fueled by the rapid advancements in mobile technologies.

REFERENCES

Adegbuyi, P., & Uhomoibhi, J. (2008). Trends in the development of technology and engineering education in emerging economies. *Multicultural Education & Technology Journal*, 2(3), 132–139. doi:10.1108/17504970810900432

Anderson, L. W., & Krathwohl, D. R. (Eds.). (2001). *A taxonomy for learning, teaching, and assessing: A revision of Bloom's taxonomy of educational objectives*. Boston, MA: Allyn & Bacon.

Benmamoun, M., Kalliny, M., & Cropf, R. (2012). The Arab spring, MNEs, and virtual public spheres. *Multinational Business Review*, 20(1), 26–43. doi:10.1108/15253831211217189

Berkley University. (2011). *Digital youth research: Kids' informal learning via digital media*. Retrieved October 12, 2011 from http://digitalyouth.ischool.berkeley.edu/

Berkman Center for Internet and Society. (2010). *Next generation connectivity: A review of broadband, internet, transitions and policy from around the world*. Retrieved from http://cyber.law.harvard.edu

Berkovich, I. (2011). No we won't! Teachers' resistance to educational reform. *Journal of Educational Administration*, *49*(5), 563–578. doi:10.1108/09578231111159548

Birbeck, M. (2005). *Xform and Internet applications*. Retrieved February 27, 2007 from http://internet-apps.blogspot.com/2005/08/delicious-link-manager-written-in.html

Bloom, B. S. (1956). *Taxonomy of educational objectives*. Boston, MA: Allyn and Bacon.

Boyer, E. L. (1995). *The basic school: A community for learning*. San Francisco, CA: Jossey-Bass Inc.

Carroll, J. B. (1963). *A model of school learning*. New York, NY: McGraw-Hill.

Carroll, J. M., & Bishop, A. P. (2005). Special section on learning in communities. *The Journal of Community Informatics*, *1*(2), 116–133. Retrieved from http://ci-journal.net/index.php/ciej/article/view/335/243

Cave, D. (2011, September 27). Mexico turns to social media for information and survival. *The New York Times*. Retrieved November 1, 2011, from http://www.nytimes.com/2011/09/25/world/americas/mexico-turns-to-twitter-and-facebook-for-information-and-survival.html?r=2&scp=2&sq=crowd%20sourcing%20political%20global&st=cse

Chakravarthy, B., & Coughlan, S. (2011). Emerging market strategy: Innovating both products and delivery systems. *Strategy and Leadership*, *40*(1), 27–32. doi:10.1108/10878571211191675

Daniels, P. (2005). Technology revolutions and social development: Prospects for a green technoeconomic paradigm in lower income countries. *International Journal of Social Economics*, *32*(5), 454–482. doi:10.1108/03068290510591290

Digital Youth Network. (2011). *Digital youth network organization*. Retrieved November 1, 2011 from http://www.digitalyouthnetwork.org/

Drake, W. (2000). *Carnegie endowment for international peace: Impact on global economic structures and processes*. Retrieved November 12, 2007 from http://www.carnegieendowment.org/events/index.cfm?fa=eventDetail&id=11&

Drucker, S., & Gumpert, G. (2007). Through the looking glass: Illusions of transparency and the cult of information. *Journal of Management Development*, *26*(5), 493–498. doi:10.1108/02621710710748329

Drumheller, K., & Lawler, G. (2011). Capture their attention: Capturing lessons using screen capture software. *College Teaching*, *59*(2), 93. doi:10.1080/87567550903252793

Dudley-Nicholson, J. (2011, June 22). The internet's silent sentinel. *Herald Sun*. Retrieved from http://www.heraldsun.com.au/ipad/the-internets-silent-sentinel/story-fn6bn9st-1226079510340

Eco, U. (1980). *The name of the rose*. Snzogno, Spain: Gruppo Editorial-Fabbri-Bompiani.

Edutopia.org. (2012). *The George Lucas educational foundation*. Retrieved from http://www.edutopia.org

Eurostat. (2012). *Indicators, households which have broadband access*. Retrieved from http://epp.eurostat.ec.europa.eu/portal/page/portal/information_society/data/main_tables

Fischer, G., Rohde, M., & Wulf, V. (2007). Community-based learning: The core competency of residential, research-based universities. *International Journal of Computer-Supported Collaborative Learning*, *2*(1), 9–40. Retrieved from http://www.springerlink.com.libdata.lib.ua.edu/content/x7m1270830277315/ doi:10.1007/s11412-007-9009-1

Garrity, R. (2010). Future leaders: Putting learning and knowledge to work. *Horizon*, *18*(3), 266–278. doi:10.1108/10748121011072717

Girod, S., & Bellin, J. (2011). Revisiting the "modern" multinational enterprise theory: An emerging-market multinational perspective. *Research in Global Strategic Management, 15*, 167–210. doi:10.1108/S1064-4857(2011)0000015013

Hamilton, R. (2011, October 6). Out of the smoke-filled room and onto the internet. *The New York Times*. Retrieved from http://www.nytimes.com/2011/10/07/us/for-public-input-crowdsourcing-online.html

Hargittai, E. (2010). Digital natives? Variation in internet skills and uses among members of the "net generation". *Sociological Inquiry, 80*(1), 92–113. doi:10.1111/j.1475-682X.2009.00317.x

Henschen, D., Stodder, D., Crosman, P., Mcciellan, M., Mcwhorter, N., & Patterson, D. (2007). Seven business and tech trends for '07. *Intelligent Enterprise*. Retrieved January 2, 2007, from http://www.crn.com/sections/breakingnews/breakingnews.jhtml?articleId=196800329

Hertz, M. B. (2011, October 24). A new understanding of the digital divide. *Edutopia*. Retrieved on November 2, 2011 from http://www.edutopia.org/blog/digital-divide-technology-internet-access-mary-beth-hertz

Hesselbein, F., Goldsmith, M., & Beckhard, R. (1996). *The Drucker foundation: The leader of the future*. San Francisco, CA: Jossey-Bass.

Johnson, N. (2008). Online reviews second only to word of mouth in purchase decisions. *Small Business Network*. Retrieved from http://searchenginewatch.com/article/2053296/Online-Reviews-Second-Only-to-Word-of-Mouth-in-Purchase-Decisions

Kelleher, C., Whalley, A., & Helkkula, A. (2011). Collaborative value co-creation in crowd-sourced online communities: Acknowledging and resolving competing commercial and communal orientations. *Research in Consumer Behavior, 13*, 1–18. doi:10.1108/S0885-2111(2011)0000013004

Ketterer, J., & Marsh, G. (2006). Re-conceptualizing intimacy and distance in instructional models. *Online Journal of Distance Learning Administration*. Retrieved from http://www.westga.edu/%7Edistance/ojdla/spring91/ketterer91.pdf

Korstanje, M. (2011). Swine flu in Buenos Aires: Beyond the principle of resilience. *International Journal of Disaster Resilience in the Built Environment, 2*(1), 59–73. doi:10.1108/17595901111108371

Kuflik, T. (2011). A visitor's guide in an active museum: Presentations, communications and reflection. *Journal on Computing and Cultural Heritage, 3*(3). doi:10.1145/1921614.1921618

LaFraniere, S., & Barboza, D. (2011, March 21). China tightens censorship of electronic communications. *The New York Times*. Retrieved November 2, 2011, from http://www.nytimes.com/2011/03/22/world/asia/22china.html?_r=1&ref=internetcensorship

Lankes, D. (2006). *The social internet: A new community role for libraries?* Retrieved March 3, 2007 from http://quartz.syr.edu/rdlankes/blog/?p=156http://quartz.syr.edu/rdlankes/blog/?p=156

Levine, J. (2006). *The shifted librarian*. Retrieved March 26, 2007 from http://www.theshiftedlibrarian.com/archives/2005/11/07/digital_utes.html

Libecap, G. (2011). Introduction - Entrepreneurship and global competitiveness in regional economies: Determinants and policy implications. *Advances in the Study of Entrepreneurship. Innovation & Economic Growth, 22*, ix–xii.

Mansour, E. (2012). The role of social networking sites (SNSs) in the January 25th revolution in Egypt. *Library Review, 61*(2), 128–159. doi:10.1108/00242531211220753

McFadden, A. C. (2008). Podcasting and RSS. In Kelsey, S., & St. Armant, K. (Eds.), *The Handbook on Research on Computer-Mediated Communications*. Hershey, PA: IGI Global.

Millership, P. (2011, October 11). World intrigued by "occupy wall street" movement. *Reuters*. Retrieved November 5, 2011, from http://www. reuters.com/article/2011/10/11/us-usa-wallstreet-world-idUSTRE79A3OB20111011

Mital, M., Israel, D., & Agarwal, S. (2010). Information exchange and information disclosure in social networking web sites: Mediating role of trust. *The Learning Organization*, *17*(6), 479–490. doi:10.1108/09696471011082349

Nagel, D. (2011, February 2). Will smartphones eliminate the digital divide? *The Journal*. Retrieved November 1, 2011, from http://thejournal. com/Articles/2011/02/01/Will-Smart-Phones-Eliminate-the-Digital-Divide.aspx?Page=1

Nelson, B. (2011, April 1). The role of social media in the Middle East uprising. *Ahramonline*. Retrieved from http://english.ahram.org.eg/News-ContentP/4/9021/Opinion/The-Role-of-Social-Media-in-the-Middle-East-Uprisi.aspx

Notten, N., Peter, J., Kraaykamp, G., & Valkenbury, P. M. (2008). Research note: Digital divide across borders – A cross-national study of adolescents' use of digital technologies. *European Sociological Review*, *25*(5), 551–560. doi:10.1093/esr/jcn071

Palfrey, J., & Gasser, U. (2008). *Born digital: Understanding the first generation of digital natives*. New York, NY: Basic Books.

Pink, D. (2011). *Forget shareholders, maximise consumer value instead*. Retrieved November 9, 2011 from http://www.telegraph.co.uk/finance/comment/8583476/Forget-shareholders-maximise-consumer-value-instead.html

Prensky, M. (2001a). Digital natives, digital immigrants. *On the Horizon, 9*(5), 1-6. Retrieved November 1, 2011, from http://www.marcprensky.com/writing/Prensky%20-%20Digital%20Natives,%20Digital%20Immigrants%20-%20Part1.pdf

Prensky, M. (2001b). Digital natives, digital immigrants, part II: Do they really think differently? *On the Horizon, 9*(6), 1-6. Retrieved November 1, 2011, from http://www.marcprensky.com/writing/Prensky%20-%20Digital%20Natives,%20Digital%20Immigrants%20-%20Part2.pdf

Price, B. J. (2008). Computer-mediated collaboration. In Kelsey, S., & St. Armant, K. (Eds.), *The Handbook on Research on Computer-Mediated Communications*. Hershey, PA: IGI Global. doi:10.4018/978-1-59904-863-5.ch037

Rainie, L. (2006). How the internet is changing consumer behavior and expectations. *Pew Internet and American Life Project*. Retrieved from http://www.pewtrusts.org/uploadedFiles/wwwpewtrustsorg/Fact_Sheets/Society_and_the_Internet/PewInternetSOCAP050906.pdf

Rajala, J. (2003). Wireless technology in education. *The Journal*. Retrieved November 10, 2011 from http://thejournal.com/articles/16482

Relly, J. (2011). Corruption, secrecy, and access-to-information legislation in Africa: A cross-national study of political institutions. *Research in Social Problems and Public Policy*, 19.

Schllinger, R. (2011, September 20). Social media and the Arab spring: What have we learned? *The Huffington Post*. Retrieved October 10, 2011 from http://www.huffingtonpost.com/raymond-schillinger/arab-spring-social-media_b_970165.html

Shin, D., Shin, Y., Choo, H., & Beom, K. (2011). Smartphones and smart pedagogical tools: Implications of smartphones as u-learning devices. *Computers in Human Behavior*, *27*(6), 2207–2214. doi:10.1016/j.chb.2011.06.017

Shirky, C. (2011, January/February). The political power of social media. *Foreign Affairs.* Retrieved November 5, 2011, from http://www. foreignaffairs.com/articles/67038/clay-shirky/ the-political-power-of-social-media

Smith, A. (2010). The internet and campaign 2010. *Pew Internet & American Life Project.* Retrieved November 4, 2011, from http://www. pewinternet.org/Reports/2011/The-Internet-and-Campaign-2010/Summary.aspx

Steele, J. (2011). Tunisia's clean elections lead the way. *The Guardian.* Retrieved October 25, 2011 from http://www.guardian.co.uk/commentisfree/2011/oct/25/tunisia-election-middle-east?intcmp=239

Stelter, B. (2011). F.C.C. push to expand net access gains help. *The New York Times.* Retrieved November 9, 2011 from http://www.nytimes. com/2011/11/09/business/media/fcc-and-cable-companies-push-to-close-digital-divide.html

Surin, J. A. (2010). Occupying the internet: Responding to the shifting power balance. *The Round Table, 99*(407), 195–209. doi:10.1080/00358531003656388

Szekely, L., & Nagy, A. (2011). Online youth work and eYouth - A guide to the world of digital natives. *Children and Youth Services Review, 33*(11), 2186–2197. doi:10.1016/j.childyouth.2011.07.002

Tamin, R., Bernard, R., Borokhovski, E., Abrami, P., & Schmid, R. (2011). What forty years of research says about the impact of technology on learning: A second-order meta-analysis and validation study. *Review of Educational Research, 81*, 4-28. Retrieved October 12, 2011 from http://rer. sagepub.com/cgi/content/long/81/1/4

Taylor, K. (2011). Arab spring was really a social media revolution. *TG Daily.* Retrieved October 12, 2011 from http://www.tgdaily.com/software-features/58426-arab-spring-really-was-social-media-revolution

Time Magazine. (2009). *The future of work.* Retrieved November 10, 2011 from http://www. time.com/time/covers/0,16641,20090525,00.html

Tyler, C. (2010). *Australian internet censorship: Necessary evil or nanny state gone mad?* Retrieved November 7, 2011, from http://www. associatedcontent.com/article/2749033/australian_internet_censorship.html?cat=25

Tyler, J., & Pillers, R. (2011). Unsustainability in today's international development. *USA Today Magazine, 139*(I2788), 26-28.

Vajoczki, S., Watt, S., Marquis, N., Liao, R., & Vine, M. (2011). Students approach to learning and their use of lecture capture. *Journal of Educational Multimedia and Hypermedia, 20*(2), 195–214.

Wald, J. (Producer). (2011, November 10). *Piers Morgan Tonight* [Television broadcast]. Los Angeles, CA: Cable News Network. Retrieved from http://piersmorgan.blogs.cnn.com/2011/11/10/ gen-colin-powells-advice-for-america-i-think-our-system-needs-to-take-a-deep-breath/

Wallsten, S. (2009). *Understanding international broadband comparisons.* Washington, DC: Technology Policy Institute.

Wang, H., & Hong, Y. (2009). China: Technology development and management in the context of economic reform and opening. *Journal of Technology Management in China, 4*(1), 4–25. doi:10.1108/17468770910942816

Warschauer, M., & Matuchniak, T. (2010). New technology and digital worlds: Analyzing evidence of equity in access, use, and outcomes. *Review of Research in Education, 34*(1), 179–225. doi:10.3102/0091732X09349791

Waters, J. K. (2009). The kids are all right. *The Journal, 36*(3), 38–42.

Whittaker, Z. (2011). London's met police uses 'blanket tracking system' to intercept, remotely shut down mobile phones. *ZDNet.com*. Retrieved November 2, 2011, from http://www.zdnet.com/blog/london/londons-met-police-uses-8216blanket-tracking-system-to-intercept-remotely-shutdown-mobile-phones/422?tag=search-results-rivers;item1

Yang, J., Chen, C., & Jeng, M. (2010). Integrating video-capture virtual reality technology into a physically interactive learning environment for English learning. *Computers & Education, 55*(3), 1346–1356. doi:10.1016/j.compedu.2010.06.005

Young, P. A. (2008). Integrating culture in the design of ICTs. *British Journal of Educational Technology, 39*(1), 6–17.

Yunus Center. (2012). *The Muhammad Yunus center*. Retrieved from http://www.muhammadyunus.org

Chapter 6
Diversity Technology, Cultural DNA, and Personality:
The Impact on Educational, Medical, Business, and Military Organizations

Dorothy Guy Bonvillain
Love-Based Leadership Consultants, USA

David R. Faulkner
Defense Equal Opportunity Management Institute, USA

William Gary McGuire
Defense Equal Opportunity Management Institute, USA

ABSTRACT

For the last sixty years, personality and personality traits (or characteristics) have been studied, researched, and applied to managing individuals and organizations. Some practitioners say that personality research predates the Roman Empire and the Great Greek Philosophers. The use of personality identification as a form of diversity leadership and possible technology is becoming more popular in helping people and organizations assign tasks within the organization as well as to enhance the performance in the organization. The Myers Briggs Type Instrument (MBTI) is one personality tool that strategically links diversity to cultural DNA and enhances the performance of educational, medical, business, and military organizations worldwide. There are other personality instruments that can provide similar results, but the authors have chosen the MBTI to best depict how personality can easily be applied to diverse systems to measure individual and organizational change. The impact of these and other diversity characteristics, competencies, and technologies must be filtered through formal instructional systems, design processes, and evaluation procedures to help leadership identify strengths and weaknesses within the organization regardless of the type of organization. There will be a need for varied evaluation and measures to help sustain effectiveness and outcomes. The authors present a brief framework for these measures.

DOI: 10.4018/978-1-4666-2668-3.ch006

INTRODUCTION

Diversity is complex and is still questioned as a way to enhance individual and organizational performance as well as effectiveness today as it was in the early beginnings of the 1970s. The trains carrying the flags for diversity seem to be going full speed toward making it mandatory for employers regardless of educational institute, business, medical organization, or military. Skeptics call diversity the 'new age Civil Rights Act.' There are no laws dictating the need to make diversity a hiring incentive or benefit, but, in 2011, the President of the United States, Barack Obama, signed an Executive Order requiring the federal government to take actions establishing diversity programs for civilian and military employees. The Office of Personnel Management (OPM) has the lead on accomplishing this task by the end of 2011.

The topic of diversity in any form tends to encourage discussions across the halls of many organizations. Some members will say that diversity is the best way to show employees that organizational leadership is willing to include everyone as part of the 'organizational team' regardless of what differences they bring to the table. Other members will report to human resources that diversity is just another way to justify Affirmative Action or even 'legally discriminate' against people that are different. While we must consider the meaning of diversity, we might also consider the various forms of diversity we are seeing in the early beginnings of the 21ˢᵗ Century. During the last five years, the United States military developed diversity programs that would demonstrate to the community the need for such programs. While having several hundred thousand military and civilian members deployed to at least two war theaters (theater in this case is considered to be the area in which the war is taking place), there was a significant need for diversity to take on the form of more meaning than 'just the typical human demographics.'

DIVERSITY TECHNOLOGY

A Way to Save Human Lives

The need for advanced technology in *Educational, Medical, Business, and Military Organizations* crosses many dimensions in our daily lives. Diversity technology continues to be the way ahead in this growing age of cyberspace and instant need for the newest gadgets. Such technology as virtual reality in computer development brings us one-step closer to the original Star Trek television show where the term 'Beam me up Scotty' takes on a new meaning. Some examples include:

- The development of prostheses in the medical field is opening doors for 'double amputees' and other wounded warriors to bring members back to the work force when they would likely not be motivated to otherwise work or even live
- Robotics in the aerospace field brings us the 'drone' or the UAV (Unmanned Aircraft Vehicle) that can be flown remotely from a workstation in the United States using 'gaming computers' that are directly linked to commercial satellites built to track people, places, and events all over the world.
- The ability to drop a bomb into a cave in the mountains of Afghanistan from an air-conditioned trailer on a military base in the United States without risking life is a sign of the times for the future for our military. The more we develop this type of technology, the less we face the harm to or loss of human life during any conflict or disaster.
- Local police and firefighter forces are using more monitoring of traffic lights, banking facilities, grocery stores and other facilities that would have required humans to facilitate or intervene when there are such things as an accident, robbery, or traffic jam.

- NASA ended the Space Shuttle Program after more than 25 years of operations and now they are looking forward to the development of the 'next generation' of spacecraft that could have humans on Mars by 2025.
- The cellular phone has taken on a new meaning as we move from 2011 to 2012. The ability to 'bank online' or make payments on credit cards or even 'shop online' is being done from most 'cell phones' with the stroke of a key.
- The uses of texting (swyping – a new term for Android Phone texting) and skyping have taken over the old letter writing or even email system.
- There is no reason to have a camera when the cell phone is a camera and video recorder.

Everything seems to be instantly achievable with technology. What once took a computer the size of a small home to launch spacecraft into orbit will now require one only the size of a small notebook to launch into deep space, return it to Earth, and land it without a human touching any of the instruments in the cockpit.

Robotics take on different meanings when used in the medical career as doctors use microsurgery that is so minimally invasive that a six- to ten-inch incision normally made a few years ago is less than a quarter of an inch today.

CULTURAL DNA

Variety, Diversity, and Differences

The need to have our military members culturally aware is not an easy task, as they are deployed to areas in the world that are different than back home. There is very little education and training for our military or civilians in the diversity of cultures they may encounter as they occupy areas

completely different than ever imagined. Several years ago, Dorothy Bonvillain, and Gary McGuire (2009) presented a framework for what they called 'Cultural DNA' (a metaphoric description of various learned and instinctive components of our own US culture) and how our lack of cultural awareness might be driven by our lack of knowledge concerning the diversity of racial, social, ethnic groups that exist in the United States. Our Cultural DNA, which Bonvillain and McGuire (2009) say is part of our cultural makeup, could be driven by personality. After delivering their research paper at the American University in Washington DC, they discovered that personality on a global scale is a significant contributor to diversity and the differences of people. The next few pages provide the discussion Bonvillain and McGuire (2009) had with a group of diversity and cultural practitioners attending the conference at the American University. The artwork for the cover page of their work (Figure 1) was designed by Mr. Peter Hemmer from the Defense Equal Opportunity Management Institute (DEOMI). The DNA Strands are Mr. Hemmer's metaphoric depiction of cultural DNA as used by Drs. Bonvillain and McGuire. The discussion centers on the use of various personality instruments to show how groups of people might be diverse in more than the typical 'protected characteristics' of the US Civil Rights Act of 1964 (As Amended). The

Figure 1. Cultural DNA

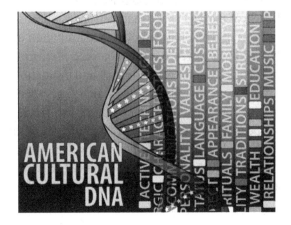

typical demographic approach does not include personality as a form of diversity. The reader of this chapter might better appreciate the overall setup as well as the detail the authors have taken to explain their work.

SIMPLE AND PROFOUND

When Dr. Bonvillain and Dr. McGuire wrote the article *Cultural DNA,* they thought they had well-defined American Cultural DNA. However, when they presented their work at American University, a colleague at the University of Maryland suggested the presentation had omitted something they all agreed should be included in any further discussion and development on cultural DNA and related diversity issues--the inclusion of personality types. The primary personality instrument and method discussed is the Myers Briggs Type Indicator (MBTI) and the Personality Shapes Model (PSM).

Most of us are readily familiar with the useful application of MBTI in managing today's diverse work environments, although some will argue that it is no longer the 'tool of choice' for the workplace. The United States Military uses the MBTI in most of the Armed Services, although the Air Force is using an instrument identified as 'The Four Lenses' to help human relations practitioners to better appreciate differences. The authors suggest that the Consulting Psychology Press (CPP) is as active today as it ever was with the use of the MBTI and that they have collected millions of data on its validity. One limitation of the MBTI, however, is that it requires administrator certification for proper testing and evaluation in the use of this instrument, which leads us to propose a more simplified approach that we call 'shapes.' This method was actually drawn on a lunch napkin for Dr. Bonvillain by Dr. Maria Church, who had previously acquired it while attending a teambuilding workshop wherein this

simple conceptual model was presented. The basic simplicity of this model allows anyone to utilize this tool to better understand diversity and build more effective teams.

This method attaches knowledge and meaning to four basic geometric shapes and in doing so, offers a simple but profound methodology for developing a better understanding of how to leverage diversity in the workplace. It resembles the MBTI and the Four Lenses but it is far less complicated—actually brilliant in its simplicity! Before we discuss the various shapes, it is only fair to state that we did not create this theory and unfortunately, we have not been able to locate the original source (even though several people have staked claim to it) so we cannot credit the theorist.

WHAT SHAPE BEST DESCRIBES YOUR PERSONALITY?

The following four logo shapes represent different types of people from a personality perspective. Keep in mind, that because we are multi-dimensional, we do not completely align with just one shape; however, we have a strong tendency (preference) to relate more readily to one shape over the others.

The triangle represents vision and goal-oriented achievement. Typically, people that identify with this personality type are perceived as driven, type-A personalities. Goal setting, and even more importantly, goal achieving is what drives these types of people. Make sure you get out of their way when they are focused, as they could run you over! Triangles are always looking to the stars, reaching for the moon, and trying to shoot right past all of it, aiming for the next universe. They are often like the Energizer bunny—they just keep on going.

The circle represents the heart of the organization. Typically, the circles are those in the organization who just want peace and harmony. They want everyone to get along and cannot understand why they do not! Care and compassion are daily behaviors demonstrated by these personality types. The circles are typically the ones that plan the office parties, company picnics, and always remember each employee's birthday.

The square represents knowledge and the mind. These are people who are very analytical. These people typically thrive in well-organized environments and feel very comfortable with structure, well-defined policies and procedures. The squares are in-the-box thinkers and do not like to bend the rules or waste their time with "creativity." The people who identify with this shape are often the accountants, engineers, and analytical employees. I have found that if I ask a square which form to fill out for travel, they will not only tell me what form to fill out, but how to fill it out, and to whom it is distributed!

Scratching your head on the squiggle line? That is because the squiggle line represents the spirit—creative energy. People in the organization who identify with the squiggle line are the creative force, not to be contained by any box, but always outside of it. They are often the ones people describe as *dancing to the beat of their own drum*. They are freethinkers and far outside of the box.

The authors have conducted data collection to confirm that the model has been effectively used as one pragmatic way to depict and further understand diversity in people throughout organizations.

TEAM BUILDING: HOW PERSONALITY SHAPES MIGHT DRIVE ORGANIZATIONS

The likelihood of having an organization with limited diversity of personality shapes is almost impossible today, but let us imagine for a moment that we did. This is what we might find: If we had an organization filled with triangles, it would be a very dynamic one—full of goal-oriented, motivated people reaching for the stars, but probably stepping on each other and elbowing their team members to get out of the way. Resources would be scattered and budgets overrun; it would be chaos. We might classify such organizations as the Central Intelligence Agency (CIA), Dot. coms, Marketing and Sales, and even the National Aeronautics and Space Agency (NASA) are good examples of Triangle organizations.

If we had an organization filled with squares, we would always be within budget, follow the rules, and do everything by the book; however, we would probably lose market-share because we were not thinking outside of the box, not innovating, and not growing. Some of the organizations we might attach to the Square personality are; The National Security Agency (NSA), The State Department, Financial Institutions (whether National or local). Square Types thrive in this environment, as there is no room for "outside the box" thinking.

If we had an organization that was full of circles, it sure would be a fun place to work; unfortunately, we probably would not get much work done! Some might think 'fun is work' or 'work is fun' when they are employed at theme parks such as The Six Flags Parks or Disney. The cast are dressed in attire that puts each person in a character role during their scheduled work time. The working staff, such as; maintenance crews, food staff, technicians, etc. are assigned to certain tasks within the park boundaries and their jobs (though not labeled as fun) are more focused on keeping the park running smoothly and accommodating the guests. There are some people that believe such jobs as social workers and even the Peace Corps are fun places to work. We can see such places filled with 'Circles.'

In addition, if we had an organization full of squiggle lines, it would feel amazing, full of energy and creativity; however, we would venture to guess that the organization would be over budget in six-months and projects may not be fully completed! Such organizations as those involved in art, music, inventions, and even rocket science could be the types of organizations filled with 'squiggle lines' in positions of responsibility. Their energy levels as well as creativity could have them overcompensating during planning and thus cause budget shortfalls and chaos with projects not being completed.

The authors are not saying 'there is or is not a perfect shape personality for any individual or organization. As described in the rudimentary examples mentioned above, one particular personality shape could be a negative or positive impact on the effectiveness of any organization.

The importance of having a balance of diversity in organizations cannot be over-emphasized. As we desire to have diversity of thought, primary and secondary dimensions (Loden, 1998) and diversity of personality in our organizations, we must be aware of the strengths each area brings to the performance and willingness to support the goals, vision, and mission of the organization. At the same time, we must also recognize that Diversity and Inclusion should not be considered another program for 'forcing' organizations to apply a more modern method of affirmative action or characteristic protection under the Civil Rights Act of 1964 (As Amended). In order to build successful teams, we must seek balance. Is that not a key success element for life? We *need* all shapes represented so that the squares can keep the triangles and squiggles grounded. We need circles to soften the abruptness that squares can sometimes bring to the workplace. We also need the vision and focus of triangles and the creativity of the developers (the squiggles). We

should strive to have all four personality shapes represented in order to provide diverse thinking and different frames of reference so the team does not succumb to Janis' '*groupthink.*' In essence, we need all of these to achieve balance, innovation, and maximum productivity.

So what if your team does not have one of the shapes represented? As a leader, it is up to you to sometimes take on that role, providing balance to the team. Remember, we are multi-dimensional and can relate to several of these shapes, so it is not too difficult to temporarily put on the hat of a different shape to balance the team. Being that heredity has provided us the ability to adapt to changing situations; we can choose to be plugged in to a given combination of team members to either function as a missing member or to be a catalyst to others. Using the MBTI or Personality Shapes, just as there are animals (chameleons) who can change to match a background, there are team members not strongly Extroverts (Triangles) or Introverts (other shapes) who can "morph" to take leadership roles in the absence of strong Extroverts. The strong introverts may want to stay in the background to steadily do the work, but they need "catalysts" in order to lead them into a group solution. There are also teams that have been assembled where inexperienced members may have latent leadership abilities and who lack the confidence to effectively "take the reins" as the saying goes. At any rate, someone may act as a catalyst, someone temporarily empowered or anointed to energize the group until a leader either joins the group or arises from within it.

For example, let us look at how Netflix and Blockbuster (BB) conducted business throughout the past decade (plus). Blockbuster had cornered the market share for in-home videos until Netflix came up with better way of doing business that leveraged technology and client convenience, which, over time, drastically reduced BB market share. The Netflix team most likely consists of a majority of squiggles and triangles. The people that planned or came up with the idea to use the 'in-store video rental machines' never supported the project with sufficient budget to sustain the program and over a period of years, other rental companies copied their process, but maintained the budget to support and sustain the process. Thanks to some dynamic 'triangles' at Blockbuster, the organizational goals shifted to accommodate customers through an open rental program that eventually won customers back to BB. Netflix customers started 'coming back' to the BB stores to try their new inventions for rentals and sales. Today, it is difficult to find a city or town without both Netflix and Blockbuster in competition for the quickest and most recent movies to rent. The battle continues as two companies can't see that personality shapes (PSM) or MBTI could be the solution for all of the chaos.

In many ways, the DNA structure mirrors a composite team in that a team will generally have components and skills distributed throughout to accomplish particular tasks. The Cultural (or Cross Cultural) DNA components of language (regional dialect or other), traditions, family customs, values, etc. must be considered when putting the team together to accomplish tasks. Imagine sending a team of Circles into an area having only Triangles with the task of assimilating into the culture. That would be like sending a team of extroverts into an area having only introverts. It would be easy to sort or pick out the differences whether those differences are Personality Shapes or Myers Briggs Type.

Interestingly, when we consider the theoretical basis of the shapes (above) and view it from a scientific lens, we can compare it to the DNA Double Helix and the constituents of DNA. There are four amino acids (Adenine, Cytosine, Guanine, and Thymine). Amino acids consist of various structures of four elements (Hydrogen, Carbon, Oxygen, and Nitrogen). The constituents all work together in synergy. There are chemical bonds throughout the structure—each team needs bonds and shared characteristics (electrons). Therefore, there are chemical and physical bonds (which can

amplify an analogy exploding into a whole new trail). The Double Helix goes through replication, which is a splitting of the DNA into two helices (like a zipper) and recombining into two new DNA molecules. The purpose or goal is always the same (master design) and the identity does not drastically change, yet the recombination results in a new (unique) molecule. Our point here is that there are an infinite number of possibilities, but the outcome is unique and may not be exactly duplicated. Herein, we see the dynamic of the team and of its members: the synergy of the diversity of components—or team members—yields a definitive powerful product. Human Terrain Teams have different Cultural DNA that can help them accomplish various components of a given mission or task. While one (or more) component might have the language skills to negotiate with elders or even youngsters in a particular location, other team members might have the Cultural DNA component of Personality Type that helps the team to understand people who differ from the team. This whole process might sound complex, but the reality of this plays out every day in places where organizations such as the US Military are trained to 'win the hearts and minds' of the very people whom they were previously fighting to 'win the war' on terrorism.

Physically, we are not identical to anyone else. This uniqueness is transmitted genetically through our DNA. Notice the structure in the drawing, how it is diverse yet organized. Just as nearly every cell in your body is comprised of basic components, so is your culture. And just as you need a microscope as a tool to look into cellular make-up, you need some conceptual way to assess your own cultural DNA—and others.

There are two types of cultural DNA: (1) Learned and (2) Acquired. The Instinctive type relates to your race, gender, and other physiological factors. Sometimes you act the way you do on the basis of hormonal or chemical influence. Elevated chemical levels in your body may affect your outlook on things and even change your values.

The second type, Learned, is just that—learned (or acquired) from your environment (family, surroundings, peers, television, etc.). The influence of all parts of your life from your birth to present have basically made you what you are. Interestingly, we all would like for everyone to be like us in many ways, or perhaps, on the other hand, we judge others based on our cultural value(s). Many times the things we judge as not valuable in others are characteristics we possess. So the question arises: Do you know yourself? Is your "self" readily identifiable?

In this information age of rapidly increasing knowledge, there is an inclination or fear that technology can successfully replace human social interaction, and thus eliminate the need for teachers. Although it has been shown that the Constructivist Learning Environments (CLEs) are advancing knowledge to a great degree, most researchers (Rieber, 1996) agree that media will not replace human interaction. Kozma (1994) recognized technology as a facilitation tool, and, though media has a great hand in teaching numerous concepts and ideas, it falls short of the human being. The old saying "You can't fool Mother Nature" is not to be taken lightly; there are social, familial, and spiritual aspects that cannot be artificially communicated, masked—and duplicated in form—but not totally reproduced, just like the strands of DNA. Therefore, the old proverb, "Iron sharpens iron, so does a man the countenance of his friend" bears out in truth—the true aspect of the human was not designed to be replaced by bionics. Cultural DNA possesses all the genetic information for all human traits...

One important aspect of Cultural DNA that may be impacted by technology is its societal imaging. Television programs, for example, are alleged to have negative effects on people to the point that many "act out" violent scenarios they view. Tons of studies by Jennings Bryant and Dolph Zillman at the University of Alabama (Roll Tide, Gary) asked this question, but there was no significant difference between experimental and control groups. Programs like 'Sesame Street,' probably THE most-studied program in the history of media, did have sociological effects on the many children and adults who watched it. So one could say "the jury is divided" on media effects, but effects are considered significant.

David shared a "funny, media influence" story: While single and living in Mobile, Alabama, David attended a large church that had a very active prayer room. The room was located in the rear of what became the Chapel, and the coordinator had placed tables, chairs, a sofa, a rolodex, a teletype machine, and two telephones in it so to equip it for individuals or small groups. My responsibility was to cover it on Monday nights from 7:00 to 8:00. As time passed, a young lady named Lee Ann would call and ask for prayer for individuals she had seen during the day. She was a shut-in and we could not figure why she called in these same people each week until one of my fellow prayer warriors recognized the names were from soap operas she had been watching during the day. This was stopped, but it had gone on for months (so much so that we had the names memorized and listed on the rolodex).

Technology also has social effects in computer gaming. It is becoming evident that interactive Internet computer games are bringing a type of diversity that could be quasi- human. I, for one, like to know with whom I am interacting, but that is not the case with my son who interacts with the same group of players each week. Through virtual interaction, he is building a rapport with strangers. His rapport with strangers (to us) seems perfectly normal and acceptable for him, but very questionable to parents as we might suspect 'computer gaming is at least suspect, especially when most gaming generally happens between the hours of ten at night until the wee hours of the next morning.' It seems that the younger the generation, the more involved or 'interconnected' they are with technology, even at home. The Cultural DNA make-up for this generation must and will always include the most current forms of technology as common day-to-day items.

SUMMARY

The complete impact of Diversity Technology, Cultural DNA, and Personality on Educational, Medical, Business, and Military Organizations is yet to be determined and will more than likely be a continuing item of interest as we move into the 21st Century. As our global networks for sharing information expand to cultures different from the United States, so shall our diversity knowledge expand? The authors have provided various impacts throughout the chapter to show the need for individual and organization diversity awareness. When we think of the Diversity Technologies; The advancements in Education through electronic medium, Medical equipment and surgical procedures, Business marketing and material production, and our Military war-fighting, we should consider the improvements we are making with learning and life saving. We have come a long way since the days of 'horse drawn carriages' to rocketry that takes people to the Moon. Predictions from this point can easily be as real as the vision for the 1960s television show 'Star Trek.'

The authors discuss the propensity of our different Cultural DNA and how we all have these differences yet we are all so similar. When we look at our differences as strengths versus negative weaknesses, we can predict behaviors in groups of people in their culture. Our Hyphenated American cultures should not be exempt from such visions.

In the last part of the chapter, the authors presented a different approach for determining Personality Type while working in the confines of any organizational culture. The use of personality shapes as compared the Myers Briggs Type Indicator (MBTI) provides the reader another option for consideration in determining workers and managers they may desire to employ in an organization. Personality Type can influence the overall organizational culture if not clearly understood. Personality Type provides another dimension of diversity that managers and leaders can use to maintain overall efficiency.

The way ahead for Diversity Initiatives is in our hands today. What Technology, Cultural DNA, and Personality Type we decide to use as potential mechanisms will make individuals and organizations open to the changes for our future. In the diversity community, there is a saying; 'I don't want to be seen as different from you. I want to be seen as different like you.'

REFERENCES

Bonvillain, D. G., & McGuire, W. G. (2009). *Cultural DNA*. Washington, DC: American University.

Church, Maria. J. (2011).*Three strategies for team success*. Retrieved from http://www.love-basedleadership.com

Kozma, R. B. (1994). A reply: Media and methods. *Educational Technology Research and Development, 42*(3), 11–14. doi:10.1007/BF02298091

McDonald, D., & Parks, K. (2011). *Managing diversity in the military: The value of inclusion in a culture of uniformity*. New York, NY: Routledge.

Payne, C. M., Payne, J. S., & Craig, J. B. (2011). *ISLET: A comparative study of face-to-face and online Iraqi culture training and the development of cross-cultural competence, studies 4 & 5*. Paper presented at the Academic Consortium for Global Education. New York, NY.

Rieber, L. P. (1996). Seriously considering play: Designing interactive learning environments based on the blending of microworlds, simulations, and games. *Educational Technology Research and Development, 44*(2), 43–58. doi:10.1007/BF02300540

KEY TERMS AND DEFINITIONS

Cultural DNA: Another way to view culture—metaphorically—comparing American Culture to DNA. Every individual has his or her own unique DNA, the basic building block for cellular development in all forms of life. In other words, DNA represents the nucleus of identity. Our approach is to show that in today's global system, knowledge and understanding of 'American DNA' is as critical to understanding, analyzing, interpreting, and predicting behaviors of people from different cultures as genetic DNA is to cellular development (as defined by Bonvillain & McGuire, 2009).

Diversity Dimensions: Depending on the author, the two or four dimension categories of diversity describe by various authors. The Marylyn Loden Diversity Wheel shows two dimensions that include Primary and Secondary dimensions, while other authors include personality and organizational dimensions as two additional dimensions.

Diversity Technology: The use of electronic medium, surgical equipment, rocket science, and other technologies that improve the efficiency and effectiveness of a given process. Such examples as; telephones, motor craft, aircraft, missilery, are but a few we are seeing as we move into the 21st Century.

DNA Double Helix: Strands that twist together to form a helix. Each strand consists of alternating phosphate (PO4) and pentose sugar (2-deoxyribose), and attached on the sugar is a nitrogenous base, which can be adenine, thymine, guanine, or cytosine. In DNA, these bases pair; adenine pairs with thymine and guanine with cytosine. Hence, DNA is a ladder-like helical structure (Biology Online, 2011).

Extroverts/Introverts: Based upon personal preference, do you prefer to focus on the outer world or on your own inner world? This is called Extraversion (E) or Introversion (I).

Human Terrain Teams: Established by the U.S. Military during the military wars in Iraq and Afghanistan (2001 through 2011 and ongoing) to assist battlefield commanders in understanding the people and the culture of the occupied area. These teams consist of; social scientists, anthropologists, linguist, medical staff, and others who can help 'win the hearts and minds' of the people to resolve conflicts in and around the battle area that are not tactical.

MBTI: The purpose of the Myers-Briggs Type Indicator (MBTI) personality inventory is to make the theory of psychological types described by C. G. Jung understandable and useful in people's lives. The essence of the theory is that much seemingly random variation in behavior is actually quite orderly and consistent, being due to basic differences in the ways individuals prefer to use their perception and judgment and other traits identified by the NBTI.

Personality Shapes: This method for managing diversity attaches knowledge and meaning to four basic geometric shapes and in doing so, offers a simple but profound methodology for developing a better understanding of how to leverage diversity in the workplace. It resembles the MBTI and the Four Lenses but it is far less complicated.

Personality Types: Are based on the well-known research of Carl Jung, Katharine C. Briggs, and Isabel Briggs Myers. Carl Jung first developed the theory that individuals each had a psychological type. He believed that there were two basic kinds of "functions" which humans used in their lives: how we take in information (how we "perceive" things) and how we make decisions. He believed that within these two categories, there were two opposite ways of functioning. We can perceive information via 1) our senses, or 2) our intuition. We can make decisions based on 1) objective logic, or 2) subjective feelings. Jung believed that we all use these four functions in our lives, but that each individual uses the different functions with a varying amount of success and frequency. He believed that we could identify an order of preference for these functions within individuals. The function which someone uses most frequently is their "dominant" function. The dominant function is supported by an auxiliary (2nd) function, tertiary (3rd) function, and inferior (4th) function. He asserted that individuals either "extraverted" or "introverted" their dominant function. He felt that the dominant function was so important, that it overshadowed all of the other functions in terms of defining personality type.

Chapter 7

The Role of Emerging Technologies in Developing and Sustaining Diverse Suppliers in Competitive Markets

Alvin J. Williams
University of South Alabama, USA

ABSTRACT

As organizations seek to maintain competitiveness in an ever-challenging global economic environment, considerable attention has been focused on rationalizing and realigning supply bases to match market realities. Firms are reducing and restructuring the number and types of suppliers from which they buy goods and services worldwide. This restructuring has a direct impact on minority suppliers. This chapter focuses on how minority suppliers can use technology, with particular focus on electronic procurement systems and related methods, to strengthen performance and attractiveness to potential business-to-business customers. Through the use of e-procurement, electronic auctions, and multiple customer relationship management processes, minority firms can strengthen relationships that lead to long-term success.

INTRODUCTION AND BACKGROUND

The concept of supplier diversity has evolved into an important component of strategic supply chain management, as well as being a significant metric for overall business performance. In their work on the purchasing function's contribution to socially responsible management of the supply chain, Carter and Jennings (2000, p. 27) included diversity as a key component of the social responsibility domain. Thus, they viewed supplier diversity as a critical piece of the organizational landscape as firms work to better understand and contribute to the broader environment in which they function. In particular, this characterizes the sourcing function, where organizations identify firms from which to procure a wide range of inputs necessary for an ongoing business concern.

DOI: 10.4018/978-1-4666-2668-3.ch007

Purchasing social responsibility (PSR) is an outgrowth of, and thus a subset of, the concept of Corporate Social Responsibility (CSR). As organizations interface with their respective environments, it is important for them to craft the appropriate kinds of relationships across a range of publics and stakeholders. Under the CSR umbrella, organizations may address a plethora of concerns, ranging from environmental policies, ethics, safety, and purchases from minority-owned enterprises. While most firms see these behaviors as good ones in which to engage, these activities are certainly not singularly altruistic. There are both calculable and non-calculable competitive benefits that accrue from cumulative CSR behaviors.

The key aim of the current chapter is to focus on PSR as a component of CSR and to examine how supplier diversity as a resource can be shaped through technology to become an even more meaningful component of organizational strategy. The guiding question becomes 'how can astute use of technology reinforce, complement, and expand the reach of supplier diversity as a tool to enhance organizational performance and contributions to the broader society?' To that end, this chapter focuses on the role of supplier diversity in corporate strategy, the business case for supplier diversity, conceptual views of diversity as a competitive resource, the role of technology in supply chain management, and the implications of technology for increased supplier diversity initiatives in global markets.

Supplier diversity has transitioned from a 'feel good' activity on the part of business organizations into one that makes 'good business sense,' contributing to strategic objectives and long-term profitability. It is viewed as a means to creating value for the organization. As options for value creation proliferate, there are many opportunities for organizations to simultaneously increase competitiveness and support minority business development. One key component of value creation is leveraging the latent potential of diverse customers, suppliers, and employees. Thus, it is important to focus on the business-to-business context, in which diverse enterprises use the full range of competitive tools to grow market share and to enhance stakeholder satisfaction.

The chapter addresses the role, purpose, and importance of supplier diversity in contributing to sustained success in competitive marketplaces, and the pivotal, facilitating role offered by technology. As supplier diversity increases in importance, how can technology serve as an enabling factor, capable of delivering higher quality and quantity of exchanges of goods and services? This question becomes even more critical as organizations in general undergo considerable supply base consolidation. Adobor and McMullen (2007) suggests that even in an era of supplier consolidation, supplier diversity has considerable potential as a tool of competitive advantage, if integrated properly into the fabric of corporate strategy. Since much of supply base reduction impacts smaller organizations, of which minority firms are represented in large numbers, gaining and maintaining in-supplier status becomes even more challenging. Thus, technology offers a facilitating path to competitiveness for minority suppliers during periods of retrenchment and belt-tightening.

Building conceptually on the resource-based view of the firm, the chapter addresses supplier diversity as a dynamic resource capable of contributing, in both tangible and intangible ways, to the capacity of organizations to enhance customer profitability and well-being. A discussion of the extent of minority business participation in the array of technology-driven processes and methodologies, offers insight into the growth potential of diverse organizations.

The link between supplier diversity and technology is laden with unrealized potential. As minority suppliers compete more adroitly in global marketplaces, there must be a concerted effort to use all aspects of technology more innovatively. From a technology perspective, the chapter focuses on e-procurement, reverse electronic auctions, and to a lesser extent, social networking. Increasingly, organizations are conducting purchasing and related functions through a series of processes labeled electronic purchasing. Greater attention to the full use of e-procurement can strengthen the position of minority firms. Concomitantly, online reverse auctions offer a number of possibilities for business. In reverse auctions, suppliers bid on buyer specifications with the intent of decreasing the price and other terms. This is quite different from traditional auctions, especially in the business-to-consumer context, where multiple prospective buyers bid and sellers sell to the highest bidder. Many organizations are using online reverse auctions to reduce the costs of doing business and to enhance the overall efficiency and effectiveness of the buyer-seller interaction. Thus, minority suppliers are encouraged to examine the long-term possibilities of including online reverse auctions as integral elements of their strategic marketing efforts.

In summary, the chapter addresses the importance of diverse suppliers, at both the macro and micro levels, and the corresponding impact of technology on the growth and development of these institutions. From a content perspective, the chapter links, both conceptually and managerially, a range of technology-related tools to the strategic and operational processes of minority firms in business-to-business marketing. Minority firms seeking to grow market share, sales, and profitability will benefit from considering some of the suggestions as they extend the reach of technology on the path to long-term success.

CONCEPTUAL PERSPECTIVES ON SUPPLIER DIVERSITY

The idea that all resources, tangible and intangible, including corporate reputation, should be managed adroitly to achieve organizational objectives is a key tenet of management. If diversity is viewed as a resource to be managed properly, it is an asset with considerable potential.

This perspective is consistent with Barney's seminal work on the Resource-Based View (RBV) of the firm (Barney, 1991, 2001). His viewpoint of an integrative approach to RBV as a path to sustained competitive advantage, offered a more strategic angle from which to analyze organizations. Barney (1991) considered an expansive definition of firm resources to include all assets, capabilities, processes, and knowledge at the disposal of the organization to promote efficiency and effectiveness in meeting the uncertain demands of market opportunities and threats. While economists and others viewed resource management as critical to success, Barney offered a more macro perspective and a wider range of resources to consider when determining organizational outcomes. At the same time that RBV focuses on internal resource management, it does so within the context of numerous external settings and scenarios, both large and small. More specifically, the mix of internal resources is mitigated and shaped by the confluence of myriad external variables – competitive, economic, political, legal, social, cultural, and technological.

This interplay between the internal forces/resources and the external environment gives rise to the marriage between Corporate Social Responsibility (CSR) and the Resource-Based View (RBV) of the firm. Branco and Rodriques (2006, p. 643) use RBV to explain why firms engage in CSR. Firms want to be viewed as responsible corporate citizens. Much of this is embodied in the concept of corporate reputation—an almost immeasurably valuable resource. Key to understanding the construct of reputation is to recognize its impact on resource acquisition, resource strategy, and resource deployment. Corporate reputation as an intangible resource influences suppliers, customers, employees, competitors, and a host of facilitating agents, including financial institutions, regulatory agencies, and global partners. Thus, it is reasonable to expect firms to carefully consider each of the constituent variables of corporate reputation, including interfaces with diverse populations, as both suppliers and customers.

Specifically, Branco and Rodriques (2006, p. 243) asked the following question of organizations regarding CSR:

Should they undertake actions designed to avoid or repair the negative impact of their operations on society or even to have a beneficial impact by promoting socially desirable ends?

This question embodies the extent to which many see the challenges and opportunities associated with CSR. Quite often firms elect to focus on the 'beneficial impact of promoting socially desirable ends.' While the promotion of socially desirable ends is a motivation for supplier diversity efforts, frequently and increasingly, firms are more driven by the business case for diversity. Worthington (2009) makes a strong business case for diversity and focuses on how socially responsible purchasing pays off for organizations.

More specifically Worthington (2009) cites several potential areas of improved performance resulting from a more diverse supply base. First, there are revenue-generating activities, which include greater knowledge of and access to local ethnic markets, which in turn may impact local and regional economic development. Concomitantly, a positive corporate reputation may ensue resulting in other tangible and intangible benefits.

Second, cost-control and/or cost-reduction benefits accrue from supplier diversity, including reduced costs of local/regional sourcing, which could lead to lower inventory costs. Associatively, lower transportation and logistics costs could be linked to local sourcing. Greater flexibility in procurement processes may also be a benefit of local diversity sourcing. A third area Worthington (2009) identifies as a potential advantage for diverse sourcing is that of risk mitigation. This construct embodies several areas, including diminished dependence on the current supply base, development of alternative supply bases during periods of crisis, and overall enhanced reputations across external stakeholder groups. Having

a relationship with minority suppliers strengthens and broadens the supply network and allows for opportunities to increase supply agility, especially during periods of supply uncertainty.

Collectively, Worthington (2009) makes an exceptionally potent business case for diversity within the supply chain. While some of the benefits are more tangible than others, on balance the positive contributions offer far more weight than the negatives. Ultimately, the success of all diversity initiatives is unalterably linked to the strength of the business case associated with the effort.

In a case-based, cross-national study of the drivers of socially responsible purchasing, Worthington, Ram, Boyal, and Shah (2008) identify government and policy developments, economic factors, stakeholder concerns, and ethical influences as key forces shaping the responses of organizations regarding supplier diversity initiatives. They also indicate the rise of the minority population rate and the attendant implications for supplying and consuming markets as an impetus to more adroitly address supplier diversity concerns.

To further strengthen the business case for supplier diversity, Heffes (2006) finds that doing business with minority-owned firms does not 'cost' organizational buyers any more than other suppliers. In some cases, firms are using minority suppliers creatively to generate new sources of revenue. Heffes further notes that typical firms allocate about 8 percent of corporate spending to minority firms, which constitutes approximately 10 percent of the overall supply base.

Additionally, Greenhalgh's (2008, p. 8) work suggests that increasing minority business enterprise competitiveness through strategic alliances is a viable option to be pursued by firms. Strengthening linkages through alliances heightens the probability of synergy and longer-term relationships. In particular, Greenhalgh (2008) finds that strategic relationships with minority firms are shaped by what each party has to offer, the value creation potential of the minority firm, and the needs of targeted customers.

EXTENT AND REACH OF MINORITY FIRM OWNERSHIP

To appreciate the depth and breadth of minority firm ownership, it is important to get some perspective. The Minority Business Development Agency (a division of the U.S. Department of Commerce), indicated that in 2007 there were almost 5.8 million minority firms, with gross receipts of $1 trillion, and employing over 5.8 million paid employees. Additionally, MBDA numbers indicated that during the 2002 to 2007 time period, minority-owned enterprises exceeded the growth of non-minority organizations in gross receipts (55% minority growth), employment (24%), and number of firms (45%).

Additionally, MBDA indicates that minority-owned firms traverse various industry landscapes, including health care and social assistance (13%); construction (10%); real estate, rental, and leasing (6%); administrative, support, waste management, and remediation services (11%); accommodation and food services (4%); transportation and warehousing (8%); professional, scientific, and technical services (10%); retail trade (9%); and all other sectors (30%). Given the richness and considerable variety of minority firms, the nature of the goods and services offered for sale can also be expected to follow suit, which bodes well for the capacity of these organizations to attract business, both domestically and internationally.

The rich variety of minority enterprises bodes well for inclusion in organizational supply bases. As firms seek to procure a broader variety of goods and services to satisfy the ever-growing demand of global customers, diverse suppliers should be in an increasingly more attractive position to expand their businesses.

SUPPLY BASE REDUCTION AND MINORITY SUPPLIERS

Increasingly organizations are focusing on the management of the entire supply network for in-creased savings, greater revenue, additional value creation, and higher levels of customer satisfaction. To achieve these goals in complex, global supply settings requires considerable integration, focus, information, and determination. One of the key cogs in the supply chain system is determining how many and which suppliers are optimal, given the goals and the competitive narrative. Parmar, Wu, Callarman, Fowler, and Wolfe (2010) reinforce the need for manufacturers to reduce supply base size. In fact, they offer an algorithm that clusters like suppliers into smaller units that are more manageable.

Increased global competition has mandated a more serious and microscopic look at all suppliers. Thus, more stringent performance measures are exacted in determining long-term fit for a range of suppliers, including minority suppliers. Progressively more competitive business environments have demanded more formal and structured approaches to supply base rationalization. Firms undertake a variety of means when considering supply base reductions, including eliminating or phasing out current suppliers, identification of suppliers that are finalists, or choosing suppliers to be strategic partners (Monczka, Handfield, Guinipero, & Patterson, 2011, p. 328). Each of these options represents varying degrees of commitment to either one or a group of particular suppliers.

Duffy (2005) offered various criteria in the selection of the appropriate number of suppliers, including supplier capabilities, the firm's level of risk aversion, defining the desired relationship with retained suppliers, and the customer's need for a range of choices. Given some of these selection criteria, a central concern is the preparation of small and minority suppliers for surviving some of the challenges associated with supplier reductions. One key avenue to ensuring and assuring long-term relevance of minority suppliers during periods of supply base optimization is to focus consistently on delivering value.

In particular, minority firms must constantly assess and reassess their value propositions. Specifically, a value proposition is the particular means in which the firm delivers usefulness and worth to a range of stakeholders. In developing value propositions, firms must delineate strategic focal areas, harness the necessary resources, and match these resources with marketplace opportunities. Fundamentally, minority firms must focus on how value is created, delivered, sustained, and measured.

Organizations that craft the most relevant value equations are the most likely survivors during times of major supplier realignment. An important component of survival as a supplier is fully understanding and being engaged in the supplier performance evaluation process. On what key criteria will performance be measured? Comprehension of performance metrics heightens the probability of continued existence for diverse suppliers. Monczka, Handfield, Guinipero, and Patterson (2011, p. 238), identify a fairly comprehensive list of important criteria for supplier selection, including the capability of the management team and employees, cost structure, level of quality sophistication, process and technological capacity, financial stability, E-systems capability, overall sourcing strategies, the likelihood for long-term relationship development, and sustainability orientation. As minority firms craft value propositions, they should be prepared from the perspective of the key performance metrics used for supplier evaluation, selection, and development. At the intersection of supplier and buyer expectations, firms explore common ground on which to pursue areas of mutual financial interest.

INTEGRATING TECHNOLOGY, SUPPLIER DIVERSITY, AND SUPPLY BASE RATIONALIZATION

Duffy (2005) suggests that technology is a key factor to consider during supply base reduction considerations. Given the pivotal role of technol-

ogy in buyer-seller relationships in general, it seems all the more important for minority firms to embrace technology as a conduit to gaining competitive advantage and to long-term success. Wiengarten, Fynes, Humphreys, Chavez, and McKittrick (2011) examine the extent to which e-business applications enhance value creation processes in the supply chain. Their findings, rooted in part in the Resource-Based View (RBV) of the firm, suggest that e-business applications have a positive influence on operational performance, especially when suppliers embrace e-business systems. If technology, especially e-systems, creates value within the supply chain, then diverse suppliers should move toward adoption of relevant technologies to strengthen their competitive postures within the marketplace.

While there are certainly initiatives that minority suppliers can undertake to be better positioned to capture e-related opportunities, Young (2001) suggests in a study of corporate Web-based supplier diversity initiatives, that organizations can do a better job of using their Web presence as tools to encourage using minority firms as suppliers. Young examined and categorized the supplier diversity-related content on the websites of Fortune 500 firms. Findings indicated that supplier diversity content spanned three areas—promotion efforts, application-related, and gatekeeper information. Some firms actively marketed their supplier diversity efforts, others focused on the forms and application assistance to take advantage of diversity programs, while still others used corporate websites as gatekeepers, especially when sharing information on certification as minority suppliers.

In their discussion of the evolution of Electronic-Supply Chain Management (E-SCM) systems, Monczka, Handfield, Giunipero, and Patterson (2011, p. 693) describe the influence of the desire for greater efficiencies in supply chains, coupled with intense competitive pressures, led to reconfigured and leaner supply chains. This necessitated considerable restructuring of business processes, information systems, people, and other resources.

Concomitantly, it heightened the need for greater supply chain integration. Out of this environment was born the predecessor of e-procurement and auxiliary electronic processes designed to improve overall performance. E-systems evolved to include Enterprise Resource Planning (ERP), which focused on the integration of all key business functions, Supplier Relationship Management (SRM), Customer Relationship Management (CRM), and social networking. Thus, as firms work to strengthen supply chain relationships and processes, there are various technological and electronic platforms from which to select. Supplying firms, including diverse organizations, must configure the appropriate type of technology matrix to match the needs and demands of customers.

Akyuz and Rehan (2009) identify several reasons for establishing e-supply chains. One of the foremost reasons is to leverage the power of the Internet to reconfigure, automate, and integrate key business functions. This level of supply chain integration bodes well for long term cost savings and overall effectiveness. Additional benefits include seamless coupling of supply chain processes through the Web and real-time collaboration and synchronization. Akyuz and Rehan (2009) further offer specific models of how to integrate the supply chain to achieve targeted performance goals. Approaches to supply chain integration are a function of supply chain goals, competitive circumstances, market structure, and the unique circumstances confronting the organization.

The following discussion focuses on specific e-supply chain management-related systems and what they offer minority suppliers in ever-increasing competitive environments, characterized by supply base reductions and restructuring. The first tool is that of e-procurement. Teo and Lai (2009) describe e-procurement as a way to achieve a host of objectives, including operational cost reductions, facilitation of volume purchases, broader buyer-seller choices, reduced processing costs, and improved overall functioning of the supply

area. Teo and Lai further state that e-procurement systems simplify purchasing processes and help leverage the entire technical infrastructure for greater levels of efficiency. They also examine some of the characteristics of e-procurement, including volume (the extent of Internet use for procurement); diversity (variety of types of procurement processes on the Internet); breadth (the extent of procurement-related linkages with other partners); and depth (extent to which business processes are interconnected with other organizations).

In his article on supplier diversity and e-procurement, Reese (2001) suggests that there is somewhat of a conundrum regarding e-procurement and minority suppliers. E-procurement generally emphasizes agreements over the long term, preferred suppliers, and those classified as strategic partners. These emphases by definition seem to favor much larger firms with far wider product and service assortments. This runs counter to the usual characteristics of minority firms – smaller in scope, fewer product/service lines, less depth and breadth in expertise, and generally limited capitalization. However, Reese touts the social benefits of supplier diversity as part of an organization's overall strategy. Additionally, Reese (2001) indicates that e-procurement has opened opportunities for minority firms by 'leveling the playing field' and by expanding the geographic and customer reach. Minority suppliers viewed e-procurement as a path to enhanced sales and profitability.

Thus, it is important for minority suppliers to consider instituting and upgrading e-procurement systems to broaden the quantity and quality of prospective sales options in the marketplace. Reese (2001) also suggests that diverse organizations partner with larger firms to leverage their resources and expertise in acquiring business from a larger variety of firms. If Firm A (diverse supplier) partners with Firm B (larger firm) in getting business from Firm C (a larger buying firm), there is a greater likelihood of having a win-win-win scenario. Given the myriad and rapid changes in the global and domestic economies and in particular industries, it behooves minority firms to leverage all resources and relationships in both supplying and buying markets.

A second suite of e-supply chain management-related options include reverse auctions. Kumar and Chang (2007) describe reverse auctions as 'competitive bidding events where multiple sellers compete for business of a single supplier.' They further characterize online reverse auctions as 'dynamic pricing with real-time bidding within a fixed time duration.' As can be inferred from the name, reverse auctions focus on price reductions throughout the process, while traditional auctions focus on price increases during the bidding session. While price reductions are the key benefit of reverse auctions, firms can also negotiate other terms, including service and related concerns.

Pearcy, Giunipero, and Wilson (2007) indicate that time-consuming activities associated with the procurement process may be substantially reduced through online reverse auctions. They describe reductions in the time to request quotes, evaluation of responses, and other procurement-related functions. Thus, it is important for firms, especially smaller organizations considering this exchange medium, to evaluate the total costs and benefits associated with reverse auctions. There are a number of opportunities for cost savings when using reverse auctions in the business-to-business setting.

At a higher level of supply chain system integration is Customer Relationship Management (CRM). Peelen, van Montfort, Beltman, and Klerkx (2009) describe CRM as uniting the potential of relationship marketing strategies and information technology. They further state that this process involves vision, strategy, valued customer experiences, organizational collaboration, CRM processes, CRM information, and CRM technology. CRM technology is the essential glue required to maintain the system. Technology sup-

ports every component of customer relationship management, which in turn complements overall organizational strategy.

Wisner, Tan, and Leong (2012, pp. 345-370) describe CRM as 'building and maintaining profitable long-term customer relationships.' They suggest including the following as tools and components of CRM—customer segmentation, understanding buyer behavior, deciding on the dimensions of customer value, personalized customer communications, sales force automation, and customer service management. They also refer to cloud computing (also known as on-demand computing) as a CRM-related tool that has implications for a range of business applications. Cloud computing allows for greater flexibility, more customization, and more sophisticated functionality.

Collectively, e-procurement, reverse auctions, and CRM offer tremendous opportunities to minority firms to ensure inclusion as suppliers during periods of supply base rationalization. While investment in these technologies may require additional effort, long-term it is a strategic decision that will help define the future of supplier diversity.

THE NEXT STEPS: DIVERSITY, TECHNOLOGY, AND COMPETITIVE MARKETPLACES

Increasingly, firms of all sizes will have to adapt more quickly to an ever-evolving marketplace. The challenges for diverse suppliers will be no less stringent and demanding. Berlak and Weber (2004), in their work on making e-procurement a viable tool for Small and Medium-Sized Enterprises (SMEs), suggest various types of cooperative arrangements to combat some of the fray of market turbulence. Specifically, small firms should work through competence networks to build dynamic enterprise relationships that combine their competencies to enhance competitiveness. E-procurement and related tools offer joint possibilities in building synergies that are lacking in a small, solo organizational environment.

Building on the work of Mintzberg, Ahlstrand, and Lampel (1998), Berlak and Weber (2004) identify different types of networks that offer varying benefits to SMEs, depending upon the situation and the needs of the organizations involved. Of particular interest to SMEs and minority firms are operational networks, compound networks, and virtual enterprises. Operational networks attempt to enhance value creation capacities by changing how resources are deployed to improve some aspect of the operation that offers additional efficiencies. In compound networks, the organizations are more or less equal, but come together to manage a particular set of tasks. Lastly, the virtual enterprise is more short-term in focus, opportunistic, and consists of joint efforts of independent organizations for purposes of improved efficiencies and effectiveness. Each of these three options can be enhanced through the use of technology, especially focusing on e-procurement-related tasks in SMEs. Thus, the critical question becomes how can diverse suppliers configure resources and value in tandem with other organizations to effect high-performing, technology-based exchanges with buyers across networks? Ultimately, diverse suppliers must become more technologically innovative in order to take advantage of strategic and operational opportunities in a very dynamic marketplace.

CONCLUDING THOUGHTS

In part, the future of supplier diversity is defined by the capacity of minority suppliers to adapt technologically. A very strong business case can be made for including diverse suppliers as part of the supplier set for myriad organizations. However, given the direct parallels between technological sophistication, especially in e-procurement-related

areas and inclusion on supply lists, it behooves diverse suppliers to move more quickly and more innovatively in that direction.

The National Minority Supplier Development Council (NMSDC) has served as a link between diverse firms and corporate America since 1972 (www.nmsdc.org). It continues to lead, encourage, and provide a range of support systems required for long-term success of diverse suppliers. According to NMSDC, minorities account for 34% of the total U.S. population, 21% of total businesses, 7% of gross receipts, and only 3% of total corporate purchases. Given these numbers, there is much left to be accomplished, especially with respect to corporate purchases. One key theme of this chapter has been to highlight how technology can be used as a conduit to increase corporate purchases well beyond the current three percent figure. There is considerable opportunity to expand the reach of diverse suppliers and thus have a greater overall economic footprint.

As minority firms broaden the types of businesses in which they are engaged, adopt more technologically sophisticated systems and processes, and gain access to additional markets, domestically and globally, market growth and overall performance are strengthened. Collectively, it is important for majority and minority firms to make stronger commitments to enhancing supplier diversity in ever more competitive marketplaces. Ultimately, this becomes a win economically, organizationally, and for society as a whole.

REFERENCES

Adobor, H., & McMullen, R. (2007). Supplier diversity and supply chain management: A strategic approach. *Business Horizons*, *50*(3), 219–229. doi:10.1016/j.bushor.2006.10.003

Akyuz, G., & Rehan, M. (2009). Requirements for forming an e-supply chain. *International Journal of Production Research*, *47*(12), 3265–3287. doi:10.1080/00207540701802460

Barney, J. (1991). Firm resources and sustained competitive advantage. *Journal of Management, 17*(1), 99–120. doi:10.1177/014920639101700108

Barney, J. (1999). How a firm's capabilities affect boundary decisions. *Sloan Management Review, 40*, 137–145.

Barney, J. (2001). Resource-based theories of competitive advantage: A ten-year perspective on the resource-based view. *Journal of Management, 27*, 643–650. doi:10.1177/014920630102700602

Barney, J., Wright, M., & Ketchen, D. (2001). The resource-based view of the firm: ten years after 1991. *Journal of Management, 27*(6), 625–641. doi:10.1177/014920630102700601

Berlak, J., & Weber, V. (2004). How to make e-procurement viable for SME suppliers. *Production Planning and Control, 15*(7), 671–677. doi:10.1080/09537280412331298139

Carter, C., & Jennings, M. (2000). *Purchasing's contribution to the socially responsible management of the supply chain.* Phoenix, AZ: CAPS Research.

Duffy, R. (2005). *Supply base rationalization.* Phoenix, AZ: CAPS Research.

Greenhalgh, L. (2008). *Increasing MBE competitiveness through strategic alliances.* Washington, DC: U.S. Department of Commerce.

Heffes, E. (2006, November 1). Diversifying suppliers isn't costly. *Financial Executive.*

Kumar, S., & Chang, C. (2007). Reverse auctions: How much total supply chain cost savings are there? A conceptual overview. *Journal of Revenue and Pricing Management, 6*(2), 77–85. doi:10.1057/palgrave.rpm.5160077

Minority Business Development Agency. (2012). *Minority-owned business growth and global reach.* Retrieved from http://www.mbda.gov/sites/default/files/Minority-OwnedBusinessGrowthand-GlobalReach_Final.pdf

Mintzberg, H., Ahlstrand, B., & Lampel, J. (1998). *Strategy safari: A guided tour through the wilds of strategic management.* New York, NY: Simon & Schuster.

Monczka, R., Handfield, R., Giunipero, L., & Patterson, J. (2011). *Purchasing & supply chain management* (5th ed.). Mason, OH: South-Western/Cengage Learning.

Parmara, D., Wu, T., Callarman, T., Fowler, J., & Wolfe, P. (2010). A clustering algorithm for supplier base management. *International Journal of Production Research, 48*(13), 3803–3821. doi:10.1080/00207540902942891

Pearcy, D., Giunipero, L., & Wilson, A. (2007, Winter). A model of relational governance in reverse auctions. *Journal of Supply Chain Management*, 4-15.

Peelen, E., Kees, V., Beltman, R., & Klerkxc, A. (2009). An empirical study into the foundations of CRM success. *Journal of Strategic Marketing, 17*(6), 453–471. doi:10.1080/09652540903371695

Porter, A. (1997). Supply-base 'optimization' stokes market competition. *Purchasing, 123*(6), 18–21.

Reese, A. (2001, August 1). Supplier diversity and e-procurement: Why your initiatives are not at odds. *Supply & Demand Chain Executive.*

Teo, T., & Lai, K. (2009). Usage and performance impact of electronic procurement. *Journal of Business Logistics, 30*(2), 125–139. doi:10.1002/j.2158-1592.2009.tb00115.x

Wiengarten, F., Fynes, B., Humphreys, P., Chavez, R., & McKittrick, A. (2011). Assessing the value creation process of e-business along the supply chain. *Supply Chain Management. International Journal (Toronto, Ont.), 16*(4), 207–219.

Wisner, J., Tan, K., & Leong, G. (2012). *Principles of supply chain management: A balanced approach* (3rd ed.). Mason, OH: South-Western/Cengage Learning.

Worthington, I. (2009). Corporate perceptions of the business case for supplier diversity: How socially responsible purchasing can pay. *Journal of Business Ethics*, *90*, 47–60. doi:10.1007/s10551-008-0025-5

Worthington, I., Ram, M., Boyal, H., & Shah, M. (2008). Researching the drivers of socially responsible purchasing: A cross-national study of supplier diversity initiatives. *Journal of Business Ethics*, *79*, 319–331. doi:10.1007/s10551-007-9400-x

Young, D. (2001, Winter). Categorizing corporate web-based supplier diversity initiatives. *Journal of Computer Information Systems*, 57–68.

KEY TERMS AND DEFINITIONS

Corporate Social Responsibility: Thoughtful actions of organizations to extend the reach and influence of firms to benefit various stakeholders.

E-Procurement: A group of integrative, Internet-based, techniques that facilitate exchanges between buyers and sellers that reduce the overall costs associated with the exchange processes.

Online Reverse Auctions: An Internet-based pricing model that focuses on reducing prices as the auction progresses.

Purchasing Social Responsibility: Efforts of corporate purchasing and supply managers to actively pursue strategies designed to buy goods and services from minority suppliers.

Resource-Based View of the Firm: A theoretical foundation on which to see organizations as managers of both internal and external resources to further the aims of the firm.

Supply Base Rationalization: A systematic review of the numbers and types of suppliers required to ensure long-term customer satisfaction and maximum value for each member of the supply chain.

Supplier Diversity: Coordinated efforts of majority organizations to meaningfully engage minority suppliers in the exchange of goods and services as a way to encourage minority enterprise growth and development.

Section 3
Design of Diversity Leadership

Chapter 8

The Analysis–Evaluation Cycle:
What are the Keys to Designing Effective Diversity Instruction?

David R. Faulkner
Defense Equal Opportunity Management Institute, USA

ABSTRACT

This chapter focuses on where diversity programs in the government and military intersect, which meets the definition and essence of diversity, how some instructional design process(es) may be undertaken to ensure that the real meaning of diversity is projected into the programs, and how to improve programs to ensure diversity training is effectively impacting organizations.

INTRODUCTION AND BACKGROUND

Anyone who has ever played in or listened to an orchestra is familiar with how important it is for all its instruments to be in tune. Tuning is a process based upon identifying a standard pitch and then meeting it. For all instruments, the standard is the 440-A, though the reeds and brass generally tune to a B-flat. Those not tuning to an A are usually termed B-flat instruments. To begin with, the oboe is tuned to the standard A, which establishes the foundation from which even the B-flat instruments tuning is based. Without both the A and B-flat instruments being in tune, there will still be a clash between the two.

Just as there is a standard tuning for symphony orchestras, there needs to be one for Instructional Design and Development, especially between the various phases and steps. As it is often difficult to determine which model works best, instructional designers 'invented' a notional model they call ADDIE (Molenda, Pershing, & Reigeluth, 2003), an acronym representing the various stages of Instructional Systems Design (ISD): Analysis, Design, Development, Implementation, and Evaluation. In reality, this ADDIE notion sprang from the Interservice Procedures for Instructional Systems Development (IPISD) and is attributed to Robert Branson, though based in the military (U.S. Army). Instructional Design itself originated in the military in the late-1940s, and was instituted into higher learning at Wayne State and

DOI: 10.4018/978-1-4666-2668-3.ch008

Indiana Universities in 1950. Over the years, the military model has evolved into the Instructional Systems Design/Systems Approach to Training, or ISD/SAT (Department of Defense, 2001). This document basically lays out the ISD plan as the ADDIE Model.

It is evident throughout the ISD business world that the term "instructional designer" means different things. Simply peruse the advertisements on any 'headhunter' website and a number of variations immerge. Some want the instructional designer to know programming, e-learning, program management, and how to clean kitchen sinks in order to effectively perform the job, while concurrently meeting the requirement of having a bachelor's degree. Interestingly, the number of colleges and universities offering that level of degree are few and far between—most recognized College or University programs start at the Master's degree level. In addition to degrees, there are some certification programs (Embry-Riddle, Nova Southeastern, etc.) that may advance those with a Bachelor's degree to meet the basic requirements.

Several years ago, the term "e-learning" appeared and ransacked the literature and marketplace. Conferences were held focusing on e-learning and promising many new methods to e-learn. Regardless of the way one approaches it, e-learning is not learning. Just because a lesson is termed "e-learning" does not guarantee that learning takes place. It seems that e-learning has also become synonymous with Computer-Based Training (CBT). Electronically Delivered Learning (EDL for short), however, is not all computer-based. Filmstrips, slide-tape presentations, video snippets, and others—all run by electricity pre-date CBT. The 'learning' connotation is a misnomer, because none of the above guaranteed learning retention and transfer.

More recently, e-learning has become so commonplace that many people do not realize that there are other platforms that can effectively deliver the instruction. One of the areas that comes to mind is the intrapersonal-interpersonal skill interaction in small groups. We should note that it is very difficult (if not impossible) to teach and evaluate empathy and other soft skills through non-human media.

Many organizations have posited that technology is the primary choice for presenting instructional programs; it is usually the recommended choice. Using this in an effort to build a "one-size-fits-all" platform, administrators have directed strategists to use technology in the face of "good ole common sense." This seems to polarize to Bob Kozma's (1994) initial stand that media influences learning as opposed to Richard Clark's (1994) media being a mere vehicle to deliver it.

So what is the purpose of media in teaching? Whatever technology (or perhaps *medium*) we use should be considered as a vessel to carry the content. A good analogy here would be the facilitated transport of proteins though an animal cell membrane—a carrier molecule transporting the protein—just like the medium carries the message from the sender to the receiver. In like manner, the instructional medium can transport a near-realistic schema- or mental model-building strategy, but falls short in replicating elements in the affective-spiritual domains. Therefore, it should be concluded that Media or Technology would not completely replace the social interaction of people. We can, however, effectively use it to transfer concepts, rules, cognitive strategies, metacognition, and other learning outcomes, into the mental makeup of a learner.

There has been a surge over the past decade or so for organizations to address equal opportunity (the military) and equal employment opportunity. One one of the areas of great interest is diversity. Diversity is often misconstrued to mean just racial and gender equality, but it covers much more than that. McGuire's and Parks' chapters in this book go much more into detail on this, so it is recommended that the reader refer to them. It is more apropos in this chapter to look at some of the instructional design issues that arise.

It is not uncommon for instruction to be developed that, in reality, has no impact on the behavior of the student following the sequence of events. The ultimate event in Gagne's Nine Events of Instruction (Table 1), *Retention and Transfer*, seems to indicate that ALL instruction developed according to the Model is powerful or effective. Just by "going through the motions" does not guarantee learning, just as performing swimming strokes on the dock ensures that an individual can swim. Neither does a series of Bloom's knowledge and comprehension objectives empower a lifeguard to have lifesaving ability—it takes some application or problem solving to pull someone from the deep waters.

As researchers have shown in media comparison studies, students exposed to media have higher retention rates than those learning from traditional methods. However, in numerous studies (ISLET, 2011, for example) the researchers did not reveal the details of the control group's substance—were the instructional strategies the same in the control group as was the experimental group? Using Computer-Based Training (CBT), sometimes referred to as Advanced Distributed Learning (ADL), is effective because of intrinsic factors—it does gain Attention, and is an inherent attention sustainer. If, however, we go back to before CBT, we see that the types of e-learning were not as motivating in comparison. Motivating the learner, therefore, is the challenge facing instructional designers and developers. Gagne's *Events of Instruction* has already called attention to engaging the learner, but there is a motivational strategy developed by John Keller that should be utilized: The ARCS Model of Motivation (Keller). ARCS is an acronym for Attention, Relevance, Confidence, and Satisfaction. Perhaps the four parts in the ARCS Model are distributed into two hemispheres—one migrating towards Kozma (Attention) and the other three towards the strategy elements.

So what are the keys to successfully designing Diversity, or more generally, any type of, instruction?

Key 1: Following an ISD Model is Essential to Planning and Execution

Every trained instructional designer will employ some type of model to design instruction. However, just using a model and inserting the components does not guarantee that the instruction will achieve its greatest impact. Most instructional designers employing the ADDIE concept begin at the analysis stage (or phase). Perhaps, though, we really need to look at the typical way things work. The administration generally identifies a possible training need and presents it to some agency to advertise for a Request For Quote (RFQ)

Table 1. Gagne's nine events of instruction

Level	Instructional Event	Internal Mental Process
1	Gain attention	Stimuli activates receptors
2	Inform learners of objectives	Creates level of expectation for learning
3	Stimulate recall of prior learning	Retrieval and activation of short-term memory
4	Present the content	Selective perception of content
5	Provide "learning guidance"	Semantic encoding for storage long-term memory
6	Elicit performance (practice)	Responds to questions to enhance encoding and verification
7	Provide feedback	Reinforcement and assessment of correct performance
8	Assess performance	as final evaluation
9	Enhance retention and transfer to the job	Retrieval and generalization of learned skill to new situation

or Request For Bid (RFB). This advertisement will identify a number of needs and constraints in the organization, and often provides a cost ceiling bidders should not exceed. Where this training need immerges brings us query: Is the need really in training or education, or is it in some environmental effect or materiel malfunction? On many occasions, early steps can help identify the path one should take before excessively spending a lot of money on needless tasking. The steps to the Analysis phase of the ISD/SAT are listed in Figure 1. (Please note: The ISD/SAT is presently under reconstruction and may differ slightly when updated.) In the approach taken by the author of this chapter, however, this strict set of steps will not be totally followed.

Many instructional designers misconstrue the use of an instructional model. Models, of course, do provide us a framework from which to plan and develop instruction, but most are sequential in nature: one-step or sub-step precedes another. A wise instructional designer can multi-task a design model to save time. Some models have lengthy cycles, and others have short ones. The ISD/SAT is one entailing a lengthy schedule. The Layers of Necessity (LON) Model (Tessmer & Wedman, 1990) was generated to accommodate

Figure 1. ISD/SAT model

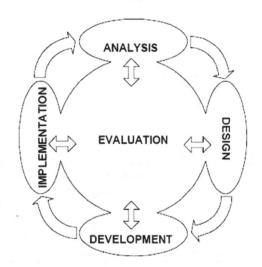

designers who have little time or resources to produce prototypes in a short time or with minimal players. Steps may be shortcut at first, but the reality of not returning and adequately covering these steps is ill-advised. In addition to the LON, Tripp and Bichelmeyer (1990) contributed to short time processing with their 'Rapid Prototyping.' These were not developed to supplant the phases of ADDIE, but to produce a temporary solution for a long-term process. The steps to these usually result in a prototype to pilot the design and development of the product as a whole.

As we address the issue of time constraints on the instructional design process, we need to realize that many tasks in a model can require somewhat-longer completion times. These steps will be addressed later as we encounter them. One of the drawbacks, however, to lengthy instructional design projects, such as in equal opportunity, diversity, culture, and others, is the amount of societal change occurring between start to completion. So herein is where the instructional design-Subject-Matter Expert team must be current on research, trends, and issues.

Key 2: Evaluation is Key to Analysis and must be Thorough

If you learned Instructional Design from an Academic Institution, or if you went through one of the certification programs, you were led to believe that Analysis was the first stage of Instructional Design. Analysis is dissecting the job and building instruction to the sum of its parts. However, Analysis does not stand by itself. It is highly dependent on Evaluation. Before you can define a standard, you need a target. Where, then do you find the person performing the job who qualifies as the master of the skills required to perform the task? Standards are nothing new, but consider finding it like classifying a type specimen in Biological Nomenclature. When formulating a new species of animal, naming it, and classifying it as distinct from others, one specimen is used as the prime example. This "Type" specimen becomes the standard to which all others sharing similar characteristics is compared. This is good for science, but, in a task analysis, it is not always something you can place in a jar in a museum. It is, however, something on which a majority must agree. If not, it can be an analyst's nightmare to ascertain which form should be THE Standard. Then, an analyst may need to try to hit a moving target to encapsulate the target. This standard in the ISD process is found in Levels 3 and 4 of the Kirkpatrick Model.

The standard, of course, is not the final target in the instructional design plan. Behavior and its Results are. Instructional design's final 'chapter' is in its success—what impact will the product have in the community, organization, and in the current trainees or graduates? Herein, we can see a synergy of intersecting models and paradigms—Keller's ARCS, Gagne's *Events of Instruction,* Constructivism, and Eclecticism—meaning that ignorance in hiring an inexperienced instructional designer can be costly. This cost becomes even more magnified when adding *Evaluation* to the mix. Instructional designing requires a higher level in Bloom's (1956; Anderson & Krathwohl, 2001) (Figure 2).

While on Instructional Models, it must be noted that not all are based on ADDIE. Due to the lack of space and time, it is inappropriate here to cover the ISD models (Reigeluth, 2000, and others have far more detailed descriptions and coverage), the approaches in a few platforms will be mentioned. The Dick and Carey Systems Approach Model (Figure 3), so often the model of choice in academic ISD, is one that follows the ADDIE scheme. The ISD/SAT also addresses these steps in great detail, and is quite lengthy, but we will address just a few areas of note.

Besides ADDIE, another approach has received a lot of attention: Competencies-Based. DuBois (1993) was one of a Google hit list of authors using Human Resource Development (HRD) to generate an array of competencies required in organizations. These competencies are very difficult for the Instructional Designer to grasp, in that they require a different approach to task mastery than does the ADDIE. This area appears to be more highly subjective than objective in its assessments, and it requires a higher level of inter-rater reliability to evaluate the 'skills' in it than traditional methods. This approach is creeping into Government/Military training more and more, as we have seen it in the High Performance Development Model (HPDM), used by the Veteran's Benefits Administration (VBA) (2004) and other associated organizations. Rather than solely identifying tasks, the HPDM addresses eight leadership competencies in Executive, Manager, and Supervisor roles in an organization. The three provide a hierarchy of "umbrellas" with Executive at the summit. These competencies include: Technical Skills, Personal Mastery, Interpersonal Effectiveness, Customer Service, Flexibility/Adaptability,

Figure 2. Bloom's taxonomy

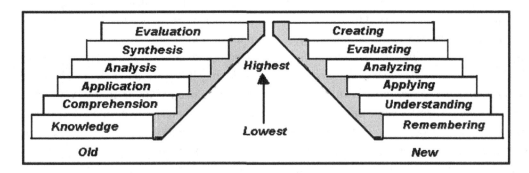

Figure 3. Dick and Carey: ISD/SAT graphic

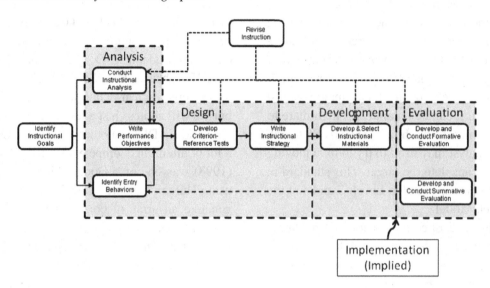

Creative Thinking, Systems Thinking, and Organizational Stewardship. Interestingly, Diversity and Cross-Cultural Competency (3C) are not directly mentioned. It appears from the many Diversity programs perused in the literature that this competency-based thinking will gradually 'invade' the workplace and subsume traditional performance-based efforts. At this point, however, the writer views it out of scope and a discussion for another time and place. Therefore, we will continue with the ADDIE/ISD/SAT approach.

KEY 3: Go-NoGo Decisions must be Implemented Throughout the ISD Process

Before we consider engaging any possible direction towards training, we need to evaluate if it is necessary to do so. This is referred to as a *Needs Analysis.* To quote the ISD/SAT Handbook, *If a problem is caused by equipment, organizational, doctrinal, and/or other inadequacies, then instruction is not an appropriate solution. Trying to use instruction to solve such problems results in wasted training resources. The challenge is to select the solution that targets the cause of the problem* (p. 4). It is at this point that program managers and administrators must evaluate the next actions by the organization. Is the performance problem in the field one of training, environment, equipment, or other? If other than training, it would seem logical to "stop the train." In an organization this may be feasible, but the quandary comes if a problem has been found after a contract has been signed, what does a contractor do? Well obviously, the best it can. However, it should be done before a contract is signed to do the work. There are programs commonly identified that have no business going farther. On the other hand, if it is in an organization where no contract is necessary, the determination to stop is economically sound. Why spend resources and time performing unnecessary tasks? The Analysis phase can be very expensive even if a training need is identified. Unfortunately, many organizations and institutions may fail to recognize that projects need to be stopped and spend a lot of potentially creative energy and funds on needless tasking. This cessation of the project is what may be referred to as a "Go-NoGo": 'Go' if a training need, 'NoGo' if not. A 'Go-NoGo' can be inserted at any key point in the process (at the end of the Analysis phase is a good example), but there needs to be evaluation points of this nature throughout the project.

As we address some issues in ISD, one that is extremely common is to have Subject-Matter-Experts (SMEs) design and develop curricula or lessons. Unless these individuals have some background in ISD, the instructional sequencing and strategies will be out of sync. For instance, it is quite common for the naïve lesson designer/developer to construct lessons without advance organizers (Ausubel, 1960), chunking (Miller, 1956), contiguous flow, and testing in a contextual substrate. Of course, even academically trained instructional designers may fail to follow this. A recent project in the DoD in the area of Cross-Cultural Competency has very good media but has a lengthy introduction (2-3 hours) and seems to go around in circles. The learner gets lost in the branching and has no navigational hints as to where they are or how to 'get through the maze.' In the diversity area, learning may fail in the technology area alone, but should thrive in the hybrid type of instruction, where technology and classroom instruction 'collide.' These programs must be thoroughly thought out and continually evaluated.

In order to continue toward the goal of describing the Analysis-Evaluation Cycle, we now look at the next Key.

Key 4: The Analysis-Evaluation Cycle is Essential to Ensure Standards

Probably the first REAL stage in instructional design processes is *Evaluation*. Evaluation should be planned early in the ISD process. How could Evaluation possibly precede Analysis? Answer: Analysis is first established in Evaluation and moves "backwards" from it. The "Standard" (described previously) and its impact relate to Levels 3 (Behavior) and 4 (Results, or Return on Expectations) in Donald Kirkpatrick's Four-Level Evaluation Model (Figure 4) (Phillips, 1996, published a similar model, based on Kirkpatrick, that has five

Figure 4. Kirkpatrick's ADDIE

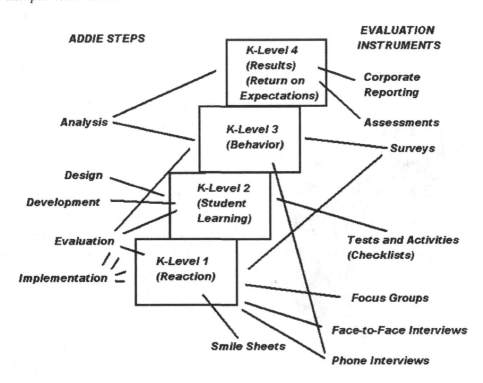

levels, splitting the Results level of Kirkpatrick into *Business Results* and *Return on Investment*). Two of the four levels (1 and 2) in this model relate to the instruction itself (physiology of the instruction), and the other two (3 and 4) to its environment (or ecology). To re-emphasize, as instructional design, ARCS, and Kirkpatrick's approach, combine to form a 360-degree approach to instructional design and development. This should be the approach mandated by academic institutions and by organizations rather than just hiring or moving someone to fit a slot. Rather than go further into how teams function, refer to the McGuire, Bonvillain, and Faulkner chapter elsewhere in this book.

We should return to our initial focus here and address the steps in the (notional) ADDIE "Model" (Figure 5). We need to pause here to acknowledge that numerous models have been introduced (nearly as many as toads in a springtime pond), but nearly all (if not all) have the same basic phases.

Key 5: The Analysis Phase Lays the Groundwork for Teaching the Components

The Analysis Phase mainly deals with requirements of performing a job and the tasks that answer

Figure 5. ADDIE model

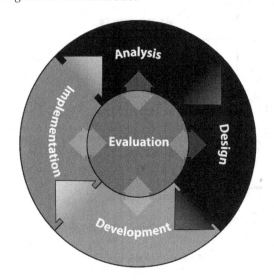

to those requirements. The basic approach is to observe the performance of individuals who have mastered a set of tasks comprising a job. It seems like it is simple, but, in reality, it is not.

The SAT Analysis plan is pictured in Figure 2. From this depiction, one can assume it is run sequentially, but indeed it does not need to be. Depending on the job, the ability and availability of data collectors (analysts), the amount of concentration or attention on it by those assigned to run the Analysis, the amount of Client-Furnished Information available, the establishment of standards and requirements, and other factors, an analysis can take from a few months up to two years to be conducted effectively. To some, the analysis is known as the Front-End Analysis (FEA). 'Front-End' is really redundant here—the alternatives, Back-End and Middle Analysis, are never mentioned, but are sometimes done if a FEA has not been done prior to the development of an existing course. The Analysis of the Equal Opportunity Advisor (EOA) position conducted at DEOMI was conducted after years of successfully conducting the course, so it could be a Middle-Analysis. The FEA of the EOA, however, was conducted more as an evaluation tool than to establish the tasks. A simplified sample of a FEA plan conducted at DEOMI can be seen in Table 2. It differs slightly from the ISD/SAT, but covers the same areas. It should be noted that the steps need not be run in the order listed, but the Training Situation Analysis (TSA) should always be conducted first.

The list of steps in Table 3 presumes that the question of training-or-not-to-train has already been addressed.

After the need to train (or educate) has been established, the Training Situation Analysis (TSA) is conducted to ascertain such things as the educational and occupational requirements. Establishing these will set the stage for any baselines and prerequisites to be met prior to training. Sometimes this may bring an added expense to the organization beyond budget, so it, along with other Analysis steps, may be planned into the project timeline.

Table 2. FEA plan

Milestone/Deliverable	Planned Completion Date
Completed project charter	06 January 2010
Approved project charter	06 January 2010
Project kickoff meeting	20 January 2010
Training situation analysis completion	17 March 2010
Determine GO/NO-GO for continuance (if training need)	17 March 2010
Occupational analysis completion	26 May 2010
Mission analysis completion	21 April 2010
Educational requirements analysis completion	05 April 2010
Job analysis completion	20 August 2010
Perform task analysis completion	26 September 2010
Complete the training task list	22 October 2010
Completion of clustering and categorizing tasks	16 November 2010
Determine GO/NO-GO for ROI and continuance	16 November 2010
Development/categorization of learning objective completion	22 December 2010
Learning analysis hierarchies completion	20 January 2011
Completion of test item development	18 February 2011
Instructional strategy determination completion	18 March 2011
Instructional method selection completion	26 April 2011
FEA document completion/final submission	15 June 2011
Determine GO/NO-GO for continuance	15 June 2011
Transition to further design/development	15 June 2011
Review and update model culmination	21 June 2011

Table 3. ISD/SAT analysis steps

Step	Title	Description
1	Training Situation Analysis (TSA)	Process of identifying a requirement to develop or revise an instructional program. Includes educational and occupational analyses.
2	Mission Analysis	Tasks lists primarily designed by military mission directives. Usually performed when new unit is formed, new manuals are printed, a new threat is realized, etc. (Would apply to new directions in an organization for a new Diversity program.)
3	Job/Task Analysis (JTA)	Actually two steps in the ISD/SAT combined into one. Involves dissection of the job performed to obtain details of its performance steps. Can also involve attitudes and competencies. Initially obtained through observation and interviewing key personnel who perform and supervise the job. Occasionally done prior to contract award. Can be obtained from previous documentation and records, but should be based on all points of interaction with performers.
3.a	Master Task List (MTL)	This is a part of the JTA but involves listing all the tasks resulting from it. Each task has components, conditions, and standards.
3.b	Constructing Task Statements	Articulating the tasks into statements having an action verb, object, and qualifier. Action verbs are written as Knowledge, Skills, and Attitudes (KSAs).
4	Training Task List (TTL)	Selection and listing of the tasks from the MTL to be trained. Usually involves Subject-Matter Expert (SME) and Analyst coordination to determine training tasks, but may be accomplished through a model or other process.

We seemingly have focused more on ISD, but what about diversity? The identified NEED for a Diversity training program in an organization should be based on requirements. Is the purpose of the organization focused on (a) having a more robust diversity in the workplace, or (b) to just have something on the shelf to show an organization's complicity to a requirement, using it more as an item to be checked off a list? If asked, most would answer in the affirmative, but, in many cases, it winds up as the latter (b).

Connecting the Analysis Phase with Kirkpatrick Level 4 results will be a key to incorporating Diversity, or any other successful training program, for that matter, into the workplace. However, getting Level 4 results into the workplace drives the analysts back to the standard question "What is the missing link between Level 4 (Results) and the Analysis Phase?" Kirkpatrick and Kirkpatrick (2009) identify this "missing link" as Level 3, *Behavior*. Rather than address that here, we will discuss it in the Evaluation section, and return to the discussion on Analysis.

ANALYSIS BEYOND THE GO-NOGO

In many instances in military and Government, we find that a Go-NoGo has already been performed when the contract is awarded. At the kick-off, which is typical of all contracts, supporting documentation (Government-Furnished Information, or GFI) and equipment (Government-Furnished Equipment, or GFE) is requested by the contractor. During this meeting, the scope, Integrated Product Team (IPT), and other essentials are established as well. Many of the materials provided are those required in the Analysis steps (Table 1).

Environmental Analysis

Perhaps an area that may be outside the Task Analysis, but very important, is the environment in which the tasks are performed. Many

instructional designers fail to see that test item mastery in an environment must be relevant to the substrate in which it is placed. For example, if a task in the analysis addressed how to tune a guitar, doing so on a violin would not be the same, though similar. The analyst/instructional designer must ask the questions: 'Where are the tasks being performed?' Another may be: 'How much of this task is transferable from one substrate to another?' We will address this later as we consider mastering the tasks.

KSAOS AND TASK LISTS

As the project begins, the steps following the TSA are conducted, sometimes necessitating interviews or observing experts performing the tasks. Some tasks, however, are way beyond the time needed for observation, so tasks are either provided as GFI or can be provided through a Job-Task Analysis (JTA). The JTA provides the Knowledge, Skills, Attitudes, and Other abilities (KSAOs). Many of the knowledge, skills, and some abilities can easily be articulated into tasks. However, some projects involve the identification of competencies in the Affective domain, which are a challenge to evaluate. In the past, attitudes were primarily shelved as being too difficult to measure, but some courses today necessitate the incorporation of 'soft-skill' strategies. Soft skills do include attitudes, but also empathy, compassion, and a number of others. Perhaps a new classification should be introduced: KSAOCs—Knowledge, Skills, Attitudes, Other abilities, and Competencies. 'Soft skills' are becoming a little easier to measure, but the results are more qualitative and subjective than the quantitatively-measured performance tasks.

Master Task List (MTL)

As tasks are identified, they are included in a Master Task List (MTL). The analyst's next chore is to pare them down through eliminating duplicates and synonyms to a list that is manageable. In one project, analysts scrubbed a list of 20,000 tasks to a few hundred.

At times, the MTL is part of the GFI and GFE. A task list for diversity, however, was more difficult to acquire, because many of the tasks are in the affective domain. A literature search for requirements and tasks for diversity courses produced no FEA or task list were few and far between, but the areas for training were quite common. No task analysis per se was found. Usually, there is a 'thread' that connects each task and its testing through the ISD process, being 'empowered' by a learning objective to elicit a specific behavior in a certain environment. The task is addressed in the instruction and then measured in the field as a Kirkpatrick Level 3 Behavior. Testing of tasks in the lesson is assigned to Kirkpatrick Level 2 (Learning), but there are some tasks that project into the workplace as on-the-Job Training (OJT).

There seems to be some question as to whom to follow when establishing characteristics of diversity. Which task analysis do you follow? Yes, there are tasks for people to follow for *diversity management*, but how can you measure 'diversity'? A literature review produced only a few visible references. No Diversity FEA was found. Many courses or programs were based primarily on legal mandates—the Civil Rights Act of 1964 and amendments. Loden's (1996) *Diversity Wheel* lists the dimensions of diversity based on her experience in the field. Thiederman (2003) appears to have an excellent task analysis if the chapter titles are followed. Thomas (1999) also has skills and abilities mingled in throughout his work. Although these and others have a 'fruit' of training, they do not have a visible 'root.' Follow the recipe and you generally will cook a good cake.

Some of the tasks (or goals) of diversity instruction address what the instructor will do in class, not what the student will do. For example, "define diversity" is an overt task (one possessing behavior that is observable and measureable by test method); 'understand' or 'know' is a covert task, one whose behavior is not well observed or measured. Covert tasks will be very difficult to perform to a standard—if 'know' is used, to which level?

Key 6: The Training Task List is Essential for Establishing the Learning Hierarchy

Once the task statements have been written, the Subject-Matter Experts and Instructional Designers meet and determine which tasks are to be trained. This is based on several factors: criticality (or importance), frequency, difficulty, and some others. Once established, it is a good practice to send these to practitioners to verify this list as accurate. Although not all may on all tasks agree, majority rules.

At some point, either before or after the verification, tasks are gathered into clusters according to system, subsystem, elements, and attributes. Some tasks may cross cluster areas, but they are listed separately in the clusters because they may have slight differences in their performance. This is the approach for performance tasks, but how should we treat the soft skills (attitudes) or competencies? In some ways, the same, but we would need to design instruments to test them later in the Design Phase. It is at this stage where we can organize the tasks into hierarchies, but, according to the ISD/SAT, we reserve that until after the Learning Objectives are constructed.

THE DESIGN PHASE

The Design Phase consists of several steps: (1) Developing and Categorizing the Learning Objectives, (2) Constructing the Learning Hierarchies, (3) Developing Test Items, (4) Determining Instructional Strategies, (5) Selecting Instructional Methods, and (6) Selecting Instructional Media. These will not be covered here because they do not directly relate to the Kirkpatrick-ISD Model scheme we are addressing, but they are important none the less. We will, however address a few concerns.

Key 7: Learning Objectives Must Interact with K-Level 2 to Empower Maximum Student Learning and Application

We can nearly transfuse the task statements constructed in the latter steps of the Analysis Phase into learning objectives. Depending on the platform, they can either be written as 'Terminal and Enabling' objectives or 'Cognitive and Sample Behaviors.' This is even the case among the Armed Services. Affective Objectives may or may not be addressed. At any rate, many of the learning objectives found in lesson plans direct the action to the incorrect testing substrate. For instance, if the testing platform is solely multiple-choice, one would not write an objective for explaining a concept. The action must match the test, otherwise how can we be sure the task specified in the learning objective was mastered? Much of the above has been addressed in Mager's (1997) chapter *Matching the Conditions*. In addition, if we have a terminal objective written on the same level of Bloom's Taxonomy as its enablers, how can we say we have supported the terminal objective? A group of knowledge- and comprehension-level tasks should have an application test or activity wherein those skills can combine to complete the terminal. This hierarchical "tree" is the activity of the next step in the ISD/SAT, Constructing the Learning Hierarchies.

As the learning objectives are written (whether cognitive or affective), the instructional designer should have an idea or two where they should be tested, the strategies used to elicit learning, the methods to be used, and the strategies to implement. We have already addressed the media/strategy issue (Kozma and Clark), and it should not be relevant to return there, but there are excellent models and methods to generate the products

from these steps. The instructional designer should not, however, pre-suppose any media as a 'one-size-fits-all,' as there are times when a mix is the best formula.

As for the Kirkpatrick Model, the testing of the Learning Objectives falls into Level 2 (Student Learning). Kirkpatrick Level 1 (Reaction) has little to do with the Behavior (Level 3), but the mastery of the tasks in Level 2 'radiate' into the field—on the job—to have the greatest effect on the organization. How the students mastered the objectives and then bring the Return on Expectations (Level 4) to its greatest level of productivity by performing masterfully is of prime importance.

DEVELOPMENT

It needs to be mentioned that the ISD has two types of products: Materials, and People. Occasionally, in the former, the Software Development Team (graphic artists, programmers, etc.) will be carried away with the 'bells and whistles' and 'overdevelop' the product. The focus of excellent-quality instruction should be on student learning, not on making it 'artsy.' This does not say that the substrate is to be drab, but it does mean that development is within scope of the instructional strategy and contract constraints. As for people as being developed, motivation (ARCS Model), and Reaction-Attentiveness (see later discussion on Kirkpatrick Level 1) are keys.

IMPLEMENTATION

In the contracting arena, most projects terminate when the product is delivered, tested, and approved. This culminates the project. Perhaps, though, when training people, this area parallels Kirkpatrick's Level 3 (Behavior), in that people, rather than materials, are incorporated into the workplace, similar to a tree in a garden. When we transplant a tree, we usually add some of the dirt from its pot to its new location. This helps it adjust to its new environment, just like much of our preparation of the student does.

Key 8: Evaluation in Itself is Essential for Everything

As we reflect back on the Models listed earlier (ISD/SAT, ADDIE, Dick and Carey, and Competency-Based), we see Evaluation as separate. As we have described the parallels between the Kirkpatrick and other models, we see that evaluation is included at every stage and step in the ISD process. Two types of evaluation are identified in the Dick and Carey Model: Formative and Summative. The SAT Model adds 'Operational,' consisting of Internal and External substages. Walter Dick and many others cover the Formative Evaluation to the point we do not need address it here, but the Formative, Summative, and Operational relate to Kirkpatrick Levels—Level 2 to the Formative and Summative, and Levels 1, 3, and 4 to Operational.

KIRKPATRICK LEVELS

We have addressed much of Kirkpatrick Levels 2, 3, and 4, but not much in Level 1. Rather than cover the Kirkpatrick Model exhaustively, the reader is directed to the works of Kirkpatrick and Kirkpatrick (and Phillips for courseware, strategies, and materials. What will be covered in the next few statements are areas of note.

Level 1 (Reaction)

Student reaction is necessary to Courseware construction and maintenance because it both strengthens the 'good' and spots the 'bad.' In order to elicit student reaction, carefully-designed questions are generated for their responses on surveys, focus groups, and activities. At DEOMI, evaluators divide the courseware (constituting of

up to several dozen lessons over several weeks) into segments wherein students are asked for their opinions—in the focus groups, they are asked how they reacted to the lesson and its presentation, as well as to identify areas where the environment may contribute to frustration (contributing to cognitive load), and where the instructors are strong and need improvement. One could say that the focus groups are a venting platform as well (sometimes bordering on whining), if conditions in the lessons are not conducive to learning. The surveys are designed to assess how well the students predict they can perform the tasks identified in the learning objectives, as well as to identify areas of concern.

Workplace Effectiveness (Workplace Characteristics during K-Levels 3 and 4)

If we are dealing with people as products, how effective are they as performers in the workplace after graduating? Is there support for workers once they enter or return to the workplace after they have been trained? Are there barriers hindering or blocking graduates from performing their jobs? Effectiveness may highly affect training, because it impacts productivity (Kirkpatrick Levels 3 and 4) and can neutralize readiness. It is highly recommended that Institutions track graduates after they complete training to get a picture of whether or not the standard is being met. In this respect, training then becomes suspect, and administrators will begin to inquire about whether their monies were well placed.

SUMMARY

This chapter covered quite a bit of ground in the Instructional Design Field, identifying eight essential keys for course analysis, design, development, and evaluation. These keys are:

1. Following an ISD Model is essential to planning and execution
2. Evaluation is key to Analysis and must be thorough
3. Go-NoGo decisions must be implemented throughout the ISD Process
4. The Analysis-Evaluation Cycle is essential to ensure standards
5. The Analysis Phase lays the groundwork for teaching the components
6. The Training Task List is essential for establishing the learning hierarchy
7. Learning Objectives must interact with K-Level 2 to empower maximum student learning and application
8. Evaluation in itself is essential for everything

It is recommended that these Keys be kept in mind when designing, developing, and evaluating on-line and classroom diversity instruction, as well as other subject areas.

ACKNOWLEDGMENT

The author expresses deep gratitude to Drs. Dorothy Guy Bonvillain and William Gary McGuire for their willing assistance on reviewing and making suggestions for this work.

REFERENCES

Ausubel, D. P. (1960). The use of advance organizers in the learning and retention of meaningful verbal material. *Journal of Educational Psychology*, *51*, 267–272. doi:10.1037/h0046669

Bloom, B. S. (1956). *Taxonomy of educational objectives, handbook I: The cognitive domain.* New York, NY: David McKay Co Inc.

Clark, R. E. (1994). Media will never influence learning. *Educational Technology Research and Development*, *42*(2), 21–29. doi:10.1007/BF02299088

Department of Defense. (2001). *MIL-HD-BK-29612, part 2A: Department of defense handbook, instructional systems development/systems approach to training and education (part 2 of 5 parts)*. Washington, DC: Department of Defense.

Dick, W., & Carey, L. (1996). *The systematic design of instruction* (4th ed.). New York, NY: Harper Collins.

Gagne, R. M., Briggs, L. J., & Wager, W. W. (1988). *Principles of instructional design* (3rd ed.). New York, NY: Holt, Rinehart, Winston.

Keller, J. M. (1983). Motivational design of instruction. In Reigeluth, C. M. (Ed.), *Instructional-Design Theories and Models: An Overview of their Current Status*. Hillsdale, NJ: Lawrence Erlbaum Associates.

Kirkpatrick, J., & Kirkpatrick, W. (2009). *Kirkpatrick then and now: A strong foundation for the future*. New York, NY: Kirkpatrick Publishing.

Kozma, R. B. (1994). A reply: Media and methods. *Educational Technology Research and Development*, *42*(3), 11–14. doi:10.1007/BF02298091

Loden, M. (1995). *Implementing diversity*. New York, NY: McGraw-Hill.

Mager, R. F. (1997). *Measuring instructional results: Or got a match?* Atlanta, GA: CEP Press.

Molenda, M., Pershing, J. A., & Reigeluth, C. M. (1996). Designing instructional systems. In Craig, R. L. (Ed.), *The ASTD Training and Development Handbook* (4th ed., pp. 266–293). New York, NY: McGraw-Hill.

Payne, C. M., Payne, J. S., & Craig. (2011). *A comparative study of face-to-face and online Iraqi culture training and the development of cross-cultural competence: Studies 4 and 5*. IS-LET (Integrated System for Learning Education and Training).

Phillips, J. (1996). Measuring the results of training. In Craig, R. (Ed.), *The ASTD Training — Development Handbook*. New York, NY: McGraw-Hill.

Reigeluth, C. M. (1999). *Instructional-design theories and models*. London, UK: Routledge.

Tessmer, M., & Wedman, J. F. (1990). A layers-of-necessity instructional development model. *Educational Technology Research and Development*, *38*(2), 77–85. doi:10.1007/BF02298271

Thiederman, S. (2003). *Making diversity work: Seven steps for defeating bias in the workplace*. Chicago, IL: Dearborn Publishing Co.

Thomas, R. R. (1996). *Redefining diversity*. New York, NY: American Management Association.

Tripp, S., & Bichelmeyer, B. (1990). Rapid prototyping: An alternative instructional design strategy. *Educational Technology Research and Development*, *38*(1), 31–44. doi:10.1007/BF02298246

KEY TERMS AND DEFINITIONS

ADDIE Model: A notional model of Instructional Design and Development derived from systems theory. Comprised of five stages (or phases): analysis, design, development, implementation, and evaluation.

Diversity: Diversity is a variety of characteristics that impact individuals' values, opportunities, and perceptions of self and others. The concept of diversity encompasses acceptance and respect, understanding of each other, and embracing the dimensions of diversity contained in each individual.

Results: Kirkpatrick Level 3 (K-Level 3) title; level in which graduates of a course apply what the learned in Level 2 (Student Learning).

Return on Expectations: Kirkpatrick Level 4 (K-Level 4) title; the extent to which targeted outcomes occur as a result of the instruction and subsequent feedback/reinforcement.

Chapter 9
Measuring the Right Objectives

Kizzy M. Parks
K. Parks Consulting, Inc., USA

Felicia O. Mokuolu
Florida Institute of Technology, USA

Daniel P. McDonald
Defense Equal Opportunity Management Institute, USA

ABSTRACT

For businesses to keep pace with contemporary workforce changes, it is imperative to foster an inclusive work environment that empowers, values, identifies, and capitalizes on the workforces' talents, skills, and abilities. Although diversity is recognized as a crucial element for organizational performance, its measurement lacks standardization. Organizations tend to follow simplistic assessment approaches, typically by tracking and measuring salient areas (i.e., easily measured areas such as the demographics of the organization and/or promotion rates). Thus, they fail to evaluate the actual effectiveness of diversity initiatives. Given that this approach is limited and lacks the substance that would inform organizational strategies of the need to increase employee engagement and productivity, the authors leveraged the expertise of two practitioners to discuss methods for measuring the effectiveness of diversity and inclusion programs. In addition, diversity is discussed as related to innovation, employee engagement, and change management, thereby leading to suggestions for future research.

INTRODUCTION

The change in workforce demographics, increased use of cross-functional work teams and reliance on global talent indicate that workforce diversity is not merely a passing phenomenon. To remain competitive in a global business environment,

organizations rely on workforce diversity and inclusion to achieve mission success (Pugh, Dietz, Brief, & Wiley, 2008; Gonzalez & DeNisi, 2009). A diverse workforce is equipped with unique capabilities, talents, knowledge, and skills that can be utilized to accomplish organizational goals. Despite the fact that diversity is a crucial element for organizational performance, it is frequently regarded as a human resource concern,

DOI: 10.4018/978-1-4666-2668-3.ch009

and often relegated to the background in harsh economic times. In order to capitalize on these diverse skills and expertise, organizations must foster an inclusive work environment that values, integrates, and embraces individual differences, as well as similarities (Cox, 1993; Hicks-Clarke & Iles, 2000; Kossek & Zonia, 1993; McKay, Avery, Tonidandel, Morris, Hernandez, & Hebl, 2007; Schneider, Gunnarson, & Niles-Jolly, 1994; Van Knippenberg, De Dreu, & Homan, 2004; Van Knippenberg & Schippers, 2007). Nonetheless, the concept of diversity management is still evolving in general, and lacks standardization, especially in the area of measurement.

To gauge correctly the progress of diversity and inclusion initiatives, top diversity organizations rely on analytics and metrics. Assessments and measures afford organizations the opportunity to track the progress of diversity and inclusion efforts as well as determine the success of such programs. Likewise, metrics and goal setting focus on results and provide direction as well as motivation to reach the targets. Such metrics offer guidance, motivation, and much needed feedback to inform organizations if their diversity efforts are making the progress the organization expected. Given such, a method for monitoring progress in ways that allow for responsive action is imperative. Organizations need to develop appropriate metrics to assess and measure diversity and inclusion. Unfortunately, many diversity and inclusion analytic journeys are misguided. Often organizations are unaware of the strategic diversity and inclusion objectives within their organizations. This neglect fosters misguided assessment strategies. Further, while diversity management is recognized as a crucial element for organizational performance, its measurement lacks standardization. Organizations tend to follow simplistic assessment approaches, typically by tracking and measuring salient areas (i.e., easily measured areas such as the demographics of the organization and/or promotion rates). Thus, they fail to evaluate the actual effectiveness of diversity initiatives. Given that this approach is

limited, it lacks substance to inform organizational strategies to impact business measures. This void highlights the need to discuss the next generation of Diversity and Inclusion (D&I) metrics that are commonly excluded from current research. Two practitioners with a combined experience of over thirty years were interviewed for this chapter. These practitioners are Philip Berry, who currently serves as the Executive Director of the Association of Diversity Councils and is the previous Vice President, Global Workplace Initiatives for Colgate-Palmolive, and Dr. Renée Yuengling, President of Renée Yuengling and Associates and a former Senior Fellow with ICF International and the previous Manager of Inclusion Training with Bank of America. During the interviews, the diversity thought leaders identified barriers to diversity and inclusion success, discussed viable diversity metrics, and raised key areas for future research. Given that a gap exists between research and practice in these areas, the aim of this chapter is to use the insight provided by the practitioners to assist in bridging the gap by providing research from a human resource perspective. We raise questions concerning the barriers to diversity initiatives that are rarely measured, such as employee perceptions of inclusion and their stake in diversity initiative success, organizational culture, middle manager support, perceptions of social isolation, and minority employee burnout. Finally, in this chapter we provide information on the Defense Equal Opportunity Management Institute Diversity Climate Survey (DDMCS), an assessment that measures the contemporary vision of diversity and inclusion.

DIFFERENTIATING DIVERSITY FROM INCLUSION

The term diversity has evolved over the years and its meaning has expanded in scope. During the early 1990s, the term diversity was conceptualized as differences between people based on primary (e.g., race, sex, and age) and secondary (e.g., religion, sexual orientation, and personality) characteristics (Loden & Rosener, 1991; Riche & Kraus, 2009). Over time, the definition has grown in sophistication; presently, diversity has become a broad term that includes overt and covert dimensions, and characteristics that may be used to group individuals. Researchers and practitioners commonly categorize diversity into three areas—internal (e.g., race, sex, ethnicity, and sexual orientation), secondary (e.g., religion, personality, skills, abilities, socioeconomic status, and education level), and structural dimensions (e.g., position in an organization, department, status) (Giovannini, 2004; Kreitz, 2008; Thomas, 2005). In essence, diversity is the mix of who we are (Berry).

As compared to diversity, inclusion refers to the extent to which an organization (organization, supervisor, and co-workers) creates a culture of respect, trust, and support for the workforce, in order to increase business success. The organization's culture, leadership, policies, and practices drive inclusion. Inclusion has to do with behaviors, strategy, and competences, essentially how we are working together (Berry). An inclusive organization recognizes and integrates the attributes of the workforce to successfully accomplish goals (Giovannini, 2004; Parks, Crepeau, & McDonald, 2008). When both diversity and inclusion are integrated into the organization, success can be expected (Giovannini, 2004). Conversely, when diversity is unmanaged and inclusion is missing, marginalized (culture, race, power, and ethnicity) employees will not work to their highest potential. Instead, they are withdrawn and disengaged. They have no energy or desire to be innovative, for example (Yuengling).

A suggestion for leaders is that *diversity* should be separated from *inclusion* in the process of diversity measurement. It is suggested to measure inclusion much like you measure engagement, with surveys (look at the differentials among groups) and focus groups (Yuengling). Another

idea for leaders is to compare organizations that assess diversity and inclusion initiatives at each phase of their process with companies that do not perform this periodic evaluation.

ECONOMIC RECESSION AND DIVERSITY

The current recession has forced many organizations to downsize their diversity efforts. It has been estimated that 7.2 million U.S. jobs have been lost since December 2007 (Davis, 2010). Some organizations have slashed diversity and inclusion budgets, decreased training, and/or reduced departments. In response to this downward spiral, we posed questions to our practitioners to inquire about the nature of this trend. We asked whether this is a sign that diversity and inclusion is simply a fad, or is it a true business imperative? In response, Mr. Berry explained, "The reason for downsizing is because organizations are trying to get to the business critical functions (need for departments to demonstrate value, e.g., generated sales, revenue or decreased costs) and where diversity has not aligned itself with the business purpose in a strong way, these and similar departments (training and development, human resources, marketing) have been downsized." Dr. Yuengling stated, "It could be, but maybe D&I departments are downsized because they are not effective; or else they were effective, and put diversity into the DNA. I do not think organizations believe diversity is a fad, much like they do not think EEO is a fad—but we haven't, as a group, sold line managers and leaders on the fact that it is business imperative."

The comments offered by our practitioners expose a need for research to address the role of middle managers in the effectiveness of diversity and inclusion programs. Middle managers are the vital links between the c-suite and the workforce (Hornsby, Kuratko, & Zahra, 2002); they are typically charged with executing the organization's vision and strategy. In light of this notion, research that investigates factors associated with diversity and inclusion efforts that provide a strong business rationale in terms of organizational productivity would benefit the current literature. Nevertheless, it is evident that middle managers should be regarded as valuable members of diversity councils, and their inputs should inform diversity and inclusion initiatives in organizations.

METHODS TO MEASURE DIVERSITY AND INCLUSION PROGRAM EFFECTIVENESS

A "one-size fits all" measurement strategy, or addressing the issue with a non-systemic approach, is a grave business mistake that could result in wasted resources, decreased performance or a defunct diversity and inclusion strategy. Unfortunately, many researchers and practitioners alike have incorrectly defined the term *diversity* by using it interchangeably with Equal Employment Opportunity (EEO) (racial/ethnic or gender representation). As a result, the bulk of diversity-labeled assessments and metrics have focused on representation or head counting, specifically with regard to race and gender (e.g., Herring, 2009; Richard, 2000). Likewise, this practice is prevalent in industry, and used commonly as a criterion by numerous professional organizations and magazines (i.e., DiversityInc and LATINA Style) to compile and profile top companies for diversity. Frequently, organizations use head counting as a key performance indicator to evaluate diversity success. This common practice of head counting perpetuates a quota mentality, and rewards bounty-hunting activities, which further segregate inclusion from the equation, and may result in a negative image.

With regard to the aforementioned issue, Dr. Yuengling stated, "Head counting is used as a common metric for two reasons—it is easy, and it suits the ideological needs of the community that is interested in representation as opposed

diversity. It is not flawed if all you want to know is 'how many of what types?' Other than that, it is flawed for two reasons:

1. It sets up a mindset for white men that the organization is filling quotas of unqualified women and minorities to meet the head count.
2. It is descriptive about how the organization looks, but it cannot tell you why the organization looks that way. Without the 'why,' you cannot build a diversity strategy or develop metrics."

Head counting is a common metric, since many professionals are tied to the EEO framework, and feel safer relying on demographic data (Berry). In theory, head counting is not flawed, but foundational, and at the very least, organizations need to know the demographics and distribution of their workforce. Since most "head counting" focuses on front line individual contributors, a higher order evaluation is needed to track the progression of minorities throughout organizational ranks. Head counting is especially needed in careers or positions that are known to have glass ceilings, or those positions tied to bonuses and stock options. This is an area that organizations need to explore and make foundational, since diverse talent should be distributed throughout the organization, not to front line positions only (Berry).

On the other hand, head counting becomes flawed when it is the only index or metric that organizations use. Other metrics or key performance indicators should be used in unison with head counting to be most effective, such as supplier diversity goals, training effectiveness, safety problems, movement of people through organizations (succession planning), participation in key external events, number of honors and awards, such as best place to work. Additional indicators include attrition rates, disparities in salary compensation, (e.g., we have accepted that minorities and women receive less compensation than white men), how many individuals are bonus and stock option eligible, are high potentials diverse, who is getting promoted, how often, what is the timeline for promotion and what is the complexion of these individuals. The bottom line is that metrics need to be customized (Yuengling) and should be indisputable and achievable as well as increase buy-in and perhaps utilization. These aforementioned indicators are considered hard metrics that are typically linked to human resources' strategic goals. On the marketplace or business side, possible metrics include examining the connection among employee resource groups and diversity councils with eliminating costs, product innovations and/or increasing sales or expanding into new markets (Berry).

DIVERSITY TRAINING

Prior research indicates that the effectiveness of diversity training programs is contingent on organizations devoting resources to optimizing inclusion and minimizing resistance on the part of the stakeholders (Kalev, Dobbins, & Kelly, 2006; Stevens, Plaut, & Sanchez-Burke, 2008). Although it has been estimated that diversity training is an over $8 B industry (Hansen, 2003), more research is required to examine the longitudinal effectiveness of such training. Commonly, diversity training effectiveness is measured by participation rates. Dr. Yuengling offered more precise methods; she suggested measuring the value of diversity training based on changes in behavior, changes in the organization, and changes in employee engagement. These areas could be evaluated through differentials in self-report surveys or 360-degree assessments. While it is difficult to evaluate any type of training, the way to evaluate training is not by examining what individuals feel or what they learned in the course, but by examining the application of the course material back to the work environment. Thus, the strongest piece is (training) transfer. Did the material carry over

into the workforce and have lasting change, or do the same patterns exist after the training? (Berry)

Along these lines, leaders should clarify the effects of diversity and inclusion training on employee burnout and counterproductive work behaviors such as deliberate sloppy work, tardiness, and absenteeism (Gruys & Sackett, 2003). Furthermore, the employee engagement construct should be examined in relation to diversity training transfer, and perceptions of social isolation in the workplace, which may lead to various forms of aggression.

DIVERSITY AND ACCOUNTABILITY

Researchers and practitioners alike have provided evidence to support the benefits associated with diversity management in the workplace, including increased effectiveness, competitiveness, and enhanced mission readiness (Cox, 1994; Ely & Thomas, 2001; GAO Report, 2005; van Knippenberg, Haslam, & Platow, 2007). For organizations to realize these aforementioned benefits and reach diversity goals, diversity initiatives must be sustained and reinforced through an accountability system (Berry; Friday & Friday, 2003). Employees automatically focus on what they get paid for and therefore the most effective way to link metrics to compensation is not through an individual's pay increase. Going higher in the industry rankings, you will see that senior ranking individuals are mostly rewarded through bonuses and stocks options. If there is a way to tie those types of benefits to diversity goals, it may lead to increased success, especially since most employees may already receive an annual 2-3% increase and maybe 5% in a good year. Therefore, a traditional percent increase is not as motivating.

In general, because Dr. Yuengling works primarily with the Federal Sector the clients she works with do not typically hold themselves accountable in the traditional sense. For Senior Executive Service members there is generally a question on their performance reviews about "supporting EEO" but is it typically a check-off-the-box type of activity. There is also a pervasive but untrue belief that awards (federal version of bonuses) cannot be tied to performance. The Navy (uniformed Navy, not Department of Navy) has started an accountability program wherein the two-stars must report activity to the three-stars and up to the four-star.

For leaders to measure and assess accountability they should explore the following questions: Does compensation (e.g., bonuses and stock options) lead to higher rates of diversity achievement and/or increase the longevity of the diversity initiate? What happens to such programs if an organization is unable to provide compensation for diversity goals? Since some organizations in the Federal Sector do not offer compensation, perhaps comparison research could be conducted between the private and Federal Sectors.

Lastly, leaders should consider implementing a scorecard accountability system. This best practice allows organizations to understand where they currently stand in order to know where they are headed. A typical scorecard is customized to meet the needs of the organization by assigning metrics to initiatives allowing comparison among programs. The scorecard can include any key indicator (e.g., representation, survey results, turnover data, promotion data, and reputation of the organization) that the organization would like to track. The results of the scorecard can be used to track progress overtime and show trends across business units, and departments.

CHANGE MANAGEMENT

Incorporating a new diversity management strategy within any organization is a major change affecting the entire workforce. Therefore, a planned diversity change strategy is favored to align the diversity initiates with the goals, strategy, and culture of the organization (Friday & Friday,

2003). A planned strategic approach best aligns diversity within the organizations strategic goals, missions and inculcates diversity into the culture of the organization. Dr. Yuengling commented, "When you think about it, all diversity really is, is change management. The demographic transition was an exogenous change on organizations; all the rest is adaptation to that change. We use traditional change management techniques and traditional Organizational Development (OD) methodologies and just tweak them for diversity. That is one of the methods to inculcate diversity into the DNA of an organization. However, we must make sure it is driven through recruitment, on-boarding, training, leadership development, performance management, workforce planning, succession planning, mentoring, etc." She continued by stating that "While more and more organizations are managing diversity using change management techniques, they tend to focus on bits and pieces of the strategy such as recruitment or communication and fail to follow a comprehensive strategy."

Based on this understanding, we urge leaders to examine the effectiveness of a planned diversity change approach; specifically, we implore them to study the proposed change phases in the diversity strategy against the executed changes. Furthermore, an investigation is warranted to review the strategic fit and alignment between the diversity plan and an organization's overall strategic position, policies, systems, etc.

DIVERSITY AND INNOVATION

Diversity has been linked to talent management, innovation, and increased productivity, higher quality problem solving, and increased organizational effectiveness (Bell & Berry, 2007; Egge, 1999; O'Reilley, Williams, & Barsade, 1997). Given these trends, diversity and inclusion is often framed as a strategy to gain a competitive edge in the marketplace. Dr. Yuengling commented that diversity and inclusion is not a competitive edge, but it is an imperative, since a competitive advantage implies a unique approach, technology, etc. that one organization possess over its competitors. It was a competitive advantage in the 1980s, but is no longer one; it is a business imperative. She went on to say that all organizations have diversity and if they don't use it they will lose out. Essentially, these types of organizations will be at a disadvantage and fall behind. She then went on to discuss the "woman advantage" and that several studies have concluded that women executives or board members lead to increased profits. This notion was discussed in a recent article that summarized research connecting woman senior leadership with financial success (Dubrow, 2009).

Mr. Berry stated that diversity is a dynamic concept with several levels. Commonly, organizations address social cultural issues through monthly observances such as Black History month. Beyond socio-cultural concerns, the next level is career development, and then to attach diversity to innovation. As Einstein stated, *"when everyone is thinking alike, then somebody isn't thinking."* When we are able to get diverse mindsets to expand a product, such as toothpaste, potato chips, or beverages, this is being innovative. The goal is to determine how we can generate more market share in a community while being more sensitive to those customers' needs. The catalyst for this is inclusiveness. An inclusive climate is tied to behaviors and competencies, and employees who feel included will take into account differences and use these for market insight and develop innovations to reach communities of interest. For example, an organization may involve the millennial generation to use social media to develop a product that incorporates the views of consumers through social media networks in order to get innovation (Berry).

Considering the deficit of research that investigates the connection between an inclusive environment and innovation, we challenge researchers to investigate factors associated with a leader's role and fostering a pro-diversity and inclusion climate

in the workplace. Additionally, we extend the call to examine the impact of an inclusive culture on product innovation and/or performance.

STRATEGIC ALLIANCE BETWEEN STAKEHOLDERS

The structure of diversity and inclusion varies by organization. Some diversity and inclusion departments report directly to the vice president of human resources, while others report to a chief talent management officer (Berry). The important issue is that regardless of the diversity and inclusion reporting structure, these professionals should not operate in a silo. If strategies developed by diversity and inclusion professionals are not aligned with other human resources strategies (e.g., training development, employee relations, benefits, and compensation), the diversity and inclusion efforts will be ineffective (Berry).

In order for diversity and inclusion initiatives to be successful, leaders and D&I professionals must secure a strong alliance with other functions in the organization, especially Human Resources. Since Human Resources own many of the diversity and inclusion initiatives and systems, it is imperative for diversity champions to align with this department, to gain the requisite buy-in and support (Roseboro, 2010). Dr. Yuengling believes that this relationship is a two-edged sword. Partnering with HR is a necessary and relevant part of being a diversity practitioner; however, to the extent that diversity is perceived as an "HR" issue and not a leadership issue, the effort will be less successful in other areas of the organization. It is a sad but true fact that HR professionals are viewed by line officers as irrelevant and not understanding the business. Diversity and inclusion receives more traction when the message is sent by line of business leaders and is not perceived as an HR issue. Further, diversity and inclusion should partner with the training department to ensure that the training curriculum reflects the correct language, and pictures and examples to reflect a diverse environment.

Given this information, leaders and researchers should examine the antecedents and outcomes associated with diversity and inclusion professionals partnering with Human Resources and/or other departments in an organization. Moreover, our practitioners expressed keen interest for researchers to investigate the impact of on-line recruiting of women and minorities, the role of cross-cultural competencies in fostering a pro-diversity climate, and the manner in which diversity issues affect virtual teams.

CLIMATE ASSESSMENT

Research, best practice, and our diversity and inclusion thought leaders emphasized the importance of conducting workplace climate assessments (Sandoval & Yuengling, 2011), also known as employee satisfaction surveys. The concept of organizational climate was originally developed by Reichers and Schneider (1990, p. 22) who defined it as "shared perceptions of the way things are around here." Climate perceptions evolve as part of a sense-making process, in which individual employees retrieve and interpret certain information from their work environment (Schneider, 1975; Schneider & Reichers, 1983). If colleagues sufficiently share this information on relevant organizational events and characteristics, a collective climate perception may emerge.

Over the past 20 years, many different forms of climate have been proposed and empirically tested, such as diversity and inclusion (e.g., Avery, McKay, Wilson, & Tonidandel, 2007), cooperation climate (e.g., Collins & Smith, 2006), procedural justice climate (e.g., Naumann & Bennett, 2000), and safety climate (e.g., Yagil & Luria, 2010). Today, diversity climate is commonly defined as individual, unit, or organizational perceptions of how employees feel their organization values and

maximizes their potential advantages (Cox, 1993; Mor Barak, Cherin, & Beckman, 1998). Specifically, a diversity climate consists of the perceptions that an employer utilizes fair personnel practices and integrates the attributes of the workforce into the work environment so all employees can reach their fullest potential while working toward mission effectiveness. This is accomplished at all levels of the organization through valuing diversity and implementing policies that demonstrate a commitment to diversity management (Cox, 1993; Parks, 2008). Thus, diversity climate is strategic in focus and reflects perceptions of initiatives aimed at capitalizing on the strengths and minimizing potential weaknesses of a employing a demographically diverse workforce (Cox, 1993; Mor Barak, Cherin, & Beckman, 1998).

In order to accurately track the progress of a diversity and inclusion program, top diversity organizations rely on climate assessments to measure the workforces' attitudes and values regarding the climate of the organization. The climate assessment process can generate the data needed to conduct an analysis to evaluate the current organizational culture and work environment as it relates to diversity and inclusion. One such workplace climate assessment is the DEOMI Diversity Climate Survey (DDMCS), which measures climate factors associated with diversity and inclusion. The sixty-five item survey consists of a blend of rating scale and short answer items to measure nine climate factors associated with diversity and organizational effectiveness.

1. Benefits
2. Inclusion
3. Mentoring
4. Justice
5. Personal Accountability
6. Training and Development
7. Leadership
8. Perceived Work Group Effectiveness
9. Work Group Cohesion

The DDMCS allows leaders to proactively assess critical diversity climate dimensions that can impact their organization's effectiveness. The survey allows insight into the perceptions prevalent in the workforces' culture overall and within significant subgroups in the organization. Given such, various groups and entities can be compared and contrasted to provide insight into potentially inequitable perceptions.

CONCLUSION

Based on the expertise of researchers and two seasoned practitioners, the current work presents a practical framework for measuring the success of diversity and inclusion programs in organizations. Although it may appear that the economic recession has shifted the attention of top management to other pressing matters, and reduced the resources allocated to promoting inclusion, diversity is far from being a "fair weather" construct. Our practitioners have reinforced the notion that diversity is not purely an organizational concern to prevent litigation by succumbing to the bounty hunter mentality of focusing on mere representation. Diversity is a business imperative that will equip organizations to survive in their various strategic groups. For this reason, it is vital for practitioners to utilize viable diversity metrics to evaluate the effectiveness of their diversity and inclusion programs. Similarly, it is crucial for researchers to work in tandem with leaders and practitioners to pursue future investigations that explore diversity and inclusion in relation to employee engagement and product innovation in order to advance the state of diversity and inclusion in the workplace.

ACKNOWLEDGMENT

The notions articulated in this chapter do not necessarily reflect the stance of the U.S. Department of Defense, the Defense Equal Opportunity Management Institute, or any other federal agencies on the subject matter. We would like to thank Philip Berry and Dr. Renée Yuengling for assisting with this chapter.

REFERENCES

Avery, D. R., McKay, P. F., Wilson, D. C., & Tonidandel, S. (2007). Unequal attendance: The relationships between race, organizational diversity cues, and absenteeism. *Personnel Psychology*, 60(4), 875–902. doi:10.1111/j.1744-6570.2007.00094.x

Bell, M. P., & Berry, D. P. (2007). Viewing diversity through different lenses: Avoiding a few blind spots. *The Academy of Management Perspectives*, 21(4), 21–25. doi:10.5465/AMP.2007.27895336

Collins, C. J., & Smith, K. G. (2006). Knowledge exchange and combination: The role of human resource practices in the performance of high-technology firms. *Academy of Management Journal*, 49, 544–560. doi:10.5465/AMJ.2006.21794671

Cox, T. (1993). *Diversity in organizations: Theory, research, and practice*. San Francisco, CA: Berrett-Koehler.

Davis, N. M. (2010, February). The great recession's lasting legacy. *HRMagazine*.

Dubrow, R. T. (2009). *The female advantage*. Retrieved from http://www.boston.com/bostonglobe/ideas/articles/2009/05/03/the_female_advantage/?page=1

Egge, S. A. M. (1999). Creating an environment of mutual respect within the multicultural workplace both at home and globally. *Management Decision*, 37(1), 24–28. doi:10.1108/00251749910251996

Friday, E., & Friday, S. S. (2003). Managing diversity using a strategic planned change approach. *Journal of Management Development*, 22, 863–880. doi:10.1108/02621710310505467

Gonzalez, J. A., & DeNisi, A. S. (2009). Cross-level effects of demography and diversity climate on organizational attachment and firm effectiveness. *Journal of Organizational Behavior, 30,* 21–40. doi:10.1002/job.498

Gruys, M. L., & Sackett, P. R. (2003). Investigating the dimensionality of counterproductive work behavior. *Journal of Selection and Assessment, 11,* 30–42. doi:10.1111/1468-2389.00224

Hansen, F. (2003). Diversity's business case: Doesn't add up. *Workforce, 82*(4), 28–32.

Herring, C. (2009). Does diversity pay? Race, gender, and the business case for diversity. *American Sociological Review, 74,* 208–224. doi:10.1177/000312240907400203

Hicks-Clarke, D., & Iles, P. (2000). Climate for diversity and its effects on career and organizational attitudes and perceptions. *Personnel Review, 29*(3), 324–345. doi:10.1108/00483480010324689

Hornsby, J. S., Kuratko, D. F., & Zahra, S. A. (2002). Middle managers' perception of the internal environment for corporate entrepreneurship: assessing a measurement scale. *Journal of Business Venturing, 17,* 253–273. doi:10.1016/S0883-9026(00)00059-8

Kalev, A., Dobbin, F., & Kelly, E. (2006). Best practices or best guesses? Assessing the efficacy of corporate affirmative action and diversity policies. *American Sociological Review, 71,* 589–617. doi:10.1177/000312240607100404

Kossek, E. E., & Zonia, S. C. (1993). Assessing diversity climate: A field study of reactions to employer efforts to promote diversity. *Journal of Organizational Behavior, 14,* 61–81. doi:10.1002/job.4030140107

Kreitz, P. A. (2008). Best practices for managing organizational diversity. *Journal of Academic Librarianship, 34*(2), 101–120. doi:10.1016/j.acalib.2007.12.001

Loden, M., & Rosener, J. (1991). *Workforce America! Managing employee diversity as a vital resource.* Homewood, IL: Irwin.

McKay, P. F., Avery, D. R., Tonidandel, S., Morris, M. A., Hernandez, M., & Hebl, M. R. (2007). Racial differences in employee retention: Are diversity climate perceptions the key? *Personnel Psychology, 60,* 35–62. doi:10.1111/j.1744-6570.2007.00064.x

Mor Barak, M. E., Cherin, D. A., & Berkman, S. (1998). Organizational and personal dimensions in diversity climate: Ethnic and gender differences in employee perceptions. *The Journal of Applied Behavioral Science, 34,* 82–104. doi:10.1177/0021886398341006

Naumann, S. E., & Bennett, N. (2000). A case for procedural justice climate: Development and test of a multilevel model. *Academy of Management Journal, 43,* 881–889. doi:10.2307/1556416

O'Reilley, C., Williams, K., & Barsade, S. (1997). Group demography and innovation: Does diversity help? In Huber, G., & Glick, W. (Eds.), *Organizational Change and Redesign.* Oxford, UK: Oxford University Press.

Parks, K. Crepeau, L., & McDonald, D. (2008). *Psychometric properties for the DEOMI diversity climate scale (DDCS): Overview and final scale.* DEOMI Technical Report. DEOMI.

Parks, K. M. (2008). *Diversity management solutions and the DoD: For defense equal parks, opportunity management institute (DEOMI).* DEOMI Technical Report. DEOMI.

Pugh, S. D., Dietz, J., Brief, A. P., & Wiley, J. W. (2008). Looking inside and out: The impact of employee and community demographic composition on organizational diversity climate. *The Journal of Applied Psychology, 93,* 1422–1428. doi:10.1037/a0012696

Reichers, A. E., & Schneider, B. (1990). Climate and culture: An evolution of constructs. In Schneider, B. (Ed.), *Organizational Climate and Culture* (pp. 5–39). San Francisco, CA: Jossey-Bass.

Richard, O. C. (2000). Racial diversity, business strategy, and firm performance: A resource-based view. *Academy of Management Journal, 43*(2), 164–177. doi:10.2307/1556374

Riche, M. F., & Kraus, A. (2009). *Approaches to and tools for successful diversity management: Results from 360-degree diversity management case studies.* CNA searchMemorandum D00203153. A2. Retrieved from http://diversity.defense.gov/ Resources/Commission/docs/Business%20Case/ Approaches%20To%20and%20Tools%20for%20 Successful%20Diversity%20Management.pdf

Sandoval, B. A., & Yuengling, R. (2011). Getting to "ground truth" in the military: Conducing diversity assessments. In D. P. McDonald & K. P. Parks (Eds.), *Managing Diversity in the Military: The Value of Inclusion in a Culture of Uniformity.* Abingdon, UK: Routledge Taylor and Francis Group.

Schneider, B. (1975). Organizational climates: An essay. *Personnel Psychology, 28*, 447–479. doi:10.1111/j.1744-6570.1975.tb01386.x

Schneider, B., Gunnarson, S. K., & Niles-Jolly, K. (1994). Creating the climate and culture of success. *Organizational Dynamics, 23*(1), 17–29. doi:10.1016/0090-2616(94)90085-X

Schneider, B., & Reichers, A. E. (1983). On the etiology of climates. *Personnel Psychology, 36*, 19–39. doi:10.1111/j.1744-6570.1983.tb00500.x

Stevens, F. G., Plaut, V. C., & Sanchez-Burke, J. (2008). Unlocking the benefits of diversity: All-inclusive multiculturalism and positive organizational change. *The Journal of Applied Behavioral Science, 44*, 116–133. doi:10.1177/0021886308314460

Thomas, K. (2005). *Diversity dynamics in the workplace.* Belmont, CA: Wadsworth.

United States Government Accountability Office. (2005). *Report to the ranking minority member, committee on homeland security and government affairs, U.S. senate.* Retrieved from http://www. gao.gov/new.items/d0590.pdf

Van Knippenberg, D., De Dreu, C. K. W., & Homan, A. C. (2004). Work group diversity and group performance: An integrative model and research agenda. *The Journal of Applied Psychology, 89*, 1008–1022. doi:10.1037/0021-9010.89.6.1008

Van Knippenberg, D., Haslam, S. A., & Platow, J. (2007). Unity through diversity: Value in diversity beliefs, work group diversity, and group identification. *Group Dynamics, 11*(3), 207–222. doi:10.1037/1089-2699.11.3.207

Van Knippenberg, D., & Schippers, M. C. (2007). Work group diversity. *Annual Review of Psychology, 58*, 1–27. doi:10.1146/annurev. psych.58.110405.085546

Yagil, D., & Luria, G. (2010). Friends in need: The protective effect of social relationships under low-safety climate. *Group & Organization Management, 35*, 727–750. doi:10.1177/1059601110390936

Chapter 10
Emerging Technology Trends and Implications for Diversity Management

Mike A. Guest
Defense Equal Opportunity Management Institute, USA

Elizabeth Culhane
Defense Equal Opportunity Management Institute, USA

Daniel P. McDonald
Defense Equal Opportunity Management Institute, USA

ABSTRACT

The rapid pace of globalization around the world is associated with profound changes to how individuals and organizations communicate. Emerging technologies and applications in recent years, such as social networks and virtual workspace tools, are dramatically opening communication, collaboration, and learning opportunities. Such technologies provide a platform for efficient communication among individuals around the world. In parallel, evolution of simulation technologies (e.g., Virtual Environments [VE] and online gaming) over the last decade has resulted in cost-effective, widely-accessible interactive environments that provide rich user experiences (e.g., 3-dimensional). These technology developments represent significant changes in the way that individuals interact with one another, and bring new challenges and opportunities for diversity management. This chapter discusses the current state of emerging technologies and implications for diversity management.

INTRODUCTION

"Globalization means an increase in the permeability of traditional boundaries, including those around countries, economies, industries, and organizations" (Thomas & Inkson, 2003, p. 6).

As these boundaries are removed, the cultural differences between individuals and groups become increasingly relevant. Held (1999) described globalization as "the widening, deepening and speeding up of worldwide interconnectedness in all aspects of contemporary social life, from the cultural to the criminal, the financial to the spiritual" (p. 2).

DOI: 10.4018/978-1-4666-2668-3.ch010

Thomas and Inkson argue that globalization is accelerating due to numerous factors in international business settings such as growth in international trade, international migration expansion, technology allowing for communication and information to transcend quicker and greater distance, organizations restructuring and downsizing, an increase in multinational corporations, and the privatization of state enterprise. The increasing prevalence of cultural differences, coupled with the wider geographic distribution of resources (e.g., personnel, equipment), challenges conventional approaches to organizational management (e.g., centralized versus decentralized).

As with traditional (centralized) organizations, globalized organizations still rely critically on teams that bring together diverse perspectives and utilize multiple resources. In order to coordinate teams, this requires communication, distribution, and incorporation of task-relevant information, harnessing collective effort and information analysis, and making decisions. Coordination of teams becomes increasingly difficult when team members are culturally diverse and distributed physically in different times and spaces. Accordingly, organizational effectiveness will become more dependent on how well it navigates and optimizes within this global landscape (see Caligiuri, Lepak, & Bonache, 2010, for a discussion of globalization trends).

An inseparable aspect of globalization is the underlying evolution of technology that is so profoundly changing how people interact. Consider that the number of people in the world with Internet access in 2006 was over 1 billion, compared to less than 100 million about a decade earlier (Computer Industry Almanac). Over the past fifty years, there have been tremendous developments in computer-based training, interactive simulation, intelligent tutoring systems, animated pedagogical agents, serious games, multimedia, hypertext and hypermedia, inquiry-based information retrieval, virtual environments with agents and computer-supported collaborative learning (Blascovich

& Hartel, 2007). More recently, the explosive popularity of social networking and online gaming has made online interactions an essential platform for communication and coordination. Organizations or teams that are able to capitalize on these technological developments gain an enormous advantage over competitors. Accordingly, diversity management may be strongly enhanced, or hindered, by how well it takes advantage of available or emerging technology.

Diversity management involves leveraging human potential and tapping into unique skill sets. As technology developments are facilitating a changing landscape in communication and interaction, diversity management initiatives must take into account, and take advantage of, this changing dynamic. This chapter reviews recent and emerging trends in technology that have implications for diversity management. In particular, social networking and simulation technologies are discussed with specific examples of recent and ongoing research and development projects applicable to diversity management. Additionally, solutions and recommendations are addressed; specifically, recruiting and outreach, training and education, resource optimization, and program tracking and measurement.

DIVERSITY MANAGEMENT

One of the questions frequently posed by companies is why we should be concerned with diversity? Of course, certain forms of discrimination are illegal (e.g., gender discrimination) and require adherence. Beyond legal adherence, some research has challenged the premise that diversity is always a good thing. For example, Thomas, Mack, and Montaglianai (2004) discuss several potential pitfalls of diversity, including increased conflict among members with diverse backgrounds, increased miscommunication, exclusion of organization members from networks, and lower group cohesion. On the other hand, there is an extensive base of research that has documented many potential benefits of diversity, including better problem solving (Karsten, 2006), better critical analysis (Thomas, 2005), more flexibility (Cox, 2001), and more innovation (Hays-Thomas, 2004). Further, recent research is showing that a more diverse workforce can help companies by increasing their effectiveness of achieving objectives, opening up more access to different segments of the marketplace, increasing morale, and enhancing productivity (Keil, et al., 2007). We may summarize that diversity is not *always* good, but there are major potential team and organizational benefits when diversity is optimized. Ultimately, organizations must understand the business case for effective diversity management and then execute appropriate diversity management initiatives.

Diversity management refers to how a company strategically and actively deals with diversity; it is how a company makes diversity an asset and what strategies it employs to enhance it. Keil et al. (2007) define diversity management as "the active and conscious development of future oriented, value driven strategic, communicative and managerial

process of accepting and using certain differences and similarities as a potential in an organization, a process which creates added value to the company" (p. 6). Keil and colleagues also suggest a number of key factors that are associated with organizational improvements when diversity is increased. The first being effecting culture change and enhancing organizational capital, followed by improving workforce diversity and cultural mix, which is a human capital benefit. Additionally, diversity can enhance market opportunities and expand external recognition and image.

Once an organization recognizes the business case for diversity, it must develop strategic plans for executing those initiatives. McDonald and Parks (2008) have provided an organizational approach to diversity management that identifies unique functions and processes that should be considered in defining diversity management programs. At a high level, the Institutional Diversity Management and Measurement Model (ID3M; see Figure 1) suggest that diversity management success is possible through initiatives in education and training, recruiting/assignment/promotion, operations support, and systems acquisition/development.

Figure 1. Institutionalized diversity management and measurement model (Dr. Daniel McDonald and Dr. Kizzy Parks; used with permission)

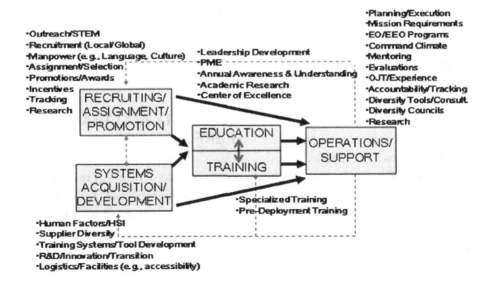

A more detailed review of the ID3M model by McDonald and Parks poses several key potential areas where technology may have a current or future impact. In particular, we will discuss solutions and recommendations for recruiting and outreach, education and training, training systems/ tool development, and accountability/tracking.

DIVERSITY MANAGEMENT CONSIDERATIONS AND CHALLENGES

As developments in technology such as social networking and virtual collaboration tools have emerged, a transformation in communication behavior is occurring. Increasingly, interactions occur in cyberspace via email, chat, or other online collaboration tools. Researchers have demonstrated that 65 to 90% of communication is Non-Verbal Behavior (NVB) such as facial expressions and hand gestures, voice tone, and body language (Yager, Ruark, & Metcalf, 2010). Yet, a majority of online communication, such as email and chat, occurs without such NVB cues, which may have negative consequences on team performance (see Blascovich, et al., 2007).

On the other hand, technology affords some profound benefits to team coordination, and offers potential enhancements and capabilities that exceed existing real-world capabilities. The simple capability to connect individuals in a common communication platform around the globe, in real-time, with minimal cost, provided the explosive foundation that we have witnessed with the Internet in the last decade or so.

On top of this Internet platform, new communication tools and features in recent years have further enhanced interactions. For example, voice-over-Internet protocol (VOIP) applications such as Skype provide the capability to have real-time, "face-to-face" interactions. In addition, virtual collaboration tools such as NetMeeting provide online meeting features such as document and/or screen sharing, file hosting, and chat.

Therefore, what differences might there be between managing diversity in a real-world setting versus an online setting? Are common diversity management issues such as gender discrimination, sexual assault, and racism similar? Although much remains to be researched in these areas, one can speculate that many of these issues could be significantly different. Information about physical appearance (clothes, skin color, etc.) and non-verbal behavior (facial expressions, body language, etc.), are either not available or can be altered with online interactions. Issues of a direct physical nature (e.g. assault) also do not exist with online interactions, although verbal offenses would still be of concern. In addition, consider that in a virtual world, individuals can assume whatever characteristics that they might choose, such as through avatars. That is, a person can choose to have an avatar representation that is of any race, gender, or physical representation. Practical anonymity is also an option. Therefore, there are quite interesting questions about the implications of new technologies on effective diversity management.

Taking this "online workforce" concept further, most (and in some cases, all) interactions among individuals will be captured. Diversity management functions such as case investigation will have unprecedented access to review interactions and online behavior. Not only would this greatly improve investigative data, but also would provide exciting opportunities for researchers and practitioners to analyze and understand social behavior.

DIVERSITY AND TEAM PERFORMANCE

In the context of diversity management, the rapid growth of Internet-based technologies has created new challenges and opportunities. Organizations have unprecedented access to, and utilization of, diverse populations. Diverse teams are increasingly working together on common tasks. This greater access to diverse skills and expertise creates significant potential for increased efficiency and productivity. Conversely, this same affordance to easily connect diverse populations raises important questions about how to best manage and utilize - and not hinder or disrupt - a diverse workforce. What are the applicable theories and practical implications for combining diverse individuals? What is the best combination of skills that might be available for a given situation, and what considerations should there be regarding diversity issues (e.g., communication differences)?

Is diversity good or bad for team performance? It depends. Two primary hypotheses have been proposed to explain the positive or negative effect of diversity on team performance (see National Research Council, 2007). One hypothesis proposes that increased diversity (e.g., of diverse skill sets) results in a wider range of skills and perspectives which is beneficial to team performance. A second hypothesis proposes that more diversity increases the probability of communication and efficiency decrements, and, therefore has a negative impact team performance.

In a review of existing research on diversity, Mannix and Neale (2006) concluded that, "whether or not the diversity effect of the expanded resource pool is positive depends on the nature of the tasks to be performed" (p. 5). A well-defined, static task domain where communication is important might benefit more from redundant or common skill sets and homogenous communication behavior (i.e., to maximize communication efficiency and minimize communication errors.) Conversely, a task domain that has a shifting or unpredictable task domain (e.g., combat mission), might benefit more from having a more diverse skill set so that there is more coverage and expertise across a wider range of possible skill needs. There is a growing need for more research into the impact of different combinations of personalities and skills, and further development of technologies for tracking and managing diverse populations.

CURRENT AND EMERGING TECHNOLOGY TRENDS

Social Networking and Online Gaming

The rapid growth in recent years of online applications for social and entertainment purposes, along with the overall explosion in Web usage, has transformed how people learn, communicate, and express themselves. Online applications such as Facebook, Twitter, and LinkedIn provide a free, widely accessible platform for anyone with access to a computer. Users have readily available features to connect with others such as image hosting, friend/group networking, chatting, and messaging.

The power of social networks as a platform for communication has prompted research into potential applications toward business and other practical uses. For example, Mills (2011) discuss the "Open Sim for Wounded Warriors" project, which developed an online (virtual) social environment for wounded warriors to connect and collaborate. Such applications have great potential to enhance outreach efforts to recruit and include groups that are not otherwise easily accessible.

In addition to social networking, online gaming has seen a surge in popularity. Like traditional games, the variety of online games is extensive. Generally, games provide entertainment for users through engaging individual or group, goal-based scenarios. Yee (2006) reported that "serious teenage gamers" play approximately 20 hours per week. Beyond entertainment, "serious games" are being researched and developed as training tools. Existing gaming features such as shooting, navigation, multi-person coordination, performance tracking (i.e., scores), and replay are frequently the same as training system requirements.

Virtual Collaboration Tools

The ongoing proliferation of Internet usage and Web technologies has prompted businesses and organizations around the world to adopt and develop online collaboration tools aimed at efficiency, productivity, and global reach. These tools greatly expand an organization's pool of potential workers, and strongly impact productivity and management. Existing tools include real-time document sharing and editing, whiteboards, and chatting, all of which are available within virtual environments to create a highly collaborative meeting space for distributed teams.

Current applications of VEs include many interactive and learning experiences (e.g., gaming), global collaboration tools (e.g., virtual meeting spaces), and training domains (e.g., military training). Utilization of these VE features promotes group engagement, enhances conversational efficiency and documentation, maintains group coordination and motivation, and increases overall individual and organizational proficiency.

A recent example of virtual collaboration tool utilization is "Teleplace" (Malan, 2011). Teleplace is an online virtual communication and collaboration environment designed to facilitate effective team coordination for distributed teams. The environment provides a wide variety of collaboration features such as Webcam, voice/chat, meeting recording and playback, digitized meeting artifacts, and shared applications. Users of this technology have reported benefits to distributed teamwork and improved efficiency. Significant reductions in travel and coordination costs are also important business drivers for utilization of this technology.

Simulation and Training

Simulation-based training has a broad and deep research and development community aimed at training solutions. Simulation training has been validated as an effective training and education tool for an extensive range of tasks and domains including aviation, team coordination, spatial learning, medical procedures, and combat operations (Singer, Kring, & Hamilton, 2006; Ragusa, 2004; Bliss, Tidwell, & Guest, 1997). Given the ubiquity of Internet usage, and increased computing bandwidth (i.e., to distribute Web-based simulations), simulations provide a powerful tool for delivering widespread training and education solutions.

Recent trends in simulation and gaming development have resulted in products that are highly interactive and immersive, relatively inexpensive, and widely accessible. Up until recently, for example, virtual environments were prohibitively expensive for individuals, complex to implement and manage, and with technical barriers and limited access. Currently, more affordable, practical virtual environments are commonly available via Internet and desktop connections. Consequently, these technologies are now becoming readily applicable for organizational, training, and entertainment purposes.

The variety of simulation design and implementation options is continuing to expand rapidly. Features such as avatars provide computer-based characters that represent real or simulated, interactive entities. Virtual training developers have great flexibility to create realistic (or beyond realistic) training environments. In some cases, simulated training environments provide essential training opportunities that would otherwise be unsafe or impossible such as aviation emergency procedures and combat operations. In addition, simulation developers have great opportunities to combine various forms of media, such as video, avatars, and computer-based training options, into a unified training experience.

Data Collection and Utilization

In general, the variety of existing and emerging technologies also provide the enhancement of highly beneficial data collection and tracking capabilities. Potentially, all user interactions and behavior within an online environment can be captured, analyzed, and replayed. Simulation systems can capture tremendous amounts of data, including:

- Text, speech, and non-verbal actions (mouse clicks)
- Decisions, interactions, discussions
- Outside documents, presentations, multimedia
- Quantitative data, statistics, metrics

This data can provide organizations with powerful training assessment and measurement options. Further, because much data can be analyzed in real-time, it affords the potential to facilitate immediate feedback or interventions as events are occurring. This capability to monitor, analyze, and track interactions poses exciting opportunities for diversity management, and provides an unprecedented amount of (and access to) data on social interactions and team performance.

SOLUTIONS AND RECOMMENDATIONS

Diversity management programs can benefit substantially by utilizing existing technologies to facilitate diversity initiatives. Primary diversity management functions, such as recruiting and outreach, should be evaluated to identify opportunities to apply available technologies.

Recruiting and Outreach

In the Gore (2000) report to the U.S. Department of Commerce on "Best Practices in Achieving Workforce Diversity," the authors iterate the impact of technology on globalization, and point out the importance of creative strategies to recruit and retain an effective, competitive workforce:

To achieve success and maintain a competitive advantage, we must be able to draw on the most important resource – the skills of the workforce. With the increasing richness of diversity in the world and in the workforce, we need to expand our outlook and use creative strategies to be successful (p. 5).

Access to a wider population increases the potential for identifying and hiring more qualified individuals, which increases organizational effectiveness and reduces operating costs through lower turnover (Keil, et al., 2007). Social media tools such as Facebook provide a platform for marketing initiatives and targeted recruiting for specialized groups.

The capability to provide efficient connectivity to persons around the world greatly extends the reach of organizations to recruit and provide a work platform for persons that might otherwise not be accessible. Consider disability programs that promote and facilitate access to the workforce for disabled persons. Virtual environments have proven effective in coordination of work activities by distributed teams in a variety of task domains (see Ragusa, 2004) and further, have provided a foundation for connecting individuals in realistic (or modified) social environments. This easy access to work activities and social environments (e.g., virtual conferences) supports the notion of engagement of all employees, as well as the importance of diversity in promoting organizational effectiveness.

The accessibility of online VEs to recruiting and outreach programs will allow organizations to attain much broader audiences, and has the potential to save valuable time and resources by allowing individuals and groups to connect without traveling. Virtual career fairs, events, programs, ceremonies, and interviews could take place in a VE. Partnerships could be formulated among minority- and disability-serving institutions.

Training and Education

An essential function of diversity management is the ongoing training and education of personnel regarding diversity policies and organizational culture. A variety of technology options are available to facilitate these efforts, including multimedia simulation, diversity awareness products (e.g., observance materials), and online training. Multimedia simulations can provide interactive scenarios via avatars or other animated agents that provide training based on situational judgments. This type of training is commonly hosted through online learning management systems, which provide widespread distribution and performance tracking. Consequently, diversity education and training efforts can be more efficiently delivered and measured. In addition, straightforward utilization of website hosting (and other online features) is an excellent tool for diversity management functions (see DEOMI Resource Network for an example: http://www.deomi.org).

Innovative ideas are also available to further diversity management efforts. Online games and other training and educational tools can be integrated into overall diversity awareness approaches. For example, online games have been used as supplemental learning tools by providing entertaining and engaging experiences that also have educational value. One can envision games being developed and utilized that demonstrate positive influences of diversity, for example. Interactive simulations can also be used as a training tool. For example, the "EOA Avatar Introduction Demo" (http://www.deomi.org/TrainingMedia/index.cfm) is used to train Equal Opportunity Advisors (EOA) in promoting the value of EOAs to unit commanders. Users interact in a simulated conversation with a Commander to learn about common barriers to overcome in the initial introduction of the EOA role. The same approach could easily be applied to diversity management training, as well as a tool for organizational awareness.

VEs allow one or more users to inhabit and interact with virtual objects, in real-time, including other actual or simulated users (i.e., agents). The immersive nature of VEs facilitates users' "presence," which refers to the psychological sense of "being there" in the (virtual) environment, and interacting first-hand with VE objects. This capability of VEs to immerse users into an environment and promote a sense of presence has proven beneficial to various learning and training domains (e.g., distributed team coordination) (see Singer, Kring, & Hamilton, 2006; Ragusa, 2004).

One decade ago, potential applications of VEs were being researched and developed. VE systems at that time were very expensive to purchase and maintain. Consequently, these systems were not readily accessible to most people. More recently, VEs are now being utilized in gaming technologies, training, and interactive applications that can be accessed from desktop computers, and are drastically lower in cost, and widely available.

Workforce Inclusion and Optimization

While emerging technologies such as social networking are rapidly increasing organizational reach to identify and recruit high-quality personnel, workforces are increasingly becoming virtual, thereby placing significant importance on technologies as essential to ongoing operations (e.g., team coordination). As previously mentioned, virtual workforce applications are already emerging that provide access to populations that might otherwise not be accessible. Geographic constraints are also eliminated in virtual environments, so the potential workforce is exponentially higher.

Consider the common example of technical support organizations. In many cases, technical support personnel may be physically located around the world, and can be further organized according to specialty areas (e.g., hardware support, software support, etc.). As incoming customer support requests are defined, they may be transferred to the appropriate specialty area (e.g., hardware). In some cases, a combined skill set (e.g., hardware and software) is needed. Existing telecommunication and computing technologies are utilized to efficiently connect the right personnel for the task at hand. This capability to connect and utilize combinations of personnel and skill sets is rapidly expanding, and issues of resource optimization and implications of diversity will become paramount as these technology developments continue.

With this increase in virtual workspace utilization, and the associated business drivers (i.e., cost reduction, increased productivity), there will inevitably be a push to migrate tasks and teams toward these technologies as they become more readily available and cost effective. The benefits will certainly prove true in many cases, but organizations must also be cautious of the pitfalls of more distributed and culturally diverse teams. Identifying the optimal methods for integrating such technologies across an organization will require careful consideration for individual and team- work requirements. In addition, given the capability to rapidly connect diverse skill sets, diversity management efforts will need to support workforce optimization through considering combinations of workforce skills (i.e., personnel).

Program Tracking and Measurement

To accurately track the progress of a diversity and inclusion program, top diversity organizations rely on established metrics. Assessments and measures afford organizations the opportunity to track the status and progress of diversity and inclusion efforts, and determine the success of such programs. A consultant with Novations summarized it cogently when she wrote, "What gets measured gets done" (Giovannini, 2004, p. 21). In other words, organizations focus time, energy, and resources on criteria outlined in a measurement plan, while ignoring all other systems that may influence diversity management.

Tracking and measuring diversity program effectiveness should take advantage of available data and measurement tools. Tools such as the DEOMI Diversity Management Climate Survey (DDMCS) (http://www.deocs.net/ddmcs/public/index.cfm) are designed and available to assess overall organizational climate as it relates to diversity. Key areas of emphasis (i.e., areas in need of improvement) can be identified for diversity management initiatives, and organizational trends can be tracked over time as one measure of program effectiveness.

Online survey and measurement tools, such as the DDMCS, should be increasingly utilized as more organizational data becomes available. That is, as more interactions among personnel move into a digital realm (i.e., computer-based), more data will be available for analysis regarding different populations and behaviors.

FUTURE RESEARCH

As new technologies evolve and impact social and behavioral dynamics, new questions arise regarding the appropriate application of those technologies. Both positive and negative consequences can result in this changing environment. In addition, much remains to be researched regarding the implications of new technology on human interaction. Technology must be developed and implemented in ways that complements and enhances, versus hindering, human interaction.

Given the increasing capability to efficiently form teams of diverse individuals and skills, such as in a virtual environment, the essential questions of how to optimize and manage team performance become paramount. Resource managers might emphasize the best straightforward combination of skill sets, but also need to consider potential issues such as personalities, communication styles, leadership and subordinate composition, as well as cultural differences that may arise such as religious accommodation and geographic time differences.

Another important focus of research going forward will be a better understanding of how online interactions are similar or different from real-world interactions. Although some types of online interactions can be very similar to real-world interactions, others can be wildly different. For example, VOIP technologies such as Skype, provide an Internet communication method that is similar to video-conferencing, where relatively direct, real-time conversations among individuals may occur with "real" visual representations of those individuals. Conversely, many virtual environments or other online social environments, allow users a very high degree of anonymity and options for visual presentation (if chosen). Individuals could choose an avatar of essentially any race, gender, or other physical presentation; and, they can remain essentially anonymous if desired. The choice of, and utilization of such technologies, must consider how it might impact interactions and organizational effectiveness.

In addition to implications for different social dynamics, online interactions may be greatly enhanced in innovative ways. Consider the available technology that translates conversation in one language into another. By integrating this type of tool into an online environment, for example, the barrier to communication among individuals that speak different languages is greatly minimized.

Existing knowledge about human behavior can also be integrated into new technologies to further facilitate human interaction. Much research has already established theories and principles of NVB, for example. Online NVB training is available for recognizing facial expressions, aggression detection, and deception. Within a virtual environment, such behaviors could be monitored in real-time to identify behavioral patterns that might otherwise go unnoticed.

There are also great training and education features afforded through simulation and gaming applications. Simulations and games can provide enhanced learning experiences that exceed real-world options. Online training systems provide ef-

ficient, persistent (i.e., 24-hour) access to training around the world, and allow individuals to practice repeatedly. Further, these training technologies provide excellent measurement and tracking options (i.e., trainee performance tracking) to further enhance training effectiveness.

Other enhanced training features are emerging that show great promise to create engaging, innovative learning experiences. As online environments become more integrated with computer-generated agents, these agents may be used to promote learning and interaction for progressive training. "Agents" refer to computer-generated entities that are embedded within online, interactive environments, frequently for the purpose of enhancing learning, training, or entertainment scenarios (see National Research Council, 2007, for a discussion).

As described in the National Research Council (2007) review of agent technologies,

…the potential power of these agents, from the standpoint of learning environments, is that they can mimic face-to-face communication with human tutors, instructors, mentors, peers, and people in other roles….Both single agents and ensembles of agents can be carefully choreographed to mimic virtually any social situation: curious learning, negotiation, interrogation, arguments, empathetic support, helping, and so on. Agent technologies have the potential for a revolutionary impact on behavioral and social science research (p. 10).

CONCLUSION

As discussed in this chapter, advances in technologies are changing how people interact with one another socially as well as within work contexts. Geographic limitations are essentially being eliminated in many cases through online interaction options. In addition, these online interactions have important differences from traditional interactions such as face-to-face meetings. Organizations need to consider the implications for how this changing technology landscape will impact diversity management efforts.

The ubiquity of online interactions is being fueled by a variety of online entertainment and collaboration tools. Online games are continuing to see a rapid growth in popularity, and social networking is now well established as a foundation for social interactions. Complemented by other essential computing tools such as email, chat, and file-sharing, online environments are evolving into an unprecedented "virtual" world with distinct affordances and constraints.

Online users of today have easy access to an extensive variety training and education tools. Accordingly, organizations have a powerful platform to create, deliver, and manage training and education programs. Increased awareness of diversity issues can be extended through online products such as diversity awareness videos. Training tools, such as simulation training for diversity managers, are becoming readily available.

In order for the field of diversity management to keep up with the evolution in technologies, it must take into account this new landscape in human interaction and pursue to adapt progressively. This adaptation should seek to both understand how interactions are evolving, and also how technologies can be utilized and developed that enhance the scope and objectives for diversity management.

REFERENCES

Bell, M. P., & Berry, D. P. (2007). Viewing diversity through different lenses: Avoiding a few blind spots. *The Academy of Management Perspectives*, *21*(4), 21–25. doi:10.5465/AMP.2007.27895336

Blascovich, J. J., & Hartel, C. R. (2007). *Human behavior in military contexts*. Washington, DC: The National Academies Press.

Bliss, J. P., Tidwell, P. D., & Guest, M. A. (1997). The effectiveness of virtual reality for administering spatial navigation training to firefighters. *Presence (Cambridge, Mass.)*, *6*(1), 73–86.

Caligiuri, P., Lepak, D., & Bonache, J. (2010). *Managing the global workforce*. West Sussex, UK: John Wiley & Sons.

Cox, T. (1994). *Diversity in organizations: Theory, research, and practice*. San Francisco, CA: Berrett-Koehler.

Cox, T. (2001). *Creating the multicultural organization: A strategy for capturing the power of diversity*. San Francisco, CA: Jossey Bass.

Egge, S. A. M. (1999). Creating an environment of mutual respect within the multicultural workplace both at home and globally. *Management Decision*, *37*(1), 24–28. doi:10.1108/00251749910251996

Giovannini, M. (2004). What gets measured gets done: Achieving results through diversity and inclusion. *Journal for Quality and Participation*, *27*(4), 21–27.

Gore, A. (2000). *Best practices in achieving workforce diversity*. Washington, DC: U.S. Department of Commerce and Vice President Al Gore's National Partnership for Reinventing Government Benchmark Study.

Graesser, A. C., & King, B. (2007). Technology-based training. In Blascovich, J. J., & Hartel, C. R. (Eds.), *Human Behavior in Military Contexts* (pp. 1–22). Washington, DC: The National Academies Press.

Hays-Thomas, R. (2004). Why now? The contemporary focus on managing diversity. In Stockdate, M. S., & Crosby, F. J. (Eds.), *The Psychology and Management of Workplace Diversity* (pp. 3–30). Malden, MA: Blackwell.

Held, D. (1999). *Global transformations*. Stanford, CA: Stanford University Press.

Karsten, M. F. (2006). *Management, gender, and race in the 21st century*. New York, NY: University Press of America.

Keil, M., Amershi, B., Holmes, S., Jablonski, H., Luthi, E., & Matoba, K. … von Unruh, K. (2007). *Training manual for diversity management*. Washington, DC: International Society for Diversity Management.

Malan, R. (2011). *Immersive virtual workspaces for collaboration*. Paper presented at the Defense GameTech User Conference. Orlando, FL.

Mannix, E., & Neale, M. A. (2006). What differences make a difference? *Psychological Science in the Public Interest, 6*, 31–55. doi:10.1111/j.1529-1006.2005.00022.x

McDonald, D. P., & Parks, K. M. (2008). *3C identifying, applying & assessing. DEOMI Technical Presentation*. Washington, DC: DEOMI.

Mills, J. (2011). *Open sim for wounded warriors*. Paper presented at the 2011 Advanced Distributed Learning iFest Conference. Orlando, FL.

National Research Council. (2008). Human behavior in military contexts. In Blascovich, J. J., & Hartel, C. R. (Eds.), *Committee on Opportunities in Basic Research in the Behavioral and Social Sciences for the U.S. Military*. Washington, DC: National Academies Press.

Ragusa, J. M. (2004, June). Improving integrated project team interaction through virtual (3D) collaboration. *Engineering Management Journal*.

Singer, M. J., Kring, J. P., & Hamilton, R. M. (2006). *Instructional features for training in virtual environments*. Technical Report A103554. Orlando, FL: Army Research Institute.

Thomas, D. C., & Inkson, K. (2003). Does your CQ measure up? In Thomas, D. C., & Inkson, K. (Eds.), *Cultural Intelligence: People Skills for Global Business*. New York, NY: Berrett-Koehler Publishers.

Thomas, K. M. (2005). *Diversity dynamics in the workplace*. Belmont, CA: Thomson Wadsworth.

Thomas, K. M., Mack, D. A., & Montagliani, A. (2004). The arguments against diversity: Are they valid? In Stockdale, M. S., & Crosby, F. J. (Eds.), *The Psychology and Management of Workplace Diversity* (pp. 31–52). Malden, MA: Blackwell.

United States Government Accountability Office. (2005). *Report to the ranking minority member, committee on homeland security and government affairs, U.S. senate*. Retrieved from http://www.gao.gov/new.items/d0590.pdf

van Knippenberg, D., Haslam, S. A., & Platow, J. (2007). Unity through diversity: Value in diversity beliefs, work group diversity, and group identification. *Group Dynamics, 11*(3), 207–222. doi:10.1037/1089-2699.11.3.207

Yager, M., Ruark, G., & Metcalf, K. (2010). *A comparison of instructor-led and computer-based delivery methods for a curriculum to interpret nonverbal behavior in cross-cultural interactions*. White Paper. Unpublished.

Yee, N. (2006). The labor of fun: How video games blur the boundaries of work and play. *Games and Culture, 1*(1), 68–71. doi:10.1177/1555412005281819

ADDITIONAL READING

Bassett-Jones, N. (2005). The paradox of diversity management, creativity and innovation. *Creativity and Innovation Management, 14*, 169–175. doi:10.1111/j.1467-8691.00337.x

Chatham, R. E. (2007). Games for training. *Communications of the ACM*, *50*(7), 37–43. doi:10.1145/1272516.1272537

Driskell, J. E., Goodwin, G. F., Salas, E., & O'Shea, P. G. (2006). What makes a good team player? Personality and team effectiveness. *Group Dynamics: Research. Theory into Practice*, *10*(4), 249–271.

Fletcher, J. D. (2009). Education and training technology in the military. *Science AAAS*. Retrieved from http://www.sciencemag.org/cgi/content/full/323/5910/72

Fong, G. (2004). Adapting COTS games for military simulation. *Association for Computing Machinery*. Retrieved from http://www.ceng.metu.edu.tr/~e120353/fong.pdf

Glastra, F., Meerman, M., & Sjiera de Vries, P. S. (2000). Broadening the scope of diversity management: Strategic implications in the case of the Netherlands. *Industrial Relations*, *55*, 698–724.

Ivancevich, J. M., & Gilbert, J. A. (2000). Diversity management: Time for a new approach. *Public Personnel Management*, *29*, 75–92.

Kalev, A., Dobbin, F., & Kelly, E. (2006). *Best practices of best guesses? Diversity management and the remediation of inequality*. Retrieved on November 9, 2011, from http://rwj.berkeley.edu/akalev/papers/AAPractices041006.pdf

Karr, C. R., Reece, D., & Franceschini, R. (2002). *Synthetic soldiers: Military training simulators*. Retrieved from http://ieeexplore.ieee.org/xpls/abs_all.jsp?arnumber=576007&tag=1

Landis, D., Brislin, R. W., & Hulgus, J. F. (1985). Attributional training versus contact in acculturative learning: A laboratory study. *Journal of Applied Social Psychology*, *15*, 466–482. doi:10.1111/j.1559-1816.1985.tb02266.x

Macedonia, M. (2012). *Games, simulation, and the military education dilemma. U.S. Army Simulation, Training and Instrumentation Command (STRICOM)*. Washington, DC: US Army.

McGraw, K. O., Tew, M. D., & Williams, J. E. (2000). The integrity of web-delivered experiments: Can you trust the data? *Psychological Science*, *11*, 502–506. doi:10.1111/1467-9280.00296

Meyer, B., & Schermuly, C. C. (2012). When beliefs are not enough: Examining the interaction of diversity faultlines, task motivation, and diversity beliefs on team performance. *European Journal of Work and Organizational Psychology*, *21*, 456–487. doi:10.1080/1359432X.2011.560383

Meyer, B., & Scholl, W. (2009). Complex problem solving after unstructured discussion: Effects of information distribution and experience. *Group Processes & Intergroup Relations*, *12*, 495–515. doi:10.1177/1368430209105045

Meyer, B., Shemla, M., & Schermuly, C. C. (2011). Social category salience moderates the effect of diversity faultlines on information elaboration. *Small Group Research*, *42*, 257–282. doi:10.1177/1046496411398396

Musch, J., & Reips, U. D. (2000). A brief history of web experimenting. In Birnbaum, M. H. (Ed.), *Psychological Experiments on the Internet* (pp. 61–87). San Diego, CA: Academic Press. doi:10.1016/B978-012099980-4/50004-6

Ng, E. S. W., & Burke, R. J. (2005). Person-organization fit and the war for talent: Does diversity management make a difference? *International Journal of Human Resource Management*, *16*, 1195–1210. doi:10.1080/09585190500144038

Page, E. H., & Smith, R. (1998). Introduction to military training simulation: A guide for discrete event simulationists. In *Proceedings of the 1998 Winter Simulation Conference*. IEEE.

Piper, A. I. (1998). Conducting social science laboratory experiments on the world wide web. *Library & Information Science Research*, *20*, 5–21. doi:10.1016/S0740-8188(98)90003-2

Pitts, D. (2009). Diversity management, job satisfaction and performance: Evidence from U.S. federal agencies. *Public Administration Review*, *69*, 328–338. doi:10.1111/j.1540-6210.2008.01977.x

Salas, E., & Burke, C. S. (2002). Simulation for training is effective when. *Quality in Health Care*, *11*, 119–120. doi:10.1136/qhc.11.2.119

Salas, E., Milham, L. M., & Bowers, C. A. (2003). Training evaluation in the military: misconceptions, opportunities, and challenges. *Military Psychology*, *15*(1), 3–16. doi:10.1207/S15327876MP1501_01

Sanchez, J. I., & Brock, P. (1996). Outcomes of perceived discrimination among Hispanic employees: Is diversity management a luxury or a necessity? *Academy of Management Journal*, *39*, 704–719. doi:10.2307/256660

Scalese, R. J., Obeso, V. T., & Issenberg, S. B. (2008). Simulation technology for skills training and competency assessment in medical education. *Journal of General Internal Medicine*, *1*, 46–49. doi:10.1007/s11606-007-0283-4

Steadman, R. H., Coates, W. C., Huang, Y. M., Matevosian, R., Larmon, B., McCullough, L., & Ariel, D. (2006). Simulation-based training is superior to problem-based learning for acquisition of critical assessment and management skills. *Critical Care Medicine*, *34*(1), 151–157. doi:10.1097/01.CCM.0000190619.42013.94

Wiseman, R. L., Hammer, M. R., & Nishida, H. (1989). Predictors of intercultural communication competence. *International Journal of Intercultural Relations*, *13*, 349–370. doi:10.1016/0147-1767(89)90017-5

KEY TERMS AND DEFINITIONS

Agents: Computer-generated representations of real or virtual, interactive, entities within a virtual environment.

Diversity Management: Refers to an organized effort to effectively manage organizational issues that relate to diversity.

Emerging Technologies: Technologies that have recently become available, that are undergoing a significant near-term evolution, or that are being applied to one or more new domains.

Resource Optimization: Efforts to maximize the utilization of existing personnel to best achieve organizational or team objectives.

Social Networks: Online communication tools, such as Facebook, that facilitate online social interactions.

Virtual Collaboration Tools: Online work tools that emphasize coordination among multiple users within a real-time, virtual environment platform.

Virtual Environments: Computer-generated environments, which present users with an interactive, real-time, immersive experience.

Chapter 11
The Impact of Culture Bump and Technology on Creating Effective Diversity Leadership

Stacey C. Nickson
Auburn University, USA

Carol M. Archer
University of Houston, USA

S. Raj Chaudhury
Auburn University, USA

ABSTRACT

One practical application of technology to promote diversity leadership can be found in the Culture Bump Approach to cross-cultural communication. This approach to dealing with differences offers the opportunity for leaders to understand the process of connecting beyond differences in a sustainable way. When this is combined with the advantages of delivering training via technology, a new possibility for diversity emerges. In this chapter, the authors examine the culture bump approach to dealing with differences, the impact of diversity leadership being framed within the culture bump approach, and technology's contribution to both.

More than a century of electronic technology, we have extended our central nervous system itself in a global embrace, abolishing both space and time as far as our planet is concerned (Marshall McLuhan, 1994).

DOI: 10.4018/978-1-4666-2668-3.ch011

CULTURE BUMP APPROACH

The Culture Bump Approach emerges from the concept of a culture bump. Archer (1991) defines a culture bump as a cultural difference. Specifically, it is the phenomenon that occurs when an individual has expectations of a particular behavior within a particular situation and encounters a different behavior when interacting with an individual from another culture. Expectations as used in the above definition, refer to the expectations of "normal behavior" as learned in one's own culture (p. 45). Far more than a definition, culture bump includes a theory revolving around the phenomenon and a methodology emanating from the theory. The Culture Bump Approach to dealing with differences (cultural, gender, ethnic, etc.) evolved from this concept and its theoretical underpinnings. The Approach includes culture specific and culture general content and incorporates experiential activities as well as cognitive activities. It includes units on (1) cultural perceptions, (2) cultural communication styles, (3) cultural values, (4) cross-cultural adaptation, (5) emotional intelligence, (6) human commonalities, and (7) culture bumps.

UNIQUE ASPECTS OF CULTURE BUMP APPROACH

While the first four items listed above might be found in any traditional intercultural training program, the last three are unique. The unit on culture bumps explains the concept and the theory and provides a structured strategy for analyzing one's culture bumps. The unit on human commonalities provides two levels of universals including examples of cultural relativism and human existentialism. Along with focusing on the behavior (or culture bump), another aspect of the Culture Bump Approach that distinguishes it from other approaches to dealing with differences is the emphasis on managing one's own emotions about encountering differences. As Kerr, Garvin, Heaton, and Boyle (2006) suggest, the relationship between emotional intelligence and leadership effectiveness is quite strong. When training in emotional intelligence is part and parcel of training for cross-cultural effectiveness as it is in the Culture Bump Approach, the impact on diversity leadership can be very powerful. The Culture Bump Approach provides the means for an organization to move diversity from their periphery, as a separate, ad

hoc responsibility, to a central position recognized as an essential component for success, the concept of diversity leadership emerges. The context for understanding these three content areas is found in a basic assumption about the point of origin for understanding differences.

FUNDAMENTAL ASSUMPTION OF CULTURE BUMP APPROACH

A critical distinction of the Culture Bump Approach is its assumption that the point of origin for intercultural understanding is a specific observable difference, which Archer (1991) termed a culture bump. The Culture Bump Approach is, therefore, interpersonal and represents a paradigm shift from more traditional approaches to learning about cultural and other differences, which focused on the construct of culture. This traditional approach, which relies on understanding the values, beliefs, and certain behaviors of cultural groups, is insufficient for understanding the complexity of human interactions. Abdallah-Pretceille (2006) calls for a paradigm shift away from the concept of culture saying that "cultural traces" or "cultural fragments" are more consistent with the reality of cross-cultural interactions in today's global society. The Culture Bump Approach represents this paradigm shift by shifting the point of origin to a specific behavior that any individual may experience. Thus, a specific, personal experience becomes the driving force for developing four specific skills that are essential in effectively communicating with those from another culture.

CULTURE BUMP SKILLS AND STEPS

Archer (2004) describes these as (1) being able to identify and objectively describe one's own culture bumps, (2) being able to describe exactly what you expect yourself (and others) to do in any situation and then being able to ascribe a meaning to having those expectations met, (3) being able to extrapolate universal characteristics and situations embedded in the culture bump, and (4) recognize and manage one's emotional response to a culture bump. These skills are honed through the practice of the eight steps for culture bump analysis, which Archer (1996) described as:

Step 1: Pinpoint a culture bump

Step 2: Describe the behavior of the other(s)

Step 3: Describe your own behavior

Step 4: List your feelings during the incident

Step 5: Extrapolate the universal situation out of the specific incident.

Step 6: What behavior would you expect from someone from your own culture in that universal situation?

Step 7: What "human" characteristic do you assign to that normal behavior when it occurs in your own culture?

Step 8: How do individuals in the other culture know if and when someone has or does not have that "human" characteristic? What are the criteria that they use to evaluate the presence or absence of that characteristic in their own culture?

OUTCOME OF THE CULTURE BUMP STEPS

Step Eight moves the individual beyond the question of why "they" are different into the question of how "we" are the same. Steps one through four ensure that a personal experience anchors the learning process and includes emotional reactions as an integral part of the process. In addition, rather than defining emotions as negative or positive, it acknowledges their importance and builds in developing emotional intelligence as being essential in communicating effectively across cultures. However, emotional intelligence—as well as perceptions, communication, and cultural values—are all integrated into the culture bump

process rather than being presented as separate components. This grounding of the content into the personal experience ensures that Culture Bump Programs hold the potential for personal change.

CULTURE BUMP AS ORGANIZING PRINCIPLE

Furthermore, as Archer and Nickson (2012) point out, it provides an instructional process that unifies all the elements of a cross-cultural program. It is the organizing principle for integrating content as well as providing a coherent organizational structure for any activity within the content areas. Thus, the Culture Bump Approach builds on the content areas that have emerged through the practice of cross-cultural training along with the types of experiential and cognitive activities and provides integration and personal skill development. Indeed, as Archer (2001) writes:

in culture bump training, the content emerges from the cultural differences of the participants themselves. An important aspect of this approach is that the participants define their own cultural identity and beliefs and in the process of uncovering and sharing their own cultural criteria, their prejudice and ethnocentric "blind spots" are surfaced. This process that is both synergistic and transformational leads to a cognitive and an affective awareness of cultural relativism. It then continues a step further by exploring various patterns for dealing with universal life situations. With this approach, prejudice and ethnocentric "blind spots" are not eliminated but are identified, acknowledged, and become a part of the process itself.

The end result of the process is not only a conscious awareness of one's own values and expectations, but also a starting point for a conversation with the Other that leads to a deep human connection. In fact, the culture bump proves to be the key to rich, authentic human relationships.

CULTURE BUMP APPROACH AND OTHER CROSS CULTURAL APPROACHES

The Culture Bump Approach both represents a paradigm shift in its focus and an incorporation of the experience and knowledge developed through the decades by intercultural communication practitioners.

While cross-cultural communication is as old as the first Homo sapiens who stumbled across someone from a different clan, cross-cultural communication as a discipline has only been developing for a little over half a century. Archer (2001) and Samovar and Porter (1976), among others, have described the historical background from which this multi-disciplined approach to understanding cultural differences evolved in the United States. Multicultural education stemmed from the 1954 decision of the Supreme Court regarding Brown vs. the Board of Education in an attempt to acknowledge the diversity of the American experience and provide equity of opportunity for all groups of Americans—particularly those that had remained outside the national consciousness. Cross-cultural or intercultural communication evolved from the experience of Peace Corps volunteers who delved into the question of how best to prepare anyone for living and working in an environment that is different. An awareness of the many aspects involved in training or educating people in cross-cultural communication emerged from these two approaches to dealing with differences—one domestic in focus and the other international in focus.

THREE IMPORTANT ASPECTS IN CROSS CULTURAL TRAINING

Three of these aspects are clarity about the goals of a training, identifying the types of training and identifying the methodology used in training. The goals in training fall into the categories of skill development, attitudinal change, and information acquisition. L. Robert Kohls (1979) developed a basic list of seventeen characteristics necessary to be successful in intercultural interactions and Hannigan (1990) refined this awareness by distinguishing between traits, attitudes and skills that are associated with effective cross-cultural communication. The goal of developing these characteristics led to various types of trainings. Hoopes and Ventura (1979) list two types of training including culture specific training which gives information about a particular culture or group as well as training using concepts such as "culture," "perception," and "values" or a combination of the two. This type of training can be either didactic or it may be experiential or both.

METHODOLOGY IN CROSS CULTURAL TRAINING

Through the history of the discipline, because of the variables mentioned above, a great deal of attention has focused on the methodology. Fowler and Blohm (2004) and Fowler and Pusch (2010) focus on specific methodologies that have developed in the discipline. These include role plays, cultural assimilators, bicultural communication workshops, lecture with participation, cross-cultural dialogues, videos, games, values-clarification exercises, field trips, readings, and simulations. All owe a debt to Kolb's Model of Experiential Learning. Sugarman (1985) points out that this model posits that experiential learning occurs in a cyclical manner in that an experience leads to observation and reflection, which then leads to a conceptualization about the experience, which is then tested, and this then leads to still another experience. This structured approach to learning is reflected in the culture bump approach to cross-cultural communication. The culture bump itself is the experience and the eight steps each represent various aspects of observation, reflection, and conceptualization. All together, the culture bump steps provide the backbone for Kolb's Model of Experiential Learning within a cross-cultural situation while incorporating human commonalities or universals as an integral part of the self-reflective process. The shift from a macro-cultural approach in Multicultural Education and Cross-Cultural Communication to the culture bump micro-cultural approach (Archer & Nickson, 2012) is a fundamental difference in training for cross-cultural understanding. When the culture bump process is combined with the various types of methods outlined above, a training design for developing effective leadership emerges. *The Toolkit for Culture and Communication* is an example of how that specific combination of process, content, and methodology is applied.

AN APPLICATION OF THE CULTURE BUMP APPROACH

The Toolkit for Culture and Communication, was developed by Archer (2004) for the University of Houston. It also provides an example of the myriad of possibilities for expanding the development of diversity leadership via technology. While the Toolkit was originally used in stand-up training, it was re-designed to take advantage of technology and has been used for training on-line since January 2012. It provides a safe and structured way for individuals from various cultural backgrounds to interact and create a cross-cultural e-community as well as providing a nexus for different organizations to collaborate. Taking a functional training design and adapting it for on-line delivery allows for some possibilities that are unavailable in stand-up training.

ADVANTAGE OF CULTURE BUMP APPROACH ON-LINE

The ability to modularize the contents of the *Toolkit for Culture and Communication* allowed the participant to view the seven segments multiple times either for language (for ESL students) or for meaning. This also allows for much more flexibility than in face-to-face teaching or training. By embedding the links to the videos as well as visuals stimuli, the on-line version is more consistent with younger users' experience of on-line learning (Fowler & Pusch, 2010). Other examples of using technology to reach this generation with cross cultural communication include Botha, Vosloo, Kuner, and Berg's (2008) use of mobile phones to connect young people from South Africa and San Francisco and Engaging Diversity's use of on-line programs to train for diversity in Welsh workforces. Challenges to adapting the learning situations can be met with different technologies.

The recent emergence of social media technologies that connect people based on an individually expressed set of preferences holds promise for a new vision of technology-enhanced culture bump training. Many people are familiar with Facebook and its suggestions of new 'friends' we could make based on demographics, our other 'friends,' etc. A more promising approach that is adaptable to Culture Bump exercises would be a Google Plus-type technology that allows people to create 'circles' of contacts based on a specific criterion. In the Web space of culture bump training, we would have participants placed automatically into certain circles based on their particular responses to visual and other stimuli in the Toolkit. Since real time human-human interactions are paramount to the success of the traditional approach, Google Plus would allow us to seamlessly transition participants who chose this option to enter into 'Hangouts'—places where video/audio chat in real time with several other 'friends' is possible. These hangouts could be time-dependent (existing for a short time while the online training course is ongoing) or they could lead to long-term friendships based on new levels of cultural communication. Another promising technology is the type of collaborative reading and note-taking abilities that can be embedded in a website using *Highlighter. com* code. This technology allows readers of a particular piece of text to 'highlight' a passage, save it to a shared account, comment on it (ala comments in other social media sites) and share it with others. Thus, a redesign of the Toolkit in this type of Web-enabled format would allow participants to automatically connect with others who share similar culture bump experiences. Groups of participants could be easily created who could use the Toolkit materials to negotiate their common culture bumps without ever having to meet face to face. The human component of negotiating differences could flourish without the constraints of time and space required for in-person training and the trainer could easily continue to monitor and guide the process as before.

The Toolkit for Culture and Communication has been used to facilitate educational organizations such as ESL programs to connect with other organizations (Tesh & Archer, 2012; Archer & Nickson, 2012). It demonstrates that the possibility of large groups of students from very different backgrounds being able to contextualize their disparate cross-cultural experiences simultaneously is possible. However, on-line participation allows for large numbers of individuals to be in proximity within the culture bump process and communicating via boards or blogs. The trade-off, of course, is in the level of intensity. For the flexibility and security offered on-line at the same time limits the relational impact of dealing with individuals with whom one may have culture bumps. The laboratory of culture bump training that depends on individuals having authentic culture bump experiences and being given the skills and practice to manage them within context is eliminated by the computer screen. Another concern with technology is the lack of depth of relationship. While social media encourages vast numbers of on-line connections, the intricate interactions that are involved in developing authentic relationships are unavailable with even the most sophisticated of technologies. As Google Plus type technologies evolve, we feel that the future is bright for studying how we maintain and nurture relationships in this new world. This nascent experience

of using the Culture Bump Approach on-line suggests vast possibilities for training diversity leadership when combined with other research on leadership development.

Multi-cultural, cross-cultural, and global leadership, while serving as euphemisms for some, are inter-related terms that share the same goal as diversity leadership; guiding others in building organizations that achieve maximum success. According to Durbin (2007), "A multicultural leader is a leader with the skills and attitudes to relate effectively to and motivate people across race, gender, age, social attitudes, and lifestyles" (p. 426). Durbin further asserts that "cross-cultural leaders must possess cultural sensitivity, cultural intelligence and…global leadership skills…essential for inspiring people from cultures other than their own" (p. 432).

Culture Bump offers an approach to dealing with differences (Archer, 1991). Owens and Valesky (2007) assert "the individual brings unique personal characteristics to the dynamic social interaction process of the group. The characteristics of these internal capacities literally determine how one perceives the environment and makes judgments about it" (p. 370), supports the role of the Culture Bump Approach as a potential tool of diversity leadership. Owens and Valesky (2007) suggest we do not view individual perceptions, feelings, and behaviors as "shortcomings that need to be corrected" (p. 371), so as not to seek individual conformity to expectations and to allow for an understanding of the patterns of those differences and to create productive outcomes for ourselves.

Marx (2006) offers "True leaders…are constantly engaging broad circles of people in the process of generative thinking. They believe that genius can spring from anyone, despite differences in demographic characteristics or values. A 21st century leader…finds discontinuity downright exciting, a breeding ground for new ideas and opportunities" (p. 151). As Marx further examines the goals of educational leaders in preparing students for diversity and change, he asserts "strategic, culturally sensitive communication" (p. 144) as the only possible means to achieve these goals.

Thomas and Ely (2007), suggest "Diversity should be understood as the varied perspectives and approaches to work members of different identity groups bring" (p. 270). This leads them to view a holistic approach to diversity as the key to gleaning the benefits of diversity. As such, Thomas and Ely infer that diversity leadership extends beyond the belief that simply diversifying employees improves effectiveness, to understanding real impact comes from "how a company defines diversity and what it does with the experience of being a diverse organization" (p. 271).

Three successive diversity paradigms are offered by Thomas and Ely (2007), mirroring the evolving social, political/legal and emerging climates of their time. The first is the "discrimination-and-fairness paradigm" (p. 271). They identify leaders that use this lens as those that focus on equality, fairness and Equal Employment Opportunity act compliance. This paradigm, according to Thomas and Ely, engages mentoring, career development, and diversity training to support women and minorities. Success is measured by recruitment and retention goals, not the diversification of work, based on the utilization of new and unique perspectives. Organizations led in this manner tend to operate with fairness, however the quest for color and gender-blindness encourages a "we are the same" (p. 271) approach. Leaders of these organizations diminish the strategic and practical advantages that could be gained from the presence of a diverse workforce.

The second paradigm proposed by Thomas and Ely (2007), is the "access-and-legitimacy paradigm" (p. 275). With this view, developed in the 1980s and 1990s, leaders ought to promote the celebration of diversity in an effort to legitimize their organizations to consumers and constituents and tap into ethnic niche markets with authenticity. This leadership approach, while recognizing differences, does so without analyzing diversity with depth, resulting in minimal understanding

of its impact. Diverse employees hired in these organizations risk being pigeonholed, and are frequently not brought into the organization's cultural mainstream.

The third paradigm, coined by Thomas and Ely, "the learning-and-effectiveness paradigm" (p. 278) recognizes the importance of employee integration, equal opportunity and valuing differences. Leadership however focuses on "letting the organization internalize differences among employees so that it learns and grows because of them" (p. 280). In their research, Thomas and Ely identified eight preconditions leadership must satisfy, in order for their organizations to benefit from diversity in terms of new knowledge, growth, and renewal. They contend leadership must:

- Value diverse opinions and insights
- Acknowledge learning opportunities and challenges that come with diversity
- Hold high performance expectations for all
- Encourage personal development
- Promote open debate and conflict that is constructive
- Offer workers a sense of value
- Have a well stated and understood mission
- Reduce bureaucracy and promote egalitarianism

These changes by leadership will allow an organization to advance from the first or second paradigm to the third. Trying to enter the third without satisfying the prerequisites however will be incompatible with obtaining the benefits of diversity, according to Thomas and Ely. They go on to identify the four actions leaders take, having shifted to the third paradigm. Those include:

- "Making the mental connection" (p. 283) that allows them to understand the impact of membership identity on the social structure of the organization and how the subsequent work is distributed and accomplished.

- "...legitimating open discussion" (p. 285) encouraging employees to openly utilize their experiences (cultural and other) to enhance the organization.
- "...actively work against forms of dominance and subordination that inhibit full contribution" (p. 285), removing barriers that do not promote tolerance of any differences they may have (cultural, racial, religious, sexual orientation, etc.).
- "...making sure organizational trust stays intact" (p. 287) to provide a safe and secure environment for employee authenticity.

Although Thomas and Ely's research identified the third paradigm as the preferred state of being for organizational success, the research did not identify the means by which an organization could achieve the eight prerequisites leading to engagement in the four actions. In this chapter, we contend that the Culture Bump approach is the transformational model that could garner the desired results, especially as practically applied using the various technology resources suggested in this chapter. This truly opens the possibility on a very large scale of Clark's (2004) vision becoming a reality.

The essence of diversity should NOT be to picture diversity as race, religion, sex, age; but to picture it as the uniqueness of every individual. Only by accepting this distinctiveness in others, will people want to help the team as a whole to succeed (Clark, 2004, p. 4).

REFERENCES

Abdallah-Pretceille, M. (2006). Interculturalism as a paradigm for thinking about diversity. *Intercultural Education, 17*(5), 475–483. doi:10.1080/14675980601065764

Archer, C. M. (1996). *A qualitative study of the communicative experience of a Venezuelan and a North American.* (Unpublished Doctoral Dissertation). University of Houston. Houston, TX.

Archer, C. M. (2001). *Training for effective cross-cultural communication.* Retrieved from http://culturebump.com/relatedmaterials.htm

Archer, C. M. (2004). *Toolkit for culture and communication.* Houston, TX: University of Houston.

Archer, C. M. (1991). *Living with strangers in the USA: Communicating beyond culture.* Englewood Cliffs, NJ: Prentice-Hall.

Archer, C. M., & Nickson, S. C. (2012). Culturebump: An instructional process for cultural insight. In Grocci, J., Alsudairi, M., & Buskist, B. (Eds.), *Handbook of College and University Teaching: Global Perspectives.* Thousand Oaks, CA: Sage Publications. doi:10.4135/9781412996891.n26

Archer, C. M., & Nickson, S. C. (2012). The role of culture bump in developing intercultural communication competency. *Psychology Learning & Teaching, 11*(3). doi:10.2304/plat.2012.11.3.335

Clark, D. R. (2004). *The art and science of leadership.* Retrieved December 17, 2011 from http://nwlink.com/~donclark/leader/diverse.html

Durbin, A. J. (2007). *Leadership: Research findings, practice and skills* (5th ed.). New York, NY: Houghton Mifflin.

Fowler, S. M., & Blohm, J. M. (2004). An analysis of methods for intercultural training. In Landis, D., Bennett, J. M., & Bennett, M. J. (Eds.), *Handbook of Intercultural Training* (pp. 37–84). Thousand Oaks, CA: Sage Publications. doi:10.4135/9781452231129.n3

Fowler, S. M., & Pusch, M. D. (2010). *Intercultural simulation games: A review of the United States and beyond.* Retrieved from http://sag.sagepubl.com/content/41/1/94.refs.html

Goleman, D. (1995). *Emotional intelligence*. New York, NY: Bantam.

Hannigan, T. P. (1990). Traits, attitudes, and skills that are related to intercultural effectiveness and their implications for cross-cultural training: A review of the literature. *International Journal of Intercultural Relations*, *14*(1), 89–111. doi:10.1016/0147-1767(90)90049-3

Kerr, R., Garvin, J., Heaton, N., & Boyle, E. (2006). Emotional intelligence and leadership effectiveness. *Leadership and Organization Development Journal*, *27*(4), 265–279. doi:10.1108/01437730610666028

McLuhan, M. (1994). *Understanding media: The extensions of man*. Cambridge, MA: MIT Press.

Owens, R. G., & Valesky, T. C. (2007). *Organizational behavior in education: Adaptive leadership and school reform* (9th ed.). Boston, MA: Pearson.

Samover, L. A., & Porter, R. E. (1976). *Intercultural communication: A reader* (2nd ed.). Belmont, CA: Wadsworth Publishing Company.

Sugarman, L. (1985). Kolb's model of experiential learning: Touchstone for trainers, students, counselors, and clients. *Journal of Counseling and Development*, *64*(4), 264–268. doi:10.1002/j.1556-6676.1985.tb01097.x

Tesh, G., & Archer, C. M. (2012). *Culture bump guides: Culture bump kids*. Retrieved from http://textesoliv.org/culture-bump-guides-culture-bump-kids/

Thomas, D. A., & Ely, R. J. (2007). Making differences matter. In *The Jossey-Bass Reader on Educational Leadership* (2nd ed.). San Francisco, CA: Jossey-Bass.

Chapter 12
Effective Diversity Management in the 21st Century

William Gary McGuire
Defense Equal Opportunity Management Institute, USA

ABSTRACT

The chapter establishes who determines the effectiveness of organizational diversity management while providing a sustainment plan for the coming years. Additional experiences from the author as a diversity practitioner help to establish how culture impacts diversity effectiveness in the U.S. Military as well as business and industry in the United States. Finally, as personality types tend to validate certain behaviors in the international community with respect to culture, the U.S. Military and supporting commercial contractors could easily change the mindset of diversity leaders when they imply that personality type has no bearing on the culture of the occupied country and the willingness to win the hearts and minds (Patreaus, et al., 2006) of those occupied. The Consulting Psychology Press (CPP) and the Myers Briggs Type Indicator (MBTI) can help us to better understand the diverse personalities required to help make organizations effective. At the end of the day, organizational leaders (regardless of their affiliation with the military, education and training, or business and industry) who receive various forms of diversity and inclusion education and training can enhance their overall effectiveness and diversity management programs.

EFFECTIVE DIVERSITY MANAGEMENT IN THE 21ST CENTURY

The use of the term 'Diversity Management' is not as new as some may think. Though we are starting to see and hear more about the use of Diversity Management in the 21st Century, we can be sure

that it is not a 21st Century term. In 1970, a husband and wife team (Merlin and Patricia Pope, Pope and Associates) coined the word 'Diversity' to describe various demographic components needed in organizations across the United States. Merlin Pope passed away during a time when Diversity and Inclusion were being presented as ways to improve the efficiency of organizations. Since his passing, Patricia Pope pushed the 'Diversity and Inclusion' concept from a dream to a major

DOI: 10.4018/978-1-4666-2668-3.ch012

business for Diversity Consulting. Patricia Pope is well known and a leading spokesperson for making Diversity and Inclusion work today. She works with educational, business, medical and military organizations across the United States to show how Diversity Frameworks enhance organizations. One of her most popular topics of discussion is what she has titled *The Illusion of Inclusion,* where she reminds listeners that organizational management tends to present an illusion that they are open to practicing the most effective diversity and inclusion, but when it comes down to people and technology, organizations will become more technologically diverse long before they will have diversity among their people. She has worked with education, medical, business, and the military for the last 30 years on making diversity and inclusion work.

Another person that can be compared to the 'Popes' is Dr. Samuel Betances from Betances and Souder and Associates. Dr. Betances built his diversity company during a time when affirmative action programs were presented as negative actions that would place minorities ahead of whites in hiring and educational programs. These programs were considered positive for minorities, but at the expense of harassment and negative comments for 'getting ahead,' as majority members would say. Dr. Betances developed a Diversity and Inclusion Program that would inspire thousands of organizations to build teams of 'differences' as the strength of the organization. The basic premise of his model is to recognize the contributions from all members that make the organization work. He provides lectures to educational, medical, business, and military organizations across the world to show how performance is not about a person's race or gender, but more about, as Dr. Betances would say, putting *'faces to spaces.'* Managing Diversity in any organization is the primary topic of his lectures. Like the Popes, Dr. Betances has authored many articles and books to help get the word out about making diversity and inclusion enhance the overall effectiveness in the organization.

WHO DETERMINES HOW EFFECTIVE DIVERSITY MANAGEMENT IS IN AN ORGANIZATION?

It is difficult to determine the effectiveness of a diversity management program in an organization. There have been numerous consulting firms that say they have framed the model for the future, but few provided a model that could be used in educational, medical, business, and military organizations. For sure, there are no programs that determine effectiveness. There are people in the organization that can help with determining effectiveness of diversity and inclusion programs. When an organization is a profit-producing organization, it is pretty obvious that the effectiveness of their diversity and inclusion program can be charted through the human relations and budget or finance officers. One way to determine effectiveness might be to have the Chief Executive Officers (CEOs) of organizations provide reports on effectiveness. This could show significant declines or improvements in the effectiveness of an organization, but the truth is, the effectiveness is determined by the leadership and that could be determined at various levels of leadership.

The military uses various surveys to determine the effectiveness of programs as well as the impact of those programs in organizations. The Defense Manpower Data Center (DMDC) is one of the controlling agencies for various surveys and data collection on diversity and inclusion across the Federal Government. Another agency is the Defense Equal Opportunity Management Institute (DEOMI), where the primary survey used is the DEOMI Equal Opportunity Climate Survey (DEOCS). This survey provides the commanders and leaders in organizations a detailed report on the command climate, and it shows the possible effectiveness commanders and leaders may be having on their personnel and their performance. The DEOCS averages more than a half million responses from organizational members each year.

The DEOMI Diversity Management Climate Survey (DDMCS) is another survey used to provide commanders and leaders a 'snapshot' of their organizations' diversity effectiveness. This survey is relatively new, but it is becoming the survey of choice for the military to use in determining effectiveness of diversity and inclusion.

HOW DOES THE ORGANIZATION SUSTAIN THIS EFFECTIVENESS?

Sustaining any effective diversity program can be difficult. The way demographics are shifting and the numbers of people in the majority group today (Whites) are not predicted to be that way by 2050. Today's U.S. population shows that there are roughly 51.8% women (United States Census, 2010), but only half of that population is employed in the workforce. Managing the diversity and inclusion differences of men and women is difficult, but how do we overcome the population of demographics as they shift early in the 21st Century, or do we even consider how to overcome the shift? There is still a high percentage of White males in positions of responsibility across education, business, medical, and the military. For several of these organizations, it will take a significant change in the 'promotion pipeline' to break through the structure that has been 'one-sided' for more than a century. The United States has tried 'Affirmative Actions and Affirmative Employment' as a way to embrace change, but even good intentions have not prospered well for accepting programs that tend to give one group 'status and position' over another group. If we sustain a diversity and inclusion program, it must be a program that includes everyone and it must be managed in a way that shows everyone is included. Team members will not have to say that 'they are different from you,' but will say 'they are different like you.'

The idea of sustaining diversity and inclusion might tend to make some workers and managers uncomfortable. There are people that have concluded diversity and inclusion is 'just another way to give minorities an advantage or get ahead' in the workplace and, with these programs still considered 'optional,' managers are not fully engaged in making them work to the benefit of the organization.

HOW THE CULTURE OF THE ORGANIZATION HELPS TO DETERMINE DIVERSITY EFFECTIVENESS?

The culture of the organization is the baseline for which all programs operate. Each organization has its own culture and each member of the organization brings their individual culture into the organization. The organizational leadership takes on the culture of the organization while anticipating each member (whether new or tenured) has assimilated, but in reality, there are significant differences between organizational and individual culture. If we were to label these differences as diversity and inclusion, then the United States would have the most diverse and inclusive organizations in the world. Since we do not typically equate culture to diversity and inclusion, we might struggle with a concept that attempts to show how culture helps to determine diversity effectiveness.

An organization's Cultural DNA (Bonvillain & McGuire, 2009) consists of various dimensions of diversity such as skills, experiences, styles of leadership, personality type, etc. The leadership (President, CEO, and Chief Operating Officer [COO]) are the culture and, while an organization can function as a small team of leaders, the working members of the organization are what constitute its' culture. Individual culture has additional dimensions that are not necessarily the same as the leadership, but these dimensions must be considered to help determine the effectiveness of the diversity and inclusiveness in the organization. Some of the dimensions might include, but are not limited to, education level, gender, race, ethnicity, language, personality, etc. There is one other cultural dimension that is not considered much in an organization, but is considered as a key to diversity and Cultural DNA: Our American Cultural Identity, or, as I tend to call it, our Hyphenated American Culture. The American Culture is probably more diverse than any country in the world. The Cultural Groups in the United States are not as diverse as the Religious Groups, but they are significantly different. There are many commonalities in our American Culture as well. We may all be classified as American, especially when we visit another country, and American through the eyes of the international community, but we are still very different. Our racial and ethnic makeup, as well as how others see and describe us, will put us into an American Group regardless of whether or not actually belonging to that particular group. As an example, light skin and other physical features may infer someone to be a White American, yet are classified as Caucasoid by Anthropologists. White Americans are as culturally different as 'the planets in our galaxy.' They are German, Irish, Berber, Scandinavian, Australian, British, Canadian, French, and others. This group could be separated by language and custom differences others might assume are common when they are all grouped as White. Every group of Hyphenated Americans will have similar diversity differences, but will still be categorized by their Cultural DNA. We might have better effectiveness in our diversity programs if we could better understand our cultural makeup. We are American, but we are also different (diverse).

WHAT ARE THE DIFFERENCES IN DIVERSITY MANAGEMENT IN THE UNITED STATES MILITARY, EDUCATIONAL INSTITUTIONS, MEDICAL, AND BUSINESS AND INDUSTRY?

The term 'diversity management' is not clearly defined by any particular organization. The *U.S. Military* could be one of very few organizations that specifically define such terms as *diversity* and *diversity management*. The military is as diverse as the society from which it recruits. Diversity management includes the ability to use all of those dimensions to accomplish the mission.

The military is deployed in two completely different cultural environments today. These leaders and managers have been able to change the military culture of 'winning wars by defeating the enemy,' to that of 'winning the hearts and minds of the people while winning the war.' This is a significant diversity management challenge as we are changing the religious accommodations for a diverse force by using our deployed military women to engage women in the towns and villages, when formerly it was considered 'taboo' for anyone in our military to strike up conversations with village women.

There are various definitions in *Educational Institutions* that articulate how to manage diversity; however, none of those definitions are inclusive enough to capture primary, secondary (Loden, 1995), organizational, and personality dimensions of diversity necessary to maintain diversity management effectiveness. The significant changes that have been very positive in long-standing institutions of learning can be perceived as negative though the institution itself believes they are moving forward by identifying particular changes. You might notice some of these particular diversity changes in educational institutions right away. Examples include:(1) gender-separate colleges from the 1950s, 1960s, and 1970s, that are now 'Co-ed' (there are some private institutions not receiving federal funding that remain gender-separate in the 21st Century), (2) racially-separated colleges and universities are now inclusive of all racial groups (some colleges remain labeled as 'Historically Black or other group' while including many racially different groups into the school – this might be perceived to be an affirmative employment program), and (3) grants and scholarships that were given to one group over the other are now distributed to a diverse population on campus. As we look across educational institutions today, it should be very obvious through the eyes (or lenses) of diversity that diversity management remains complex, yet more effective today than in previous decades in the United States.

There has been significant growth in diversity management in the *Medical* community as compared to any time in the last 50 years. There has been a steady increase in the percentages of racially and ethnically different doctors and nurses from exclusively White people to those from the 'immigrant pool,' coming to America to either apply skills they already possessed or to extend newly learned skills in this new and diverse culture, prepared to practice medicine where major disasters have occurred amongst people from a completely different and diverse group. The advances in technology in medical applications have escalated to the point where doctors conduct major surgery through electronic medium from across a major ocean on a patient in a war-torn environment. The likelihood of these types of medical advancements might have never been seen by 'dreamers from the past,' but these changes are but a few we can see that help manage more effective and efficient diversity today and in the

future. The by-gone days of 'Beam me up Scotty' (Star Trek, 1968, television show) are becoming closer to reality as we become more diverse and inclusive with varying types of diversity. In parallel, we see a great example of diversity of people from just observing the bridge in Star Trek.

The last area of diversity management includes *Business and Industry* and how these organizations have included diversity as an opportunity for enhancing outcomes. The commercialization of products and goods, as well as people differences in advertising globalized what was otherwise considered a part of an American-centric product and business. The McDonald's Company, Kentucky Fried Chicken, Pizza Hut, and many other businesses common to the United States found tremendous profits by taking their business to the global market. Today, while we still fight military wars in two major areas, military members can find any of the three previously mentioned companies within a short HMMVE (Hummer) drive from the battle zones.

WHAT ARE SOME EFFECTIVE DIVERSITY PROGRAMS THAT CAN BE APPLIED TO MILITARY, EDUCATION AND TRAINING, MEDICAL, AND BUSINESS AND INDUSTRY ENVIRONMENTS?

The key to any successful and effective diversity program is the organizational cultural awareness. The sustainment of such awareness is a charter for all organizational leadership and the members; Sustainment begins at organizational entry and continues through the indoctrination period for the employee or organizational member. There are no specified time schedules that establish a formal indoctrination, however, organizational members can and will quickly let you know that they have accomplished their 'grace period' (or other word use that says the same thing) and now feel as if they are fully indoctrinated members of the organization.

Several programs encourage diversity and inclusion; recruiting members having specific skills as experienced members depart for various reasons, builds a solid foundation for an effective program; Retaining those members and providing incentives (additional pay, time off to manage family and other quality of life events, etc.) for continued assimilation into the culture of the organization are but a few items that enhance the effectiveness of any diversity program. The military uses such incentives as reenlistment bonuses, potential attendance at schools or training (language schools where a person can pick up a second language), assignments to global regions needing such skills, back-home recruiting, and many others that might help to sustain an effective global military force.

The other types of organizations mentioned in this question and part of the chapter all have similar incentives. Some elect to publicize those incentives to their entire organization while others 'mask' the incentives in ways that force members to 'investigate' existing ways they might help to make and keep the diversity and inclusion program effective. There should not be a member searching for incentives offered to everyone; fair and equal should be the organizational standard for diversity.

HOW DOES PERSONALITY TYPE HELP TO DEVELOP EFFECTIVE DIVERSITY MANAGEMENT?

The primary personality type instrument is the Myers Briggs Type Indicator (MBTI). The MBTI is not the only instrument being used today. There are varying personality instruments diagnosing leaders, managers, and everyone in the workforce regardless of position in the organization. The Five Factor Model, the Four Lenses, and the DiSc are but three of many used to place personalities into positions in an organization as leaders or followers. It is not my intent to justify that one particular personality type is better than or worse than any

other in an organization. Personality types are as different as the number of organizational members and because no two similar personality types are the same, we cannot state that the best or most effective leaders and managers are a particular type. As I think about the use of the Myers Briggs or MBTI, for example, I can only imagine working in an organization that includes the entire group from top management to lowest level worker as having the type identity of ISTJ (Introverted, Sensing, Thinking, and Judging) versus ENFP (Extroverted, Intuitive, Feeling, and Perceiving). The 'I' part tells me *how people get their energy* (this translates to 'internally driven'). The 'S' letter tells me *how people take in information* (this translates to using the five senses versus looking for the possibilities). The 'T' letter tells me *how people make decisions* (this translates to making logical versus compassionate heart decisions). The 'J' letter tells me a person's outer world orientation (this translates to structured and organized world and experiences versus flexible and spontaneous). The ISTJ might not be expected to start work daily before 8AM, but they all show up at 7AM just to show that they are committed to the organization and their need for structure would not be functional if they arrive at five minutes before starting. The fact they are at work early is of no concern to them as they expect arriving early validates their job and organizational commitment. This type of personality loves 'cube city' and can comfortably operate in the confines of the 'cube' with a computer for as long as needed. Of course, they are 'mentally drained' at the end of the day and, for them to be re-energized, they will go home for the day and self-reflect (read or enjoy some quiet time) to get their energy levels peaked for the next day's events. They operate very independently and do not require much supervision. What piques my interests in an organization such as this is: there is minimal (if any) time for socializing (perhaps the term 'venting' could be used, but this environment generates internal anxieties that, if not put in check, could cause significant emotional and physical problems for the organization), blinding you from seeing through the behaviors around the organization. I am not saying 'a smiling face is a happy employee,' or a team member with a 'smiling face' can be hiding or masking internal emotional items. However, I am saying employees or team members will perform much better regardless of their personality type when they are satisfied their leadership is confident in the skills and behaviors and provides a scaffolding environment to work in that is free from any and all emotional organizational time bombs. If the employees and leadership are both ISTJ types and they both 'retreat' to their office for their daily routine, it is difficult for me to understand the effectiveness of the organization.

Personality type must be as diverse (and understood to be) as the dimensions of diversity in the Loden Wheel (Loden, 1995) or the organizational effectiveness could be doomed to failure.

DIVERSITY CHARACTERISTICS THAT CAN INFLUENCE THE EFFECTIVENESS IN ORGANIZATIONS

There are many characteristics that enhance organizational effectiveness. It would be foolish of me to list all of the dimensions at the risk of forgetting one that might be more important to the reader than what I might believe, but I will provide some that seem to be on the 'tip of the spear' for Human Relations Managers and Chief Operating Officers. The one thing that concerns me about this list is that it might lead me into the trap that many organizations find themselves in with respect to diversity and inclusion, which is: the application of 'diversity and inclusion' is the latest way to show Equal Opportunity(EO) and Equal Employment Opportunity EEO) and Affirmative Action (AA) to minority groups. The typical organization will automatically include race, gender, religion, ethnicity, age and ability differences as

its goals for diversity. In other words, 'We have met our vision, mission, and goal by including all of these particular groups.' The organization will forget about the other dimensions that are vital to the effectiveness if they consider only the 'primary' (Loden, 1995) dimensions. There must be leaders looking for skills, experience, education, language (multilingual) fluency, technology familiarization, and many other dimensions that can, and will, benefit the team. A friend of mine who has also been my boss on two different occasions recently made the statement 'Diversity should not and must not stand alone,' and I really had to think about what was being said—but not for long—as I realized the message for me was that diversity—'standing alone'—will never make an organization effective. I do not like being identified as 'different from someone' as much as I like being identified as 'different like someone.' That is my story and I am sticking to it!

SUMMARY AND CONCLUSION

It should be clear from the material presented in this chapter that the leadership is most critical in determining the effectiveness of diversity in the organization. The leadership cannot determine the effectiveness without feedback and actions from the members of the organization. We might find we can sustain effective diversity management by using the philosophy of 'managing by walking around' versus 'managing by sending electronic messages.' This is not to say leaders who use email as their way to communicate in the organization are wrong. The leadership could use a combination of techniques to keep the 'pulse of the organization.'

There seems to be more similarities than differences in diversity management in business and industry, educational institutions, medical facilities, and the military. The need to recruit and retain the best performers and sustain performance is indicative of positive organizational effectiveness. The old saying 'a happy team member' (employee, soldier, etc.) creates an effective organization can certainly help leaders to reduce the number of negative issues when the members are satisfied. The effective diversity and inclusion programs mirroring the community membership having varied racial, gender, ethnic identity, educational background, abilities, experiences, religious beliefs, and others, will be the programs 'of choice' in Americas' future for organizations and the community. The culture and personality type included in the organization should also be considered as we look at building and sustaining effective diversity management. There is nothing wrong with having a group of rocket scientist or explosive ordnance disposal members that are quiet and structured in their approach to work. The task might require more inner thinking and following step-by-step processes to complete the job. The effectiveness of the organization can and will be influenced by varying personality type. There might be organizations having only one personality type? If so, I would like to see how the diversity program is measured.

To summarize the diversity characteristics I see influencing the effectiveness in organizations, I would need to write a separate chapter, so I will not do that. However, I should note 'all of the characteristics discussed throughout the chapter can influence diversity effectiveness in an organization.' Diversity researchers continue to show more diversity does make the organization more effective (Military Leadership Diversity Commission, 2011).

In conclusion, the United States is a 'Salad Bowl' for diversity and inclusion and a 'stew' for culture. The cultural, personality, and diversity dimensions from our community helps us to solidify organizational effectiveness. We can no longer aspire to be a 'melting pot' nation believing the melting together of many will form one American. The ability to maintain our numerous inner cultural differences while remaining American seems to be the solution for the future of diversity. The more we accept our differences, the more alike we become.

REFERENCES

Betances, S. (2001). *Ten steps to the head of the class: A challenge to students*. Chicago, IL: New Century Forum.

Bonvillain, D., & McGuire, W. G. (2009). *Cultural DNA*. Washington, DC: American University.

LeBaron, M. (2003). *Bridging cultural conflicts: A new approach for a changing world*. San Francisco, CA: Jossey-Bass Publishing.

Loden, M. (1995). *Implementing diversity*. New York, NY: McGraw-Hill.

Lustig, M. W. (2009). *Intercultural competence: Interpersonal communications across cultures* (6th ed.). Reading, MA: Allyn & Bacon.

McDonald, D., & Parks, K. (2012). *Managing diversity in the military: The value of inclusion in a culture of uniformity*. New York, NY: Routledge.

Moran, R. T. (2007). *Managing cultural differences* (7th ed.). Burlington, MA: Butterworth-Heinemann.

Pope, P. (2002). *Relationship mapping: A tool for diagnosing relationships*. West Chester, OH: M.A.P. Publishing, Inc.

Steele, C. M. (2010). *Whistling Vivaldi: And other clues to how stereotypes affect us*. New York, NY: W.W. Norton and Company, Inc.

Thomas, R. (1999). *Building a house for diversity: A fable about a giraffe & an elephant offers new strategies for today's workforce*. New York, NY: AMACOM.

Thomas, R. (2001). *Harvard business review on managing diversity*. Boston, MA: Harvard Business School Publishing. doi:10.1007/978-3-322-84445-3

Yuengling, R. (2002). *The 2003 annual: Consulting*. New York, NY: Wiley.

KEY TERMS AND DEFINITIONS

Affirmative Action: Affirmative action is intended as an attempt to promote equal opportunity. It is often instituted in government and educational settings to ensure that minority groups within a society are included in all programs. The justification for affirmative action is that it helps to compensate for past discrimination, persecution or exploitation by the ruling class of a culture, and to address existing discrimination. The implementation of affirmative action, especially in the United States, is considered by its proponents to be justified by disparate impact.

Affirmative Employment: The AEP is designed to eliminate underrepresentation of women, minorities and persons with disabilities, and identify programs to conduct affirmative recruitment for underrepresented occupations and pay grades. The plan includes a comprehensive work force analysis by occupational categories, grade groupings, and series. It identifies barriers to the recruitment and retention of under-represented groups and identifies action items to eliminate those barriers.

Cultural DNA: Extracted from the American University Intercultural Quarterly on Culture (Bonvillain & McGuire, 2009). Our purpose in this article is to metaphorically compare those biological perspectives to what we elect to call American Cultural DNA. Our approach is to look at American Cultural DNA components as having the same labels (or identities) across cultures in America. The difference is the way those identities operate in their given American Cultural Experience. After all, we are all the same in the United States, right?

Culture: The integrated pattern of human knowledge, belief, and behavior that depends upon the capacity for learning and transmitting knowledge to succeeding generations *b* : the customary beliefs, social forms, and material traits of a racial, religious, or social group; *also* : the characteristic features of everyday existence (as diversions or a way of life} shared by people in a place or time <popular *culture*> <southern *culture*> *c* : the set of shared attitudes, values, goals, and practices that characterizes an institution or organization <a corporate *culture* focused on the bottom line> *d* : the set of values, conventions, or social practices associated with a particular field, activity, or societal characteristic <studying the effect of computers on print *culture*> <changing the *culture* of materialism will take time.> Merriam Webster Dictionary.

DISC: The DISC Model continues to be one of the most popular four quadrant behavioral and personality models. The online DISC profile and other disc profiles are based on the research of William Moulton Marston Ph.D. (1893-1947). Marston, who was influenced by such contemporaries as Carl Jung, sought to find theory to explain the behavior of "normal" "healthy" people within a specific situation or environment. Marston, the father of the DISC, was a graduate of Harvard University. It was Marston's 1928 "Emotions of Normal People," which introduced the theory of DISC. He classified four categories of human behavioral type, style or temperament—Dominance, Influence (Marston chose the term inducement), Steadiness or Stability (originally submission), and Compliant, Conscientious, or Cautious, (originally compliance).

Diversity: The condition of having or being composed of differing elements : VARIETY; *especially* : the inclusion of different types of people (as people of different races or cultures) in a group or organization <programs intended to promote *diversity* in schools> Merriam Webster Dictionary.

Diversity in the Air Force: Diversity in the Air Force is broadly defined as a composite of individual characteristics, experiences, and abilities consistent with the Air Force Core Values and the Air Force Mission. Air Force diversity includes, but is not limited to, personal life experiences, geographic background, socioeconomic background, cultural knowledge, educational background, work background, language abilities, physical abilities, philosophical/spiritual perspectives, age, race, ethnicity, and gender.

Diversity in the Army: The Army defines diversity as the different attributes, experiences, and backgrounds of our Soldiers, Civilians and Family Members that further enhance our global capabilities and contribute to an adaptive, culturally astute Army.

Diversity in the Coast Guard: Diversity, though not easily captured in a single definition, allows the Coast Guard to benefit from the talents, abilities, ideas, and viewpoints of a workforce drawn from the richness of American society, including men, women, minority groups, people with disabilities and veterans. Diversity is vital to mission readiness and excellence. It is after all, part of our mission to become the volunteer organization of choice.

Diversity in the Marine Corps: The United States Marine Corps uses the same definition as the US Navy. They do not specifically define diversity.

Diversity in the Navy: Diversity is all the different characteristics and attributes of individual sailors and civilians that enhance the mission readiness of the Navy.

Effective Diversity Management: As determined by the leadership (management) of any organization might include such events as; the balance of race, ethnicity, gender, age, sexual orientation, ability, and other 'primary or secondary dimensions of diversity used to claim diversity effectiveness.

Four Lenses: The 4 Lenses™ assessment is a proven personality assessment which helps organizations build a solid understanding of the innate talent and potential of its individuals. The 4-Lenses™ instrument was created from the research of the Myers Briggs' Personality Type Indicator, as well as David Keirsey's modifications to this instrument in his book, Please Understand Me. This instrument has been simplified to create a more enjoyable experience with longer-lasting application retention.

MBTI: The Myers-Briggs Type Indicator (MBTI) assessment is a psychometric questionnaire designed to measure psychological preferences in how people perceive the world and make decisions. These preferences were extrapolated from the typological theories proposed by Carl Gustav Jung and first published in his 1921 book *Psychological Types* (English edition, 1923). The original developers of the personality inventory were Katharine Cook Briggs and her daughter, Isabel Briggs Myers. They began creating the indicator during World War II, believing that a knowledge of personality preferences would help women who were entering the industrial workforce for the first time to identify the sort of war-time jobs where they would be "most comfortable and effective." The initial questionnaire grew into the Myers-Briggs Type Indicator, which was first published in 1962. The MBTI focuses on normal populations and emphasizes the value of naturally occurring differences.

Chapter 13

Religious Diversity and Technology:
Traditional Enemies Made Friends for Leaders

Charlotte E. Hunter
Defense Equal Opportunity Management Institute, USA

Lyman M. Smith
University of Florida, USA

ABSTRACT

Religious and humanist identity and values, although often invisible, may affect (a) job performance, (b) conduct, and (c) organizational commitment. A 2009 research survey of active-duty service members in the U.S. armed forces investigated religious and humanist identification and values; results revealed areas that may significantly affect a leader's ability to successfully exercise command. A military leader's diversity management plan cannot be effective without a means of discerning, then understanding implications to the military mission of religious/humanist beliefs/values present among personnel. This chapter explores the benefits of survey technology in providing military leaders with needed information, implications for leadership policy and future research areas.

INTRODUCTION

Religious faith and technology are often thought to be mortal enemies. Yet when considered within the parameters of diversity management, these two phenomena may, in fact, be best friends. In this chapter we examine the role religion plays in

a comprehensive diversity management plan and demonstrate the usefulness technology in supporting belief/practice needs, assisting leadership in making informed decisions, and maximizing contributions from all personnel involved while realizing mission objectives.

According to social science research, religious identity and values comprise essential components in the lives of many individuals and groups. This

DOI: 10.4018/978-1-4666-2668-3.ch013

remains true even as increasing numbers of individuals reject the majority religious identity in the United States—Christianity, in its myriad forms—and embrace non-traditional religious systems or identify as having no religious beliefs. Although more than 80% of the U.S. population embraces some form of religious faith, non-believers (a broad group that includes atheists and agnostics and which is described herein as *Humanist*) form their individual identity and establish personal and professional values in conjunction with the majority system, even if their individual reaction to religious belief is one of rejection (Kosmin & Keysar, 2008; Pew, 2008). We contend, therefore, that the rise of non-traditional faith and humanist expressions validates the importance of carefully exploring and identifying the belief systems of all organizational members.

The need to explore and understand religious/humanist identity and values, and their effect on behavior receives further impetus from the fact that, unlike other aspects of diversity (e.g., race, gender, nationality, ability, and age), religious and humanist identities usually are not immediately apparent, nor necessarily known to others via non-intrusive means. Yet, however difficult to discern, religious/humanist identity have been shown to affect not only an individual's personal outlook and contributions made to the organization, but the individual's ability to interact and cooperate with others within the organization (Clair, et al., 2005).

Within a bureaucratic organization such as the military, however, inquiries concerning personal religious identity and religious values may evoke feelings of discomfort, suspicion, and even offense. Intelligent use of survey technology thus becomes a critical and useful tool that allows religious diversity data to be gathered in confidence, ameliorating or eliminating suspicions, and allowing leaders and researchers to explore the effects of this diversity. To illustrate the interaction of religious/humanist characteristics with other personal and community attributes and their implications we use results from the Religious Identification and Practices Survey (RIPS), conducted among over 6,000 active-duty personnel in the U.S. armed forces in 2009.

BACKGROUND

Religion, which in part comprises the individual and societal human response to the divine, in all its complexity and variety (Otto, 1923), exists as an integral, even primary, cultural element and a leading source of personal and collective identity (Geertz, 1973; Bellah, 2006). The last decade of the twentieth century and the first decade of the twenty-first have afforded U.S. citizens – and members of the U.S. armed forces – evidence of the power of religious and humanist belief, adherence, practice, and allegiance in national, international, and local circumstances. In the shocked aftermath of the 11 September 2001 bombings, religious rhetoric was used to inform American public opinion as the Bush administration engaged in militaristic moves, helping to "shape American responses toward both the issues of Iraqi disarmament and an invasion of Iraq" (Smidt, 2005, p. 260).

Within the military, religion acts as an institutional source of power, strength, insight, and confusion depending on the context and the manner in which it is embraced by leaders and subordinates. For those in uniform, thrust into the maelstrom of two violent wars, religion was called upon to play three prominent, visible roles. President Bush employed religious rhetoric to inspire and motivate all who would hear his words. Standing on the deck of the aircraft carrier *Abraham Lincoln*, Bush announced to the ship's sailors and Marines (and, by means of media, to all military personnel and the nation): "[W]herever you go, you carry a message of hope, a message that is ancient and ever new. In the words of the prophet Isaiah, 'To the captives, come out; and to those in darkness, be free.' Thank you for serving our country and our cause. May God bless you all. And may God continue to bless America" (Bush, 2003).

As ethical compass, religion—and humanist values—guided those engaged in the midst of morally equivocal combatant operations (Burdette, 2009; Eberle, 2007; Bess, 2006; Fahey, 2005). In addition, in a third capacity, religion's comforts were widely touted and employed as military men and women struggled to cope with the emotional aftermath of violent actions and situations, to include PTSD, suicidal ideations, suicide attempts, murder, abuse, and the like (Ringdal, 2010; Benimoff, 2009; Lawrence, 2007; Drescher, et al., 2007; Shay, 2002; Verkamp, 1988; Marin, 1981).

These roles (motivator, moral compass, and comforter) seem facially uncontroversial and indeed seem to encompass the best religion offers in times of trial. But from what source, other than personal beliefs and prejudices, do military leaders gain information that allows them to address these and other religiously-suffused policy and leadership questions without violating their constitutional mandate to protect religious freedoms, without demoralizing their troops by playing favorites among the bewildering and increasingly diverse religious/humanist beliefs and practices? How do leaders do this while remaining focused on the successful execution of the military mission?

EXPLORING, UNDERSTANDING, AND ACCOMMODATING RELIGIOUS DIVERSITY IN THE DEPARTMENT OF DEFENSE

Accommodation of Religious Diversity

Claims and perceptions of religious discrimination are not uncommon in the Armed Forces. In 2008, for example, an atheist Army soldier filed suit against the DOD, alleging discrimination directed toward him by Christians offended by

his disbelief, his unwillingness to participate in public prayers, and his desire to hold meetings with fellow military atheists (Kaye, 2008; Blumner, 2008). More recently, evangelical Christian military chaplains (and some civilian counterparts) have claimed the DOD's lifting of restrictions upon sexual orientation—the repeal of Don't Ask, Don't Tell—constitutes discrimination on a chaplain's ability to preach, teach, counsel, and conduct ceremonies in accordance with his or her faith group beliefs (Noah, 2011).

Requests for religious accommodation can also be a source of perceived discrimination and can become important beyond the level of the individual command. Since 1981, for example, Army policy has prohibited anyone in uniform from having a beard or wearing a turban over unshorn hair, all three of which are religiously mandated grooming or apparel for baptized Sikh men (Jordan, 2009). In 2008, however, the Army's recruiting command allowed two Sikh doctors-in-training to retain their religious distinctiveness (unshorn hair, turbans, beards) when they were commissioned and while they underwent basic and follow-on training; when these training periods neared completion, both Sikhs faced pressure to conform to Army grooming and apparel policies. When accommodation of their visible religious distinctiveness was denied at the unit level, both appealed to a civilian Sikh lobbying group, whose members promptly enlisted the support and aid of congressional leaders (Congress, 2009; Singh & Kaur, 2009). Eventually the Army Deputy Chief of Staff (G-1), who presides over Army personnel policy, stepped into this quickly escalating public controversy and approved the religious accommodation requests of both men, allowing them to be exempted, during their current assignments, from the strict, conformist grooming and apparel policies.

Current military policy leaves many such accommodation decisions in the hands of unit commanders who may not possess the training or informational resources to respond in a manner which meets the needs of the overall organization as well as the individuals directly affected. This case illustrates the importance of a comprehensive and consistent approach to religious accommodation at the enterprise level, an approach based on up-to-date, accurate information on religious/humanist identities and beliefs and their implications for organizational success (Hunter & Smith, 2011).

Identifying Religious Diversity in the Armed Forces

Civilian researchers report significant changes within the American religious landscape during the past two decades (Kosmin & Keysar, 2008; Pew, 2008; Wuthnow & Hackett, 2003; Kosmin & Mayer, 2001). New Religious Movements (NRMs) seem to bubble to America's religious surface on a daily basis (Eck, 2002; Grammich, 2004; Rice, 2003; Melton, 1995), while immigrants introduce new faiths or new cultural manifestations of already existing faiths (Wuthnow & Hackett, 2003; Kurien, 2004). Denominational adherence among Christian churches appears to be declining (Cheyne, 2010; Kosmin & Keysar, 2008; Kosmin & Mayer, 2001; Pew, 2008), along with attendance at formal services (Presser & Chaves, 2007; Redden, 2007), with "home" churches reportedly in the ascendant (Barna Group, 2006). Scholars strain to divine the cultural, sociological, political, and economic implications of a nation whose citizens often declare themselves religious, but who deny possessing any religious preference (Steensland, et al., 2000; Hout & Fischer, 2002), and still others wrestle with the dynamics surrounding perceptions of religious discrimination (Wuthnow & Hackett, 2003; Edgell, et al., 2006; Edgell & Tranby, 2007; Harper, 2007; Froese, et al., 2008).

Within this turbulent and ever shifting national landscape, DOD leaders, ever in pursuit of volunteers from all segments of society, may well ask: What does the U.S. military population look like religiously? Until recently little related data existed, and what did exist often did not, could

not, provide accurate answers. Civilian surveys cannot provide the desired information for several reasons. First, despite common myths to the contrary, military members are not representative of the larger civilian population. Rather, military ranks are filled by a self-selecting portion of the nation's population and possess distinctive characteristics in terms of age, gender, education, ethnicity, race, physical ability, and geographic origin, to name only a few (Segal & Segal, 2004). Second, religious surveys conducted in the civilian domain, the primary resources for statistical information on religion in the U.S., address the population at large or specific demographic groups, and provide little or no information on military service. Third, access to military members by social science researchers is tightly controlled, with most surveys conducted only by or under the auspices of the Defense Manpower Data Center (DMDC) and related entities within the individual services. Fourth, many civilian surveys ask questions with the explicit goal of equating religious belief with political activity (Wald, 1989; Owen, 1991; Mockabee, 2007); politically-saturated sampling, if conducted in the DOD, would run afoul of the Hatch Act and military regulations (DODD 1344.10, 2008; Schultz, 2006; Hatch Act, 1993). Finally, the limitations and complexity of religious identification sampling and survey work become amplified in the military's hierarchical, authoritarian culture. Religious/humanist identification and beliefs cannot, for example, be considered in conjunction with determining official evaluations, current or future assignments, or other consideration of an individual's performance or suitability for advancement; only when an individual requests an accommodation in support of his or her religious preference does a service member's religious/humanist identification become a legitimate concern of leaders (DODI 1300.17, 2009).

This information abyss is particularly ominous in light of the growth and influence of minority religious/humanist groups in the nation and, consequently, within the U.S. military and DOD workforces, and is of special concern when considering religiously focused sampling procedures within the DOD setting.[1] Because the number of individuals who identify with a minority faith is small relative to the total U.S. population, social scientists using survey methodologies standard in large-scale national polls rarely achieve sufficient numbers of minority religious adherents to achieve statistical significance, whose members regularly are relegated to the "other" category.

These common logistical and statistical constraints complicate exploration of the content and implications of minority faith-group and humanist characteristics. The inability to study minority groups results in a distressing lack of empirical information that might be of interest and assistance to military leaders, particularly if it includes data concerning those faith groups whose presence in the military is increasing or decreasing, even if in small increments. Military members from these communities may claim and/or require special accommodations, and in the DOD, where the religious identification and needs of every military member are strongly protected by policy and law, all requests for accommodation of faith-related practices must be afforded careful consideration; denial or approval may prompt high-level review and, occasionally, revision of military policies and doctrinal standards (DODI 1300.17, 2009; Jolly, 2007; RFRA, 2006; Rosenzweig, 1996).

Additionally, military leaders must anticipate and manage the unique stresses and demands placed upon a population whose work and training are focused on a national defense mission twenty-four hours a day, every day of the year. This population does not enjoy the freedom of returning home each evening or attending faith-specific houses of worship on their Sabbath; instead, they often abide together in field training environments, in barracks, or in remote or combat areas in which they are isolated from friends, family, and familiar cultural support for months at a time. In such tight circumstances, religious differences may and do gain significance not normally encountered in the civilian world. The quest for answers to these real world issues drive surveys (those conducted in the military context) to be less focused on theoretical concerns and more focused on information directly applicable to religious/humanist identification and its impact on other personnel and mission concerns.

Two Indispensables: DMDC and DEOMI Religious Surveys in the DOD

Within the DOD, responsibility for gathering information on the religious beliefs and practices of military personnel is shared between the individual services and the Defense Manpower and Data Center (DMDC). The DMDC gathers and maintains official demographic data on military members, aggregating a wide variety of personnel-related data collected about military members by the individual services at the time of enlistment, including voluntarily supplied information on religious/humanist affiliation. DMDC figures then, are not statistics as such, but rather are parameters accounting for 100% of the population. Religious/humanist identification data are based on self-reported information collected from new military members who respond to direct questions regarding religious identity at a Military Entrance Processing Station (MEPS).

DMDC data provide a picture of military members at entry. Significant concerns exist, however, regarding the accuracy of the Center's data collected and published when applied to the current force, questions that affect the utilitarian knowledge needs of military commanders. First, the atmosphere within each MEPS may be described as stressful, even intimidating. In such an atmosphere, members of minority faith groups and/or humanists may avoid advertising themselves as different and may avoid the question regarding religious/humanist identification altogether (Eisman, 2008). Second, after initial entry onto active duty (or the reserves/Guard), updates regarding religious identification occur only if service members voluntarily, deliberately choose and know how to do so. RIPS revealed 18% of respondents changed religious affiliation after entering the military. Relying solely on entry level identification presents a knowledge gap of potentially significant consequence for military leaders. Third, the accuracy of the information collected at MEPS may be compromised through the data transfer and interpretation process due to the differing programs used by the two organizations.

The RIPS serves as a complimentary and, we believe, essential source of data regarding religion/humanism in the military setting in that it provides a high level of detail with regard to this aspect of cultural identity and beliefs. Because it is integral to the overall research efforts of the Defense Equal Opportunity Management Institute (DEOMI), it has the additional benefit of tie-in with DEOMI's Defense Equal Opportunity Climate Survey (DEOCS), a commander's management tool that permits proactive assessment of critical organizational climate dimensions that may affect a military unit's effectiveness.[2] The DEOCS assesses thirteen climate factors in three areas—military Equal Opportunity (EO), civilian Equal Employment Opportunity (EEO), and Organizational Effectiveness (OE)—by posing questions answered via a five-point Likert-type scale.

In 2009, DEOMI pioneered the RIPS, an extension to the DEOCS focused on religious/humanist identification and beliefs. The RIPS was designed as a thirty-question, voluntary extension presented to DEOCS participants upon completion of the standard question set. Each participant was given the opportunity to opt out of the RIPS, and all were assured of confidentiality. Attaching the RIPS to the DEOCS permitted the comparison of religious/humanist identity and beliefs to other aspects of diversity management without compromising the identity of respondents.

The initial RIPS was designed to investigate nine factors believed to provide reliable estimates of an individual's religious/humanist identity,

behaviors, and how these are intertwined with leadership imperatives regarding military education and training, personnel policy, and operational planning. A major design objective separated religious/humanist beliefs into component factors not specifically related to one or a few religious traditions. After asking respondents about their views, beliefs, and behavior, the RIPS solicited respondents' religious identification in terms of denominational affiliation (or other appropriate category) and asked if respondents' identification or beliefs had changed since entering the military.

Technological Advantages of the RIPS

Religious faiths are nothing if not multitudinous, and to include every variation of Islam, or the myriad Baptist offshoots, in traditional paper-and-pencil survey instruments would be cumbersome and possibly counterproductive. One principal advantage of the RIPS lies in the use of a drop-down menu that allowed respondents to choose from a wide variety of historical denominations and new (or newer) religious/humanist associations. For example, those who initially chose *Islam* as their primary identification then saw a drop-down menu that listed sixteen theologically distinct Muslim groups from which respondents could choose; ten of these were claimed by respondents among the total of twenty-seven individuals who identified as *Muslim*. This indicated greater diversity among *Muslims* in the military than normally is assumed or reported by the DMDC. Certainly, there can be no doubt that significant theological and *praxis* variations exist between *Muslim* sects, and knowledge of this diversity may serve military leaders by prompting consideration of Islamic variations among military members.

A second advantage of the RIPS lay in the path by which individuals found, and then identified, their religious/humanist traditions. For example, evangelical Christianity constitutes a variously defined and large group that does not necessarily coincide with traditional Christian denominational structures in the U.S. (Smith, 2008; Yong, 2007; Clairborne, 2005). To allow respondents the greatest possible flexibility in self-identification, the drop-down menu included a category entitled *Evangelical*, positioned at the same level as major denominational identities. A service member, therefore, who self-identified principally as an evangelical Christian, and secondarily expressed his or her evangelical faith through membership in or affiliation with the Presbyterian Church in America (an evangelical church), could find that faith group listing by accessing the *Evangelical* menu, then reviewing the list of denominations in a subsequent drop-down menu. This avoids a common issue of equating evangelical, a theological distinctive with denominational identity which is an institutional characteristic (Yong, 2007; Clairborne, 2005).

Yet a third advantage of the RIPS lies in the assurance of privacy provided to participants. These men and women, most of whom have at least a few months of service time under their belts, may be more likely to reveal their religious identification than was the case when asked at the MEPS, particularly if they identify as a religious minority or humanist. This confidentiality is critical not only in gaining more accurate information but also being able to apply it for education, training, and doctrine.

Military Religious Demographics

Table 1 contains figures obtained from DMDC and RIPS illustrating differences in results obtained for the same population, but obtained at differing points in military service (entry versus post-entry).

A significant difference between the two methods is seen in the data error; the RIPS has an error of less than 1%, compared with DMDC's data error of nearly 9%. This may be due to the result of the increased numbers of specific religious/humanist groups in the DEOMI data as well as the potential loss of records involved in the DMDC data transfer process and coding limitations.

The other significant difference between the two surveys lies in the relatively higher percentages of minority faith/humanist traditions reported in the RIPS. RIPS data provide higher numbers of people who self-identify as *Jews, Muslim, Pagan, Eastern*, and *Humanist* than does DMDC, and these figures are more similar to those reported in the American Religious Identification Survey (Kosmin & Keysar, 2008) and the Pew Religious Landscape Survey (Pew, 2008) than are the DMDC figures. This, in conjunction with the decrease in data error, may reflect and reinforce the advantages already discussed of administering a religious

Table 1. Faith group identification from DEOMI and DMDC

Faith Group	DEOMI (%)	DMDC (%)
Adventist	2.77	0.34
Baptist	17.56	13.88
Brethren	0.27	0.04
Congregational	2.23	0.55
Episcopal	0.86	0.66
Evangelical	0.99	0.55
Lutheran	2.57	2.36
Methodist	3.7	3.61
Pentecostal/Charismatic	2.89	1.52
Presbyterian	1.69	0.93
Other Protestant	6.54	4.92
Catholic	20.11	20.22
Orthodox	0.4	0.11
Other Christian	3.28	19.56
Jewish	1.09	0.32
Muslim	0.45	0.25
Pagan	1.18	0.17
Eastern	0.87	0.42
Less common	1.19	0.62
Humanist	3.61	0.55
No religious preference	25.5	19.55
Data error	0.25	8.87
Total	100	100

identification survey in a confidential setting and *after* a military member has become comfortable in their military identity and culture.

Job Performance

The RIPS permitted comparison of self-reported religious/humanist identity to other factors of interest such as job performance. The data revealed that those who identified as *Pagans, Jews, Catholics, Humanists*, and *No Religious Preference* viewed their religious beliefs as less important in how they do their jobs than did *Mainline Protestants* (the control group). In contrast, *Other Protestants* (those groups known to be more conservative than mainline denominations) and *Muslims* viewed religious beliefs as more important to job performance than the control group (see Table 2).

These findings pose a challenge to traditional leadership methods within the armed forces, particularly in light of the large numbers who

Table 2. How important is religion to job performance?

Independent Variable	Coefficient	t statistic	Significance
Other Protestant	-0.2302705	-3.46	0.001
Roman Catholic	0.2927883	6.38	0
Jewish	0.341673	2.22	0.026
Muslim	-0.3810857	-1.61	0.108
Pagan	0.5623333	3.78	0
Humanist	1.821697	20.89	0
NRP	1.315561	32.83	0
Gender	-0.1822409	-4.14	0
Age	-0.1530204	-8.41	0
Officer/Enlisted	0.0622062	2.18	0.029
Hispanic	-0.2876433	-6.25	0
American Indian	-0.1037085	-1.21	0.225
Asian	-0.1866827	-2.31	0.021
Black	-0.5150359	-11.39	0
Hawaiian	0.0277092	0.23	0.816
Constant	2.947442	28.73	0

identified as *Humanist* or *NRP*. The military's dangerous mission has resulted in widespread use of motivational messages believed to encourage service members to push hard toward realization of the military goal, even at the expense of personal safety or one's life. Often these motivational messages include language that proclaims special gifts and blessings bestowed by God upon the United States and that exhorts service members to consider themselves part of a mission both divinely authorized and intended to bring righteousness into places where evil prevails. Commanding officers may reinforce these sentiments by openly invoking God's blessings upon the unit, and they often receive support from theistic military chaplains, who validate such messages with officially sponsored prayers. RIPS results, however, indicate over 30% of military members may find such messages uninspiring, unimportant, or offensive (Dao, 2011). In contrast and as noted above, a significant portion of the population *does* value such forms of encouragement (*Other Protestants* and *Muslims*). The fact no easy answer to this leadership conundrum exists does not and should not suggest avoidance as the best means to proceed; rather, these results indicate that leaders may be wise to engage re-evaluation of traditional, familiar conduct.

RIPS also finds older respondents indicate faith is relatively more important in job performance than do younger respondents. Who are these older military members? They are the leaders, the commanders, charged with motivating and inspiring younger and/or junior troops. These are also the leaders currently charged with making decisions on religious accommodation requests, leaders for whom the importance and content of faith may vary significantly from those they lead.

On a practical management level, therefore, RIPS data provide leaders with food for leadership thought with regard to their own language and behaviors, those of their peers, and those of the men and women who are mentored by these leaders. Religion and leadership language have often intertwined, and this mingling has at times resulted in high-profile complaints and lawsuits, such as erupted at the U.S. Air Force Academy in 2004-2005, where cadets claimed overt evangelical Christian messages were the norm among Academy leaders, messages a number of cadets and their parents claimed amounted to religious discrimination (Cook, 2007; Parco, 2007; Goodstein, 2005). In this case, in which religious identity and negative climate situations were obviously entangled, investigation results indicated that actions and words on the part of overly zealous evangelical Christian military members, especially senior leaders, comprised the nexus of disharmony (Hajjar, 2010). Overt religiosity and expressions of civil religion are a part of the American ethos (Bellah, 2006), and any attempt to promote a religion-free military would create legal and emotional chaos among military members and the country that supports them. At the very least, and by using a tool such as the RIPS, leaders can become and remain better aware of the religious/humanist sentiments of unit personnel and make informed, rather than automatic, decisions concerning the use of religious tropes in addressing real needs in the lives of their people.

Conduct

On today's battlefields, concepts of right and wrong are more important than ever in achieving mission success in line with national principles and priorities. In a combat environment, lapses of moral judgment can escalate a seemingly simple, localized action into an international incident, resulting in public scrutiny that has a profound impact on strategic concerns. With this in mind, the RIPS asked service members whether religious/humanist identification had an impact on determinations of right and wrong and if religious/humanist identification affected one's attitude toward those who differ in belief.

One question in particular illustrates the results of this inquiry. Respondents were asked to respond to the following: "The world would be better if people got rid of their religious beliefs and dealt with each other as equals." In examining the results (MLR, Table 3), members identifying as *Other Protestant* indicated a greater tendency to disagree with the statement than did those identifying with other religious traditions.

This finding comports with social science research that has noted religious people tend to be more intolerant of those differing from themselves (Cunningham, 2010; Balkin, et al., 2009; Wilcox & Jelen, 1990; Herek, 1987). RIPS results also indicate that those who come from minority or non-dominant faith groups are more willing than *Mainline Protestants* to accept others as equals, regardless of religious beliefs, as evidenced by responses from *Jews, Catholics, Pagans, Humanists*, and *NRP*.

This knowledge may be important when planning missions in countries, which have a

Table 3. Dealing with others as equals

Independent Variable	Coefficient	t statistic	Significance
Other Protestant	0.3077118	4.83	0
Roman Catholic	-0.2235655	-5.09	0
Jewish	-0.7222333	-4.91	0
Muslim	-0.0486777	-0.21	0.83
Pagan	-0.7233397	-5.09	0
Humanist	-1.522454	-18.25	0
NRP	-0.7878785	-20.57	0
Gender	0.2493224	5.92	0
Age	0.1107566	6.36	0
Officer/Enlisted	-0.102785	-3.77	0
Hispanic	-0.068002	-1.55	0.122
American Indian	-0.0615093	-0.75	0.451
Asian	-0.1201679	-1.56	0.12
Black	0.0328173	0.76	0.448
Hawaiian	-0.2719564	-2.39	0.017
Constant	3.744566	38.18	0

non-Christian majority religion. In such settings *NRPs, Humanists*, and *Pagans*, who are more likely to affirm others as equals regardless of religion, may be less troubled than *Other Protestants*, who have a greater tendency to see differing religious beliefs as an obstacle to equality. Indeed, considerable controversy erupted in the media and courts during the last decade regarding actions taken by evangelical Protestant Christians in military venues (Hajjar, 2010; Jonsson, 2010; Mount, 2009; Leopold, 2009; Allen, 2009; Jordan, 2009; Hanna, 2008; Paley, 2008; Shane, 2008; Jordan, 2008; Eisman, 2008; Rittgers, 2007; Cook, 2007; DOD IG Report, 2007). One particularly egregious example occurred in Iraq in 2004, when a squad of soldiers displayed provocative Christian triumphalist messages on their military vehicles, thus publicly demeaning Islam (Sharlet, 2009). Employing a detailed and confidential survey, such as the RIPS, permits leaders to gauge the effect that religious/humanist attitudes and perceptions may have upon mission accomplishment.

Organizational Commitment

Every organization is concerned with the loyalty of its members, and the military may be even more so than most. Does religious/humanist identity play a role in this, and if so, what other factors may affect a member's commitment to the unit? One means to explore this question was incorporated in the RIPS, in conjunction with its link to the DEOCS. The DEOCS contains an Organizational Commitment factor that measures the extent to which one's personal values and goals match those perceived as prevalent or dominant within the unit. As shown in Table 4, it is reverse-coded from the factors considered above, meaning a negative sign for the coefficient indicates lack of commitment to the organization.

Pagans, Humanists, and *NRPs* tended to view their organizational commitment more negatively than those of the control group, *Mainline Protestant*. These results may speak to underlying

assumptions about leadership and values inherent in military organizations, both of which tend to endorse and reinforce a hegemonic Christian privilege with regard to organizational behavior. The three groups whose responses register lower levels of commitment are those whose members have consciously rejected traditional religion as an organized venture worthy of their loyalty, even after controlling for age. As such, we suspect these three groups tended to distrust the military organization to the extent the organization relies on organizational values and goals that reflect specifically Christian principles. Growing consciousness of religious assumptions in leadership strategies, organizational structure, and policies has potent implications for military leaders.

These same implications reach into the critical areas of retention and recruitment. Just as military leaders seek to be mindful of individuals with specific racial and ethnic characteristics (e.g., Hispanics, Blacks, Asians) when seeking to ensure

Table 4. Organizational commitment

Independent Variable	Coefficient	t statistic	Significance
Other Protestant	-0.0095458	-0.2	0.843
Roman Catholic	0.0487527	1.46	0.143
Jewish	-0.1142174	-1.02	0.306
Muslim	-0.2121968	-1.23	0.217
Pagan	-0.2908834	-2.7	0.007
Humanist	-0.3515323	-5.56	0
NRP	-0.0770481	-2.65	0.008
Gender	-0.0469813	-1.47	0.141
Age	0.1572289	11.91	0
Officer/Enlisted	-0.2160689	-10.43	0
Hispanic	-0.1032322	-3.09	0.002
American Indian	-0.1556973	-2.51	0.012
Asian	-0.0348662	-0.59	0.552
Black	-0.0741689	-2.26	0.024
Hawaiian	-0.1034141	-1.2	0.231
Constant	1.471269	17.93	0

a favorable EO climate within units, so also should they be mindful of minority religious/humanist military members.

SOLUTIONS AND RECOMMENDATIONS

How might military and federal leaders benefit from RIPS type surveys, the technology that supports them, and the statistically valid information derived about the religious identification and practices of personnel? Creating a supportive workplace and environment is a proved contributor to a mission-ready workforce and is intimately tied to other aspects of environmental concerns within a diversity-oriented establishment. In view of the power religion wields within the human cultural terrain, DOD leaders need accurate and descriptive information about the religious/humanist identification of military members (Hajjar, 2010; Benjamin, 1998).

First, while little scholarly attention has been given to this subject to date it is worthwhile to speculate what might be the reaction of family members, relatives, and friends of those who, as members of minority faith/humanist groups, received positive or negative reinforcement of their beliefs and practices during their tenure within the DOD (Pacifism Blogspot, 2006). Respectful and informed attention given to the religious/humanist beliefs and practices of military personnel, reinforced by knowledge gained through sound sampling results, cannot help but add to the ability of commanders and civilian supervisors to address two leading indicators: (1) recruitment of new personnel and (2) retention of currently-serving active-duty members, Reservists, and DOD civilians (Lancaster, et al., 2004).

Second, because military leaders bear a responsibility to negotiate this complex cultural arena, accurate and up-to-date information allows greater facilitation in taking care of religiously diverse service members and providing for their needs.

Service members whose religious beliefs and practices require the provision of faith-specific supplies (for example, host used in Eucharist celebrations, kosher and halal meals-ready-to-eat) could be anticipated and provisions made to accommodate their needs, and those who require time, space, apparel, or other permissions beyond what policy specifically addresses or allows, likewise could be managed with foresight, rather than with reactive impatience or out of ignorance.

Third, accurate measures and analysis of religious diversity would empower military leaders to examine current and planned policies, regulations, and military law to determine what, if any, religious biases are reflected in these and how such biases affect personnel. If, as we believe, religious/humanist beliefs inform a military member's decision to remain in the armed forces as well as their ability to act in accord with mission requirements, leaders who fail to appreciate these beliefs risk a potentially great cost to the military organization.

FUTURE RESEARCH DIRECTIONS

This chapter has focused on general issues regarding the religious/humanist identities and beliefs of service members. The majority of respondents to the RIPS were enlisted and junior officers (their numbers exceeding by far those of senior leaders in the military population). It is clear, however, from numerous allegations, complaints, and lawsuits that military leaders themselves possess salient religious/humanist identities that complicate the effective management of this diversity. Worden (2005) addressed the salience of a leader's religiosity in business organizations, and future research focused on the military would benefit from addressing the question of the implicit and explicit articulation of a leader's religious/humanist identity and beliefs and if/how these affect leadership effectiveness within the organizational unit.

This is not to deny, however, the rich potential for research that still exists with regard to the generalized military population. What types of religiosity or humanist identity, for example, result in the highest degrees of impact upon job performance, conduct, and interpersonal relationships? How does an individual's religiously based authority-mindedness, a term used by research exploring religiously motivated political behavior, affect that person's ability to cope with the ambiguities of religious and humanist diversity and accommodation (Wald, et al., 1989; Owen, et al., 1991; Mockabee, 2007)? Answers to these questions will enrich the ongoing leadership debates within the military services.

RIPS-type research permits a holistic investigation of specific aspects of human diversity. Such investigations may seek to incorporate and integrate all current dimensions of diversity research along with potentially new ones such as decision making and social categorization processes into a unified whole. In such a setting, all diversity would be recognized to possess both positive and negative attributes and the entire spectrum would be considered in view of the end in sight and other values established by the leadership. Principles elaborated by van Knippenberg (2004), in discussion of the categorization-elaboration model, could be incorporated in such an effort. The RIPS concept of including in-depth investigation of religious/humanist principles could be expanded to include networking, decision-making, and other aspects of an individual's identity to explore what mix best facilitates productive work units.

CONCLUSION

Today's DOD leaders work within an environment in which demographic diversity is obvious, equality of all within diversity is proclaimed if not always actualized, and mission success is tied to respect for diversity of all kinds, cultural and demographic even as certain cultural elements are favored over others (Lim, et al., 2008). At the same time, military culture values uniformity and conformity, often equating these with unity of purpose, a culture that seeks always to promote unit cohesion and *esprit de corps*. These are truths, seemingly distinct and disparate, in search of a unifying principle, and the leadership task involved in balancing these factors is neither simple nor easy.

One of the principal goals of using a confidential survey such as the RIPS is to encourage systematic, integrated study of religion, humanism, and related attitudes and practices in this little-studied, rich arena of human interaction. We believe this research contributes a more nuanced and complex understanding of religion/humanism to military leaders and social researchers working within the military environment. Our findings indicate that, when careful attention is paid to the nature and the evidence of this identity component, consistent and meaningful relationships emerge that can and do have an impact on leadership methods and, subsequently, on military readiness.

Dealing intelligently and forthrightly with different perspectives on religion—just as leaders are required to do regarding issues regarding race, ethnicity, and gender—will, we believe, enhance unity of effort within an increasingly diverse workforce. Leaders who possess an understanding of the role of religion in their diverse workforce, based on verifiable information supplied by surveys such as the RIPS, are positioned to succeed.

REFERENCES

Allen, B. (2009, April 6). Top army chaplain raises Jewish ire with call for fasting during Passover. *Associated Baptist Press*. Retrieved from http://www.abpnews.com/content/view/3977/53/

Balkin, R. S., Schlosser, L. Z., & Heller Levitt, D. (2009). Religious identity and cultural diversity: Exploring the relationships between religious identity, sexism, homophobia, and multicultural competence. *Journal of Counseling and Development*, *87*(4), 420–427. doi:10.1002/j.1556-6678.2009.tb00126.x

Barna Group. (2006). *Barna update: House church involvement is growing*. Retrieved from http://www.barna.org/

Bellah, R. N., & Tipton, S. M. (2006). *The Robert Bellah reader*. Durham, NC: Duke University Press.

Benimoff, R. (2009). *Faith under fire: An army chaplain's memoir*. New York, NY: Crown.

Benjamin, M. J. (1998). Justice, justice shall you pursue: Legal analysis of religious issues in the army. *The Army Lawyer, 1,* 1–18.

Bess, M. (2006). *Choices under fire: Moral dimensions of World War II*. New York, NY: Knopf.

Blumner, R. E. (2008, May 4). This atheist finds he needs a foxhole. *St. Petersburg Times*. Retrieved from http://www.tampabay.com/opinion/columns/article483665.ece

Burdette, A. M., Wang, V., Elder, G. H., Hill, T. D., & Benson, J. (2009). Serving god and country? Religious involvement and military service among young adult men. *Journal for the Scientific Study of Religion, 48*(4), 794–804. doi:10.1111/j.1468-5906.2009.01481.x

Bush, G. W. (2003). Address to the nation on Iraq from the U.S.S. Abraham Lincoln. *Weekly Compilation of Presidential Documents, 39,* 516-518. Retrieved from http://frwebgate2.access.gpo.gov/cgi-bin/TEXTgate.cgi?WAISdocID=ij6veJ/22/1/0&WAISaction=retrieve

Cheyne, J. A. (2010). The rise of the nones and the growth of religious indifference. *Skeptic, 15*(4), 56–60.

Clair, J. A., Beatty, J. E., & Maclean, T. L. (2005). Out of sight but not out of mind: Managing invisible social identities in the workplace. *Academy of Management Review, 30*(1), 78–95. doi:10.5465/AMR.2005.15281431

Clairborne, S. (2005). On evangelicals and interfaith cooperation: An interview with Tony Campolo. *Cross Currents, 55*(1), 54–65.

Congress (2009, August 18). *Letter to the honorable Robert M. Gates*. Retrieved from https://salsa.wiredforchange.com/o/1607/images/House%20Letter%20Final.pdf

Cook, H. (2007). Service before self? Evangelicals flying high at the U.S. air force academy. *Journal of Law and Education, 36*(1), 1–33.

Cunningham, G. B. (2010). The influence of religious personal identity on the relationships among religious dissimilarity, value dissimilarity, and job satisfaction. *Social Justice Research, 23*(1), 60–76. doi:10.1007/s11211-010-0109-0

Dao, J. (2011, April 26). Atheists seek chaplain role in the military. *The New York Times*. Retrieved from http://www.nytimes.com/2011/04/27/us/27atheists.html?_r=1&scp=1&sq=Atheists%20seek%20chaplain%20role%20in%20the%20military&st=cse

DoD Instruction 1304.28. (2004). *Guidance for the appointment of chaplains for the military departments*. Washington, DC: DOD.

DODD. 1344.10. (2008). *Political activities by members of the armed forces*. Washington, DC: DOD.

DODI. 1300.06. (2007). *Conscientious objectors*. Washington, DC: DOD.

DODI. 1300.17. (2009). *Accommodation of religious practices within the military services*. Washington, DC: DOD.

Drescher, K. C., Smith, M. W., & Foy, D. W. (2007). Spirituality and readjustment following war-zone experiences. In Figley, C. R., & Nash, W. P. (Eds.), *Combat Stress Injury: Theory, Research, and Management*. New York, NY: Routledge.

Eberle, C. (2007). God, war, and conscience. *The Journal of Religious Ethics*, *35*(3), 479–507. doi:10.1111/j.1467-9795.2007.00316.x

Eck, D. L. (2002). *A new religious America: How a "Christian country" has become the world's most religiously diverse nation*. New York, NY: HarperOne.

Edgell, P., Gerteis, J., & Hartmann, D. (2006). Atheists as 'other': Moral boundaries and cultural membership in American society. *American Sociological Review*, *71*(2), 211–234. doi:10.1177/000312240607100203

Edgell, P., & Tranby, E. (2007). Religious influences on understandings of racial inequality in the United States. *Social Problems*, *54*(2), 263–288. doi:10.1525/sp.2007.54.2.263

Eisman, D. (2008, December 28). Military aims to muzzle evangelizing at recruiting sites. *The Virginia Pilot*. Retrieved from http://hamptonroads.com/2008/12/military-aims-muzzle-evangelizing-recruiting-sites

Fahey, J. J. (2005). *War and the Christian conscience: Where do you stand?* Maryknoll, NY: Orbis.

Froese, P., Bader, C., & Smith, B. (2008). Political tolerance and God's wrath in the United States. *Sociology of Religion*, *69*(1), 29–44. doi:10.1093/socrel/69.1.29

Geertz, C. (1973). *The interpretation of cultures: Selected essays*. New York, NY: Basic Books.

Goodstein, L. (2005, June 23). Air force academy staff found promoting religion. *The New York Times*. Retrieved from http://www.nytimes.com/2005/06/23/politics/23academy.html?scp=1&sq=Air%20Force%20academy%20staff%20found%20promoting%20religion&st=cse

Grammich, C. (2004). Many faiths of many regions: Continuities and changes among religious adherents across U.S. counties. *RAND Labor and Population Report WR-211*. Retrieved from http://www.rand.org

Hajjar, R. M. (2010). A new angle on the U.S. military's emphasis on developing cross-cultural competence: Connecting in ranks' cultural diversity to cross-cultural competence. *Armed Forces and Society*, *36*(2), 247–263. doi:10.1177/0095327X09339898

Hanna, J. (2008, September 26). Second soldier sues over religious freedom issues. *Associated Press*. Retrieved from http://www.militaryreligiousfreedom.org/press-releases/complaint_sept.html

Harper, M. (2007). The stereotyping of nonreligious people by religious students: Contents and subtypes. *Journal for the Scientific Study of Religion*, *46*(4), 539–552. doi:10.1111/j.1468-5906.2007.00376.x

Hatch Act (5 U.S.C. 7323) (1993).

Herek, G. M. (1987). Religious orientation and prejudice: A comparison of racial and sexual attitudes. *Personality and Social Psychology Bulletin*, *13*(1), 34–44. doi:10.1177/0146167287131003

Hout, M., & Fischer, C. S. (2002). Why more Americans have no religious preference: Politics and generations. *American Sociological Review*, *67*(2), 165–190. doi:10.2307/3088891

Hunter, C. E., & Smith, L. M. (2011). Exploring the management of religious diversity within the US military. In McDonald, D. P., & Parks, K. M. (Eds.), *Managing Diversity in the Military: The Value of Inclusion in a Culture of Uniformity* (pp. 311–368). New York, NY: Routledge.

Jolly, R. S. (2007). The application of the religious freedom restoration act to appearance regulations that presumptively prohibit observant Sikh lawyers from joining the U.S. army judge advocate general corps. *Chapman Law Review*, *11*(1), 155–182.

Jonsson, P. (2010, January 22). Trijicon sights: How the 'Jesus gun' misfired. *Christian Science Monitor*. Retrieved from http://www.csmonitor.com/USA/Military/2010/0122/Trijicon-sights-How-the-Jesus-gun-misfired

Jordan, B. (2008, February 26). Flag ritual returns to Annapolis chapel. *Military.com*. Retrieved from http://militaryreligiousfreedom.org/press-releases/fowler.html

Jordan, B. (2009, April 15). Sikhs want DOD turban, hair bans lifted. *Military.com*. Retrieved from http://www.military.com/news/article/sikhs-want-dod-turban-hair-bans-lifted.html?ESRC=eb.nl

Kaye, R. (2008, July 8). Atheist soldier sues army for 'unconstitutional' discrimination. *CNN*. Retrieved from http://articles.cnn.com/2008-07-08/us/atheist.soldier_1_tours-discrimination-bible?_s=PM:US

Kosmin, B. A., & Keysar, A. (2008). *American religious identification survey (ARIS) 2008*. Hartford, CT: Institute for the Study of Secularism in Society & Culture.

Kosmin, B. A., & Mayer, E. (2001). *American religious identification survey*. New York, NY: The Graduate Center of the City University of New York.

Kurien, P. (2004). Multiculturalism, immigrant religion, and diasporic nationalism: The development of an American Hinduism. *Social Problems*, *51*(3), 362–385. doi:10.1525/sp.2004.51.3.362

Lancaster, A. R., Klein, R. M., & Wetzel, E. S. (2004). *U.S. department of defense retention trends*. Arlington, VA: Defense Manpower and Data Center.

Lawrence, L. (2007, November 20). Military chaplains: Being a cog of conscience in the military killing machine. *Christian Science Monitor*. Retrieved from http://www.csmonitor.com/2007/1120/p20s01-usmi.html

Leopold, J. (2009, April 6). Army faces backlash for scheduling 'day of fast' on feast of Passover. *The Public Record*. Retrieved from http://pubrecord.org/religion/845/army-faces-backlash-for-scheduling-day-of-fast-on-feast-of-passover/

Lim, N., Cho, M., & Curry, K. (2008). *Planning for diversity: Options and recommendations for DoD leaders*. Santa Monica, CA: RAND Corporation.

Marin, P. (1981, November 14). Living in moral pain. *Psychology Today*, 71–80.

Melton, J. G. (1995). The changing scene of new religious movements: Observations from a generation of research. *Social Compass*, *42*(2), 265–276. doi:10.1177/003776895042002009

Mockabee, S. T. (2007). A question of authority: Religion and cultural conflict in the 2004 election. *Political Behavior*, *29*(2), 221–248. doi:10.1007/s11109-006-9023-4

Mount, M. (2009, May 22). Military burns unsolicited bibles sent to Afghanistan. *CNN*. Retrieved from http://edition.cnn.com/2009/WORLD/asiapcf/05/20/us.military.bibles.burned/

Noah, M. (2011, May 23). Gays in military: 'Conscience protections' needed for chaplains, 21 entity leaders say. *Baptist Press*. Retrieved from http://www.bpnews.net/printerfriendly.asp?ID=35362

Otto, R. (1923). *The idea of the holy*. London, UK: Oxford University Press.

Owen, D. E., Walk, K. D., & Hill, S. S. (1991). Authoritarian or authority-minded? The cognitive commitments of fundamentalists and the Christian right. *Religion and American Culture*, *1*(1), 73–100. doi:10.2307/1123907

Paley, A. R. (2008, May 29). Marine in Iraq suspended over coins quoting gospel. *Washington Post*. Retrieved from http://www.washingtonpost.com/wp-dyn/content/article/2008/05/29/AR2008052903683.html?sid=ST2008053001342

Parco, J. E., & Fagin, B. S. (2007). The one true religion in the military. *The Humanist*, *67*(5), 11–17.

Pew Forum on Religion in Public Life. (2008). *U.S. religious landscape survey*. Washington, DC: Pew Research Center. Retrieved from http://religions.pewforum.org/

Presser, S., & Chaves, M. (2007). Is religious service attendance declining? *Journal for the Scientific Study of Religion*, *46*(3), 417–423. doi:10.1111/j.1468-5906.2007.00367.x

Redden, E. (2007, December 18). More spiritual, but not in church. *Inside Higher Education*. Retrieved from http://www.insidehighered.com/news/2007/12/18/spirituality

Religious Freedom Restoration Act (RFRA) (2006), 42 U.S.C. 2000bb-1.

DOD Report No. H06L102270308. (2007, July 20). *Alleged misconduct by DOD officials concerning Christian embassy*. Washington, DC: DOD.

Rice, T. W. (2003). Believe it or not: Religious and other paranormal beliefs in the United States. *Journal for the Scientific Study of Religion*, *42*(1), 95–106. doi:10.1111/1468-5906.00163

Ringdal, G. I., & Ringdal, K. (2010). Does religiosity protect against war-related distress? Evidence from Bosnia and Herzegovina. *Politics and Religion*, *3*(2), 389–405. doi:10.1017/S175504831000009X

Rittgers, D. (2007). These dishonored dead: Veteran memorials and religious preferences. *First Amendment Law Review*, *5*, 400–433.

Rosenzweig, S. A. (1996). Restoring religious freedom to the workplace: Title VII, RFRA, and religious accommodation. *University of Pennsylvania Law Review*, *144*(6), 2513–2536. doi:10.2307/3312675

Schultz, K. M. (2006). Religion as identity in postwar America: The last serious attempt to put a question on religion in the United States census. *The Journal of American History*, *93*(2), 359–384. doi:10.2307/4486234

Segal, D. R., & Segal, M. W. (2004). America's military population. *Population Bulletin*, *59*(4), 3–40.

Shane, L., III. (2008, November 12). Military atheists want new rules on prayer. *Stars and Stripes*. Retrieved from http://www.stripes.com/news/military-atheists-want-new-rules-on-prayer-1.85154

Sharlet, J. (2009, May). Jesus killed Mohammed: The crusade for a Christian military. *Harper's Magazine*. Retrieved from http://www.harpers.org/archive/2009/05/0082488

Shay, J. (2002). *Odysseus in America*. New York, NY: Scribner.

Singh, A., & Kaur, H. (2009, January 26). *Re: Captain K. S. Kalsi & Second Lieutenant T. S. Rattan (Sikh health professionals)*. [PDF document]. Letter to Secretary of Defense Robert M. Gates. Retrieved from www.sikhcoalition.org/documents/SikhCoalitionLettertoRobertGates.pdf

Smidt, C. (2005). Religion and American attitudes toward Islam and an invasion of Iraq. *Sociology of Religion*, *66*(3), 243–261. doi:10.2307/4153098

Smith, L. E. (2008). What's in a name? Scholarship and the pathology of conservative Protestantism. *Method and Theory in the Study of Religion*, *20*(3), 191–211. doi:10.1163/157006808X317446

Steensland, B., Park, J. Z., Regnerus, M. D., Robinson, L. D., Wilcox, W. B., & Woodberry, R. D. (2000). The measure of American religion: Toward improving the state of the art. *Social Forces*, *79*(1), 291–318.

Stefani. (2006, May 18). Religion in the military. *Pacifism Blogspot*. Retrieved from http://verbal-pacifism.blogspot.com/2006/05/religion-in-military.html

van Knippenberg, D., De Dreu, C. K. W., & Homan, A. C. (2004). Work group diversity and group performance: An integrative model and research agenda. *The Journal of Applied Psychology*, *89*(6), 1008–1022. doi:10.1037/0021-9010.89.6.1008

Verkamp, B. J. (1988). The moral treatment of warriors in the early middle ages. *The Journal of Religious Ethics*, *16*(2), 223–249.

Wald, K. D., Owen, D. E., & Hill, S. S. (1989). Habits of the mind? The problem of authority in the new Christian right. In Jelen, T. G. (Ed.), *Religion and Political Behavior in the United States* (pp. 93–108). New York, NY: Praeger.

Wilcox, C., & Jelen, T. (1990). Evangelicals and political tolerance. *American Politics Research*, *18*(1), 25–46. doi:10.1177/1532673X9001800102

Worden, S. (2005). Religion in strategic leadership: A positivistic, normative/theological, and strategic analysis. *Journal of Business Ethics*, *57*(3), 221–239. doi:10.1007/s10551-004-6943-y

Wuthnow, R., & Hackett, C. (2003). The social integration of practitioners of non-western religions in the United States. *Journal for the Scientific Study of Religion*, *42*(4), 651–667. doi:10.1046/j.1468-5906.2003.00209.x

Yong, A. (2007). The future of evangelical theology: Asian and Asian American interrogations. *Asia Journal of Theology*, *21*(2), 371–397.

ADDITIONAL READING

Balkin, R. S., Schlosser, L. Z., & Heller Levitt, D. (2009). Religious identity and cultural diversity: Exploring the relationships between religious identity, sexism, homophobia, and multicultural competence. *Journal of Counseling and Development*, *87*(4), 420–427. doi:10.1002/j.1556-6678.2009.tb00126.x

Barna Group. (2006). *Barna update: House church involvement is growing*. Retrieved from http://www.barna.org/

Benimoff, R. (2009). *Faith under fire: An army chaplain's memoir*. New York, NY: Crown.

Burdette, A. M., Wang, V., Elder, G. H., Hill, T. D., & Benson, J. (2009). Serving god and country? Religious involvement and military service among young adult men. *Journal for the Scientific Study of Religion*, *48*(4), 794–804. doi:10.1111/j.1468-5906.2009.01481.x

Clair, J. A., Beatty, J. E., & Maclean, T. L. (2005). Out of sight but not out of mind: Managing invisible social identities in the workplace. *Academy of Management Review*, *30*(1), 78–95. doi:10.5465/AMR.2005.15281431

Cunningham, G. B. (2010). The influence of religious personal identity on the relationships among religious dissimilarity, value dissimilarity, and job satisfaction. *Social Justice Research*, *23*(1), 60–76. doi:10.1007/s11211-010-0109-0

DODI. 1300.17. (2009). *Accommodation of religious practices within the military services*. Washington, DC: DOD.

Eberle, C. (2007). God, war, and conscience. *The Journal of Religious Ethics*, *35*(3), 479–507. doi:10.1111/j.1467-9795.2007.00316.x

Edgell, P., Gerteis, J., & Hartmann, D. (2006). Atheists as 'other': Moral boundaries and cultural membership in American society. *American Sociological Review*, *71*(2), 211–234. doi:10.1177/000312240607100203

Edgell, P., & Tranby, E. (2007). Religious influences on understandings of racial inequality in the United States. *Social Problems*, *54*(2), 263–288. doi:10.1525/sp.2007.54.2.263

Froese, P., Bader, C., & Smith, B. (2008). Political tolerance and god's wrath in the United States. *Sociology of Religion*, *69*(1), 29–44. doi:10.1093/socrel/69.1.29

Hajjar, R. M. (2010). A new angle on the U.S. military's emphasis on developing cross-cultural competence: Connecting in ranks' cultural diversity to cross-cultural competence. *Armed Forces and Society*, *36*(2), 247–263. doi:10.1177/0095327X09339898

Herek, G. M. (1987). Religious orientation and prejudice: A comparison of racial and sexual attitudes. *Personality and Social Psychology Bulletin*, *13*(1), 34–44. doi:10.1177/0146167287131003

Hunter, C. E., & Smith, L. M. (2011). Exploring the management of religious diversity within the US military. In McDonald, D. P., & Parks, K. M. (Eds.), *Managing Diversity in the Military: The Value of Inclusion in a Culture of Uniformity* (pp. 311–368). New York, NY: Routledge.

Jolly, R. S. (2007). The application of the religious freedom restoration act to appearance regulations that presumptively prohibit observant Sikh lawyers from joining the U.S. army judge advocate general corps. *Chapman Law Review*, *11*(1), 155–182.

Kosmin, B. A., & Keysar, A. (2008). *American religious identification survey (ARIS) 2008*. Hartford, CT: Institute for the Study of Secularism in Society & Culture.

Kurien, P. (2004). Multiculturalism, immigrant religion, and diasporic nationalism: The development of an American Hinduism. *Social Problems*, *51*(3), 362–385. doi:10.1525/sp.2004.51.3.362

Lim, N., Cho, M., & Curry, K. (2008). *Planning for diversity: Options and recommendations for DoD leaders*. Santa Monica, CA: RAND Corporation.

Pew Forum on Religion in Public Life. (2008). *U.S. religious landscape survey*. Washington, DC: Pew Research Center. Retrieved from http://religions.pewforum.org/

Presser, S., & Chaves, M. (2007). Is religious service attendance declining? *Journal for the Scientific Study of Religion*, *46*(3), 417–423. doi:10.1111/j.1468-5906.2007.00367.x

Religious Freedom Restoration Act (RFRA) (2006), 42 U.S.C. 2000bb-1.

DOD Report No. H06L102270308. (2007, July 20). *Alleged misconduct by DOD officials concerning Christian embassy*. Washington, DC: DOD.

Rice, T. W. (2003). Believe it or not: Religious and other paranormal beliefs in the United States. *Journal for the Scientific Study of Religion*, *42*(1), 95–106. doi:10.1111/1468-5906.00163

Ringdal, G. I., & Ringdal, K. (2010). Does religiosity protect against war-related distress? Evidence from Bosnia and Herzegovina. *Politics and Religion*, *3*(2), 389–405. doi:10.1017/S175504831000009X

Rittgers, D. (2007). These dishonored dead: Veteran memorials and religious preferences. *First Amendment Law Review*, *5*, 400–433.

Schultz, K. M. (2006). Religion as identity in postwar America: The last serious attempt to put a question on religion in the United States census. *The Journal of American History*, *93*(2), 359–384. doi:10.2307/4486234

Smidt, C. (2005). Religion and American attitudes toward Islam and an invasion of Iraq. *Sociology of Religion*, *66*(3), 243–261. doi:10.2307/4153098

Smith, L. E. (2008). What's in a name? Scholarship and the pathology of conservative Protestantism. *Method and Theory in the Study of Religion*, *20*(3), 191–211. doi:10.1163/157006808X317446

Steensland, B., Park, J. Z., Regnerus, M. D., Robinson, L. D., Wilcox, W. B., & Woodberry, R. D. (2000). The measure of American religion: Toward improving the state of the art. *Social Forces*, *79*(1), 291–318.

van Knippenberg, D., De Dreu, C. K. W., & Homan, A. C. (2004). Work group diversity and group performance: An integrative model and research agenda. *The Journal of Applied Psychology*, *89*(6), 1008–1022. doi:10.1037/0021-9010.89.6.1008

Worden, S. (2005). Religion in strategic leadership: A positivistic, normative/theological, and strategic analysis. *Journal of Business Ethics*, *57*(3), 221–239. doi:10.1007/s10551-004-6943-y

Wuthnow, R., & Hackett, C. (2003). The social integration of practitioners of non-western religions in the United States. *Journal for the Scientific Study of Religion*, *42*(4), 651–667. doi:10.1046/j.1468-5906.2003.00209.x

KEY TERMS AND DEFINITIONS

Chaplain: "A commissioned officer of the Chaplain Corps of the Army, a commissioned officer of the Chaplain Corps of the Navy, or a commissioned officer in the Air Force designated for duty as a chaplain" (DoD Instruction 1304.28, 2004). The instruction provides official guidance on the process involved and the requirements to be a military chaplain. All prospective candidates for chaplain must be willing to "function in a pluralistic environment."

Diversity: "Diversity extends to age, personal, and corporate background, education function, and personality. It includes lifestyle, sexual preference, geographic origin, tenure with the organization, exempt or non-exempt status, and management or non-management. It also shows up clearly with companies involved in acquisitions and mergers. White males are as diverse as their colleagues" (R. Roosevelt Thomas, Jr., President of the American Institute for Managing Diversity). Though this definition applies to diversity in a traditional business setting, it is broad enough to address the issues of the military and other governmental entities when applied generally. The definition permits one to immediately grasp that diversity is not simply another name for equal opportunity but constitutes another and complimentary function of leadership and management.

Faith: "Faith is both the substance of things hoped for and the evidence that things exist that are not yet perceived with the senses" (Hebrews 11.1 from the New Testament). This definition is applicable to the concepts conveyed in this chapter as it forms the source for many of the identities and attitudes being considered. It also permits extension beyond Christianity in that it is a more general expression of the human ability to see beyond the present and base current decisions on consideration of larger issues.

Humanism: "Humanism is a progressive philosophy of life that, without theism and other supernatural beliefs, affirms our ability and responsibility to lead ethical lives of personal fulfillment that aspire to the greater good of humanity" (American Humanist Association).

Leadership: "…influencing people by providing purpose, direction, and motivation, while operating to accomplish the mission and improve the organization" (Army Regulation 600-100). Though there may be a myriad of definitions of leadership, this one from the Army's manual is appropriate for the challenges considered in this chapter.

Military: "A branch of the Armed Forces of the United States, established by act of Congress, in which persons are appointed, enlisted, or inducted for military service, and which operates and is administered within a military or executive department. The Military Services are: the United States Army, the United States Navy, the United States Air Force, the United States Marine Corps, and the United States Coast Guard" (DOD Dictionary of military terms).

Religion: "A personal set or institutionalized system of attitudes, moral or ethical beliefs, and practices that are held with the strength of traditional religious views, characterized by ardor and faith, and generally evidenced through specific religious observances" (DoD Directive 1350.2). This is a working definition that is broad enough to include both theistic and nontheistic concepts and is thus useful in the military setting.

Survey: Survey research is social science inquiry based on an interview method of collecting data from the subjects of the research. The method applied in this chapter is a computer assisted self-administered survey in which participants were able to respond to the majority of given questions and statements via answers provided in five point Likert-type scales.

ENDNOTES

[1] The term "minority" refers to numbers of faith group adherents in comparison to the adherent/membership numbers of large groups such as the Roman Catholic Church, the Southern Baptist Convention, and Methodist groups.

[2] In 1971, the Secretary of Defense established the Race Relations Education Board and, subsequently, brought into being the Defense Race Relations Institute (DRRI), later renamed the DEOMI. Today DEOMI hosts education and training programs in human relations, equal opportunity, equal employment opportunity, and diversity. DEOMI includes a research arm that pioneered the Defense Equal Opportunity Climate Survey (DEOCS).

Section 4
Diversity Leadership in Education

Chapter 14
Preparing Science Teachers:
Developing a Sense of Community Using Technology

André M. Green
University of South Alabama, USA

ABSTRACT

Pathway to Science (PTS) is a nationally funded project through the National Science Foundation (Award # 0934829) involving a university's Colleges of Education, Arts and Sciences, and Engineering Departments in partnership with a local school district. All entities involved have a vested interest in increasing the number of certified secondary science teachers as all are interested in producing students who are better prepared in science at both the collegiate and secondary levels. This chapter explores how technology is used in the training of science teachers and how technology is used to retain them as science teachers once they are employed.

BACKGROUND

Pathway to Science (PTS) is a nationally funded project involving a university's Colleges of Education, Arts and Sciences, and Engineering departments in partnership with a local school district. All entities involved have a vested interest in increasing the number of certified secondary science teachers as all are interested in producing students who are better prepared in science at both the collegiate and secondary levels. The partnership between these entities is a very unique

DOI: 10.4018/978-1-4666-2668-3.ch014

partnership in that more than 80% of the teachers who teach in the district hold at least one degree from this university.

The program has the goals to:

1. Prepare a total of up to approximately 24 science teachers over a five-year period who are highly qualified and generally in science at the secondary level in grades.
2. Enhance student achievement by providing certified science teachers in those classrooms that currently have no certified teachers.
3. Create a replicable model that will provide ongoing mentoring and professional de-

velopment for novice science teachers to increase the probability that they will be retained and become career teachers.

The goals of the program fall in line with the project's desire to increase the supply of qualified science teachers for the local school district as well as for other partner school districts in rural regions of the state. The project thus far has managed to attract racially and ethnically diverse science majors (who are traditionally underrepresented among science teachers and who would likely take other career paths) into the teaching field by an extensive recruitment campaign that targets senior and recent graduates in the STEM disciplines. Currently the lack of certified science teachers is a major cause of poor achievement and low expectations for high-risk students. This problem is greatly exacerbated in both rural and urban areas because schools in these locales are most likely to serve disadvantaged children and to have teachers who are teaching out of field. For this reason, PTS immediately impacts the academic achievement of students in these target school districts. Through the Noyce scholarship program, a redesigned alternative certification program was developed to significantly increase the clinical field experiences while shortening the time to complete certification, thus putting more qualified science teachers into classrooms sooner.

The Noyce PTS program adds to the body of knowledge identifying factors that attract science majors to careers as secondary school teachers. Beyond providing incentives to commit to the program, the programs engage science education candidates in a replicable curriculum that is designed to provide a wide spectrum of teaching experiences to disadvantaged students, especially poor and minority students attending hard to staff schools. Perhaps the most critical characteristic for PTS is the mentoring of these newly minted teachers to ensure that they will provide effective instruction in their own classrooms and are set on a pathway to becoming career teachers.

DESIGN OF THE PROGRAM

Once applicants are accepted into the programs, they begin a content rich 48-hour program designed to increase their content knowledge in science and education to provide them with the foundation needed to become effective science teachers. In completing this program, participants are required to earn 15 hours of graduate level credit in science content courses. The remaining 33 credit hours are comprised of education pedagogy courses. The participants are full-time graduate students and complete the intensive program within four semesters (spring through the following spring). In the third semester, participants have a field experience at the middle school level and a field experience at the high school level. In the final semester of the program, participants complete a student teaching experience in a high needs hard to staff school under the supervision of a master teacher in the school, a university supervisor, and the program director.

In addition, Noyce Scholars in PTS are provided with a one-year membership to the Alabama Science Teachers Association (ASTA) and the National Science Teachers Association (NSTA). The program is designed for participants to have the opportunity to interact with and learn from different science teachers across the state of Alabama and across the nation. It is the intent of the program to expose its participants to the best and brightest science teachers in the state and to the best practices in the nation. Specifically, Noyce Scholars complete the following curriculum (also see Table 1):

1. Curriculum and Teaching (9 semester hours)
2. Foundations of Education (6 semester hours)
3. Evaluation of Teaching and Learning (3 semester hours)
4. Technology (3 semester hours)
5. Reading in the Content Areas (3 semester hours)

Table 1. Curriculum

Spring	Summer	Fall	Spring
Curriculum & Teaching	Curriculum & Teaching	Curriculum & Teaching	Internship
Learning Theory	Educational Foundations	Technology	Reading
Content Course	Educational Foundations	Content Course	Special Education
Content Course	Content Course	Content Course	

6. Science Content Teaching Field (15 semester hours)
7. Special Education (3 semester hours)
8. Student Teaching Internship (6 semester hours)

The alternative pathway for initial certification through the alternative master's program is a 48-hour curriculum that is designed for those students who have an undergraduate degree in a science content area. An example of exemplary teacher preparation efforts embedded in the Noyce PTS program is that the program is designed to increase the science content knowledge of its candidates, unlike many graduate level programs that only focus on teaching methodology. The certification offered is a general science certification that requires 15 semester hours of graduate level content course work in at least two science disciplines. The 15 semester hours in graduate level science content along with their existing undergraduate degree equips the Noyce scholars with a deeper understanding of the subjects that they will teach when they enter the teaching profession.

The Noyce Scholars are required to complete four sets of field experiences. They are advised and supervised by the secondary science education faculty. The students have a beginning experience in the schools, a middle school and high school level field experience, and a student teaching experience at the level of their choice. These experiences are in addition to the field experience they complete as a part of the application process. The program ensures that each student in the program has the opportunity to practice and apply the theories learned during their education classes.

Noyce Scholars commit to teach in a high needs secondary school for three years as a condition for them receiving the scholarship. After graduation these new teachers typically are employed by the local school system, a high needs school district, but some will teach in surrounding rural counties where staffing is a major problem. Scholars will participate in the Alabama Teacher Mentor Program (a statewide mentoring initiative for first year teachers) for at least one additional year. The project director also mentors the students for an additional year.

The Noyce Scholars participate in a teacher education program that is designed to meet the diverse needs of the school districts it serves in an ever-changing educational environment. The program that Noyce scholars participate in challenges them to explore their own development, background, and biases so they may critically evaluate and question how teaching in diverse schools can impact the manner in which they view cultures that are different from their own (Tatum, 2002, 1997, 1992). The scholars are challenged to confront those biases in a supportive yet demanding environment that gives them different perspectives and viewpoints to consider because the cultural diversity of students is growing rapidly and is ever changing. This approach prepares the scholars to be effective teachers of all students regardless of ethnicity or socio-economic background (Banks, et al., 2001; Darling-Hammond & Falk, 1997). The program prepares the scholars to be successful in a multicultural society by exploring strategies that deal with cultural relevant pedagogy (Ladson-Billings, 2001), cultural competence (Lindsey, Robins, & Terrell, 2003), relationship building (Irvine, 2002; Ladson-Billings, 1994), and above all else the academic achievement of their students.

MENTORING

A trained master teacher mentors the graduates during their first year of employment to help them transition successfully into the teaching field. The Noyce Programs employ critical elements of the Alabama Mentor Teacher Program (AMTP) that is provided for first year teachers. AMTP was designed to give beginning teachers assistance in three areas:

- **The school:** specific assistance with school-wide issues such as collegiality, school administration policies and procedures, and the enculturation of the new teacher into the school family;
- **The classroom:** special attention is given to issues such as classroom and student management, pacing through the curriculum, and the development of a holistic approach to inquiry based teaching;
- **A teacher's personal life and well being:** an imbalance between a teacher's work and personal life goals can be a contributing factor to the attrition of teachers. According to Ingersoll and Kralik (2004), nationally 14% of beginning teachers quit after their first year of teaching. However, 98% AMTP teachers surveyed responded that they intended to remain in the profession.

The mentoring component of this program is essential to its success because a universal truth exists for beginning teachers; "beginners in teaching are expected to do essentially the same job on the first day of employment as the 20-year veteran.

In addition, teachers spend the majority of their time isolated from their peers… furthermore, beginning teachers are often given some of the most difficult teaching assignments…" (Holden, 1995, p. 1). The mentoring component of this program is designed to offset that reality for many teachers because we know that well designed mentoring programs can help reduce the attrition rates of new teachers. These programs have the capacity to positively affect teachers' attitudes, feelings of efficacy, and their instructional skills (Carr, Herman, & Harris, 2005; Darling-Hammond, 2003).

In addition to the AMTP mentor teacher, the Noyce programs director also mentors the participants. The program director has regularly scheduled visits and program support activities for each graduate during their induction year to provide support and guidance. Additionally, graduates are required to attend quarterly seminars designed to discuss general classroom techniques, classroom demonstrations, and other projects appropriate for science and mathematics. These meetings are designed to strengthen the bond among participants by providing them with an instant network of support. In addition, graduates who may experience difficulty during these critical initial career months will receive immediate and specific intervention. Our aim is to create a community of learners that will support both groups of students.

CREATING A COMMUNITY OF LEARNERS USING TECHNOLOGY (FACEBOOK)

A major challenge in running the Noyce PTS program rests in our ability to create a community of learners where the participants feel supported and safe enough to express concerns or challenges that allow for their optimum growth as teachers. This challenge is present as they matriculate through their program of study and becomes especially challenging after they graduate to become full time science teachers.

To date various forms of technology has been used try to develop a sense of community amongst the students selected to be Noyce scholars while matriculating through the program. However, the technology mainly used that provides immediate access to students and allows for a platform with instantaneous response is Facebook. Noyce Scholars use Facebook for online discussions for their science methods course and Facebook is also used to keep the students connected to one another while they are completing their field experiences. Both will be discussed.

Using Facebook in a Science Methods Course

The Noyce PTS participants' science education methods course and all four field experiences fall under the direction of the secondary science education instructor who happens to be the principal investigator of the Noyce PTS project. Within the course, Facebook is used primarily for online discussion of topics on a private page that was established for the Noyce scholars and other methods students that correspond to the course. In order for lively and meaningful discussion to take place, a sense of community must be established or at least partially established amongst the students before they meaningfully participate in online discussions.

The Noyce Scholars take their science methods course in the third semester of their program of study and much work goes into trying to create a sense of community amongst them in the previous two semesters and throughout the program. Throughout the program scholars are treated to several dinners and also travel to a state and national science education conferences to become familiar with one another. In addition, the scholars take 14 of their 16 (students have the option of taking two science elective course of their choosing) required courses with one another to also assist in building this community of learners and support amongst them. By the time the students

enroll in their science methods course, they are familiar with one another. This familiarity makes discussing difficult topics in class or on Facebook much easier.

Due to time constraints in the science methods course enough time is not always available to discuss topics that are presented or brought up in class and Facebook provides a platform to continued discussion of important topics outside of class time. In addition, the Noyce scholars are given specific topics in which they must lead the Facebook discussion. They think of creative and relevant questions that they want to address based on the readings for the week. For example, here are some questions from a Noyce scholar regarding a case study that the class was assigned to read. The questions were in regard to controversial issues in science:

In case 8.1, Sandy decided to discuss a touchy topic within her community. I would like to know, would you have taken the same route as Sandy and when the parents got involved, would you have still continue with your debate on Friday, or called it off?

Secondly, Sandy comes from a prestigious family and she has never been "without." When I state "without," I mean she comes from a family were both parent are present, her mother was able to stay at home, her father was a physician, and she probably lived in the suburbs with a white picket fence. Being that most of us will be teaching in a title one school, and many of the students live in a poverty stricken environment, how do you as a teacher plan to relate to your students without them feeling/thinking that you are better than them, so there could not be anything in common between the two of you.

Many of the students judged Stephen Hawking and some did not even know who he was. In your class, how do you plan to avoid passing judgment on your students, especially the ones with behavioral problems? And try to help students understand that judging each other is not nice? Additionally, the textbooks are more geared towards Caucasian scientists therefore do you feel it is important for students to know scientists that come from different backgrounds and ethnicities?

With regard to the focus of this chapter, the important point here is that these questions generated 54 comments/responses and other questions from the class. Each time a student posed any question it received the same or even more responses because they were familiar with one another and knew that questions were generated from a sense of wanting to know what others would do and a sense of knowing that the others in the class wanted everyone to develop into excellent teachers. The students are diverse and come from many different backgrounds so the diversity of thought added to the richness of the Facebook discussions. It also helped that although the reading assignments were the foundation of many questions posed the students responses were grounded in the field experiences that they had completed and the field experiences that they were currently in. The discussions were also rich because the assigned readings had relevance to what they were experiencing in their program.

Facebook provides for the science methods class a space to discuss topics to a level that is much more in-depth as opposed to discussing it in class. In class, time does not permit endless conversation on any particular topic. Topics chosen for class are pre-selected and based on what the instructor deems necessary to discuss with room built in to discuss other issues that students want to discuss but again time is limited. Since many students are already Facebook users they simply just join the group created especially for them and discuss what they wanted to discuss whenever they feel like it. Using a form of technology that the students already use allows the instructor to monitor the students thinking and address possible misconceptions that students held with regard to

education or even content specific issues. The technology allows for everyone, students and instructor alike, to get to know each other better as everyone was every ones friends on Facebook and were allowed access. Students and instructor really learned a lot about each other by following one another. This was both good and bad in some instances.

Using established technology that was a companion to the course was also used and in truth the students could have used that technology for online discussions as well. However, it was mainly used to turn in assignments. This technology was not used as much for online discussions because the instructor wanted the students to get to know each other better on a personal basis and the class technology was too formal for that to happen effectively.

Field Experiences and Facebook

Keeping the Noyce Scholars connected during their field experiences, especially student teaching is challenging and in many respects many areas exists where improvement can occur. Of the seven students who were in the program none were placed at the same school so Facebook was used to keep them connected with one another along with occasional dinners and meetings that were held.

The idea was for students to participate in student teaching and then vent on the private Facebook page that was created for them to do so. Some students did so sparingly at times but most did not because the demands of student teaching were just so much for them to handle. They were constantly lesson planning and constantly working on their craft. They were trying to become a part of the school culture in which they were assigned. Their supervisors knew what they were doing because they were required to turn in reflections that showed that they were critically thinking about the activities they were engaged in their student teaching experience. Whether that activity was lesson planning, teach lessons, developing relationships with students, participating in after school activities or whatever the supervisors knew what was happening.

The problem is that the majority of the time the supervisors were the only ones that knew what each student was engaged in and their thought processes because they did not share with their peers their experiences on the platform designed for them to do so. They shared some experiences with one another at meetings, informal dinners, or within a class but the goal was to develop a community that could sustain itself without providing a catalyst for interaction to occur so that all could learn from each other's experiences.

It is a belief that teaching is a profession in which teachers isolate themselves from one another once they are in their classrooms and close the doors. Student teaching can work in the same manner in that the student teachers are typically isolated from each other in a classroom with an individual teacher and if they are not highly encouraged to interact with each other they will not do so for the most part. The goal is to develop a community of learners that engage with one another freely without them being forced to do so. As we move forward with the program closer attention will be paid to the interactions that occur between students and future cohorts will be highly encouraged to use the platform established for them to communicate with one another to developed a more tightly knit community of learners that can be sustainable beyond their graduation date.

CONCLUSION

Training science teachers can be a difficult job in itself and developing a sense of community amongst them adds to that difficulty to that endeavor. However, technology has that ability to make that job a tad bit easier if implemented correctly. The Noyce Pathway to Science program success is partially measured by being able to retain the participants of the program as career science teachers after graduation. Technology will definitely assist with that goal.

The technology that the participants use in their education program and after graduation will bring a diversity of thought to their individual experiences. This diversity of thought will assist them in developing into better science teachers and eventually into leaders at their individual schools. The technology used will help keep participants of the program connected so that they will have a stable support system of peers who will be there to encourage them in those down days that every teacher has and cheer them on when they are achieving at the highest levels.

REFERENCES

Banks, J. A., Cookson, P., Gay, G., Hawley, W. D., Irvine, J. J., & Nieto, S. (2001). Diversity within unity: Essential principles for teaching and learning in a multicultural society. *Phi Delta Kappan*, *83*(3), 196–203.

Carr, J. F., Herman, N., & Harris, D. E. (2005). *Creating dynamic schools through mentoring, coaching, and collaboration.* Alexandria, VA: ASCD.

Darling-Hammond, L. (2003). Keeping good teachers: Why it matters what leaders can do. *Educational Leadership*, *60*(8), 6–13.

Darling-Hammond, L., & Falk, B. (1997). Supporting teaching and learning for all students: Policies for authentic assessment systems. In Goodwin, A. L. (Ed.), *Assessment for Equity and Inclusion: Embracing All Our Children* (pp. 51–75). New York, NY: Routledge.

Holden, J. (1995). *Mentoring frameworks for Texas teachers.* East Lansing, MI: National Center for Research on Teacher Learning.

Ingersoll, R., & Kralik, J. (2004). *The impact of mentoring on teacher retention: What the research says*. Denver, CO: Education Commission of the States.

Irvine, J. (2002). *In search of wholeness: African American teachers and their culturally specific classroom practices*. New York, NY: Palgrave Macmillan.

Ladson-Billings, G. (1994). *The dreamkeepers: Successful teachers of African American children*. San Francisco, CA: Jossey-Bass.

Ladson-Billings, G. (2001). *Crossing over to Canaan*. San Francisco, CA: Jossey-Bass.

Lindsey, R. B., Robins, K. N., & Terrell, R. D. (2003). *Cultural proficiency: A manual for school leaders* (2nd ed.). Thousand Oaks, CA: Corwin Press.

Tatum, B. D. (1992). Talking about race, learning about racism: The application of racial identity development theory in the classroom. *Harvard Educational Review*, *62*(1), 1–24.

Tatum, B. D. (1997). *Why are all the black kids sitting together in the cafeteria? And other conversations about race*. New York, NY: Basic Books.

Tatum, B. D. (2002). Choosing to be black: The ultimate white privilege? In Singley, B. (Ed.), *When Race becomes Real: Black and White Writers confront their Personal Histories* (pp. 215–224). Chicago, IL: Lawrence Hill Books.

Chapter 15
Global Status Elevation in Today's Classroom

Susan Ferguson Martin
University of South Alabama, USA

ABSTRACT

This chapter details how technology may be implemented and utilized in K-12 and post-secondary class-rooms as a resource for inviting two-way communication between American students and educators and students and educators from other countries, as well as potential expectations and outcomes from such a teaching tool. This model demonstrates going beyond infrequent, rare communication to regular two-way communication as part of the typical curriculum, in an effort to elevate the status of people from other countries through promotion of cultural, linguistic, and interpersonal communication.

INTRODUCTION

Through the Internet, learners may access information from the world over, yet it is not only access to technological literacy that empowers students. Access to people globally as learning resources is an underutilized asset to the average classroom. Some foreign language courses access information and engage in occasional global communication beyond classroom walls, but even those resources are underused. With today's learner being more apt to learn from an online, interactive source than from a textbook or other print source, it seems

logical to take the experience a step further to live, two way interaction with people from various countries and cultural backgrounds. No longer is the power to study abroad limited to time and monetary resources; it is limited only to Internet access.

Much of the prejudice that continues to perpetuate itself across borders of nationality, race, religion, and politics, comes from a lack of familiarity. Though this era of highly accessible international news coverage has helped some become more geographically aware, continued limited contact with the global community still leaves many viewing life outside the country's borders as mystical at best, or scary and cruel, as much news

DOI: 10.4018/978-1-4666-2668-3.ch015

coverage seems to convey. The dispelling of bias is a crucial component of social change. Education has been playing a critical role in modern global culture and society; culture has had enormous impacts on education by constantly generating new demands. It is essential that students obtain cross-cultural awareness to be competitive in the global economy.

With the tools in place for global communication as a typical classroom component, students may engage in regular cultural and language learning from a primary source, rather than secondhand. They may travel to the streets and homes and historical places that were before mere images on the pages of their textbooks. Students may experience firsthand what sets them apart from the world, as well as what makes people similar. Teachers may co-teach with international counterparts. Ongoing learning and cultural and educational exchanges may be actualized through Internet based communications, such as classrooms that span multiple countries through the use of two way online communication. Additionally, relationships may easily be maintained, language skills may be enhanced, and cultural exchanges may continue to flow through ongoing relationships by email exchanges between international and American educational partners.

The opportunity for international learning partnerships is no longer limited to those who have the opportunity to travel abroad. The opportunity is now, in our classrooms, available to all.

THE WAY WE WERE (AND ARE)

In 1974 *The Equal Education Opportunities Act*, reaffirming equal education for all, and in the same year *Lau. V. Nichols,* demonstrated that the 14th amendment applied to language being tied to national origin discrimination. This was a landmark time for many born in America and others who had more recently immigrated to the United States. While discrimination in the classroom gained

attention and started a slow path to dissolving, it still remains prevalent in the today. Some of the concerns of the 1970s have remained—that too often marginalized students are not afforded the same educational opportunities as others. With a growing immigrant population, other concerns over discrimination based on language, culture, and socioeconomics have gained recent attention. Hopefully, if you are reading this book a decade or more after the copyright of this publication, the need for such a chapter on status elevation for students will be dated, and you will be able to look back at how far we have come in elevating the status of marginalized people. Until such a time, there remains the need for educating students of all ages on the necessities and merits of recognizing the value of all people for their personal merits as well as the value of interchanges between others as an aide for self edification.

Among other difficulties faced by English language learners, immigrants, and other marginalized people, are the pains with which they try to position themselves socially. What is less evident, for it is more an internal struggle, are the difficulties faced by many non-native English speakers in terms of how to begin to interact in a predominantly English language, American cultural environment. While some are willing to take risks in learning and negotiating language, many are more likely to wait for an invitation to interact. Even when such opportunities present themselves, some will participate with great hesitancy and apprehension. There is also the attitudinal consideration of status and worth. Many students may find it difficult to have a positive attitude if they perceive that they are being looked down upon. Sometimes it is easier to adopt a "tough" attitude than to appear susceptible to racial criticism or taunts about speech, dress, and culture. Likewise, those unfamiliar with different cultures are reticent to engage in conversation and academic exchanges with cultures non-similar to their own.

One way to combat the issue is through elevation of status. When students, regardless of who they are, are seen by their peers as a benefit to the greater good, stereotypes are often thrown by the wayside. Each student brings to the educational situation his or her own set of lived through experiences. While we may guess about some background knowledge, we cannot begin to know the whole of the experiences of another being. Daniels (2007) says, "The skilled teacher brings, or weaves, together pupil perspectives and understandings with those that she seeks to promote in the classroom. This process builds on pupil prior knowledge and understanding with the ideas and concepts the teacher wishes to explore with them" (Daniels, 2007, p. 325). We cannot guess what rich life experience might lead to self and fellow student discovery through. In fact, for students such experiences take the form of prior knowledge, prior lived through experiences. According to Schecter and Cummins (2003), "we set out to enhance the status of multilingual children by creating a context within the school where they would have ample opportunities to demonstrate their skills and to share aspects of their cultures, countries of origin, and personal experiences with their peers and teachers" (Schecter, 2003, p. 35).

Rosenblatt (2005) says that students have within them qualities that make them conducive to learning—qualities she refers to as "inner capital." In "The Transactional Theory of Reading and Writing," she says, "Embodying funded assumptions, attitudes, and expectations about language and about the world, this inner capital is all that each of us has to draw on in speaking, listening, writing, or reading. We 'make sense' of a new situation or transaction and make new meanings by applying, reorganizing, revising, or extending public and private elements selected from our personal linguistic-experiential reservoirs" (Rosenblatt, 2005, p. 5). Language is capital in a very global sense, and it is certainly the currency of success in the educational world. It purchases the path to a wealth of knowledge and carries with it an exchange rate of self-promotion and advancement. For marginalized students who are hesitant, for

those who do not know the score when it comes to interaction within an educational situation, we must invite them to make sense of their situation. By lowering their anxieties and raising their confidence, students become more receptive to take in the environment that surrounds them. Rosenblatt describes it as, "A nurturing environment that values the whole range of human achievements, the opportunity for stimulating experiences, cultivation of habits of observation, opportunities for satisfying natural curiosity about the world, a sense of creative freedom—all of these lay the foundation for linguistic development" (p. 81).

In their 2003 book, *Multilingual Education in Practice: Using Diversity as a Resource*, Schecter and Cummins demonstrate that, "By acknowledging to students that their L1 (first language) represents a significant accomplishment, we would encourage then to express themselves more fully through their L1 (first language) in both oral and written communication. This home language communication is particularly important during a time when they may feel inadequate about their English proficiency or frustrated by their inability to express their needs, thoughts, ideas, and knowledge" (Schecter, 2003, p. 35). Support for the L1 is important in validating students' culture, for not only does it fill students with a sense of pride that they have made in their lifetime great accomplishments, but is also illustrates for classmates that this student, too, has a background and a heritage. Freeman and Freeman (2006) explain the importance of incorporating first language textual support in terms of intrinsic value explaining, "Cultural literacy helps readers understand their own history and culture and how they fit into and also shape the social structure" (Freeman, 2006, p. 11). Through allowing students to write, express, and create in and with their first language, we demonstrate to individual students that what they already know is valid and worthwhile to us. Through incorporating live connections to various cultures into the classroom situation, we demonstrate to all students that we value their culture and other cultures, as being of as much import as our own.

Following that same line of reasoning, Miller (2003) challenges teachers to transform their classrooms into environments where Vygotsky's *Zone of Proximal Development* (ZPD) can function. She postulates that for some teachers this means changing student roles and allowing for more student interaction and whole-class discussion (Miller, 2003, pp. 292-293). The classroom then takes the form of, "a supportive social space in which mutual assistance creates new ways of talking and thinking about texts—that is, such discussion creates a zone of proximal development" (p. 312). This type of classroom environment also demands peer collaboration, playing into another Vygotskian idea. Vygotsky had, early in his work, declared that the ZPD would work when "more competent peers" and adults interacted with and aided students in their learning. Gibbons says that this "successful coordination with a partner—or assisted performance—leads learners to reach beyond what they are able to achieve alone, to participate in new situation and to tackle new tasks, or, in the case of second language learners, to learn new ways of using language" (Gibbons, 2002, p. 8). She also explains that Vygotskian theory not only sees interaction as significant, but also "views dialogue as constructing the resources for thinking" (p. 14). Gibbons translates this to the classroom when she explains that while there needs to be room for talk that allows learners to "explore and clarify concepts or to try out a line of thought through questioning, hypothesizing, making logical deductions, and responding to other's ideas." Kathleen Fay and Suzanne Whaley (2004) express the implications of Vygotsky's principle for the multicultural classroom as, "Students understand concepts by experiencing them rather than by merely being told how something works" (Fay, 2004, p. 17). Such classroom contexts demonstrate what has been known in a broad sense as the constructivist approach to education.

A GLOBAL MISSION FOR EDUCATORS

Institutions of education in the United States continue to host a growing number of speakers of English as a second language at all levels of academics and English language fluency. Likewise, global connections continue to be sought and established between institutions in the U.S. and those in other countries.

Many educators recognize that the growth in the immigrant population and the attempt to globalize government and educational institutions necessitates action to educate students in a more holistic way. Given the growing number of limited English proficient members of our society, as well as the increasing need to understand events on a global canvas, there is a growing need to educate more diverse students for successful lifelong endeavors.

Unfortunately, there is far too often a wiling learner who meets with a less than willing teacher in an environment unfavorable for promoting quality, meaningful learning experiences, thus resulting in the degradation of student motivation. While some students are able to learn in spite of the absence of educational nurture, others become discouraged learning too minimal an amount to contend in the educational arena. Many students feel that teachers do not care about them or value them as people. Since many adults continue to perpetuate (too often openly) prejudices that influence others, it is important to invite students to explore diversity in order to create their own understanding.

An underutilized way to erase global barriers incorporates technology in the classroom through two-way visual communication as well as through email and social networking. What once was possible only by way of student exchange programs, study abroad, or immigrant enrollment, is now available to all students—free. No longer is global understanding available only to those who can afford to travel. Live communication and relationship development may now perpetuate cultural understanding and advancement for all parties involved. In addition, it is educationally, as well as socially, sound!

When we consider all that we do in the classroom to promote communication as well as to advance social development, the possibilities for cultural exchange and understanding fit into most every aspect of the curriculum. What hinders many from making these classroom connections are perceived time constraints and uncertainty as to how to begin the process of inviting the world into the classroom.

MS. LENTZ'S TECHNOLOGICAL CULTURAL EXCHANGE

In her small, southeastern school district, Ms. Lentz is an advocate for English language learners as well as a secondary English language arts teacher. For years, she had looked for ways to educate her peers on global differences and similarities as the school district received growing numbers of immigrants with limited English proficiency. The main issues she kept facing were apathy on the part of her peers and prejudice by many of the American students who were not taking well to the changing demographics of the region. On the one hand, she wanted to keep all the newcomers with her, to somehow shelter them from the ridicule until their English was more fluent and they could defend themselves. On the other she wished that her fellow teachers would understand that all students have a right to an equal education, and besides language differences they are not too dissimilar to other students in the district.

It was one day after a particularly tough bullying issue among a newcomer from Venezuela and an American student on the soccer team, Ms. Lentz determined to effect change at all costs. She knew that she might not have the support of her fellow teachers. Though she would have support from the administration, that support came in the form of, "You know what's best, so do what you think," which was pretty much the equivalent to the apathy conveyed by her peers.

Ms. Lentz felt certain that what the school needed was an understanding of the similarities between the immigrant population and themselves, as well as an appreciation for the cultural differences that brought diversity and depth to the area. There must be some way to convey what seemed to obvious to her, to a doubting, disgruntled population.

One thing that had sparked some interest was a cultural food fair and arts festival. Since forty-three different cultures were represented in her school system, the fair made for interesting tastes and entertainment. Staff and students seemed to enjoy the occasion, and she felt certain that she needed more frequent cultural encounters to produce a more long lasting effect.

Ms. Lentz was also a realist. She realized she needed to start with her own classroom and perhaps a couple of teachers who would value her plan and effort for positive change, and then take the plan to the school and district as a whole.

She had a couple of students who had been in the school system for a while before returning to Brazil to live. Their father had been in the U.S. to work for his company for three years, and he had brought his family to experience the culture and language experience along with him. The brother and sister had both adapted quite well to their American surroundings. Though they spoke Portuguese fluently, they had known enough English when they arrived to feel comfortable participating in school extracurricular activities. Because of their appearance, the family blended in well with their peers and were generally well received by classmates and teachers. The entire family had kept in touch through email and online social networks, and she thought they might hold some key in helping her bridge the gap.

Ms. Lentz set up a series of online, face-to-face conversations through SKYPE. She planned the conversations around a thematic unit for her juniors and seniors who were working on interview skills.

To prepare her class she had them brainstorm questions they would want to ask someone who lived in a different country. When time came for face-to-face contact, the students were receptive to the interaction. They generally found the conversations interesting, commenting on the "cool accents" and on how the people in Brazil looked very similar to people in the United States.

The next set of conversations took place a week later. Ms. Lentz had met a professor and his family who planned to move into the area the following school year. She thought it would be interesting for the family to interview her students about life in the United States. She did not tell the students ahead of time that the family was from Mexico. She did, however, tell them that this time they were going to be on the opposite side of the interview. This time students were eager to express the positive aspects of the school. The family asked about sports and theater. They wanted to know about the weather and fun activities. They also asked about whether they would be welcome at the school and whether there were other people from Mexico that lived in the community.

In the days that followed, Ms. Lentz's students were eager to make other connections. They wanted to meet people in other countries. Some students suggested that they continue to talk to the family from Mexico to help make them feel welcome. Several students wanted to have an email exchange with the families from Mexico and Brazil. Word spread to other classes and teachers that the international conversations were taking place, and students seemed eager for other projects that could connect them with people outside the classroom setting.

Soon many made connections to the Central American and South American students in the school. Ms. Lentz invited some of the students to take part in the online and in class conversations, and while it did not fix all the prejudices, it seemed to be a start in opening lines of communication. Much psychology could be debated about how students responded in what seemed a backward way to social change, but the overall idea seemed beneficial, and in the months to come, Ms. Lentz helped her students make connections with families in Saudi Arabia, Germany, South Korea, and Ghana. Using on the resources already at her disposal, and generating conversations open to both sides, new ways of looking at people from differing cultural backgrounds were realized.

Were it not for such opportunities, some students would never speak with anyone of another cultural or linguistic background, much less someone in another country. Many people in other countries are more than happy to reciprocate, for it offers them an opportunity to learn something of the American way of life. So much of what we believe about other countries and cultures is influenced by what is apparent on the political radar. Yet we often fail to learn about the people of a nation. These personal conversations among average people are what truly helps elevate status and opinions. That can then translate to the marginalized people within a school and a community.

SOLUTIONS AND RECOMMENDATIONS

One barrier to implementing the technological approach to status elevation in the classroom is time. As with any curricular change, there is no way around the fact that activities involved with two way communication and online research are going to consume some of the hours otherwise devoted to other aspects of the curriculum. What may be done is a restructuring of how you use these initiatives in multiple aspects of your classroom. Ms. Lentz was able to use the online research component of her classroom to fulfill many of her state curricular objectives, and much of what the students found was later written up and discussed, thus fulfilling even more of the components of her language arts curriculum.

Another barrier may be access to technology within the classroom. While some classrooms and school districts seem more technologically endowed than others, there are still ways around this barrier. Many teachers get permission to use their own laptops in the classroom. Some schools have computer labs that teachers may reserve, while many are moving toward carts of laptops that may be checked out for classroom use.

Something else to consider as you seek global partnerships is time zone differences. While this will not be a complete hindrance in all situations, it is still important as you make plans to meet your neighbors abroad.

Typically, new ideas that are implemented with educational standards in mind are supported at the local and state level. With more discussion about how to best address diversity in the classroom, school districts are looking for tangible, low cost ideas to bring to their student population.

CONCLUSION

Barriers still exist that continue to marginalize people that differ from the status quo. With technology allowing teachers to reach out to the global community by way of online resources and face-to-face interaction, the path to status elevation for students in American schools and the international community will hopefully be a short one.

REFERENCES

Daniels, H. (2007). Pedagogy. In Daniels, H., Cole, M., & Wertsch, J. V. (Eds.), *The Cambridge Companion to Vygotsky* (pp. 307–331). Cambridge, UK: Cambridge University Press.

Fay, K., & Whaley, S. (2004). *Becoming one community: Reading and writing with English language learners*. Portland, OR: Stenhouse.

Freeman, Y. S., & Freeman, D. (2006). *Teaching reading and writing in Spanish and English in bilingual and dual language classrooms*. Portsmouth, UK: Heinemann.

Gibbons, P. (2002). *Scaffolding language, scaffolding learning: Teaching second language learners in the mainstream classroom*. Portsmouth, UK: Heinemann.

Miller, S. M. (2003). How literature discussion shapes thinking: ZPD's for teaching/learning habits of the heart and mind. In Kozulin, A., Gindis, B., Ageyev, V. S., & Miller, S. M. (Eds.), *Vygotsky's Educational Theory in Cultural Context* (pp. 289–316). Cambridge, UK: Cambridge University Press. doi:10.1017/CBO9780511840975.016

Rosenblatt, L. (2005). The transactional theory of reading and writing. In Rosenblatt, L. (Ed.), *Making Meaning with Texts* (pp. 1–37). Portsmouth, UK: Heinemann.

Schecter, S. R., & Cummins, J. (2003). *Multilingual education in practice: Using diversity as a resource*. Portsmouth, UK: Heinemann.

ADDITIONAL READING

Barbieri, M. (2002). *Change my life forever: Giving voice to English-language learners*. Portsmouth, UK: Heinemann.

Cary, S. (2002). *Working with second language learners: Answers to teachers' top ten questions*. Portsmouth, UK: Heinemann.

Chaiklin, S. (2003). The zone of proximal development in Vygotsky's analysis of learning and instruction. In Kozulin, A., Gindis, B., Ageyev, V. S., & Miller, S. M. (Eds.), *Vygotsky's Educational Theory in Cultural Context* (pp. 39–64). Cambridge, UK: Cambridge University Press. doi:10.1017/CBO9780511840975.004

Cranton, P. (2002). Teaching for transformation. *New Directions for Adult and Continuing Education, 93*, 63–71. doi:10.1002/ace.50

Creswell, J. W. (2007). *Qualitative inquiry and research design: Choosing among five approaches.* Thousand Oaks, CA: Sage.

Cummins, J. (1981). Empowering minority students: A framework for intervention. In Garcia, O., & Baker, C. (Eds.), *Policy and Practice in Bilingual Education* (pp. 103–117). Bristol, UK: Multilingual Matters.

de Jong, E., & Grieci, G. (2005). Mapping the ESOL curriculum: Collaborating for student success. In Kaufman, D., & Crandall, J. (Eds.), *Content-Based Instruction in Primary and Secondary School Settings.* Alexandria, VA: TESOL.

Echevarria, J., Vogt, M., & Short, D. (2004). *Making content comprehensible for English language learners: The SIOP model.* Boston, MA: Allyn & Bacon.

Fay, K., & Whaley, S. (2004). *Becoming one community: Reading and writing with English language learners.* Portland, UK: Stenhouse.

Freeman, Y. S., & Freeman, D. (2003). Struggling English language learners: Keys for academic success. *TESOL Journal, 12*(3), 5–10.

Freeman, Y. S., & Freeman, D. (2006). *Teaching reading and writing in Spanish and English in bilingual and dual language classrooms.* Portsmouth, UK: Heinemann.

Freire, P. (1972). *Pedagogy of the oppressed.* Harmondsworth, UK: Penguin.

Gibbons, P. (2002). *Scaffolding language, scaffolding learning: Teaching second language learners in the mainstream classroom.* Portsmouth, UK: Heinemann.

Giroux, H. (1997). *Pedagogy and the politics of hope: Theory, culture, and schooling.* Boulder, CO: Westview Press.

Gordon, T. (2005). Working together to raise content-based instruction into the zone of proximal development. In Kaufman, D., & Crandall, J. (Eds.), *Content-Based Instruction in Primary and Secondary School Settings.* Alexandria, VA: TESOL.

Hedegaard, M. (1990). The zone of proximal development as basis for instruction. In Moll, L. C. (Ed.), *Vygotsky and Education: Instructional Implications and Applications of Sociohistorical Psychology* (pp. 349–371). Cambridge, UK: Cambridge University Press. doi:10.1017/CBO9781139173674.017

Herrel, A., & Jordan, M. (2004). *Fifty strategies for teaching English language learners.* Upper Saddle River, NJ: Pearson.

Kaufman, D., & Crandall, J. (Eds.). (2005). *Content-based instruction in primary and secondary school settings.* Alexandria, VA: TESOL.

Krashen, S. (1981). *Second language acquisition and second language learning.* Oxford, UK: Pergamon Press.

Krashen, S. (1982). *Principles and practices in second language acquisition.* Oxford, UK: Pergamon Press.

Krashen, S. (1985). *The input hypothesis: Issues and implications.* London, UK: Longman Group.

Krashen, S. (2000). What does it take to acquire language? *ESL Magazine, 3*(3), 22–23.

Krashen, S., & Terrell, T. (1983). *The natural approach: Language acquisition in the classroom.* London, UK: Prentice Hall Europe.

Kutz, E., Groden, S., & Zamel, V. (1993). *The discovery of competence: Teaching and learning with diverse student writers.* Portsmouth, UK: Heinemann.

McCarty, T., & Dick, G. (2003). Telling the people's stories: Literacy practices and processes in a Navajo community school. In Willis, A., Garcia, G., Barrera, R., & Harris, V. (Eds.), *Multicultural Issues in Literacy: Research and Practice* (pp. 101–122). Mahwah, NJ: Lawrence Erlbaum & Associates.

Morales-Jones, C. A. (2002). Teaching for communication. In Zainuddin, H., Yahya, N., Morales-Jones, C. A., & Ariza, E. (Eds.), *Fundamentals of Teaching English to Speakers of Other Languages in K-12 Classrooms* (pp. 68–83). Dubuque, IA: Kendall/Hunt Publishing.

Nieto, S. (1999). *The light in their eyes: Creating multicultural learning communities*. New York, NY: Teachers College Press.

Rosenblatt, L. (2005a). The literary transaction: Evocation and response. In *Making Meaning with Texts* (pp. 72–88). Portsmouth, UK: Heinemann.

Rosenblatt, L. (2005b). The transactional theory of reading and writing. In Rosenblatt, L. (Ed.), *Making Meaning with Texts* (pp. 1–37). Portsmouth, UK: Heinemann.

Rueda, R., & Garcia, E. (2003). Assessing and assisting performance of diverse learners: A view of responsive teaching in action. In Willis, A., Garcia, G., Barrera, R., & Harris, V. (Eds.), *Multicultural Issues in Literacy: Research and Practice* (pp. 203–222). Mahwah, NJ: Lawrence Erlbaum & Associates.

Schecter, S. R., & Cummins, J. (2003). *Multilingual education in practice: Using diversity as a resource*. Portsmouth, UK: Heinemann.

Schmittau, J. (2003). Cultural-historical theory and mathematics education. In Kouzlin, A., Gindis, B., Ageyev, V., & Miller, S. (Eds.), *Vygotsky's Educational Theory in Cultural Context* (pp. 225–245). Cambridge, UK: Cambridge University Press. doi:10.1017/CBO9780511840975.013

Snow, D. (1992). *Myths and misconceptions about English language learning*. Washington, DC: Center for Applied Linguistics.

Valdes, G. (2001). Learning and not learning English: Latino students. In Willis, A., Garcia, G., Barrera, R., & Harris, V. (Eds.), *Multicultural Issues in Literacy: Research and Practice* (pp. 185–202). Mahwah, NJ: Lawrence Erlbaum & Associates.

Vygotsky, L. S. (1962). *Thought and language* (Hanfman, E., & Vakar, G., Trans.). Cambridge, MA: MIT Press. doi:10.1037/11193-000

Wong Fillmore, L., & Snow, C. (2000). *What teachers need to know about language. ERIC Clearinghouse on Language and Linguistics*. Washington, DC: Center for Applied Linguistics.

Chapter 16
Google Unbound:
Using Web 2.0 Tools to Develop High Literacy

Mark Mouck
American Cooperative School of Tunis, Tunisia

ABSTRACT

This chapter is an exploration of Langer's Envisioning Literature: Literary Understanding and Literature Instruction in the context of the 21st century. A social-constructivist, Langer identifies five stances that highly literate readers use to interpret a text. Noting that much of Langer's oeuvre was written prior to the advent of the Internet, the author provides transformational teachers with research-based examples of skills and lessons for using Internet technology to tap into a diversity of voices in the literature classroom. Framed in the context of a society that has recently experienced the democratization of information, where citizens need to be able to quickly interpret a variety of voices, this chapter explores the social construction of knowledge in the classroom and online to prepare them to be participants in the social construction of knowledge in the Information Age.

INTRODUCTION

Google has replaced Prometheus. The archetypal trickster is unbound, Pandora's box is loosed and the world is glutted with information. The myth of Google, the myth that information is at our fingertips (Introna & Nissenbaum, 2000; Granka, 2010), is exacerbated by an inability to handle the information overload (Lim, So, & Tan, 2010) or read it critically (Williams, Karousou,

& Mackness, 2011). Modern adolescents have access to more information than in any other time in the history of the world (Bertolt, 2009; Gray, Thomas, & Lewis, 2010; Helsper & Eynon, 2010; Pinder-Grover & Groscurth, 2009). While their complicity in the generation of information on Web 2.0 applications and platforms compounds the glut, its potential for collaboration and critical thinking is also just beginning to be explored as a pedagogical tool (Gouseti, 2010; Jukes, McCain, & Crockett, 2010; Lim, So, & Tan, 2010; Williams, Karousou, & Mackness, 2011; Bobish, 2010; Dlab

DOI: 10.4018/978-1-4666-2668-3.ch016

& Hoic-Bozic, 2011; Humrickson, 2011; Wood, 2010). Small sample sizes and studies of narrow uses of the Internet as a pedagogical tool, however, compound the paucity of research. A research-based, unified purpose and integrative approach to understanding how to harness the Internet for educational purposes on a large scale is needed (Gouseti, 2010; Jukes, McCain, & Crockett, 2010; Lim, So, & Tan, 2010). Langer's (2011a) *Envisioning Literature: Literary Understanding and Literature Instruction* offers a way forward. Over the course of the last several decades, she has developed a research-based pedagogy as well as classroom techniques that teachers can use to help students develop the high literacy that they need to sort through, tap into the richness of, and create meaning out of the glut. Much of Langer's work, however, was written prior to the advent of the Internet, and her more current work mentions the potential of the Internet only in passing (2011b). This chapter proposes ways of adapting her oeuvre for the Internet Age: it will look at ways to engage and enrich knowledge and understanding as well as critical thinking about literary texts through transformational leadership of the culturally diverse voices of the 21st century classroom using Web 2.0 applications.

The goal of Langer's pedagogy is a concept she terms "high literacy," the ability to interpret a variety of new texts through a community that taps into experiences with previous texts and life experiences. Langer (2001) defines high literacy by saying:

Although basic reading and writing skills are included in this definition of high literacy, also included are the ability to use language, content, and reasoning in ways that are appropriate for particular situations and disciplines [....] and that knowledge becomes available as options when students confront new situations (p. 838).

High literacy is the product of a process she terms "envisionment building." Envisionment building is the movement through five stances, or perspectives, that a reader occupies while developing an interpretation of a text.

Langer's approach to developing high literacy places her squarely in the social-constructivist camp, an educational approach that is the legacy of Vygotsky, Bruner, and Bahtkhin's student-centered theories of learning. Their work has direct implications for the Internet generation, whose interconnectivity means they are already versed in the contemporary activities of social-constructivism. Langer's student-centered model is in contrast to the prevailing test driven approach of content-centered models. While the content-centered model has, for generations, yielded research-based techniques for setting goals, motivating students and assessing learning, Dewey's legacy has only recently begun to generate research-based techniques that can be used in the classroom. Applebee, Langer, and Purves (1991) admit as much and thus begin their quest to rectify the problem of the teaching of high literacy over the subsequent two decades. Many of those publications present quantitative research on classroom practices that lead to both high literacy and successful achievement on standardized tests (Applebee, Langer, Nystrand, & Gamoran, 2003). Langer's (2011a) approach, however, does not address the ways in which the Internet can be tapped as an educational experience.

The first section of this chapter provides a context for social-constructivism and discusses the advantages and pitfalls of the use of socially constructed knowledge in education over content- and standards-based education. The second section reviews research on the strengths and weaknesses of the use of Web 2.0 applications in education. The third section discusses practical techniques for teaching adolescents how to achieve the five stances of envisionment building using Internet technology.

BACKGROUND

Langer's envisionment building stands in stark contrast to the practice of modern education. Based on two longitudinal studies spanning 12 years (Langer, 2011a), Langer expresses dismay in what she sees in many literary classrooms. Langer's primary critique of modern pedagogy is that it is not modern at all (Langer, 2011a; also see Prensky, 2001). Modern pedagogy, backed by the federal policies of No Child Left Behind and Race to the Top, relies on approaches that were first developed by Thorndike in a previous century to address now obsolete needs. Over the first half of the 20th century, Thorndike developed an assembly line educational system that satisfied the needs of an industrial giant and emerging superpower. Based on identifiable standards as well as valid and reliable tests of achievement, Thorndike's content-centered instructional techniques provided a quantifiable solution to the educational needs of a rapidly growing economy and its swelling workforce (Tomlinson, 1997).

What Thorndike and his legacy did not provide, however, was the development and measurement of thinking (Ketterer, 2008; Watras, 2009). Watras takes his critique one-step further by referring to the comments of a contemporary of Thorndike, Bode, saying, "Thorndike's view of learning was not appropriate for a curriculum dedicated to democracy wherein the members cooperated with each other and with other groups to pursue shared interests" (p. 121). In the 21st century and on the Internet, touted as being the platform for the democratization of information (Friedman, 2005) as well as a place where cooperation is not mutually assured (e.g. cyber bullying), adolescents have access to a variety of texts for which their content-centered education has not prepared them. Langer's social-constructivist pedagogy directly addresses Bode's nearly century-old critique by helping students to develop high literacy.

High literacy is the ability to generate meaning from a text. Meaning is generated from any number of attributes that belong to the text but also attributes that are given to the text by the reader. Attributes that belong to the text include textual, contextual, inter-textual, and discursive meanings. In this way, the meaning of the text is continually shifting depending on which lens the reader uses to view it. In this way, too, the text can claim no one truth, meaning, or interpretation: Langer's "horizons of possibilities."

A text's meaning is dependent upon other lenses that the reader brings to the text as well. Reader-generated meanings, like the meanings generated by the many contexts to which a text belongs, rely on the time and place of the reading and relevant past personal experiences of the reader. Communicating those experiences changes the reader's understanding of the text. Bruner (2004) argues that the stories we tell of our experiences, whether experiences of reading the text or personal experiences that we use to understand it, inter-dependently shape our perceptions of the text and our lives. Furthermore, we decide what the experience we relate means as we utter it. He says, "'Life' in this sense is the same kind of construction of the human imagination as 'a narrative' is" (p. 692). Likewise, audience, time, and place determine what we say and how we say it (Langer, 2001). Bakhtin argues that so much of our utterances is determined by the context of our utterances that context supersedes text (Hamston, 2006; Matusov, 2007).

The thinking that occurs in solitary encounters with a text is different from the thinking that occurs in dialogic thinking. In a discussion, where each participant contributes his or her own experiences to develop an understanding of a text, the community's understanding of the meaning of the text is made richer. Matusov (2007) describes the effects of dialogic thinking this way: through the "recursive dialogical and reflective process, a strong academic discursive community emerged" (p. 219). Bruner takes this one-step further by investigating the cultural influence on the stories we tell:

The tool kit of any culture is replete not only with a stock of canonical life narratives (heroes, Marthas, tricksters, etc.), but with combinable formal constituents from which its members can construct their own life narratives: canonical stances and circumstances, as it were (p. 694).

The greater the personal and cultural diversity of the group that discusses a text, the richer each individual's experience of the text will become: access to a greater variety of experiences of a text lead to richer meaning (Matusov, 2007). The teacher of a student-centered classroom is responsible for creating a context where the other communities to which the members of a class belong contribute to a rich and dynamic discussion.

The literature classroom is a unique community located within a Venn diagram of other communities (Langer, 2011a). Literature classrooms rely on Vygotsky's theory of social-cognition to develop high literacy (Langer, 2001). A contemporary of Bakhtin, his theory holds that knowledge and understanding are community constructs (Langer, 2001). For a community to exist, members agree to the validity of a knowledge set and terminology to describe that knowledge (Bruffee, 2009; Langer, 2001). Langer (2001) summarizes Vygotsky's concept of the role of the environment in forming knowledge saying, "environment is a fundamental part of what gets learned, how it is interpreted, and how it is used" (p 839). With the agreement of the purpose of the classroom established, dialogic thinking, which incorporates multi-vocal contributions, creates and constitutes knowledge and understanding of the text. A community of inquirers is created when both student and teacher "can participate in thoughtful examination and discourse about language and content" (Langer, 2001, p. 839).

The literature classroom asks students to enter into the community of highly literate readers, which requires a perceptual shift. Ketterer (2008) says this shift is psychological and therefore individual: "The child undergoes no less than a restructuring of the personality [...] that results in passage to a new stage" (p. 8). Bruffee (2009) says this shift is socio-cultural: "If we think of knowledge as a socially justified belief, then to teach *King Lear* seems to involve creating contexts where students undergo a sort of cultural change" (p. 560). Bakhtin argues that engaging in dialogue, where a diversity of "discourses are available for an individual to appropriate, to internalise [sic], and to speak through" is inherent to this shift (Hamston, 2006, p. 57). Tapping into both perspectives, teachers are tasked with creating projects and assessments where students see a direct relationship between what they are learning and the world in which they live (Roegiers, 2007). This shift affects not only the culture of the classroom, but also future contexts to which the students will belong. Bruner says:

The ways of telling and the ways of conceptualizing that go with them become so habitual that they finally become recipes for structuring experience itself, for laying down routes into memory, for not only guiding the life narrative up to the present but directing it into the future (p. 708).

Teachers are responsible for giving students the opportunity to try on a variety of roles and voices to develop a variety of perspectives from which to understand the text of study and prepare them for later engagements with other texts (Langer, 2001).

To bring about the perceptual shift of high literacy, the student-centered classroom must be grounded in Vygotsky's Zone of Proximal Development. Vygotsky noted that instruction is best that precedes capacity (Ketterer, 2008). Teachers create experiences that provide the scaffolding to build a concept of the text through the characteristics of personal experiences it. To create a community of inquirers in the classroom, then, is to know that which the diverse members of a community are capable and to know the type of experiences the members need to develop confidently. In a student-centered classroom, students are free to grow from creative engagement with imaginative experiences of a variety of texts (Langer, 2011a).

Navigating the glut of experiences of a text in a classroom relies on transformational leadership. Responding to the disconnect between organizational and educational leadership, Bolkan and Goodboy (2009) and Pounder (2008) sought to identify those attributes of a teacher that enhance student learning. Bolkan and Goodboy (2009) find that teacher credibility is linked to student participation. Matusov (2007) links student participation to a teacher's ability to cede discursive control. Pound (2008) finds that increased participation leads to increased effort in the classroom, which has a stronger, measureable effect on cognitive learning than transactional leadership. So the transformational teacher creates a community where students feel a sense of belonging, which provides a sense of freedom and power over their own learning and which is intellectually and emotionally safe (Barkley, 2007; Davidson, 2009; Marzano, 2007; Sullo, 2007). Transformational leadership engenders a community of diverse enquirers through dialogue. To this end, teachers must become the architects of experience.

Social-constructivism will not always develop high literacy in the classroom, and there are many criticisms of it. Among the ranks of its advocates comes the first criticism: despite teacher's best efforts, sometimes it just does not work (Blau, 2003; Bruffee, 2009; Langer, 2010). Mathews (2003) offers a significantly more scathing assessment. Using data from Project Follow Through, a 27-year study involving 75,000 students comparing student-centered pedagogy to content-centered pedagogy, Mathews shows that students in student-centered classroom performed substantially worse on a wide range of tests. He says these students performed poorly *"even on those outcomes valued in the learner centered approach"* [emphasis original] like self-esteem and higher-order thinking (p. 60). Mathews chooses to ignore the response from a variety of researchers, including House, Glass, and Walker (1978), who point out that different

pedagogies yield different results. House, Glass, and Walker question the use of content-based assessments of achievement to establish conclusions on social-constructivism.

Another criticism of student-centered pedagogy points out that collaborative work is hampered by the varied participatory styles of students, including dominating, non-participating, and off-task students (Pinder-Grover, 2009). This argument is specifically addressed in the time and reflection afforded by asynchronous tools. Finally, the artificial context of the classroom prevents transference of knowledge (Airasina & Walsh, 1997). Taken together these authors reflect the primary issues of the debate between content- and student-centered models of teaching. The first step towards creating the environment where students mold experiences into new ideas is to create an environment where students think critically through dialogue.

USING WEB 2.0 TOOLS AND ENVISIONMENT BUILDING

The Internet is also a unique community; however, extending the research on classroom discussions presented above to the Internet has many advocates. First, Prensky (2001) differentiates between the digital native, one who grew up with the Internet, and the digital immigrant, one who has had to adapt to it. Digital natives think differently than digital immigrants and have different learning needs, which are uniquely met by social-constructivism and the Internet (Arend, 2009; Bose, 2010; Gouseti, 2009; Pinder-Grover & Groscurth, 2009; Wood, 2010). Second, the Internet is ideally suited to creating or, at least, extending the creation of environments where both sets of digerati can access information for a variety of purposes (Helsper & Eynon, 2010; Jukes, McCain, & Crockett, 2010). Third, throughout the five stances of envisionment building, getting students to document and develop their ideas individually or collaboratively online can have many benefits, including a documentation of the development and organization of their ideas (Arend, 2009), deep reflection (Birrell, 2011; Heafner & Friedman, 2008; Arend, 2009), metacognition (Joyce Weill & Calhoun, 2004; Marzano, 2007), recall (Heafner & Friedman, 2008), and transference of knowledge from one context to another (Marzano, 2007).

The advent of Web 2.0 tools has not guaranteed, however, learning or collaboration (Lim, So, & Tan, 2010; Williams, Karousou, & Mackness, 2011). One reason stems from an authorized definition of Web 2.0 tools. In fact, some authors admit to concocting a working definition from a variety of other authors (Heafner & Friedman, 2008). In this way, the definition of Web 2.0 tools reflects the social construction of knowledge in the Internet age. Many others skip a definition and, instead, explain what can be done with Web 2.0 tools in a nod to the ever-shifting nature of Web 2.0 tools (Bobish, 2010; Dlab & Hoic-Bozic, 2011; Humrickson, 2011; Lim, So, & Tan, 2010; Wood, 2010). A second reason stems from teacher's use of Web 2.0 tools without providing adequate structure to an assignment or an explanation of the use of a platform (Lim, So, & Tan, 2010). Part of this problem is addressed in the section on practical advice for teachers using Web 2.0 applications at the end of this chapter. A third problem stems from the additive nature of the use of Web 2.0 tools rather than integrative use of Web 2.0 tools in the classroom, often a result of faulty attempts of a teacher-centered classroom trying to use student-centered techniques (Lim, So, & Tan, 2010; Williams, Karousou, & Mackness, 2011). The extent of this disconnect can be measured by the amount of time students spend reading and commenting on the input of others (Heafner & Friedman, 2008). A fourth problem stems from the fact that educational platforms rarely achieve the involvement saturation that social networking platforms have, and students can become resentful of educational intrusion on social sites (Willams, Karousou, & Mackness, 2011). A fifth problem stems from the way in which students interact with each other on Web 2.0 tools. Ranging from superficial comments like "that was interesting!" to grammar edits, these types of comments fail to achieve the higher-order thinking of a literary classroom and may be the result of a blurring of the line between formal and informal reading contexts (Lim, So, & Tan, 2010). Finally, the most significant problem stems from a paucity of quantitative research on the effectiveness of Web 2.0 tools (Gouseti, 2010; Williams, Karousou, & Mackness, 2011), a reflection of the problem facing the student-centered classroom. Regardless, all papers in this review point to both student appreciation of the collaborative process and the potential for increasing critical thinking skills developed with Web 2.0 tools (Brodahl, Hadjerrouit, & Hansen, 2011; Heafner & Friedman, 2008; Humrickson, 2011). Without an integrative approach to using the Internet as a pedagogical tool, however, there is no guarantee of the benefits of Web 2.0 tools. Langer's envisionment building offers an integrative approach and unified purpose for using the Internet to develop high literacy.

THE FIVE STANCES OF HIGH LITERACY

Langer (2011a) proposes fives stances that highly literate students use to create meaning from a text. She defines a "stance" in terms of understanding and interpretation. To understand a text, she says, is to interpret it. Each stance represents a different perspective from which to understand, and, therefore, interpret a text. The stances are (1) "being outside and stepping into an envisionment," (2) "being inside and moving through an envisionment," (3) "stepping out and rethinking what you know," (4) "stepping out and objectifying the experience," and (5) "leaving the envisionment and going beyond" (pp. 17-21). With each successive stance, the skills required to handle the stance become more abstract. The first three stances deal with a reader's ability to develop knowledge of and understanding of *what* the text says. The third stance, specifically, asks the reader to draw connections between what the text means and the reader's own experience of the concepts of the text. The fourth stance begins to focus more on *how* the text communicates ideas and how these ideas fit into the student's own moral and literary frameworks. The final stance, a new stance in the second edition of *Envisioning Literature: Literary Understanding and Literature Instruction*, describes our ability to generate new ideas and new texts in response to or inspired by the text of study.

The First Stance: Being Outside and Stepping into an Envisionment Building

The first stance is characterized by information gathering. In a first encounter with a text, highly literate readers are trying to establish the topic of the text or a reference point into which to gather information (Langer, 2001). Gathering information can occur as a way to prepare to read the text or while reading the text. Marzano (2007) labels the former "critical input experiences" (p. 31), while Langer (2011a) calls them "easing access" and "inviting initial understandings" (p. 102). While this stance is most prevalent in the first encounters with a text, it can occur throughout the reader's entire experience with the text. As we try to understand what the text "will be about [...] we pick up as many clues as possible" (p. 17). A large number of skills are involved in generating ideas about the meaning of a text. In the first stance, however, the teacher need only help the student accrue facts and inferences. Accruing facts will become crucial to the first and second stances where interpretations are developed.

A number of pre-reading strategies ease access to a text. Easing access often means providing students with and teaching them to develop their own framework from which to begin their reading

and into which they can gather information as they read. A first framework can be developed by having students "thumb" through a book, investigate any information they can glean from a cover, or by providing them with quotes from the text. Asking students to talk about or research and aggregate on a wiki what they know about the time-period in which the text was written or set is one framework (Heafner & Friedman, 2008). Like the Inquiry Model, which is begun with hypothesis generation, Langer's pre-reading strategies ease access and provide the platform for genuine questioning and curiosity (Davidson, 2009; Joyce, Weil, and Calhoun, 2004; Marzano, 2007).

Each of these pre-reading strategies also sets the stage for students to summarize what the text says more accurately while they are reading, an overarching standard for adolescents (Marzano, 2007). The first stance is about knowing what the text says. One simple activity in the information gathering stage includes having a reader keep a blog about what he or she is thinking while reading or when finished with an assignment. This can include questions that arose during the reading that need to be discussed or interesting ideas it inspired. It can also take the form of drawing or finding pictures based on the reading or documenting interesting words or phrases from the text and posting them (Langer, 1991). Students frequently benefit from an assignment that asks them to look for specific things, like actions, events, tone or a character's response to events, while focusing their reading (Langer, 2011a; Birrell, 2011; Arend, 2009). Students can create separate wiki pages for each character, theme, and literary technique. XTimeline allows students to document the sequence of events of a story and to augment the timeline with links, photos, videos or text and allows for comments or discussions about what should be included or not (Heafner & Friedman, 2008). Asking each student to document one original fact from the reading assignment and to aggregate those facts on a wiki creates a central repository for facts or initial ideas.

Finally, Langer (2011a) suggests getting students to write their thoughts before they join a discussion. Forums, where students are required to write a reflective post based on a reading assignment as well as comment on other posts, facilitate a nightly reading reflection and encourage online discussion, as some students will return to check on replies (Birell, 2011). To get a discussion with adolescents started, broad questions about the text like, "What did you think of the reading?," "What was it about?," "What did it make you think about?" are crucial to allow adolescents to feel comfortable about speaking their minds (Langer, 2011a). Arend (2009) and Birrell (2011) find that the audience of a forum encourages meaningful reflection, which can be stimulated by requiring students to post a comment in a forum and to reply to other's posts. Additionally, Arend (2009) finds that the asynchronous nature of Web 2.0 applications further increases reflective thinking. These can become better reference sites than the literary guides discussed in the fourth stance and hold information to be used for final projects.

Discussions on a forum or in a classroom, where members invite participation to tap individual understanding and seek clarification (Langer, 1991), are best orchestrated within community-prescribed rules. Research suggests that allowing students to develop the rules of discussion makes these ground-rules explicit, builds buy-in, whereby the community is responsible for the enforcement of the rules, fosters Bruffee's (2009) normalized language all of which develops trust among its community members (Farr, 2010; Langer, 2001; Lemov, 2010). These rules can be determined in class meetings (Marzano, 2007; Sullo, 2007) and posted to the home page of a forum or as part of a student-generated rubric for blogs. The most effective rules, though, are going to be the ones open to negotiation. As the year progresses, the rules established by the learning community at the beginning of the year should be challenged, modified, or eliminated altogether (Marzano, 2007). In this way, the teacher provides guidance to help students develop a safe environment in which to try out and compare ideas from a variety of voices. These platforms can become seeds for in-class discussions since immediate insights are introduced, perspectives are taken, and misunderstandings can be corrected.

The Second Stance: Being Inside and Moving through an Envisionment

After developing initial ideas about a text, the highly literate become immersed in the world, or framework, of the text and continually augment, modify or even abandon it for a better one. The process of "moving through" an envisionment is similar to the Inductive Model. Joyce, Weil, and Calhoun (2004) conclude their chapter on "Learning to Think Inductively" with a description of inductive reasoning: it is the "continual collecting and sifting of information, construction of ideas, particularly categories, that provide conceptual control over territories of information" (p. 48). Built on the facts and inferences of the first stance, the inductive reasoning model asks students to start to "envision" the text, or to place themselves within its context. In developing opinions about a character or theme, students can review the notes, blogs, forums, and wikis they wrote during the first stance as well as reflections recorded on forums and blogs. The notes they have generated will help them compare and contrast elements of the text, which Marzano (2007) says is a simple but powerful organizational strategy. Once they have mastered comparing characters, for example, they are able to compare and contrast scenes, and eventually texts. Wikis used as aggregators, discussed earlier, become fodder for comparisons, contrasts and synthesis in this stance (Heafner & Friedman, 2008).

In the second stance, literature readers begin to see connections between the text and their own experiences. In this stance, discussions become more personal as the text becomes more familiar.

Open-ended questions that invite elaboration are useful for initiating these types of discussions online and off (Marzano, 2007; Davidson, 2009). At this stage, discussions and forums need to be the laboratory of ideas. As with the Inquiry Model, elaboration and hypothesis generation are two characteristics of the second, third and fourth stances of envisionment building. Davidson (2009) says, "Inquiry involves ambiguity, doubt and multiple perspectives" (p. 35). Key features of the Inquiry Model include what the student is thinking about and questions that arise during the envisionment process (Langer, 2011a). To serve these features, teachers can demonstrate open-ended questions that require students to reflect on and add to what has been said, like Marzano's (2007) "Why would that be true?," and Davidson's (2009) "How do you know that?" (p. 38), which are different from the questions of the first stance. Each elicits the elaboration of possible interpretations that causes meaningful reflection and allows for the genuine exploration of an idea. It also encourages textual-based evidence for an interpretation, crucial to the development of valid conclusions. A community of inquirers will use a discussion to consider an idea carefully, exploring potential problems with the interpretation as well as its implications on other areas of the text. Hypotheses in the form of ideas and interpretations are only considered wrong once students have found a reason for it to be rejected. This type of questioning opens students to Langer's (2011a) "horizons of possibilities" that develop the stances of high literacy rather than being tied to one framework. They invite stocktaking of what the students know and how they know it as well as the first steps towards taking a critical stance and developing interpretations (Langer, 2011a). Ideas developed early on in a blog or a forum are returned to and reflected on later in new posts. Asking students to pick out early ideas that they still deem correct and to elaborate on them, or to modify early ideas to fit new understandings as part of a blog or forum post meets this purpose (Arend, 2009).

In this way, too, learner's ideas are still being expressed in a comfortable setting. Additionally, Ogle (2010) suggests that adolescents need help listening to and understanding each other. She provides them with a few starter phrases that can facilitate a discussion with their peers like, "I'm not sure what that means" and "I thought of that, too, and I also thought about…"(p. 61), which are also effective when written as online comments. These starter phrases are important for discussions on the Internet as well. These discussions then serve as a starting point for large group discussions. They offer students the ability to test ideas and comfortably generate questions about things they did not understand without a spotlight. Collaboration is an important key to the Inquiry Model and the five stances of envisionment building (Joyce, Calhoun, & Weil, 2004; Davidson, 2009; Langer, 2011a; Marzano, 2007).

The Third Stance: Stepping Out and Rethinking What You Know

Reflective thinking and talking is important for adolescents especially as they encounter new ideas and frameworks. In this stance, which occurs as easily on the first day with a text as well as the last, students are encouraged to judge the value of their knowledge of a text. In this stance, summary, inductive reasoning as well as comparison and contrast are just as important as they were in the second stance, but they are used for a different reason. It is in this stance that students start to refine their interpretation. Facts are things that a reader knows because a text states or implies them unambiguously. An interpretation, however, involves all other responses to a text and is the foundation for generating meaning from a text. Interpretations require textual evidence to support them. To develop interpretations of a text, teachers can begin with relatively safe observations like changes in the text (Langer, 2011a). These can be changes in themes, characters, tone, or even the figurative language used to convey these elements in a text. Interpretations can be a return to hypotheses that were generated at the beginning of the reading and tested for accuracy (Davidson, 2009; Marzano, 2007; Langer, 2011a). Asking students to draw from their notes, blogs, or forums about a character to show how a character has changed often forces them to return to an earlier section of a book, which causes them to rethink the ideas they generated on the first reading. Rethinking is one of the hallmarks of high literacy.

Asking students to generate a wiki page or Web page to store powerful quotes aids students in looking carefully at the language. Having them later organize those quotes according to their location in a text or attribution to a character forces them to synthesize the information in a variety of meaningful ways (Marzano, 2007). Providing students with prompts to discuss situations in which they have encountered experiences similar to the character's aids comprehension through sympathy. Cloud-based presentation platforms, like Prezi and Glogster, facilitate the sharing of visual responses and can be developed by multiple users synchronously.

Finally, asking students to use a blog, forum or wiki to share other texts, including songs, videos, poems, other blogs found on the Web, short stories or books that resemble the text in some way to be described by the student encourages reflection as well as transference of knowledge and understanding to new contexts (Heafner & Friedman, 2008; see also Langer, 2011a).

The Fourth Stance: Stepping Out and Objectifying the Experience

In this stance, students gain the skills that are specific to the comprehension of complex literary devices in order to move the framework developed in the first stance into high literacy. This stance is characterized by the ability to analyze the effect of a literary device, to assume a different perspective, personal or historical, and to see connections within the text and with other texts.

Paired opposites offer a way to begin comparing structural components of a text. As adolescents are just starting to gain the conceptual ability to handle abstract thought, paired opposites are complex enough to be stimulating, but not so complex as to be overwhelming, allowing them to work in their zone of proximal development. Some examples include contrasting the literal meaning with the figurative meaning of figurative language, exploring the construction and use of irony and sarcasm, identifying doppelgangers, and discussing textual ambiguities discovered in earlier stances. Sites specializing in online graphic organizers like Glogster, MindMeister, Visuwords, and Wordle help students to illustrate these concepts. These can be imported into cloud-based presentation software like Prezi or Google Docs (Presentations) to become part of larger projects.

A final source both for easing access to a text and gathering information about literary techniques is online literary guides. Given the ubiquity and ease of access to these guides, students will sometimes turn to them in place of reading the text. While many of these sites offer superficial understandings, banning these sites from the classroom is folly and leads to a black market in knowledge. The aim of the social-constructivist classroom is to foster close examination of textual meaning. Holding students accountable through textual evidence of their insights forces them to rely more on the text and less on the literary guides. Additionally, some of these sites can offer broader frameworks for the text, including context, organizational strategies that authors employ, as well as thematic development and the use of figurative language (Langer, 1991). Whether students are exposed to these concepts in the classroom or on-line should not matter, as long as they foster the development of ideas and as long as students are able to support these frameworks with textual evidence. Another use of literary sites asks students to review literary sites for validity, reliability, and depth of analysis and to post their responses on any variety of Web 2.0 tools. Finally, teaching students about plagiarism and how to document the source of their ideas frees them to use these sites to enrich their understanding.

The Fifth Stance: Leaving the Envisionment and Going Beyond

This stance is as much about responding to a text as it is about creating a new text. Since this stance can literally take any form, a few examples will suffice: have students create a podcast of themselves reading a poem before and after working on speaker and voice; film a scene from a narrative and post it to a video sharing website and then imbed it into a blog or presentation; turn a speech from *Macbeth* into rap or a song on an MP3 recorder and imbed it as part of an online presentation; post a pastiche of a poem side by side on a website with the poem that inspired it; create a mashup of the opening scenes from the TV show *Lost* with a voice over of a passage from *Lord of the Flies*. The possibilities are endless and the point of an education in high literacy.

CONCLUSION

The Internet is not a panacea for educational problems; it is a tool. Teachers are preparing students for the world of the Internet. Integrating Web 2.0 tools into the classroom is only effective if a teacher is able to guide a diverse population through the process of collaborative learning. Social-constructivism offers a way for students to develop the meta-cognitive processes by which they can generate interpretations as they begin to navigate progressively larger communities, including the global community found on the Internet.

There are diverse implications for this research. This research continues the process of validating the use of Internet in the classroom by providing a unified, integrative approach for its use. It directly addresses the emerging use of distance learning. It provides justification for the use of learning management systems in schools. It validates the need for a diverse population in classroom environments and a diversity of cultural representations in texts of study. Finally, it encourages a shift from didactic, transactional and management practices towards transformational leadership in the classroom.

Much research is still required, however, for using the Internet in the classroom. This chapter focuses very narrowly on the literature classroom. Other fields will require separate research. Additionally, the use of transformational leadership in the classroom is only beginning to be explored. Relatedly, the use of collaborative learning is only beginning to gain adherents. More specifically, the use of dialogic thinking as a pedagogical tool requires more qualitative research. Likewise, its application to Web 2.0 discourses is still an emergent field of study. Finally, studies on ways that the Internet can provide scaffolding for understanding as well as real world projects for study are ripe with possibilities but nascent in qualitative research.

Applications and Advice for Web 2.0 Tools

Below is advice for the teacher wishing to create a collaborative, student-centered classroom on the Internet.

1. Involve the real world. The Internet allows the teacher to design assignments that tap into, reflect upon, and respond to a larger context than just the classroom.
2. Design assignments to involve reflection on their findings and peer interaction. Ask students to comment on or provide feedback for other posts. This creates a meaningful and social interaction of ideas. Students often need direction in providing feedback to each other. This can be achieved in several inter-related ways. First, provide students with a model for feedback. Second, provide students with a task that has them focus

on a few aspects of the assignment. Third, provide students with a rubric measuring the incorporation of other's ideas as well as substantive feedback if they are to be graded on their responses.

3. Give students choice in how the assignment is completed when possible. This can take the form of asking students to do Web searches and aggregate results, and then use the results to generate analytic or creative assignments. The later encourages synthesis of multiple inputs and can take the form of a variety of media- movies, podcasts, music, essays, pastiches, and narratives written from alternative perspectives. Likewise, the community can use the results to analyze current events that reflect issues it faces. In this way, a variety of ideas can be organized and synthesized, rather than becoming a fact-finding mission.

4. Mediate student developed knowledge and understanding. Provide regular feedback and timely commentary on student-developed content.

5. Teach one platform at a time. Provide hands-on, step-by-step instructions for the use of the platform as well as links to online tutorials. Online learning environments like Moodle, Edmoto, and Schoolology sidestep this issue by allowing teachers to host relevant Web 2.0 tools in one spot.

6. Use platforms for specific purposes. For example, wikis are useful for aggregating research; cloud-based documents, like Google Docs, TitanPad and ThumbScribe, are useful for collaborative writing, peer editing and storage; cloud-based presentation applications like Prezi, Glogster, and MindMeister are useful for synchronous, dynamic organization, and presentation of ideas; blogs are useful for solitary, reflective writing; forums are useful for multi-user reflection; websites, like Google Sites, are useful for having students collect and display their best work and to reflect meta-cognitively on what they have learned throughout the year.

7. Avoid using multiple platforms for one assignment. Adequate reflection on content can be difficult when navigating multiple platforms.

8. Develop a policy and procedure for dealing with inappropriate responses to community platforms.

REFERENCES

Airasian, P., & Walsh, M. (1997). Constructivist cautions. *Phi Delta Kappan, 78*(6), 444–449.

Applebee, A., Langer, J., Nystrand, M., & Gamoran, A. (2003). Discussion based approaches to developing understanding: Classroom instruction and student performance in middle and high school English. *American Educational Research Journal, 40*(3), 685–730. doi:10.3102/00028312040003685

Applebee, A., Langer, J., & Purves, A. (1991). *Final report*. Alexandria, VA: Center for the Learning and Teaching of Literature.

Arend, B. (2009). Encouraging critical thinking in online threaded discussions. *The Journal of Educators Online, 6*(1), 1–23.

Bambrick-Santoyo, P. (2010). *Driven by data: A practical guide to improve instruction*. San Francisco, CA: Jossey-Bass.

Barkley, S. (2007). *Tapping student effort: Increasing student achievement*. Cadiz, KY: Performance Learning Systems, Inc.

Bertot, J. (2009). Public access technologies in public libraries: Effects and implications. *Information Technology & Libraries, 28*(2), 81–92.

Birrell, S. (2011). The use of blogs to prompt learner reflection during first co-operative education work terms. In *Proceedings of the International Conference on e-Learning Mexico,* (vol. 3, pp. 423 – 430). IEEE.

Blau, S. (2003). *The literature workshop: Teaching texts and their readers.* Portsmouth, NH: Heinemann.

Brodahl, C., Hadjerrouit, S., & Hansen, N. (2011). Collaborative writing with web 2.0 technologies: Education students' perceptions. *Journal of Information Technology Education, 10*(2), 73–103.

Bruffee, K. (2009). Collaborative learning and the "conversation of mankind". In Miller, S. (Ed.), *The Norton Book of Composition Studies.* New York, NY: W.W. Norton & Company.

Bruner, J. (2004). Life as narrative. *Social Research, 71*(3), 691–710.

Davidson, S. (2009). Communities of inquiry. In Davidson & Carber (Eds.), *Taking the PYP Forward: The Future of the IB Primary Years Programme,* (pp. 27-42). Melton, UK: John Catt Educational Ltd.

Dlab, M., & Hoic-Bozic, N. (2011). An approach to adaptivity and collaboration support in a web-based learning environment. *International Journal of Emerging Technologies in Learning, 3,* 28–30.

Friedman, T. (2005). *The world is flat: A brief history of the twenty-first century.* New York, NY: Farrar, Straus, and Giroux.

Gouseti, A. (2010). Web 2.0 and education: Not just another case of hype, hope and disappointment? *Learning, Media and Technology, 35*(3), 351–356. doi:10.1080/17439884.2010.509353

Granka, L. A. (2010). The politics of search: A decade retrospective. *The Information Society, 26*(5), 364–374. doi:10.1080/01972243.2010.511560

Gray, L., Thomas, N., Lewis, L., & National Center for Education Statistics. (2010). Educational technology in U.S. public schools: Fall 2008. In *Teaching as Leadership: The Highly Effective Teacher's Guide to Closing the Achievement Gap.* San Francisco, CA: Jossey-Bass.

Hamston, J. (2006). Bakhtin's theory of dialogue: A construct for pedagogy, methodology and analysis. *Australian Educational Researcher, 33*(1), 55–74. doi:10.1007/BF03246281

Heafner, T., & Friedman, A. (2008). Wikis and constructivism in secondary social studies: Fostering a deeper understanding. *Computers in the Schools, 25*(3-4), 288–302. doi:10.1080/07380560802371003

Helsper, E., & Eynon, R. (2010). Digital natives: Where is the evidence? *British Educational Research Journal, 36*(3), 503–520. doi:10.1080/01411920902989227

House, E., Glass, G., Mclean, L., & Walker, F. (1978). No simple answer- Critique of the "follow through" evaluation. *Educational Leadership, 35*(6), 462–464.

Humrickson, E. (2011). *Information literacy instruction in the Web 2.0 library.*

Introna, L., & Nissenbaum, H. (2000). Shaping the web: Why the politics of search engines matters. *The Information Society, 16*(3), 1–17.

Joyce, B., Weil, M., & Calhoun, E. (2004). *Models of teaching.* Boston, MA: Pearson Education, Inc.

Jukes, I., McCain, T., & Crockett, L. (2011). Education and the role of the educator in the future. *Phi Delta Kappan, 92*(4), 8–14.

Ketterer, J. J. (2008). Zone of proximal development. In Salkind, N. J. (Ed.), *Encyclopedia of Educational Psychology.* Thousand Oaks, CA: Sage Publications.

Langer, J. (1991). *Literary understanding and literature instruction: Report series 2.11.* Albany, NY: Center for the Learning and Teaching of Literature.

Langer, J. (2001). Beating the odds: Teaching middle and high school students to read and write well. *American Educational Research Journal, 38*(4), 837–880. doi:10.3102/00028312038004837

Langer, J. (2011a). *Envisioning literature: Literary understanding and literature instruction* (2nd ed.). New York, NY: Teachers College Press.

Langer, J. (2011b). *Envisioning knowledge: Building literacy in the academic disciplines.* New York, NY: Teachers College Press.

Lemov, D. (2010). *Teach like a champion: 49 techniques that put students on the path to college.* San Francisco, CA: Jossey-Bass.

Lim, W., So, H., & Tan, S. (2010). eLearning 2.0 and new literacies: Are social practices lagging behind? *Interactive Learning Environments, 18*(3), 203–218. doi:10.1080/10494820.2010.500507

Marzano, R. (2007). *The art and science of teaching: A comprehensive framework for effective instruction.* Alexandria, VA: The Association for Supervision and Curriculum Development.

Mathews, J. (2003). Constructivism in the classroom: Epistemology, history and empirical evidence. *Teacher Education Quarterly, 30*(3), 51–64.

Matusov, E. (2007). Applying Bakhtin scholarship on discourse in education: A critical review of essay. *Educational Theory, 57*(2), 215–237. doi:10.1111/j.1741-5446.2007.00253.x

Ogle, D. (2009). Creating contexts for inquiry: From KWL to PRC2. *Knowledge Quest, 38*(1), 56–61.

Pinder-Grover, T., & Groscurth, C. (2009). *Prinicples for teaching the millenial generation: Innovative practices of U-M faculty.* Center For Research and Teaching Learning Occasional Papers.

Pounder, J. S. (2008). Transformational classroom leadership: A novel approach to evaluating classroom performance. *Assessment & Evaluation in Higher Education, 33*(3), 233–243. doi:10.1080/02602930701292621

Prensky, M. (2001). Digital natives, digital immigrants. *Horizon, 9*(5), 1–6. doi:10.1108/10748120110424816

Roegiers, X. (2007). Curricular reforms guide schools: But, where? *Prospects, 37*(2), 155–186. doi:10.1007/s11125-007-9024-z

Subban, P. (2006). Differentiated instruction: A research basis. *International Education Journal, 7*(7), 935–947.

Sullo, B. (2004). *Activating the desire to learn.* Alexandria, VA: Association for Supervision and Curriculum Development.

Tomlinson, C., Brighton, C., Hertberg, H., Callahan, C. M., Moon, T. R., Brimijoin, K., & Reynolds, T. (2003). Differentiating instruction in response to student readiness, interest, and learning profile in academically diverse classrooms: A review of literature. *Journal for the Education of the Gifted, 27*(2-3), 119–145.

Tomlinson, S. (1997). Edward Lee Thorndike and John Dewey on the science of education. *Oxford Review of Education, 23*(3), 365–383. doi:10.1080/0305498970230307

Watras, J. (2009). Academic studies, science, and democracy: Conceptions of subject matter from Harris to Thorndike. *Philosophical Studies in Education, 40,* 113–124.

Williams, R., Karousou, R., & Mackness, J. (2011). Emergent learning and learning ecologies in web 2.0. *International Review of Research in Open and Distance Learning, 12*(3), 39–59.

Wood, S. (2010). Technology for teaching and learning: Moodle as a tool for higher education. *International Journal of Teaching and Learning in Higher Education, 22*(3), 299–307.

KEY TERMS AND DEFINITIONS

Dialogic Thinking: Literally, the type of thinking that occurs in a dialogue; while not strictly related to Marx's Dialectic, it is Bahtkin's theory that new ideas are created in the opposition of ideas.

Envisionment Building: A pedagogical technique created by Judith Langer for high literacy that builds knowledge and understanding of a text as a community through the five stances of high literacy.

Multi-Vocal Thinking: A way of describing the variety of experiences that members bring to a community's creation of knowledge and understanding of a text.

Social Constructivism: The theory that valid knowledge and understanding are created and agreed upon by a community.

Student Inquiry Model: A pedagogical approach that encourages students to develop knowledge and understanding through questions.

Synchronous vs. Asynchronous Technology: Synchronous technology allows multiple users to participate in a document's development simultaneously. Asynchronous technology allows multiple users to participate in a document's development at the user's convenience.

Web 2.0: Internet-based platforms that promote user-generated content.

Zone of Proximal Development: The theory that students learn best when teachers design lessons to build on previous knowledge and understanding while asking them to "stretch" for more difficult concepts.

Chapter 17
Technology in Mathematics Education:
A Catalyst for Diversity Leadership

Peter M. Eley
Fayetteville State University, USA

ABSTRACT

Combining both leadership and diversity, the author's define "leadership diversity" to be: leadership that engages followers that is inclusive to gender, culture, and the social context of the followers. In this chapter, a theoretical framework called "Technological Mathematical Leadership Diversity" (TMLD). TMLD refers to using technology to engage all followers' mathematic learning that is inclusive of their gender, culture, and social context. As mathematics educators, it is important to understand that our role as chief instructor is changing; students are now taking control of their education. The infusion of Web 2.0 is changing how students learn and receive their information. The author set out to answer three questions through the TMLD lens: 1) Will the technology be applied to something already done? 2) Will the technology be used in such a way that it improves upon the way an existing task is done? 3) Will the technology allow us to do things that could not easily be done before? Within this context, the authors organize the technology into two distinct categories "productivity" and "cognitive" based off their primary usage. The rising cost of higher education is driving students to find ways to obtain their education in the quickest time and least expensive way possible. While in pursuit of this, it is important that diversity leadership is maintained. Using frameworks such as TMLD, the authors are able to examine the existence and potential effectiveness of a technological tool. These changes can affect mathematics education in a drastic way.

DOI: 10.4018/978-1-4666-2668-3.ch017

INTRODUCTION

"Electronic technologies—calculators and computers—are essential tools for teaching, learning, and doing mathematics. They furnish images of mathematical ideas, they facilitate organizing and analyzing data, and they compute efficiently and accurately (NCTM, 2000). Knowing this fact, the National Council of Teachers of Mathematics (NCTM) suggests, "effective teachers maximize the potential of technology to develop students' understanding, stimulate their interest, and increase their proficiency in mathematics" (NCTM, 2008). As student learning and communication evolves so does the technologies used to teach these students. More importantly, "In the future, how we educate our children may prove to be more important than how much we educate them" (Friedman, 2005, p. 302). The No Child Left Behind Act of 2001 was developed in response to the breadth of literacy skills necessary for students to be successful in the 21st century workforce as well as the increasing need for technology literacy. The primary goal of Title II, Part D of the No Child Left Behind Act of 2001 is the improvement of "student academic achievement through the use of technology in elementary schools and secondary schools" (Butler, Chavez, & Corbeil, 2007).

Mathematics education has started to recognize the vast possibilities of the digital age for changing how students learn and how teachers teach mathematics. Rapid technological innovations are forcing reform that is bringing changes undreamt of even five years ago and unparalleled in the nation's history (U.S. Department of Education, 2005). Due to great advances in technology, students today are exposed to unlimited resources that can be adapted for mathematics learning. Students are only limited by their own creative abilities (Eley & Hines, 2011). Advances in technology have opened the door for students to explore mathematics content from real world situations, in real-time furthermore, using teacher creativity; simple computer software can easily be adapted to function in a traditional classroom situation.

Researchers have evidence that suggest; technology can be used to keep students motivated (Eley, 2008). In addition, every opportunity teachers have to use technology, should be incorporated into the classroom (NCTM, 2000; NCTM, 2008). Technology in mathematics is also used as an equity tool for students who need assistive technologies in learning mathematics to overcome disabilities. In contrast, technology can be seen as contributor to disparities because of the larger number of students who may not have access to such technologies (U.S. Department of Commerce, 2006).

Technology is a perfect instrument to introduce leadership diversity to teach mathematics with cultural relevance and rigor. According to Bass (1994), Bass and Avolio (1994) contemporary leadership demands greater emphasis on engaging the follower. However, contemporary leadership models, "have little to say about equity, social justice, or diversity; they do not strive toward inclusiveness or the removal of barriers" (Chin, 2010, p. 153). Diversity is important to the leadership so that he/she "can create an organizational culture responsive to the social contexts expected by its followers" (p. 153).

Combining both leadership and diversity, we define "leadership diversity" to be: leadership that engages followers that is inclusive to, gender, culture and social context of the followers. In this chapter we will emphasis what we will call "Technological Mathematical Leadership Diversity" (TMLD). TMLD refers to using technology to engage all followers' mathematic learning that is inclusive of their gender, culture, and social context. TMLD is a theoretical framework that was developed by Eley and Moffett (2012). This framework provides a way to categorize, research, and measure, teaching mathematics with technology and student learning. Furthermore, it makes the instructor the lead facilitator, and is inclusive to diversity and equity of learners. Throughout this chapter, we will view the various aspects of using technology to teach mathematics through the lens of TMLD.

As mathematics educators, it is important to understand that our role as chief instructor is changing; students are now taking control of their education. The infusion of Web 2.0 is changing how students learn and receive their information. Webs 2.0 are web applications that promote collaboration and information sharing among users (i.e. wikis). The role of teacher is changing from instructor of information to facilitator of information (Solomon & Schrum, 2007; Ryan & Cooper, 2010). Students can receive news as soon as it happens with Twitter and Facebook on their mobile phones before teachers get home to watch the evening news. Other countries, such as Japan, have already started making changes in their curriculum to take advantage of the opportunities that technology provides. Japan was making changes to its curriculum to foster greater creativity, artistry, and play (Solomon & Schrum, 2007).

Keeping students engaged in the learning process can be one of the toughest tasks for teachers. Teachers must come up with ways to assess students' learning and encourage critical and analytical thinking skills. Technology can easily lend itself to accomplishing these tasks (NCTM, 2008). Many different mathematical technologies exist to help students, however to use them effectively requires some training and professional development courses where the focus is, how to implement these technologies after teachers become competent in their use.

Mathematics education technologies are not limited to only digital technologies but the focus of this chapter will only consider a limited number of digital technologies that are affordable, accessible, and relatively easy to learn to use. When considering mathematical education technologies to invest in, a few things need to be considered before spending large amounts of time, energy, and financial resources.

Ryan and Cooper (2010) outline 3 important things to look at before considering any technology for educational use, with a few tweaks this outline works well for mathematics educations. We consider these suggestions below while incorporating a TMDL lens.

1. Will the technology be applied to something that we already do? (i.e., will it significantly enhance it)
2. Will the technology be used in such a way that it improves upon the way we do existing task? (i.e., trading in standard calculators for graphing calculators)
3. Will the technology allow us to do things that we could not easily do before? (i.e., modeling, mathematical simulations)

After considering the recommendations above you will be in a better position to make an investment into the few mathematics technologies discussed in this chapter and how they relate to TMDL.

TYPES OF TECHNOLOGIES AFFECTING STUDENT LEARNING IN MATHEMATICS EDUCATION

Technologies that are used in mathematics education typically can be categorized into two distinct categories, but some of the technologies can be placed into both categories depending on how they are used. Productivity and Cognitive are distinct categories that mathematical educational technologies can be aggregated into. In this chapter tools are placed into categories based on their primary use in mathematics education.

Productivity tools are technologies that are used to produce a product (Ryan & Cooper, 2010). Examples of productivity tools are word processors, email, spreadsheets, and editing software. All of these tools produce products that are used in a variety of way in mathematics education. These tools help us to work more efficiently and gives us the ability to get more done.

Cognitive tool are technologies that are used to engage and enhance thinking (Jonassen, 2005). Examples of cognitive tool are simulation programs, modeling programs, and educational computer games. These tools allow us to manage information that allows us to think more clearly, creatively, and critically (Ryan & Cooper, 2010). Cognitive tools enable us to do and see things that we were not able to easily see before without the technology.

Most of the mathematics education tools are either a productivity or cognitive tool. Within these two domains of tools exist an array of task-oriented tools that are important to mathematics education. Adapting Hammond's (2007) task from his task-oriented framework with a mathematics education lens. The following task and technology tools are considered and how they are used in mathematics education as it relates to diversity leadership.

- Research
- Collaboration
- Communication
- Composing
- Presenting
- Collecting Data
- Analyzing Data
- Acquiring and practicing skills
- Assessing
- Publishing

Research

Research in mathematics education is a growing field that has various aspects. Research in mathematics education can focus on political issues such as educational policies that affect mathematics education on the ground level or focus on how students learn mathematics. When researching

mathematics education, technology is important when it come to locating information on current research in the field. In the field researchers use search engines, online archives and databases to accomplish these task.

TMLD is clearly present in mathematics education research because the research takes into account the various mathematics fields being studied. As a result the researcher becomes more knowledgeable about that particular field and becomes a local leader in that particular field of study. The use of technology here is very inclusive to all of the research that is available on the search engines and technological resources that lend themselves to you in this particular field of study.

Commercial search engines such as Google, Bing, and Yahoo are often used to start general searches. Searching for key terms or words may result in finding some or the books and well know research papers on the areas that you are researching. Furthermore, search engines like Google Scholar searches more specifically for research articles from journals and thus leading to other electronic resources. Online archives allow researchers to have access to a variety of searchable documents from multiple journals (Lawrence & Giles, 2000). JSTOR is an online archive that has a variety of searchable journals articles form a wide variety of years to present. In spring 2011 JSTOR announced that books would start to be added to their archives (Jstor, 2011).

Databases are critical tools to researchers in mathematics education, because they allow researchers to read abstracts and find the location of research articles and books. The Education Resources Information Center (ERIC) is the worlds' largest library of education literature and is a government sponsored Internet resource (Education Resource Information Center, 2012). After gathering information about abstracts, the articles can then be located in the online archives such as JSTOR.

Collaboration

Collaboration in mathematics educations is a very large part of what we do. The very nature of education is a collaborative effort and technology makes it possible to have collaborators from the far corners of the earth. Several technological collaborations tools exist such as blogs, wikis, and social media. These tools assist TMDL because of the open format and diversity of learners that can be reached through this tool. More specifically, we will address how these technologies work in mathematics education.

Blogs and websites are where people post factual information and opinions. In mathematics education, blogs are useful as collaborative tool by students, teachers, and researchers to share learning experiences (Lynne & Solomon, 2010). The blog allows others to comment on experiences and share their opinion. The back and forth communication leads to collaboration on projects, ideas and other related experiences. This tool is powerful in that things can be posted and if you are interested in them, you can comment or start a conversation about something different. Further more you can create a learning community that may not have previously existed.

Wikis in mathematics education is a priceless collaboration tool for mathematics educators. Wikis are similar to blogs but differ because they allow approved users to changes or add to the original information that was posted. This tool is good because it allows users to work together and not be in the same place at the same time (Vara, 2006). For example, teachers in 3 different states create a math lesson on a wiki website. Each teacher can log into the website and add things to the lesson. A teacher can add or delete problems from their lesson and the other collaborator's lesson. The power of this tool is that changes are shown immediately and if you want to change things back to previous versions of the lesson you can easily do so by the click of a mouse.

Web 2.0 tools are a new phenomenon to social media with the most popular tools being Twitter and Facebook. Social media is having an expanding role in education everywhere and math is no exception. Twitter is a micro-blogging tool that allows users to express information in 140 characters or less (Priego, 2011). Facebook is a collaborative website that allows users to interactive with others exchange ideas and share video and pictures.

Twitter is important to mathematics educators because it allows usres to communicate with a large community of learners and researchers. Many of the mathematics education organizations like NCTM have twitter accounts. Organizations like NCTM pass along important information on the daily basis. Twitters helps to build a network of colleagues that have common interest and experiences in mathematics education (Priego, 2011). Twitters tweet helpful information to their followers and open users up to other people and ideas that they would not ordinary experience. Many tweet about new trends in mathematics education and others about helpful websites, people etc. The limitation of 140 characters makes sharing information concise and direct.

The use of Facebook in mathematics education is very similar to Twitter, but Facebook allows for more detail information and collaboration. Users in mathematics education can express ideas and views in a full context. They are able to share files, diagrams and have conversations with other users. One new feature on Facebook is the video chat. This will allow for real time collaboration with other teachers and researchers from anywhere via a good Internet connection.

Communication

Mathematics educators use various communication tools such as blogs, Wikis voice/chat, Listservs and Podcasting that all contribute to TMDL (Flanagan & Calandra, 2005). Blogs, wikis, and chat were addressed earlier in this chapter, because they not only serve as communication tools but also assist in collaborations. Listservs and Podcasting introduce a couple of other methods that are used to communicate.

Listservs are just mailing list that allow the emailer to send an email message to a large list of email address at once. Usually to be included on a listserv you have to subscribe to it. Subscribing to a listserv is typically done by emailing the listserv email address with the message "subscribe" in the body of the message. Listervs are important to mathematics educations because they are the communication channels, which we receive news. The type of news sent on the listserv can vary from job search information to bulletins.

Word processors are a critical tool in mathematics education. It has many different uses for instruction and conveying different types of information. Word processors such as Microsoft Word with the equation editor add on packages make it very useful for creating test and worksheet materials (Mathtype, 2012). This eliminates the hand written test, and mathematics material being written legibly. Composing programs allow mathematics educators to communicate ideas, researching findings and opinions.

Video/audio technology is vitally important to mathematics educators because of its ability to reenact what took place during the recorded time frame. Educators and researchers are able to review teaching of lessons and how students perceived to learn mathematics material during the time frame. This tool is very power because it allows educators and researchers to digest what was going on during the recorded time period and they are able to give an in-depth critical review of the material (Derry, 2007).

A new and innovative technology that is changing how teachers teach on the board is the interactive White Boards (Marzano, 2009). Interactive white boards are electronic boards that instructors can use just like a traditional blackboard without the chalkboard mess. The boards are utilized with computers and can record the strokes that are written on the board. The recording feature is really nice for teachers because they can record all of their lessons on the board (Derry, 2007). Computer programs like PowerPoint and Keynote come to life on interactive white boards because instructors are able to write directly on the slides while working with the board.

Data Collection

Finding useful data to analyze is not always an easy task for educators. However, with new found access to tool such as Google earth. Finding and collecting useful data is becoming easier and easier. Global Information Systems (GIS) are being used in classrooms to help students learn from the data that is collected in their geographical region (North Carolina State University College of Education, 2002). The data from GIS is very useful because real world connections can be made and educators are able to arrogate the data in many different ways.

When considering TMDL graphing calculators are more than just sophisticated adding machines. They are often equipped with the ability to use external probes and sensors. The probes and sensors are used to collect data for analysis in the graphing calculator (Texas Instruments, 2011). For example, a temperature sensor plugged into a graphing calculator can recorded the changing temperature of ice in a cup. Once the data collection process is completed then you can do central tendency statistics such as finding the average.

Digital still cameras play a role in data collection in mathematics education. Digital cameras are often used in digital story telling by students learning mathematics concepts. Students find the digital story telling process to be a motivational tool and can be a help to parents looking to be involved in their child's learning process (Eley & Hines, 2011). Digital cameras are helpful to mathematics educators for data collection, recording and instructional purposes.

Computers

Computers are one of the single most important technological tools for the field of mathematics education and TMDL. Computers allow researchers and educators to analyze data, acquire and practice skills, use self-paced tutorial, use educational computer based games, and data collections. Mathematics educators have only scratched the surface of the numerous uses of computers and in the future computers will continue to play an important role in mathematics education.

Analyzing data can be a very tedious task but it is necessary for researchers to gather information about what is being studied. Computers allow researchers to be able to store and easily retrieve large amounts of data. This data can be numerical or video archives of studies that were conducted. An array of computer programs exist for analyzing data exists such as SPSS and SAS to name a few (SAS, 2012; Field, 2009). Math educators use these programs to indicate statistical significance in research studies conducted among other things. A consequence of analyzing data, educators are able to make evidence based decisions that can lead to more equitable educational policies.

Acquiring and practicing skills in mathematics is essential to students' success in mathematics education. Technology can make acquiring and practicing these skills fun and rewarding (Eley & Hines, 2011). A number of computers software program exist that allow students to acquire and practice math skills. Commercial programs such as Study Island (2012) allow students to acquire and fine tune mathematical skills for continued success in mathematics education.

Self-contained tutorials are now a common technological tool for educators and students. Using technology such as self-contained tutorials in education, forces changes to the role of the teachers from educators to educational facilitators and directly address TMDL in that it considers all students ability levels. In self-contained tutorials and classes students work at their own pace (Study Island, 2012). This works well for students who learn at a faster or slower pace. The structure also supports students who may work or do not have the ability to attend a synchronous class. These types of course have a tendency to be online learning courses.

Teachers as facilitators of education are a direct result of technological advances in education and embody TMDL. The self-contained tutorials allow students to construct their own learning. The education facilitators help students where their progress is hindered. They also provide leadership and direction for students that are working alone. Facilitators help keep students on track and make sure that students are learning the material correctly without hindering their construction of knowledge.

Assessing Student Learning

Actively using technology to assess student learning is becoming a stable in K-12 education. We cannot talk about every technological assessment tool out there however; we will discuss its uses in general across the country. Classroom response systems are systems, which allow students to response in the classroom via a handheld device. The response back can be anonymous or non-anonymous depending on the system and how it is set up. Student response systems are helpful to students because it eliminates the fear of answering wrong in front of classmates or colleagues. Students using a response system are more likely to respond and really express their answers. From a teacher point of view it gives them a quick snap shot of how the students are performing (SMART, 2012). Therefore instruction can be quickly tailored to what is needed right away. Assessing this way helps teachers to use time more efficiently thus giving students more time to learn more.

Assessing not only occurs in the classroom but it can also be done effectively online using survey and quiz tools. Using online quizzes and survey help teachers assess students in the same way as classroom response systems, however the students do not have to be present. The surveys are often used to collect information from students and learning more about how to teach students whom you do not see in a face-to-face environment (Blackboard, 2012). Online technology provides the instructor the ability to assess in an asynchronous environment and keep the students engaged.

Publishing

Publishing in mathematics education is the lifeline of the field. The importance of publishing cannot be underestimated. Publishing demonstrates TMDL and allows mathematics educators to collaborate, grow professionally, and help the field reach new levels of understanding of mathematics teaching. Technology is very important to publishing in mathematics education because it allows for easier collaboration. Technology has given us the ability to post mathematics blogs and electronic journals and videos for sharing with the larger mathematics education community as a result the educator leads in the field and addresses diversity.

Websites, electronic journal and wiki are all different however, they help mathematics educator in many of the same ways. Website/electronic journals are usually static in nature, but allow its readers to easily read information from them. Wiki are a Web 2.0 tool, which simply means that readers are able to both read and contribute to the reading or information provided. Publishing a wiki is very useful for sharing information among colleagues and students sharing work.

Publishing videos to websites such as YouTube and TeacherTube are helping students and teachers in mathematics education and shares with the larger community (Youtube, 2012; Teachertube, 2012). Technology has made recording and posting videos of content very easy. Mathematics education is enhanced because of the availability of teaching content that may explore teaching tough subjects in a different format or innovative way. Students are able to visit the site and learn from other instructors.

TECHNOLOGY INTEGRATED INTO THE CURRICULUM

Integrating technology into mathematics curriculum is not always an open and shut case. Teachers have to know their content well and be comfortable with the technology (NCTM, 2008). Teachers also need continued support through professional development activities to keep their pedagogy and technology skills updated (Sztajn, Marrongelle, & Smith, 2011). The pedagogical moves needed to implement technology in the classroom are not innate. It is a skill that is taught and carries a responsibility for student learning.

Professional development activities help teachers develop skill to integrate technology when appropriate to teach key mathematical concepts (Sztajn, Marrongelle, & Smith, 2011). Contrary to popular belief a student should not be just given a piece of technology and left to figure out things on their own. Teachers teach students the key concepts that are needed for success and slowly integrate the tool as it benefits the students' workload. It will be an injustice for technology to become a crutch for students and teachers alike. Technology being used in this manner paralyzes over-time students' basics foundational conceptual understanding of the basics (Eley, 2008). As a result, you are left with students who cannot do the most basic things in mathematics without the aid of technology.

Technology is just another tool for mathematics educators to use for the end goal of getting students to have a conceptual understanding of mathematical concepts (NCTM, 2008). Technology helps teachers to discover or prove things that were not easily discovered or proven before the technology became available. Teachers are able to demonstrate concepts such as how a limit converges. Students can be easily shown things like this in a technological environment, when abstractly the ideas are hard for student to see or understand.

TECHNOLOGY AS MOTIVATOR

Technology is used as a motivational tool for students (November, 2010; Eley, 2008; Eley & Hines, 2011). Many students are consumed with using technology on the daily bases with computers, cellphones, iPads, etc. As educators, we must get our heads around the idea that the students are into technology, and if we are going to be effective in reaching them, we must now go to where they are. Unfortunately, teachers have to compete with Facebook for face-time with their students.

A teacher who uses technology effectively opens the door to reaching their students (November, 2010). The technology as motivator can help teachers develop relationships through similar interest and gives the teacher the opportunity to impart knowledge to the student because the door to learning for them is now open. Using technology engages students who otherwise would not be interested into the subject (Eley, 2008).

TECHNOLOGY AND THE FUTURE

Technology is changing the face of K-16 education. In the future, we feel that brick and mortar places of education will become a things of the past and will be only available to those who are able to afford it, thus making it a poor conduit for TMDL. The rising cost of higher education is driving students to find ways to obtain their education in the quickest time and least expensive way possible. These changes will affect mathematics education in a drastic way.

As we become even more technological as a society, the need for mathematics conceptual understanding will be more important. However, it seems that we are burning the candlestick on both ends. On one end, students are being required to learn more advance concepts sooner. This will enable them to meet the needs of our society as we call on them for more in-depth mathematical knowledge. On the other end, we are giving students technological tools with improper implementation and they become handicaps to the student because we want and expect so much out of them so soon.

Mathematics teachers are often asked from students: why do I need to learn this? Unfortunately, this question is often answered with because it's on the test. The newly adopted Common Core Standards for Mathematics (2010) (CCSM) hopes to address this issue and others. From the new standards we hope the question is how can I used this to do ... Meaning that the CCSM inspire student to be leaders in creativity and innovation.

Online learning in mathematics will continue to be an area of intensive research as to how to effectively deliverer online content to students who traditionally struggle in mathematics. Learning in an online synchronous environment would not be much different from the traditional setting but what students are demanding is an asynchronous environment that provides them with the flexibility to learn "ON Demand." Students learning this way brings with it new problems and puts a different outlook on older problems like academic fraud/cheating in online courses.

Overall, the future of technology in mathematics education is very stable with a TMDL agenda moving forward to include all. The current landscape in mathematics provides a permanent home for technological advance and their uses to forward the agenda of mathematics education. We have to remember that at some time a chalkboard was a technological advance that was not welcomed and now it is seen as a museum artifact. How long will it be before we can look back and say to someone, I remember when math class was in a building with a human teacher?

REFERENCES

Bass, B. M. (1994). *Bass and Stogdill's handbook of leadership: Theory, research, and managerial applications* (3rd ed.). New York, NY: Free Press.

Bass, B. M., & Avolio, B. J. (1994). *Improving organizational effectiveness through transformational leadership*. Thousand Oaks, CA: Sage.

Blackboard. (2012). *Blackboard*. Retrieved March 1, 2012, from http://www.blackboard.com

Butler, J. W., Chavez, J., & Corbeil, J. R. (2007). The effect of one-day traning in digital storytelling on inservice teachers' anxiety toward computers. *TCEA Educational Technology Research Symposium, 1*, 8-15.

Chin, J. L. (2010). Introduction to the special issue on diversity and leadership. *The American Psychologist, 65*(3), 150–156. doi:10.1037/a0018716

Common Core State Standards Initiative. (2010). *Common core state standards for mathematics*. Retrieved from http://www.corestandards.org/the-standards

Derry, S. J. (2007). *Guidlelines for video research in education*. Retrieved March 5, 2012, from http://drdc.uchicago.edu/what/video-research-guidelines.pdf

Education Resource Information Center. (2012). *Website*. Retrieved from http://www.eric.ed.gov/ERICWebPortal/resources/html/collection/about_collection.html

Eley, P. M. (2008). *Does using computer software make a difference in learning geometric and probability concepts?* Retrieved March 5, 2012, from repository.lib.ncsu.edu/ir/bitstream/1840.16/2652/1/etd.pdf

Eley, P. M., & Hines, K. W. (2011). Students tell the story best: Creative mathematics storytelling using narrative software. *Centroid, 37*(2), 9–13.

Eley, P. M., & Moffett, N. (2012). *Framing techological teaching from a leadership diversity point of view*. Unpublished.

Field, A. (2009). *Discovering statistics using SPSS* (3rd ed.). London, UK: Sage Publication.

Flanagan, B., & Calandra, B. (2005). Podcasting in the classroom. *Learning and Leading with Technology, 33*(3), 20–25.

Hammond, T. C. (2007). A task-oriented framework for stand-alone technology intergration classes. *Journal of Computing in Teacher Education, 23*(4), 119–124.

Jonassen, D. H. (2005). *Modeling with technology: Mindtools for contemporary change* (3rd ed.). Englewood Cliffs, NJ: Prentice Hall.

Jstor. (2011). *Books at JSTOR: Leading university presses announce plan to publish books online at JSTOR*. Retrieved October 12, 2011, from http://about.jstor.org/news-events/news/books-jstor-leading-university-presses-announce-plan-publish-books-online-jstor

Lawrence, S., & Giles, C. L. (2000). Accessibility of Information on the web. *Intelligence, 11*(1). doi:10.1145/333175.333181

Lynne, S., & Solomon, G. (2010). *Web 2.0: New tools, new school*. Eugene, OR: International Society for Technology Education.

Marzano, R. J. (2009). Teaching with interactive whiteboards. *Multiple Measures, 67*(3), 80–82.

Mathtype. (2012). *Mathtype*. Retrieved March 5, 2012, from http://www.chartwellyorke.com/mathtype.html

National Council of Teachers of Mathematics. (1989). *Curriculum and evaluation standards for school mathematics*. Reston, VA: NCTM.

National Teachers of Mathematics. (1994). Board approves statement on algebra. *NCTM News Bulletin, 6*(1).

NCTM. (2000). *National council of teachers of mathematics*. Retrieved February 8, 2010, from my.nctm.org/standards/document/chapter3/index.htm

NCTM. (2008). *The role of technology in the teaching and learning of mathematics*. Retrieved October 17, 2011, from www.nctm.org/uploadedFiles/About_NCTM/Position_Statements/Technology%20final.pdf

North Carolina State University College of Education. (2002). *GIS is an interdisciplinary technology tool*. Retrieved March 5, 2012, from http://www.ncsu.edu/gisined/text-why.html

November, A. (2010). *Empowering students with technology* (2nd ed.). Thousand Oaks, CA: Sage.

Priego, E. (2011). *How Twitter will revolutionise academic research and teaching*. Retrieved March 3, 2012, from http://www.guardian.co.uk/higher-education-network/blog/2011/sep/12/twitter-revolutionise-academia-research

Ryan, K., & Cooper, J. (2010). Those who can, teach. In Ryan, K., & Cooper, J. (Eds.), *Those Who Can, Teach* (pp. 197–234). Boston, MA: Wadsworth Cengage Lerning.

SAS. (2012). *SAS*. Retrieved March 5, 2012, from http://www.sas.com/govedu/edu/curriculum/index.html

SMART. (2012). *SMART*. Retrieved March 5, 2012, from http://smarttech.com/us/Solutions/Higher+Education+Solutions/Products+for+higher+education/Complementary+hardware+products/SMART+Response

Solomon, G., & Schrum, L. (2007). *Web 2.0: New tools, new schools*. Eugene, OR: International Society for Technology in Education.

Study Island. (2012). *Study island*. Retrieved March 5, 2012, from http://www.studyisland.com/

Sztajn, P., Marrongelle, K., & Smith, P. (2011). *Supporting implementation of the common core state standards for mathematics*. Raleigh, NC: William & Ida Friday Institue.

Teachertube. (2012). *Teachertube*. Retrieved March 2012, from http://www.teachertube.com

Texas Instruments. (2011). *Education technology*. Retrieved March 5, 2012, from http://education.ti.com/educationportal/sites/US/productDetail/us_cbl_2.html

U.S. Department of Commerce. (2006). *A nation online: Entering the broadband age*. Retrieved November 2, 2011, from http://www.ntia.doc.gov/reports/anol/NationOnlineBroadband04.pdf

Vara, V. (2006). *Offices co-op consumer web tools like "wikis" and social networking*. Retrieved October 17, 2011, from http://online.wsj.com/article/SB115802778487360244.html

Youtube. (2012). *Youtube*. Retrieved March 5, 2012, from http://www.youtube.com

Chapter 18
Teacher Leadership:
Learning and Leading

Andrea M. Kent
University of South Alabama, USA

ABSTRACT

This chapter focuses on the metamorphosis of teacher leaders, from the roles, responsibilities, and dispositions of teacher leaders, to teacher leaders using technology for self-professional development as well as leading professional development for the improvement of teaching and learning. The underlying premise is that teacher leaders work with diverse populations of both teachers and public school students who are present in schools today. It is strong leadership at the classroom level that makes a difference with colleagues and students, regardless of ethnicity, gender, or social class, and can ultimately impact an entire school culture. This chapter integrates these core tenants in an effort to guide the reader to understanding the necessity of developing teacher leaders to meet the challenges inherent in 21st century schools and classrooms.

INTRODUCTION

Teacher leaders have typically been an integral part of the daily life of P–12 schools. They generally self-identify by becoming the key persons or experts in a school for a specific curricular area. Their commitment to life-long learning lays the foundation for teachers to emerge as leaders. In today's world, technology has become the gateway for learning. Teacher leaders can and should use a variety of emerging technologies to learn new skills, to continually expand their knowledge, and to enhance their craft. In turn, teacher leaders must be able to use technology to lead diverse groups of teachers, and to show other teachers how to effectively incorporate technology into their teaching while guiding various communities of students along the path of life-long learning. Through the use of innovative and evolving technologies, teachers are able to reach students in the context of the multiple modalities of learning and the vari-

DOI: 10.4018/978-1-4666-2668-3.ch018

ous literacies that are inherent within the learning styles of students. As examined throughout this chapter, it is the premise that teacher leaders nature great teachers. Ultimately, effective teachers have an immediate impact on our communities and society at large through the P - 12 students who are our leaders of tomorrow (Chetty, Friedman, & Rockoff, 2011).

With the underlying premise of the diverse populations of both teachers and students present in today's schools, this chapter will specifically focus on:

- Define teacher leadership;
- Discuss the roles and responsibilities of teacher leaders, including their role in school reform;
- Present prevalent dispositions in teachers serving as teacher leaders;
- Elaborate on the professional development teacher leaders must engage in for continued learning, both for themselves and in leading other teachers;
- Emphasize the role of technology for 21st century teacher leaders.

DEFINING TEACHER LEADERS

Teacher leaders have been prevalent in schools for many years. The concept of teacher leadership is not new, but as their roles and responsibilities continually mature as part of school reform. In light of current challenges faced in the schools each day, the implementation and impact of teacher leaders must continually be examined (Berry, et al., 2011). Leadership characteristics generally emerge as teachers are called on to serve outside, and in addition to, their role as classroom teachers, leading in various capacities at the school level. It is the definition of teacher leadership in *Teaching 2030* (Berry, et al., 2011) that forms the premise of this chapter. In this book, a teacher leader as a *Teacherpreneur* is defined by Ariek Sacks, as:

a teacher leader of the future that has proven accomplishment and deep knowledge of how to teach, a clear understanding of what strategies must be in play to make schools highly successful, and the skills and commitment to spread their expertise to others—all while keeping one foot firmly in the classroom (p. 136).

In the recent past, the school's infrastructure has often times been put in place to support teacher leaders as they work alongside their colleagues, with the ultimate focus of improving student achievement (Berry, et al., 2011). Teacher leaders embrace the challenge of school improvement as they are given the opportunities to participate with their colleagues by facilitating the process of student inquiry, dialogue, and reflection in order to meet the challenge. A prevalent example can be seen in school-based literacy, coaches often seen in elementary schools and that have also emerged in the recent past in secondary schools (Steiner & Kowal, 2009)

ROLES AND RESPONSIBILITIES

The roles of teacher leaders have ranged from those who are recognized positions with formal titles, such as *instructional coaches, grade level chairperson* or *committee chairs*, to less formal roles such as being looked to as the instructional expert in a content area or being known for any number of strengths in an area that is consider a critical issue of the time—budget cuts, new technology, English Language Learners, etc. Often, a member of the school administrative team will recognize the leadership potential of a teacher, and work to foster those skills through committee assignments and professional development opportunities. In more recent years, teacher leader certifications have been designed and developed by state departments of education and supporting programs have been implemented in the university at the graduate level as a career path for teachers, expanding opportunities for teachers beyond staying in the classroom or being removed from classroom teaching (Teacher Leadership Exploratory Consortium, 2010). Regardless of the path, teacher leaders contribute to the success of a school, from academics to morale, and are central to its daily functions.

When considering the varied roles of teacher leaders, they are generally examined in the context of making a difference with an innovative idea, forward thinking that moves into action, or reawakening colleagues through working toward a common goal. For example, a classroom teacher writes a grant for their students to receive a laptop computer to use in class and to check out to take home. He develops the system for this to occur, and provides the professional development his student needs to make this happen. Soon, other teachers in the school are asking him for help so that they can do something similar with their students. The teacher also becomes known as the technology guru as "word gets around" regarding the activities and assignments he is implementing with his students using their laptops.

Teacher leaders must embrace the challenge of leading teachers, who are often largely unlike their students in terms of race and socio-economic backgrounds, to provide equal educational opportunities and to honor the diverse cultures and contexts inherent in schools today (Pugalee, Frykholm, & Shaka, 2001). These efforts include teacher leaders providing:

- Both the knowledge and material *resources* to their colleagues, and a willingness to model the application of these resources;
- Innovative *instructional strategies* they implement and model;
- Knowledge of the *curriculum*, the ability to lead curriculum teams, and the ability to examine and write curriculum;
- *Support* to classroom teachers, being a right hand to the daily teaching and learning activities that occurs within a classroom;

- Opportunities for their colleagues to engage in *professional development*, whereby the focus is creating a classroom and school environment that learning is central, and even craved;
- *Mentoring* to both new educators and those with experience who operates in wisdom, where guidance is not about the right answer but about the quest for knowledge and learning;
- *School leadership,* respected for their knowledge and abilities as a teacher, known for their willingness to go the extra mile for the school as a whole as well as their students, and involved in the decision-making processes at the school;
- *Data coaching*, examining the data of a given content, grade level, classroom, and/or individual student and can provide guidance on areas of strength, needed focus, and instructional strategies;
- A *catalyst for change*, exhibiting leadership qualities that promote and implement educational change when it is necessary, while never losing focus of the realities of the classroom;
- A commitment to life-long *learning*, knowing that there is so much to learn and impossible to "arrive" in knowing all there is to know, even in area of specializations;
- Creating *partnerships* outside of the school, with the business and community, focusing on the improvement of the local educational system thereby improving the quality of life in the community (Harrison & Killion, 2007; Haury, 2001).

According to a study done to better understand the roles and responsibilities of teacher leaders by Berry, Daughtrey, and Wieder (2010) self-efficacy and teaching effectiveness both improve while teachers lead other teachers. Simultaneously, student achievement greatly improves. The roles and responsibilities of teacher leaders are considered to be vital to confidence and classroom effectiveness while being involved in leadership work such as talking with other colleagues and leading other teachers.

Inherent in many of these roles are the teacher leaders who have recently evolved in the area of technology. It is the teachers who have committed themselves to keeping abreast of the latest technological innovations, who have committed themselves to acquiring the knowledge and utilizing emerging technologies on a daily basis, and who use technology as a primary tool in teaching and learning and in their role as teacher leaders. These teachers become better than proficient with implementing the technology with their own students in their own classrooms. For teacher leaders, *E-learning* is implemented seamlessly, and enhances learning opportunities for students and themselves. These leaders are then quickly looked to as a source of help by their colleagues, for guidance and mentoring on the pedagogy of technology implementation. As teachers and students experience success through implementation, the teacher leaders finds themselves inadvertently leading learning communities to sustain and improve success.

It is clear that in every school the roles of teacher leaders are varied and are identified with different labels, but all should ultimately contribute to the success of the school (Harrison & Killion, 2007). These roles are often overlapping, building on the strengths of each teacher as an individual. Teacher leaders develop as their commitment to the profession is revealed. Thus, teachers believe they can impact the diverse learning community in their classes and school, and teachers demonstrate the capacity to develop leadership qualities (Ross & Gray, 2006). Ultimately, teacher leaders directly impact the culture of the school, work to improve student learning, and have an impact on the practice of their colleagues. Teacher leaders should provide a positive impact on the school and community where they lead.

A SHARED RESPONSIBILITY

Due to the increasing demands of school leaders, teacher leaders have emerged to improve areas of student achievement by bridging the gap between administrative managers and classroom teachers (Beachum & Dentith, 2004). In the past, the concept of school administration was viewed as top-down supervision. However, current research indicates that as the principal's job is becoming more complex, their responsibilities are not adequately fulfilled by one person (Danielson, 2007). During the past decade, the view of instructional leadership has seen a paradigm shift—focusing on collaborative efforts of teachers and principals. The interaction within this paradigm forms the foundation that is the common element that defines the role of the teacher leader. As has been stated, "such paradigm shifts associated with developing teachers as leaders may include moving from isolation to collaboration, from privatization of practice to open sharing of practice, and from independence to interdependence" (Searby & Shaddix, 2008). This statement is evident as teacher leaders develop the school budget with a team of teachers, respond to a school crisis under the guidance of their administrator, and provide school-based professional development on the latest district mandate.

This shift supports the morale and buy-in needed to create successful schools. Research shows that it is crucial to build democratic practices to meet the goals of the school and respond to the diverse needs of the students (Beachum & Dentith, 2004). These practices can help establish an environment that encourages teachers and administrators to work together as a community. A teacher leader is embodied as a teacher who serves both the classroom and provides various leadership roles. Teacher participation and leadership at the local school has been emphasized in various aspects, and studies reveal that classroom teachers who had the support of teacher leaders were more likely to initiate change, felt that their opinions were valued, and took risks with less fear of failure (Beachum & Dentith, 2004).

Role in Reform

Teacher leaders have played a significant role in reform efforts among schools. They begin with a vision, and refine their vision in an ongoing process as they work with colleagues in effort to move forward to improve the quality of the education system. They:

- Have a vested interest in the continuous improvement of their school;
- Are in tune with how their colleagues think and work;
- Know the history of the school and are able to foresee elements of the future;
- Have an understanding of the values and attitudes of the community;
- Will to take a step out of their comfort zones to implement change (Roby, 2011).

Teacher leaders are not afraid to take risks as they have the knowledge and experience to have foresight on when a risk may be worth taking. Teacher leaders create an environment that is focused on the improvement of schools in order to best meet the academic needs of students. It is the notion that teacher leadership connects teachers and principals with a mutual goal, *improving learning for students*. As a result, teacher leaders have the power to impact a school culture that includes continuous learning for all students, teachers, administrators, caregivers and the community (Roby, 2011).

A Diversified Community

The importance of a classroom culture centered on learning is a vital characteristic of teacher leaders. A culture centered on learning includes meeting the learning needs of all learners, both students and adult peers, by differentiating instruction and considering learning styles. In addition, establishing a culture of learning includes knowing and understanding multicultural education, integrating these concepts into daily teaching, and adjusting teaching styles to meet the preferences of the learners. Teacher leaders must also place emphasis on mentoring teachers of color so they feel successful in their positions as they serve as change agents for the students they teach. Ultimately, minority teachers should to be encouraged and supported early in their in career to become teacher leaders as they are involved in leading students in their own classrooms as well as helping develop and enact school-wide policy decisions. Gone are the days of a one size fits all curriculum and teaching style. Teacher leaders need to be knowledgeable of the areas of strengths and desired growth of the teachers they work with, as well as the students they teach. They have to be committed to reaching all learners, regardless of the ethnic background or learning styles of the people they are teaching.

IDENTIFYING DISPOSITIONS OF TEACHER LEADERS

It seems reasonable that one may ask what "qualifies" a teacher to be a teacher leader. The answer lies in part in the innate dispositions teachers possess to be leaders outside of the classroom, and in part, the supports that are provided to develop teachers as leaders. It is the premise of Albert Bandura's social learning theory, whereby teachers (1) learn from each other, both in real time and virtually, (2) develop a positive self-efficacy, and (3) are able to synthesize knowledge and application of that knowledge to continually morph into the role of a teacher leader. The purpose a teacher has in these efforts is focused on the improvement of teaching and learning (Bandura, 1997).

For today's teachers to develop into the teacher leaders of tomorrow, a disposition of leadership must be nurtured and developed (Hunzicker,

Lubowiak, Huffman, & Johnson, 2009). This process begins by providing support for a beginning teacher. Generally, many preservice teacher preparation programs are designed so that inherently new teachers develop an understanding between the relationship and cycle of adult teaching and learning, as the preservice teacher is evaluated and provided feedback, whereby the new teacher comes to expect that feedback. This process should be continued through the induction phase as new teachers are mentored to build leadership capacity, while a disposition of leadership is nurtured. A mentor works with the new teacher and shares the responsibility for the performance and professional success of a colleague (Lambert, 2003). It is likely that if teachers are able to find success in a difficult situation, their teacher self-efficacy becomes stronger and their potential as leaders expands. The shared accountability for classroom outcomes that impacts the school maximizes teacher effectiveness through a collaborative, team approach. It is through this quality mentoring that the new teacher begins to emulate the actions and behaviors of the teacher of teachers, while the more veteran teacher becomes more skilled in the element of teacher leadership. This process is helpful for both the new teacher and the mentor, as teacher leader qualities are developing in both participants.

The concept of teacher leadership has evolved through the years and plays to the strengths of the expertise and knowledge classroom teachers possess. Though developing into a teacher leader takes time, the dispositions to lead may be instilled early, and developed through the daily life of a teacher (Riel & Becker, 2008). Being a reflective teacher, acquiring knowledge and learning from the multiple dimensions of teaching is only the first step of becoming a teacher leader. It is the personal determination to overcome the traditional structure of schools, to teach and learn from colleagues, as the culture of the school shares a collective responsibility for student learning. The dispositions of leadership that are generally apparent in teachers include:

- A positive self-esteem where teachers realizes their worth as educators, and are able to reflect on their practices as teachers with a focus on continuous improvement in the face of the ever expanding role in the classroom and school;
- A feeling of significance in the daily work of teachers as they realize the power they have to impact the lives of countless students in the academic, social, and emotional realms;
- Knowing they are competent to differentiate instruction and instructional tools in teaching today's diverse students who are tomorrow's leaders and community members of the next generation;
- Having decision making power, under the parameters set forth by administrators, whereby they are free to be creative and spontaneous in their work in order to meet the needs of a diverse group of learners and strive to meet their professional goals;
- Possessing a high self-efficacy, which may be examined in the context of a teachers' beliefs about their capability to teach, to set professional goals and to engage in reflective processes as they face teaching challenges and successes (Hunzicker, et al., 2009).

As these qualities are developed, a foundation of certainty, inspiration, and determination are solidified as teacher leaders are empowered to do their work in the classroom first and then in the community.

The Professional Development of Teacher Leaders

The work of teacher leaders may vary, but they generally serve as teacher leaders in a classroom, among a grade level or department, across the school, and beyond the walls of the school. Teacher leaders have a strong sense of who they are as teachers, reflect on their practice in order to improve their craft, and are action oriented. They channel these characteristics to better themselves by constantly learning from both professional endeavors as well as informally from their students, colleagues, and community.

Although professional development is important for any teacher, it plays a critical role in the development of a teacher leader. Professional development provides a platform for teacher leaders to enrich their confidence, content knowledge, student learning, and most importantly their leadership skills. A cross-analysis case study done on professional development in science teacher leaders revealed the importance of teacher leaders in a student's academic success (Bailey, Rehmat., Lombardi, & Keppelman, 2012). Teacher leaders strive to want more knowledge and to learn more and more each year in order to successfully development new teachers into future teacher leaders. Lieberman, Saxl, and Miles (1988) discovered that teacher leaders need to perfect on-the-job skills such as the abilities to:

- Build trust and rapport;
- Handle learning processes and manage the work;
- Diagnose organizational conditions; and,
- Build confidence and skills in others.

Inherent with these assertions is that teacher leaders are committed to life-long learning. Not only are they committed to the development of leadership skills, they are also willing to stay abreast of current educational trends and practices, especially in the area where they lead. Some of the necessary learning takes place as a natural part of leading. For example, intellectual and professional growth increases from collaborating with peers through activities such as classroom modeling and professional books studies. The challenge of trying to constantly improve classroom practice, not to mention impacting a school, forces a teacher leader to reflect on current practices and be a

leader for change. The good news is that teacher leaders have the natural inclination of wanting to learn and this is due in part to their dispositions that have been present and continually nurtured since their initial teaching endeavors. These dispositions, such as positivity, confidence, and self-efficacy provide teacher leaders with a strong power to grow and learn in their field as leaders. They crave the conversations with their colleagues that force them to reflect on their practice, they are excited to read the articles that give them affirmation about what they are doing right, and they embrace the new publication that gives them innovative ideas to implement with their students and model for their peers.

As teacher leaders instruct their students and communicate with colleagues, areas of interest begin emerge as a focus for expertise. Teacher leaders take the initiative to engage in professional learning and development. They participate in diverse communities of practice as they seek networks both inside of their school community and across various cultures to gain new ideas and information they can implement (Riel & Becker, 2008). They may read professional literature on a topic, spend time exploring professional websites, engage in simple Web exploration, present and attend at professional meetings, and even decide to further their knowledge and abilities by pursuing advanced degrees. They willingly commit the time, energy, and resources needed to obtain the knowledge and skills needed to continue to refine the art and craft of teaching beyond the four walls of their classroom. Professional growth is an on-going process that occurs naturally as teacher leaders strive to better the craft of teaching, and lead others in the process.

For teacher leaders of today, as they engage in these professional development practices, the use of technology becomes integral. The use of technology often arises as teacher leaders view technology as the beginning of professional development for themselves and others. Teacher leaders use technology to become active researchers, collecting observational data, analyzing the data, and sharing the results of the data with their peers. They take pride in using the results to initiate change within their classroom, that often carry-over to improvements that filter to other teachers and classrooms. Regardless of ethnicity or social class, e-learning becomes a great equalizer in that knowledge can be accessed at school and home as well as in many public places. The commitment to continue a quest to improve content, pedagogy, and leadership must exist, and with that comes countless opportunities through e-learning for development.

TEACHERS LEADING TEACHERS

Whether informally or formally, teachers can contribute to the success of their school in a variety of ways. As previously noted, the roles teacher leaders can encompass are varied, and include, for example, sharing professional resources with colleagues, serving as an instructional specialist by sharing teaching strategies, working as a curriculum specialist to develop standards, facilitating professional learning, mentoring new teachers, taking part in a school committee, and being a catalyst for change (Harrison & Killion, 2007). Critical to the latest paradigm of the role of the teacher leader is that the teacher leader remains an active participant in the classroom, while recognizing that the role has a place and value (Berry, et al., 2011). Within this role, the *teacherpreneur*, discussed earlier, emerges. The teacher is strategically tied to the classroom and students, while also continuing to enhance the knowledge of teaching, perfect the craft of teaching, understand the making of a successful school, and committed to working with colleagues for the betterment of the profession. The teacherpreneur recognizes excellence among teachers and works to improve school wide instructional strategies, principals of classroom management, and assessment applied to diverse settings. In this context,

the teacher leader can help teachers realize more than the power of their instruction, but also the structure of the classroom social interactions in light of their perceptions of their students and themselves. Teacherpreneur is a hybrid role, a role that builds on credibility that comes from teaching, while also investing in the betterment of the larger school community.

Today's emphasis of teacher leadership has moved away from site-based management by administrators to utilizing the classroom expertise that teacher leaders possess (Sherer, 2007). Most principals only remain in a given school as administrator for three or four years, whereas teachers in leadership positions typically spend longer periods of time in a school, leaving them with the institutional memory of programs that have been successful and those that were not (Danielson, 2007). As effective classroom teachers earn their position in leadership roles, administrators are extending the reach of these teachers beyond the classroom. This extension results in broader experiences and improved learning for the teacher as a leader, the fellow teachers who are led, and for the students who are positively impacted by improved instruction (Sherer, 2007). It is important to note that most effective teacher leaders are not *anointed* in a position by an administrator, rather they *earn* the respect of their colleagues in their diligence to improve instruction, their willingness to share their knowledge with their peers, and their dedication to the educational improvement the school and community (Austen, 2010).

Expanding leadership roles has been proven to help schools work together in a collaborative environment towards a common goal. School administrators simply cannot do it all, and cannot be the sole source of leadership in a school. The challenges that schools face today is rigorous, and it is up to the teacher to play a critical role in the school environment in order to overcome these challenges. Many of the most powerful opportunities for teacher leadership influence the daily lives of children. Research shows that in the most successful schools, teachers take the initiative to make improvements. For example, they are aware that they are most capable of teaching students most like themselves, so they engage in professional development that challenges themselves to develop the skills and dispositions required to promote an equitable education for all students. Teacher leaders are central in these efforts as they provide support for implementing effective pedagogies to meet the needs of all students throughout a school. Through encouraging teachers to act as leaders, schools can help teachers reach their full potential, which leads to positive impacts on student achievement (Danielson, 2007).

In elementary, middle, and high schools, teachers generally value the contributions, talents, and efforts of their peers in the work place as they share the common goal of positively impacting the achievement of their students. This core belief of most educators empowers teachers to become teacher leaders. Teacher leaders help to create and to expand a school's context for sustained professional learning, and model the processes for adult learning as they consistently focus on ensuring that their students are provided the maximum learning opportunities. The challenge of building and sustaining the culture of a school is focused on the ideals of teacher leaders and provides the structure to support teachers leading other teachers. When given the chance and opportunities to converse with other practitioners, teacher leaders inherit valuable information that can provide students with the maximum learning opportunities that have been proven to work by other colleagues. In order to lead effectively, teacher leaders should value the contributions of each colleague, and be able to relate to the teachers they lead while building a collaborative environment.

Conversely, teacher leaders are generally respected by their peers as valued members of the school community. Teacher leaders must fundamentally embody the philosophical belief system that is generally held by the school faculty. For example, the teacher leader practices inquiry based, student engagement in meaningful contexts. It is this earned value that empowers teacher leaders to influence others. The strength of teacher leaders is their willingness to learn from their own teaching, collaborate with their colleagues, and share their knowledge and expertise with the idea of improving the learning community and the collective responsibility of school improvement (Riel & Becker, 2008).

Likewise, the teacher leader must be valued by the school administrators. As previously noted, administrators must nurture and help develop teacher leaders in their schools. From the structuring of the school day, to providing opportunities for the teacher leader to engage in professional learning communities, to giving access to the appropriate, necessary, and innovative technologies, to respecting the diversity represented on the school faculty and student population, the administrator has a direct impact on the role and the success of a teacher leader.

TECHNOLOGY IN TEACHER LEADERSHIP

The role of technology in teacher leadership is not insignificant. In the short time span of 50 years, we have gone from typing, calculators, and shorthand, to word processing, spreadsheets, and databases, to twenty-first century digital graphics, animation, Web publishing, and video-audio editing. In this brief amount of time, technology has truly changed our world. And these rapid changes form the basis of the skills that are demanded in the workforce. It is imperative that students graduate from high school with the ability to: work with others; identify, organize, plan, and allocate resources; work with a variety of technologies; understand complex interrelationships; and acquire and evaluate information. Admittedly, students are growing up in a world of technology and are very technologically savvy. However, students must be taught how to use technology as a learning tool, as a gateway to knowledge and the application of that knowledge. That process likely begins with a teacher leader promoting the use of technology in the creation of a learning community that transcends the walls of a classroom, crosses the physical boundaries in a school, and broadens the perspectives of technology for both teachers and students (Teacher Leadership Exploratory Consortium, 2010).

Based on this foundation, teacher leaders must ask themselves if they are aware of the potential of technology in education, if they themselves integrate technology effectively, if they model the use of technology to improve teaching and learning. It is the pedagogy of technology in the classrooms, rather than the technology in and of itself that has the power to make a difference in the academic achievement of students. Research supports that teacher leaders are aware of the power of technology in schools. In fact, a study reported by Riel and Becker (2008) revealed that:

- Teacher leaders use emerging technology more than other classroom teachers;
- Are much more likely to have incorporated a variety of computer applications into their daily instructional practices; and,
- Are competent technology users themselves.

They use computers more with their students; more for professional activities such as lesson planning, posting student work to the Web, and communicating with parents. These teachers identified themselves as exemplary computer users significantly more than teachers not classified as teacher leaders. Though innovative or exemplary use of technology may be only one of a number of conditions consistently seen in a teacher leader, I believe it is a strong enough component that it merits its own section in this chapter.

The notions of technological implementation lead to that fact that being informed consumers of e-learning products and services as well as co-constructors of these tools are simply a necessity. As previously stated, P-12 students are growing up in a technology-rich world. That world is associated with global flows of information, connecting networks of people, products, and ideas across what was once geographic boundaries. Therefore, teacher leaders must be willing to engage the minds of learners in ways beyond traditional textbooks. When teacher leaders use technology successfully in their own classrooms with the students they teach, they gain the credibility from their colleagues and lead by example. Teacher leaders constantly search for ways to make technology beneficial for their teaching and for students' learning (Riel & Becker, 2008). The nature of technology speaks to teacher leaders being life-long learners. As technology changes so quickly, early adopters, in fact, all adopters, must stay abreast of current trends in order to keep up!

Technology is, in fact, about teaching and learning. As noted early in the chapter, teacher leaders use technology for their own professional development. Teacher leaders use this notion to help colleagues see the value in using technology first for their personal professional development. As teachers see that professional development is a process, not a one-time event, they realize the accessibility and ease of using technology to learn that can take place on a daily basis at any given moment. Once teachers embrace technology for learning themselves, they are generally open to learning to use technology as a tool for the teaching and learning for their students. For example, using interactive white boards, document cameras, smart phones, and computers with Internet access can all be instructional tools used in classrooms with all age students, regardless of specific content area.

Teacher leaders must be prepared to embed effective use of technology with their students, and they must also work closely with their colleagues as they develop school-wide cohesive use of technology. Many teachers realize the promise of technology and the potential impact on student learning, but most are overwhelmed with the task of keeping current and learning how to effectively use technology to support their daily instruction. They know they must change the way they teach simply to meet the learning styles of a diverse group of students, become less teacher directed to acting as a facilitator as students are engaged in constructing their own knowledge. As teacher leaders model various technology uses for teaching and learning, and as teachers embrace the use of technology, the ultimate benefit is seen in the students they teach. Effective teacher leaders guide their colleagues in implementing technology in their teaching, and helping students navigate technological tools to connect resources and promote collaborative learning (Teacher Leader Consortium, 2010). Technology speaks all languages, considers various learning styles, and promotes academic achievement in diverse learning environments. The primary purpose of technology in schools is to develop the literacy skills required to successfully participate in the global economy and today's society; and to improve the traditional academic achievement of all students, including those who experience a disproportionate underachievement (Cummins, Brown, & Sayers, 2007).

Technology in schools helps to narrow the gap of the *digital divide* in relation to poverty and minority students. However, the educational potential of technology is directly connected to the pedagogy of its implementation rather than the technology itself. Using computers as a tool for skill and drill, or test preparation type activities does not enhance students' critical thinking and problem solving skills. Using technology in schools for collaborative, critical inquiry in meaningful contexts makes a long-term difference in the academic success of all students. In this realm, the teacher leader helps colleagues actualize the power of technology, in all schools, including those serving low-income and minority students. The teacher leader must lead with a mantra of excellence and equity, and in an effort to develop school-wide communities of inquiry as they use technology and other tools

to maintain the status of highly engaged learners. A teacher leader responds to a diverse learning community by identifying the technologies that are most salient for a group of teachers and students at a given period of time, and promotes collaborative and differentiated learning opportunities for all stakeholders. It is the teachers who stay in the know with technology and discover the best technological fit for students that create a better learning environment and gain maximum learning opportunities in the classroom. These teacher leaders are often approached by other colleagues as a source of help and guidance due to their increased knowledge and effectiveness. If implemented properly, technology truly can be a great equalizer in helping to provide a quality education for all students.

FINAL THOUGHTS

Teacher leaders are not new educational concepts, yet current attention to the notion of teacher leadership gives fresh ideas and new possibilities to the role. The continuous development of teacher leadership is central to the ongoing efforts of school reform. Though there are many facets to the role of a teacher leader, it is central that teacher leaders have a deep understanding of the evolution of the teaching and learning process, the ever-changing demographics of the community in which we live, and that they stay abreast of the ever emerging and changing technologies. From committee leadership and department heads, to mentoring, modeling best practices, and asking reflective questions, teachers lead with established credibility and are focused on the improvement of teaching and learning in the school.

Critically, the social and professional networks that link a diverse group of teachers socially and academically to each other must be facilitated through the work of teacher leaders, using both technology and traditional means. Admittedly, teacher leaders have many obstacles to face such as the traditional structure of the school day, time constraints, lack of support, and ill-defined roles, but they must recognize these conditions and be proactive in working with school administrators to manage these obstacles (Collay, 2006). It is the ever-evolving leadership roles for teachers that are making a moment-by-moment positive impact on student achievement, one teacher at a time, one student at a time.

As the definition of leading teachers expands—with the focus on emphasizing the strengths of teachers and utilizing these leadership qualities to mentor the next generation of teacher leaders—the cyclical process empowers the school culture to promote change. Issues of diversity must become more vital as our schools are now a reflection of the global society represented in today's communities. Teachers must lead the call of reaching all students, enhancing their learning experiences, and preparing them for the twenty-first century, a technologically centered, global world. Therefore, for teacher leaders to be successful, they must earn the respect and be supported by the building level administration as well as by their colleagues, be given time to collaborate with their peers, be provided with the resources they need to meet the needs of their students and fellow teachers, and have the opportunity to engage in professional development. As these factors occur, teacher leaders will continue to be viewed as the expert teachers in their schools, never losing focus of the students they teach, yet ever broadening their impact in the school community.

REFERENCES

Austen, P. (2010). Informal instructional teacher leaders: How principals can support their effect on instructional reform. *Academic Leadership*, *8*(3), 1–7.

Bailey, J., Rehmat, A. P., Lombardi, D., & Keppelman, E. (2012). *Developing science teacher leaders through long-term professional development: A cross-case analysis of four teachers*. Washington, DC: National Association for Research in Science.

Bandura, A. (1997). *Self-efficacy: The exercise of control*. New York, NY: W.H. Freeman.

Beachum, F., & Dentith, A. (2004). Teacher leaders creating cultures of school renewal and transformation. *The Educational Forum*, *68*, 276–286. doi:10.1080/00131720408984639

Berry, B., Barnett, J., Betlach, K., C'de Baca, S., Highley, S., & Holland, J. M. … Wasserman, L. (2011). *Teaching 2030: What we must do for our students and for our public schools… now and in the future*. New York, NY: Teacher's College Press.

Berry, B., Daughtrey, A., & Wieder, A. (2010). *Teacher leadership: Leading the way to effective teaching and learning*. Washington, DC: Center for Teaching Quality.

Boyd-Dimock, V., & McGree, K. (1995). Leading change from the classroom: Teachers as leaders. *Issues about. Change*, *4*(4), 1–10.

Chetty, R., Friedman, J. N., & Rockoff, J. E. (2011). The long-term impacts of teachers: Teacher value-added and student outcomes in adulthood. *Executive Summary of National Bureau of Economic Research Working Paper No. 17699*. Retrieved April 1, 2012 from http://obs.rc.fas.harvard.edu/chetty/value_added.html

Collay, M. (2006). Discerning professional identity and becoming bold, socially responsible teacher-leaders. *Educational Leadership and Administration*, *18*, 131–146.

Cummins, J., Brown, K., & Sayers, D. (2007). *Literacy, technology, and diversity: Teaching for success in changing times*. Boston, MA: Allyn and Bacon.

Danielson, C. (2007). The many faces of leadership. *Educational Leadership*, *65*(1), 14–19.

Harrison, C., & Killion, J. (2007). Ten roles for teacher leaders. *Educational Leadership*, *65*(1), 74–77.

Haury, D. L. (2001). *Cultivating leadership among science and mathematics teachers*. Columbus, OH: Eric Database.

Hunzicker, J., Lukowiak, T., Huffman, V., & Johnson, C. (2009). Tomorrow's teacher leaders: Nurturing a disposition of leadership. *Academic Leadership Live: The Online Journal*, *9*(2). Retrieved December 13, 2011, from http://www.academicleadership.org/article/Tomorrow_s_Teacher_Leaders_Nurturing_a_Disposition_of_Leadership

Lambert, L. (2003). Leadership redefined: An evocative context for teacher leadership. *School Leadership & Management*, *23*(4), 421–430. doi:10.1080/1363243032000150953

Lieberman, A., Saxl, E., & Miles, M. (1988). Teacher leadership: ideology and practice. In Lieberman, A. (Ed.), *Building a Professional Culture in Schools*. New York, NY: Teachers College Press.

Pugalee, D. K., Frykholm, J., & Shaka, F. (2001). Diversity, technology, and policy: Key considerations in the development of teacher leadership. In Nesbit, C. R., Wallace, J. D., Pugalee, D. K., Miller, A. C., & DiBiase, W. J. (Eds.), *Developing Teacher Leaders: Professional Development in Science and Mathematics* (pp. 289–307). Columbus, OH: ERIC Publications.

Riel, M., & Becker, H. J. (2008). Characteristics of teacher leaders for information and communication technology. In Voogt, J., & Knezek, G. (Eds.), *International Handbook of Information Technology in Primary and Secondary Education* (pp. 397–417). New York, NY: Springer. doi:10.1007/978-0-387-73315-9_24

Roby, D. (2011). Teacher leaders impacting school culture. *Education*, *131*(4), 782–790.

Ross, J. A., & Gray, P. (2006). Transformational leadership and teacher commitment to organizational values: The mediating effects of collective teacher efficacy. *School Effectiveness and School Improvement*, *17*(2), 179–199. doi:10.1080/09243450600565795

Scherer, M. (2007). Playing to strengths. *Educational Leadership*, *65*(1), 7.

Searby, L., & Shaddix, L. (2008). Growing teacher leaders in a culture of excellence. *Professional Educator*, *32*(1), 1–6.

Steiner, L., & Kowal, L. (2009). *Instructional coaching*. Retrieved April 1, 2012 from http://www.readingrockets.org/article/25980/

Teacher Leadership Exploratory Consortium. (2010). *Model teacher leader standards*. Retrieved December 13, 2011, from http://tlstandards.weebly.com/index.html

KEY TERMS AND DEFINITIONS

Dispositions: Inherent qualities, inclinations, or tendencies.

Teacher Leaders: Teachers who are perceived as experts by their peers and administrators in some area(s) related to classroom teaching while also engaging in leadership opportunities outside that classroom that directly impact the overall school culture and achievement.

Teacherpreneur: A teacher leader of the future that has proven accomplishment and deep knowledge of how to teach, a clear understanding of what strategies must be in play to make schools highly successful, and the skills and commitment to spread their expertise to others—all while keeping one foot firmly in the classroom.

Chapter 19
Mentorship in Diversity Leadership in Higher Education:
Empowering Emerging and Established Leaders

Catherine L. Packer-Williams
Jefferson Davis Community College, USA

Kathy M. Evans
University of South Carolina, USA

ABSTRACT

The purpose of this chapter is to 1) review the need for diversity leadership in higher education, 2) explore the challenges of diversity leaders, 3) specify the need for mentorship in diversity leadership, 4) share the authors' successful e-mentoring experiences as women faculty of color engaged in diversity leadership, and 5) offer recommendations on how to incorporate technology as a tool for mentorship in diversity leadership in higher education. The term "diversity" can be considered as vast as it is vague. For the purpose of this chapter, diversity refers to the recruitment and retention of students and faculty of color in higher education as well as the incorporation of multiculturalism across disciplines and curricula.

INTRODUCTION

In 1978, the landmark case of Regents of the University of California v. Bakke was held before the U.S. Supreme Court in which a White male applicant to the University of California Medical School at Davis claimed reverse discrimination

when he was not admitted. Particularly in question was the university's diversity recruitment efforts through setting aside 16 spaces for students of color through a special admissions program. The U.S. Supreme Court decided to allow race to be considered as a factor for admissions in creating an overall diverse student body. Since the Bakke decision of 1978, institutions of higher education have been called upon to promote diversity as a

DOI: 10.4018/978-1-4666-2668-3.ch019

salient part of ensuring inclusive and equitable learning communities. According to the literature, many Traditionally White Institutions (TWIs) have historically struggled with the integration or adoption of such diversity efforts (Brayboy, 2003; Brown, 2004; Niemann, Y. & Maruyama, 2005). This struggle or reluctance towards diversity initiatives intensified with the 1998 Hopwood case. This case stated that race could no longer be used as a factor in admissions decisions. The diversity efforts of colleges and universities became even more muddled when the U.S. Supreme Court abrogated or retracted the Hopwood decision in 2003 and once again allowed race to be used a factor in the admissions process due to the educational benefits of a diverse student body (Rudenstine, 1996).

According to Aguirre and Martinez (2002), "Diversity nourishes the institutional climate in higher education much like water brings life to barren land" (p. 55). Diversity enriches the campus learning community by (1) supporting diverse perspectives and voices, which promote intellectual inquiry, (2) providing opportunities to effectively learn how to manage conflict when individuals share different points of view, and (3) establishing an example of the equitable and democratic society we aspire to become (Gurin, Dey, Hurtado, & Gurin, 2002). There has been a movement by institutions and educational organizations to establish diversity mission statements to publicize a commitment to fostering diversity in higher education (Garcia, et al., 2001; Humpreys, 2000). However, nearly a decade after the abrogation of the Hopwood decision which once again allows race to be considered as a valuable factor in diversifying campus communities, there is still arguably a disconnect between actual diversity initiatives and the educational mission statements of too many TWIs. Specifically, although more colleges and universities have a standalone diversity mission statement or have the importance of diversity embedded within a global mission statement of the institution, little change is evi-

dent in the student body, faculty, administration, or curriculum to show the fruits of institutional commitment to recruiting and retaining students and faculty of color and/or integrating diversity into the curriculum across disciplines. As a result, diversity leadership in higher education is vital to moving the importance of diversity from rhetoric to practice.

Unfortunately, most institutions do not have prominent positions in diversity leadership, such as, a Chief Diversity Officer, Associate Provost for Diversity and Inclusion, Vice President for Diversity and Equity, etc. Leadership in diversity on university and college campuses has often been relegated to the margins instead of centered in comparison to other forms of leadership in higher education with diversity work often relegated to committees. "The centering of higher education leadership practices in a Eurocentric consciousness continues to challenge the use of the diversity paradigm to change to social context for higher education and society" (Aguirre & Martinez, 2006, p. 81). According to Aguirre and Martinez (2006), this type of Eurocentric leadership paradigm, which places diversity leadership at the margins, has led diversity in higher education to have a more managerial than true leadership approach. From a managerial approach, faculty are either rewarded or punished by appointed, influential managers (Connerly & Pederson, 2005). Conversely, leaders can be appointed or emerge from the faculty and provide a vision and motivation to achieve major institutional goal changes. As a result, leadership in diversity can be thought of as a collective endeavor with the focus being to promote change as a vehicle to transform the institution.

When no clear directive or organization is put in place by administration to address pertinent issues of diversity when they arise, it is not uncommon for an individual or a collective group of faculty members to emerge as leaders to attempt to initiate diversity initiatives on a micro level (e.g., academic discipline) or macro level (e.g., college or university wide). Because of the lack of clear institutional vision and diversity leadership by administration, these faculty members require a higher level of support that is typically difficult to find at their home institution. Attempting to be a diversity change agent at an institution where no commitment to diversity is formalized into action, may have negative professional impacts such as, on tenure and promotion, as well as psychological and physical impacts such as early career burn out.

The Need for Mentoring

Even when diversity initiatives are in place at an institution of higher education, both emerging and established diversity leadership require support. Being a leader in diversity in higher education requires a strong level of commitment, tenacity, and tolerance. As an agent of change, leaders are required to disable the status quo that have kept institutional "isms" in place for decades and in some cases, centuries. This is not a task for the weak of heart. It is also a task that should not be conquered in isolation. Physical and emotional fatigue, followed by periods of burn out, disenchantment, and even anger are often experienced by diversity leaders as they fight for equity and justice (Lankau & Thomas, 2009).

Because of the many challenges they face, establishing a strong mentoring relationship is essential for both established and emerging diversity leaders. As with all good mentorship, mentors for diversity leaders can serve as buffers for avoiding confrontation, isolation, and alienation in the academy (Packer-Williams & Evans, 2011). Diversity leadership mentors can share approaches on how to create and promote strategies or policies that change biases toward the inclusion of diversity. Personal and professional challenges associated with being a change agent can also be processed and validated with a diversity competent mentor. Unfortunately, finding a mentor who possesses a solid understanding of the challenges of diversity leadership can be complicated if one does not look beyond one's own campus community. Therefore,

it is strongly recommended that both emerging and established diversity leaders participate in and foster e-mentoring relationships as part of their professional development.

E-Mentoring for Diversity Leadership

E-mentoring is defined as "a mentoring relationship which uses the tools of electronic communications either to extend and enhance an existing mentoring relationship, or to create one where it would not otherwise exist" (Muller, 2009, p. 25). It can also be referred to as "telementoring," "cybermentoring," "virtual mentoring," or "iMentoring." Research has shown that e-mentoring may not only be as beneficial but perhaps even more advantageous that face-to-face interactions (Muller, 2009). As an example, through the act of writing an email message to a mentor, diversity leaders may gain an opportunity for deeper self-reflection and evaluation than in a synchronous conversation. When writing an email to a mentor, the mentee is required to carefully and responsibly clarify the critical diversity dilemma, questions, and/or challenges that are being faced. Unlike traditional mentoring, e-mentoring also offers availability, speed, and access. Furthermore, according to Muller (2009), e-mentoring aids in building relationships between individuals who are disempowered or on the margins of mainstream groups and thus providing expanded opportunities to exchange ideas and receive support. By participating in e-mentoring, diversity leaders can address the isolation and disempowerment they may experience from being on the margins of leadership in higher education as well as gain support and ideas to foster change at their own institution.

The purpose of this chapter is to 1) review the need for diversity leadership in higher education, 2) explore the challenges of diversity leaders, 3) specify the need for mentorship in diversity leadership, 4) share our successful e-mentoring experiences as women faculty of color engaged in diversity leadership, and 5) offer recommendations on how to incorporate technology as tool for mentorship in diversity leadership in higher education. The term "diversity" can be considered as vast as it is vague. For the purpose of this chapter, diversity refers to the recruitment and retention of students and faculty of color in higher education as well as the incorporation of multiculturalism across disciplines and curricula.

REVIEW OF THE LITERATURE

There are literally hundreds of publications on mentoring, most of it relates to business and industry (Leavitt, 2011) but there is a fair amount of literature on mentoring in higher education. Most of that literature refers to the student/ mentor relationships with faculty. The resources thin considerably when the focus is on faculty mentoring faculty and thinner still on mentoring for diversity leadership. In fact, empirical studies published on mentoring diversity leadership are truly difficult to find. On the brighter side, there are a few studies focused on using technology and mentorship. What follows is a brief review of the published literature on diversity efforts in higher education, traditional mentoring practices, and technology as a tool for mentoring.

Diversity Efforts in Higher Education

It is often the mission of institutions of higher education that students will learn to live in harmony with those who differ from them and that discrimination is unfair. Several researchers have found that most faculty, administrators, and students support the idea of diversity because a diverse campus increases the level of learning for students and fulfills many mission statements about broad preparation and readiness for the global community (Aguirre & Martinez, 2006; Brown, 2004; Quezada & Louque, 2002). However, when more specific analyses are conducted, White faculty

and students have a more positive assessment of campus climate than faculty and students of color (Brown, 2004) and White faculty tend not to support diversity efforts (Brayboy, 2003; Lowe, 1999). Some suggest that these discrepancies occur because diversity efforts are marginalized and not integrated into the mainstream of college academic and social life (Aguirre & Martinez, 2006; Brown, 2004; Humphreys, 2005). In fact, Aguirre and Martinez (2006) point out that uneven progress in institutional changes relative to diversity is because "the dominant group feels threatened and actively seeks to maintain its privileged position and because institutions of higher education are rule bound and focused on maintaining homeostatic environment and culture" (p. 60).

Institutions hire diversity leaders to meet their recruitment and retention goals for diversity, yet most are unwilling to transform the culture of the university and make diversity an integral part of that culture. According to Aguirre and Martinez (2006) the challenge is for diversity leaders to design strategies to help alleviate the fears, biases and apathy and create a more positive campus culture and climate. Diversity leaders cannot meet that challenge without support and assistance and much of that support and assistance comes from a mentor.

Traditional Mentoring

Mentoring is typically divided into two categories—formal and informal. Research has shown that faculty prefer informal to formal mentorship relationships. Informal mentoring relationships typically occur naturally and are usually voluntary and egalitarian. Because the individuals have chosen one another, they meet more frequently and the relationship is more effective, meaningful, more satisfying and enduring than formal mentoring relationships. (Borders, et al., 2011; Johnson, 2002; Mullen & Hutinger, 2008; Ragins & Cotton, 1999). Formal mentoring relationships are often set up by colleges and universities for junior faculty (those new to the profession) who are matched with a senior faculty member who will help the junior member navigate through the organization and advance his or her career. Typically, these relationships are time limited and may or may not include formal training for the mentors.

A certain kind of person is ideal for mentoring new professionals. Zeller, Howard, and Barcic (2008) found in a 10-year study of faculty mentors that characteristics of good mentors included those who would "guide, protect, teach, challenge, open doors, and provide feedback. According to Smith, Howard, and Harrington's (2005) study what makes an outstanding mentor was his or her ability to act as trainer, activist, and supporter for his or her protégés. They also found that mentors believed that psychosocial support was more important than career functions. This was an interesting finding in that it was believed previously that only the protégés focused on the psychosocial aspect of the relationship.

Researchers have found that mentoring results in protégés learning relational skills (working with others) and personal skill development of the skills they need to perform their jobs. Mentors who act as role models for their protégés helped protégés to acquire the skills, attitudes, behaviors and values they need to be successful in the job (Hezlett, 2005; Lankau & Scandura, 2002; Lumpkin, 2011; Zellers, Howard, & Barcic, 2008). Role modeling is something that might be difficult for mentors to accomplish from a distance, however, recent literature suggests that protégés or mentees should have multiple mentors because no one person can fulfill all of the needs of the new professional (Benishek, et al., 2011; de Janasz & Sullivan, 2004; Evans & Cokley, 2008; Magnuson, 2002). Finally, the benefits of a mentoring relationship include greater productivity (Packer-Williams & Evans, 2011), confidence, higher career satisfaction, greater career advancement in protégés (Borders, et al., 2011), career rejuvenation, and increased job satisfaction for mentors (Pullins & Fine, 2002; Stevens-Roseman, 2009).

However, there can be some downsides to mentoring. Mentoring relationships change and deteriorate as do other relationships—especially when the needs of the protégé are no longer being met by the mentor. Also, assigned mentoring relationships can be problematic in that the professionals involved did not have a choice in the pairing (Carruthers, 1993). On occasion, the mentor can become jealous of the protégé's progress and begin to have a negative effect on the protégé's career (Carruthers, 1993). The literature is mixed as to whether cross racial and cross gender pairings are beneficial or harmful (Carruthers, 1993; Chandler, 1996; Davidson & Foster-Johnson, 2001; Dreher & Ash, 1990).

When mentoring is mentioned, the typical response is to imagine someone who is older and more experienced, paving the way into an organization for the younger inexperienced person. Kram (1983), however, suggested peer mentoring as opposed to hierarchical mentoring and it has been found that peer mentoring can be extremely effective. Because they are peers, the individuals in the peer mentoring relationship typically share the power, work collaboratively, meet psychosocial needs, and reduce isolation (Leavitt, 2011). In fact, Bryant and Terborg (2008) found that there is a relationship between the perception of high-level peer mentoring competence and higher levels of knowledge creation and sharing. As a result "organizations that are able to raise their employees' levels of peer mentoring competency through training can increase knowledge creation and sharing toward competitive advantage" (Leavitt, 2011, p. 25).

Muller (2009) suggests that planning for mentoring relationships should have eight basic components to be effective: 1) research and planning in advance, 2) the development of resources, 3) strategies for recruiting participants, 4) strategies for matching participants, 5) training for mentors and protégés, 6) communication, 7) closure, and 8) evaluation of effectiveness of the program. Some best practices in faculty mentoring would clearly apply to diversity leadership mentoring. Borders et al. (2011) suggest the following mentoring activities: communicating expectations for performance, giving feedback on performance, having a collegial review process, creating timelines for promotion or tenure, mentoring by someone senior to the mentee, recognizing the department chair as a career sponsor, supporting undergraduate learning, promoting scholarly development, and assist mentees to balance their personal and professional lives.

Technology as a Tool for Mentoring

The benefits of mentorship are numerous, as the previous studies have illustrated. Unfortunately, as Leavitt (2011) points out, mentors for diversity leaders are "woefully" unavailable in the workplace and this shortage puts them at a disadvantage for career advancement (Ely & Rhode, 2010). Therefore, many diversity leaders are compelled to find mentors outside their own institutions. In the last 10 years distance mentoring has become a great deal easier to manage with the help of technology. Muller (2009) points out that organizations develop e-mentoring programs when natural mentoring is not occurring or when segments of the population are not included in natural mentoring. Natural mentoring typically occurs when the mentor and protégé have a lot in common, especially race and gender. For diversity leaders, there are often no naturally occurring mentorships and they need to seek external mentors. According to Muller, external mentors can be more objective and "safer confidants" and can connect protégés with a broader set of contacts. E-mentoring is a way for diversity leaders to develop ongoing one-on-one relationships with experienced individuals across the county without leaving home.

E-mentoring could include e-mail exchanges exclusively or an institution could establish a technological platform designed specifically for the mentoring program. Such a platform could include Web pages, shared databases, scripts to enhance communication, and mathematical matching systems for mentors and protégés (Muller, 2009). As mentioned earlier, e-mail tends to be more thoughtful than face-to-face communication because the writers must take time to compose their correspondence and people tend to pay more attention to the written word than they do to the person delivering it and they tend to be more open and freer to communicate (Sproull & Kiesler, 1991). E-mail and other electronic communications are great equalizer in that people are less intimidated in communicating with those with authority and power (Sproul & Kiesler, 2001; Zuboff, 1988) and visible differences between mentor and protégés are minimized leading to greater trust (Muller, 2009).

OUR E-MENTORING SUCCESS STORIES

According to the literature, there is a strong need for diversity leaders to proactively identify methods of maintaining resilience (Kezar, 2008). We offer our personal experiences in hope that it will offer insight into how we as African American women faculty proactively sought and created opportunities for mentoring in diversity leadership through the use of technology.

Peer E-Mentoring as a Tool for Retention: Catherine's Story

Throughout my educational career at TWIs, as a high school student, an undergraduate, master's, and doctoral student, I found it rare to have a course with more than one other African American female student. Even rarer was the opportunity to be taught by an African American woman professor. As an aspiring academic, I relished opportunities to learn from these few African American women professors. What they taught me, directly and indirectly, was that academia can be very challenging because of the disparities in higher education that exist for African American women professors. I learned that African American women professors are the least likely in the professorate to receive tenure, are more overburdened with committee work, are least likely to receive mentoring, and receive lower teaching evaluations (particularly in courses that integrate diversity in the curriculum) than their counterparts (Packer-Williams & Evans, 2011). Their lessons not only prepared me to be proactive in addressing issues of equity and diversity but triggered an interest in leadership and multicultural diversity training.

After obtaining my first academic position, it was not long before I began to have my own testimonies regarding the disparities I was forewarned of by my professors. Determined not to become a statistic, I chose to seek mentoring to aid in my own retention. I specifically chose to explore the possibility of peer e-mentoring in an effort to have a reciprocal relationship with someone who could also voice and validate similar disparities as well as develop strategies to lessen the disparities at our respective institutions. My course of action included going to conferences and attending sessions and interest group meetings specifically for junior faculty with the purpose of finding someone with a similar story. Through this experience, I found connections with numerous women of color with stories that mirrored my own. I found one woman junior faculty member that not only shared a similar personal narrative but also shared my interest in leadership and multicultural diversity training on the teaching, research, and service areas. The two of us established the goals of our peer e-mentoring relationship, which included biweekly or monthly video conferences to process our experiences and provide/receive constructive feedback, provide accountability reports on scholarship productivity, and brainstorm methods to collaborate and turn our experiences as emerging diversity leaders into viable research projects.

This now five-year peer e-mentoring relationship has proven to serve as a method of preserving my psychological well-being. The e-mentoring relationship enabled me to feel less marginalized and disempowered. It also provided me with the courage and inspiration to continue my work in diversity leadership.

E-Mentoring as a Tool for Empowering Emerging Leaders: Kathy's Story

As I reflect on my first e-mentoring experience in diversity leadership, I recall asking a particular white, male faculty member to be a part of my dissertation committee. He agreed to do it as long as I also included one of his pet topics in my research. However, he had not done any research in the area of diversity himself. In fact, none of the faculty members on my committee had much expertise in this area of diversity leadership, research, and training. Therefore, I had to get mentoring for this part of my dissertation from outside of my own doctoral program. I e-mailed a person who was a renowned leader in the field and had published extensively in this area—another African American woman.

Throughout my graduate training (Master's and Ph.D.), I have never had an African American woman professor. I was thrilled when I received an e-mail from her almost immediately responding to my inquiry. She invited me to contact her if I had any more questions, which I did. She was always helpful, resourceful, encouraging, and patient. Without her help, I am sure my journey through the dissertation process would have been very rocky. I was immensely impressed with her and counted her as my mentor even though we had never met and all our correspondence was by e-mail.

When we finally met face to face at a national conference, she introduced me to several of her students who were doing similar research and to other leaders in the field of diversity leadership, research, and training. I was in awe of her and I could not believe the time she took to help someone who was not even a student at her university. She provided for me a model of mentoring in diversity leadership, especially for African American women. There are so few of us in the academy, it is our duty to encourage and support women who are just entering the profession even if it has to be done long distance via e-mentoring. If it had not been for her support and encouragement throughout the e-mentoring relationship, I doubt if I would have pursued a career in diversity leadership, research, and training because of institutional /individual biases that exist for diversity leaders.

RECOMMENDATIONS

Diversity leadership requires persistence, patience, being proactive, and support (Kezar, 2008). The following recommendations are offered for both emerging and established leaders as methods for incorporating technology as a tool for mentoring in diversity leadership.

- **Join online organizations that support and foster diversity leadership:** Due to time and financial constraints, it is not always feasible to join organizations and/or regularly attend national conferences that support one's values as a diversity leader. Finding organizations and e-mentoring communities can aid in locating e-mentors in the field. For example, the Association of American Colleges and Universities hosts www.DiversityWeb.org: An Interactive Resource Hub for Higher Education. This hub lists numerous organizations and websites that may be helpful to emerging and established diversity leaders.

- **Create an e-mentoring community:** Using the institution's instructional technology team as a consultant (if necessary), consider establishing and hosting a new e-mentoring community. Technology choices can include simple email lists, message boards, Web-based forums, and chat rooms. In addition, an e-mentoring community can be established using popular social media such as Facebook, iGoogle, MySpace, or Ning.

- **E-Mentor faculty on how to make diversity work "count" towards their tenure and promotion:** Because diversity leadership continues to be viewed on the margins on many university campuses, tenure track faculty may shy away from the work because it may detract from their research productivity. Collaborating and brainstorming ways to conduct diversity research may not only attract emerging diversity leaders, but it will also add to the importance of diversity work to the literature. The establishment of an interdisciplinary diversity leadership research team may also attract emerging diversity leaders.

- **Find e-mentors and allies in administrative leaders across institutions:** While some institutions continue to struggle with issues of diversity, there are institutions that can serve as models for best practice. These institutions are more likely to have senior administrative positions for their diversity leader(s), such as a Provost or Vice President of Diversity who may be able to provide e-mentoring and/or share valuable resources to aid you.

- **Consult the literature to find an e-mentor in specific disciplines:** The literature on diversity leadership has been expanding over the last ten years. Search the literature for specific areas of interest in diversity leadership and obtain the contact information of the author(s) who may be able to provide you with support or guidance.

- **Leaders in diversity are encouraged to continually engage in critical personal reflection and personal transformation as part of the e-mentoring process:** "If leaders are unable or unwilling to transform themselves to be change agents for diversity, they cannot provide the leadership necessary for building diverse and inclusive institutions of higher education" (Aguirre & Martinez, 2006, p. 81). Proficient diversity leadership requires leading by example. Therefore, diversity leaders in higher education need to be able to transform themselves by making diversity a core value in their personal and professional lives. Through the e-mentoring process, diversity leaders can be challenged to recognize and confront their own beliefs and values and gain a critical understanding or how their own worldview presents itself (positively or negatively) in their work as change agents.

- **Encourage and assist potential mentors in using technology:** Not all established leaders embrace technology to the fullest. It makes sense to perhaps have a reciprocal mentoring relationship with individuals who are still discovering the benefits of technology. Consider mentoring such diversity leaders in the use of technology while receiving mentoring from them on diversity leadership.

CONCLUSION

Institutions of higher learning continue to struggle with the incorporation of diversity in the recruitment and retention of students and faculty of color as well as the integration of multiculturalism across disciplines and curricula. Leaders in diversity across colleges and universities serve as change agents for the promotion of culturally proficient and equitable institutions. Creating change is a task filled with challenges and dilemmas for both emerging and established diversity leaders who often experience a lack of mentors to serve as buffers in the politically fueled world of diversity in higher education. E-mentoring can be a powerful technological tool that is a cost effective method of offering encouragement, guidance, training, exchange of information, and coaching, as well as building communities of collaborative agents of change across institutions.

Given the promising findings on the success of e-mentoring in various fields, future quantitative and qualitative research on the development and effectiveness of formal and informal e-mentoring relationships for diversity leadership in higher education is recommended. It is further recommended that future research consider the personal and professional implications for both the mentor and mentee participating in e-mentoring. Finally, research that illustrates the effectiveness of using technology as a tool for diversity leadership on establishing institutional change on both the macro- and micro-levels is also recommended.

REFERENCES

Aguirre, A. Jr, & Martinez, R. O. (2002). Leadership practices and diversity in higher education: Transitional and transformational frameworks. *The Journal of Leadership Studies*, *8*, 53–62. doi:10.1177/107179190200800305

Aguirre, A., Jr., & Martinez, R. O. (2006). Diversity leadership in higher education. *AHE Higher Education Report, 32*(3).

Benishek, L. A., Bieschke, K. J., Park, J., & Slattery, S. M. (2004). A multicultural feminist model of mentoring. *Journal of Multicultural Counseling and Development*, *32*, 428–442.

Borders, L. D., Young, J. S., Wester, K. L., Murray, C. E., Villalba, J. A., Lewis, T. F., & Mobley, A. K. (2011). Mentoring promotion/tenure-seeking faculty: Principles of good practice within a counselor education program. *Counselor Education and Supervision*, *50*, 171–188. doi:10.1002/j.1556-6978.2011.tb00118.x

Brayboy, B. M. J. (2003). The implementation of diversity in predominantly white colleges and universities. *Journal of Black Studies, 34,* 72–86. doi:10.1177/0021934703253679

Brown, L. (2004). Diversity: The challenge for higher education. *Race, Ethnicity and Education,* 7(1), 22–34.

Bryant, S., & Terborg, J. (2008). The impact of peer mentor training on creating and sharing organizational knowledge. *Journal of Managerial Issues, 20,* 11–29.

Carruthers, J. (1993). The principles and practice of mentoring. In Caldwell, B. J., & Carter, E. M. A. (Eds.), *The Return of the Mentor: Strategies for Workplace Learning.* London, UK: The Falmer Press.

Chandler, C. (1996). Mentoring and women in academia: Reevaluating the traditional model. *NWSA Journal, 3*(8), 79–100. doi:10.2979/NWS.1996.8.3.79

Connerly, M. L., & Pedersen, P. B. (2005). *Leadership in a diverse and multicultural environment.* Thousand Oaks, CA: Sage Publications.

Davidson, M. N., & Foster-Johnson, L. (2001). Mentoring in the preparation of graduate researchers of color. *Review of Educational Research, 71,* 549–574. doi:10.3102/00346543071004549

de Janasz, S. C., & Sullivan, S. E. (2004). Multiple mentoring in academe: Developing the professional network. *Journal of Vocational Behavior, 64,* 263–283. doi:10.1016/j.jvb.2002.07.001

Dreher, G. F., & Ash, R. A. (1990). A comparative study of mentoring among men and women in managerial, professional, and technical positions. *The Journal of Applied Psychology, 75*(5), 539–546. doi:10.1037/0021-9010.75.5.539

Ely, R. J., & Rhode, D. L. (2010). Women and leadership: Defining the challenges. In Nohria, N., & Khurana, R. (Eds.), *Handbook of Leadership Theory and Practice* (pp. 377–410). Boston, MA: Harvard Business Press.

Evans, G. L., & Cokley, K. O. (2008). African American women and the academy: Using career mentoring to increase research productivity. *Training and Education in Professional Psychology, 2,* 50–57. doi:10.1037/1931-3918.2.1.50

Garcia, M., Hudgins, C., Musil, C. M., Nettles, M. T., Sedlacek, W. E., & Smith, D. G. (2001). Assessing campus diversity initiatives: A guide for campus practitioners. In *Understanding the Difference Diversity Makes: Assessing Campus Diversity Initiatives.* Washington, DC: Association of American Colleges and Universities.

Gurin, P., Dey, E. L., Hurtado, S., & Gurin, G. (2002). Diversity in higher education: theory and impact on educational outcomes. *Harvard Educational Review, 72*(3), 330–366.

Hezlett, S. A. (2005). Proteges' learning in mentoring relationships: A review of the literature and an exploratory case study. *Advances in Developing Human Resources, 7*(4), 505–526. doi:10.1177/1523422305279686

Humphreys, D. (2000). Diversity plan trends aim to meet 21st century challenges. *Black Issues in Higher Education, 16,* 34–36.

Humpreys, D. (2000). National survey finds diversity requirements common around the country. *Diversity Digest, 5*(1), 1–2.

Johnson, W. B. (2002). The intentional mentor: Strategies and guidelines for the practice of mentoring. *Professional Psychology, Research and Practice, 33,* 88–96. doi:10.1037/0735-7028.33.1.88

Kezar, A. (2008). Understanding leadership strategies for addressing the politics of diversity. *The Journal of Higher Education, 79*(4), 406–441. doi:10.1353/jhe.0.0009

Kram, K. E. (1983). Phases of the mentor relationship. *Academy of Management Journal, 26*, 608–625. doi:10.2307/255910

Lankau, M., & Thomas, C. (2009). Preventing burnout: The effects of LMX and mentoring on socialization, role stress, and burnout. *Human Resource Management, 48*(3), 417–432. doi:10.1002/hrm.20288

Lankau, M. J., & Scandura, T. A. (2002). An investigation of personal learning in mentoring relationships: Content, antecedents, and consequences. *Academy of Management Journal, 45*(4), 779–790. doi:10.2307/3069311

Leavitt, C. C. (2011). *Developing leaders through mentoring: A brief literature review*. Columbus, OH: ERIC.

Lowe, E. (1999). Promise and dilemma: Perspectives on racial diversity and higher education. In Lowe, E. (Ed.), *Promise and Dilemma* (pp. 3–43). Princeton, NJ: Princeton University Press.

Lumpkin, A. (2011). A model for mentoring university faculty. *The Educational Forum, 75*, 357–368. doi:10.1080/00131725.2011.602466

Magnuson, S. (2002). New assistant professors of counselor education: Their 1st year. *Counselor Education and Supervision, 41*, 306–320. doi:10.1002/j.1556-6978.2002.tb01293.x

Mullen, C. A., & Hutinger, J. L. (2008). At the upping point: Role of formal faculty mentoring in changing university research cultures. *Journal of In-service Education, 34*, 181–204. doi:10.1080/13674580801951012

Muller, C. B. (2009). Understanding e-mentoring in organizations. *Adult Learning, 20*(1), 25–30.

Niemann, Y., & Maruyama, G. (2005). Inequities in higher education: Issues and promising practices in a world ambivalent about affirmative action. *The Journal of Social Issues, 61*, 407–426. doi:10.1111/j.1540-4560.2005.00414.x

Packer-Williams, C., & Evans, K. (2011). Retaining and reclaiming ourselves: Perspectives on a peer mentoring group experience for new African American women professors. *Perspectives in Peer Programs, 23*(1), 9–23.

Pullins, E. B., & Fine, L. M. (2002). How the performance of mentoring activities affects the mentor's job outcomes. *Journal of Personal Selling & Sales Management, 22*(4), 259–271.

Quezada, R., & Louque, A. (2002). Developing diverse faculty in culturally proficient education programs. *Multicultural Education, 9*, 10–14.

Ragins, B. R., & Kram, K. E. (2007). *The roots and meaning of mentoring*. Thousand Oaks, CA: Sage.

Rudenstine, N. (1996). Why a diverse student body is so important. *The Chronicle of Higher Education, 42*, B1–B2.

Scandura, T. A. (1992). Mentorship and career mobility: An empirical investigation. *Journal of Organizational Behavior, 13*(2), 169–174. doi:10.1002/job.4030130206

Smith, W. J., Howard, J. T., & Harrington, K. V. (2005). Essential formal mentor characteristics and functions in governmental and non-governmental organizations from the program administrator's and the mentor's perspective. *Public Personnel Management, 34*(1), 31–58.

Sproull, L., & Kiesler, S. (1991). *Connections: New ways of working in the networked organization*. Cambridge, MA: MIT Press.

Stevens-Roseman, E. S. (2009). Older mentors for newer workers: Impact of a worker-driven intervention on later life satisfaction. *Journal of Workplace Behavioral Health, 24*(4). doi:10.1080/15555240903358652

Zellers, D. F., Howard, V. M., & Barcic, M. A. (2008). Faculty mentoring programs: Envisioning rather than reinventing the wheel. *Review of Educational Research*, 78(3), 552–588. doi:10.3102/0034654308320966

Zuboff, S. (1988). *In the age of the smart machine*. New York, NY: Basic Books.

KEY TERMS AND DEFINITIONS

Change Agent: A leader and catalyst that collaborates with others to advocate for and create change.

Diversity Competent Mentor: A mentor that values diversity, recognizes the value of cultural differences, and engages in self-reflection regarding himself or herself as a cultural being.

E-Mentoring: A method of establishing, extending, or enhancing a mentoring relationship using electronic communication.

Formal Mentoring: Often established by colleges and universities for junior faculty who are matched with a senior faculty member who will help the junior member navigate through the organization and advance his or her career.

Hierarchical Mentoring: A type of formal, traditional mentoring relationship in which an older, more experienced person mentors a younger, less experienced protégé.

Informal Mentoring: Mentoring relationships that typically occur naturally and are usually voluntary and egalitarian.

Peer Mentoring: An alternative networking and collaboration model in which mentees are essentially equal in experience and rank.

Chapter 20
Diversity Leadership in the Community College:
Bridging the Gap

RaShaunda V. Sterling
San Jacinto College, USA

James R. Williams
Prairie View A&M University, USA

ABSTRACT

The chapter examines the disconnection between the diversity of community college students and community college administrators. The history of community colleges in the United States is presented, along with the demographics of the typical community college student. A definition of leadership is provided, and theories of diversity leadership are discussed. Methods of producing greater diversity at the administrative level are also explained. In particular, Kotter's eight-stage model for organizational change is presented as a means of altering a college's culture to promote greater diversity leadership. Further, strategies that can be used to increase diversity in community college leadership, with an emphasis on the role that technology can play in promoting diversity leadership, are presented. Directions for future research are shared.

INTRODUCTION

Because of their focus on diversity and inclusivity, community colleges have provided more avenues of access to students who have traditionally been underserved and underrepresented at Institutions of Higher Education (IHEs) (Crews & Aragon,

2004). Students who are members of the first generation in their families to attend college, those who are members of minority groups, those who are academically underprepared, and those who are low-income are more likely to enroll in a community college (Achieving the Dream, 2005). Further, of the 12.4 million community college students in the U.S., 58% are female, 45% are members of an ethnic minority, and 12% have disabilities (Crews & Aragon, 2004). Thus, the

DOI: 10.4018/978-1-4666-2668-3.ch020

average student at a community college is likely to be a minority woman who is academically unprepared and economically disadvantaged (Crews & Aragon, 2004).

Despite the cultural and ethnic diversity of community college students in the U.S., the leadership at these IHEs often does not reflect the demographics of the populations they serve. While minorities make up about 35% of students at all IHEs (colleges and universities), only 14% of presidents, and 19% of administrators are minorities (Betts, et al., 2009). To address these issues, many community colleges are implementing efforts to encourage and promote greater inclusivity and shared leadership. This chapter will examine the history of community colleges and will look at the issue of diversity from both a student and administrator perspective. Further, the disconnection between the diversity of the student populations and community college administration will be examined. Lastly, theories of diversity leadership and ways to promote greater diversity at the administrative level will be discussed.

BACKGROUND

In 1901, Joliet Junior College, the first public community college in the United States, was founded in Joliet, Illinois (American Association of Community Colleges, 2011). Today, there are 1,167 public, private, and tribal community colleges (American Association of Community Colleges, 2011). Historically, these IHEs have provided a way for students who have had limited access to post-secondary education to attain a college degree (Barnes & Piland, 2010). Because of their open admissions policies, community colleges have been able to serve a more diverse student population than universities (Crews & Aragon, 2007).

Until around 1970, community colleges were called *junior colleges* (Robinson-Neal, 2009). The main purpose of these institutions was to offer training beyond the secondary level and to prepare students for either a vocational field or for the university (Dunning, 2008). The term *community college* became more widely adopted during the 1970, as the mission of these institutions expanded to include more continuing education, job-training, and social programs (Dunning, 2008; Robinson-Neal, 2009).

First-generation, academically limited, minority, and low-income students are most likely to attend a community college (Achieving the Dream, 2005; Crews & Aragon, 2004). These factors often make it more difficult for community college students to graduate (Achieving the Dream, 2005; Astin, 1993; Pascarella & Terenzini, 1991). Because minorities are more likely to attend a community college, less likely to transfer to a four-year university, and least likely to graduate from any post-secondary institution, there is a dearth of minorities who have the education and experience to reach leadership positions at IHEs (Robinson-Neal, 2009).

PROMOTING DIVERSITY LEADERSHIP

Leaders are people who guide others, and leadership entails the method that leaders employ to motivate their followers (Gregory-Mina, 2009). According to Northhouse (2010), leadership is the process by which a person acts as an agent of influence on others in order to accomplish a shared objective. Northouse (2010) further describes leadership as a complex process that has a multitude of dimensions. Recognizing that leadership is both a process and a product is important when one is attempting to understand and define the characteristics of effective leaders. According to Nikaien et al. (2012), there is a relational process between leaders and followers. Northhouse (2010) goes further, stating that the true nature of leadership, based on research findings, reveals a more complex process than how leadership is often portrayed in texts that are written for a popular audience.

It is good and beneficial for researchers, educators, and members of organizations to discover the definition, formula, and process of leadership (Gregory-Mina, 2009). By doing so, they will be better able to train, develop, and transfer leadership styles, characteristics, and methodologies into a comprehensive theoretical framework. When they have more sophisticated knowledge of leadership and leadership theory, educational administrators and members of organizations will also be able to more effectively articulate what they need, expect, and desire from their leaders (Gregory-Mina, 2009). Andreescu and Vito (2010) state that, in order for an organization to be effective, it must have effective leadership. Stakeholders who appreciate that leadership is a sought-after skill and who can recognize that skill in others who are in line for leadership opportunities are better equipped to capitalize on individual differences in leadership styles.

According to Northhouse (2010), leadership skills are highly valued commodities.

The leadership characteristics that are acquired through experience and training are called skilled leadership qualities. Bentley (2007) explains that one view of the skills approach to leadership is the paradigm of the servant-leader. This concept can be seen in some denominations of the African American Christian church in the U.S. (Bentley, 2007). It focuses on the importance of qualities such as unselfishness, altruism, and self-sacrifice, which are all necessary when helping others reach their own personal potential. According to Smith and Roysircar (2010), those who identified themselves as servant-leaders described their own interactions with important people as awesome and motivating. Because these leaders experienced positive interactions, they wanted to help others have similar experiences. They, in turn, worked on developing skills that would allow them to have a positive impact on their organizations (Smith & Roysircar, 2010).

In certain leadership environments, there is a shortage of minorities in leadership roles be-cause of a lack of educational achievement, and consequently, a limited pool of highly qualified applicants to leadership positions (Portugal, 2006). Minority men, in particular, often lag behind their female counterparts. A U.S. Census report revealed that women of any ethnicity have more professional degrees than men (89,000 vs. 82,000), and they are more likely to have earned a doctor-ate (68,000 vs. 65,000) (United States Census Bureau, 2010). Among African Americans in the U.S., males have a small lead in professional degree attainment (82,000 vs. 81,000), but African American females lead in doctoral degree attainment (66,000 vs. 61,000) (United States Census Bureau, 2010). These statistics show that minority women are more likely to have greater educational and economic success than their male counterparts (Kaba, 2011). These women are more likely, too, to have greater access to leadership opportunities.

Minority Leaders

In their interviews with African American leaders, Smith and Roysircar (2010) found that certain qualities contribute to one's success as a leader. In interviews, the group of African American leaders described themselves as outgoing and gregarious. They had efficacious communication skills, and they valued communication. They saw themselves as people who possessed great vision. They were strong in strategic planning. The leaders who were interviewed further stated that they keep their sense of humor and their perspective. They were able to listen to and hear the concerns of stakeholders. They understood how systems worked and were able to view issues from multiple perspectives. These were identified as the characteristics of effective leaders (Smith & Roysircar, 2010).

Reed and Evans (2008) suggest that a complex interaction of race, gender, and socialization all impact minority leaders' perception and leadership skills. While a leader may not intentionally display favoritism toward a specific group, unintention-ally, the leader may have a deeper interest in and an understanding of others who share the leader's cultural heritage (Reed & Evans, 2008). There are positive and negative aspects to this partiality. Educational leaders who are minorities may have a unique perspective of the problems that plague minority students attending community colleges. Conversely, the leaders' culture may cloud their judgment, and this may negatively impact how they lead.

Reed and Evans (2008) also make the assertion that minority leaders do not share the same values and beliefs that their Anglo American counterparts possess. Further, minority leaders tend to identify and empathize with minority students more than leaders of other races (Reed & Evans, 2008). Andreescu and Vito (2010) point out that individual characteristics can influence not only managerial styles, but also leadership preferences. This suggests that race, gender, and situation all impact individual leadership styles. As such, to accommodate an increasing diverse student population, current leaders at community colleges must take into account race and gender when hiring for administrative positions, if they are truly committed to plurality of thought and to inclusivity. Creating a culture that promotes diversity initiatives is also critical to increasing minority participation at the administrative level.

Using Kotter's Model to Increase Minority Leadership Opportunities

In *Leading Change*, John Kotter (1996) discusses his eight-stage process of organizational transformation. Kotter posits that change is a reality of life and that effective leaders know how to implement changes in ways that encourage cooperation and minimize discord. While Kotter's process has typically been applied in business and industry, the model could be used by community colleges to create a shared vision for improving diversity leadership opportunities. A significant part of increasing the number of minorities in administrative roles is an IHE's commitment to diversity

initiatives (Portugal, 2006), and Kotter's model can assist in raising an organization's awareness and acceptance of diversity and inclusivity.

The first stage of Kotter's model, *Establishing a Sense of Urgency*, involves understanding the issues and potential problems that currently beset the organization. For community colleges, this means facing the reality of an increasingly diverse student population and significantly less diverse leaders (Betts, et al., 2009). By bringing this issue to the attention of the administrators, faculty, and staff at an institution, the leader who is responsible for the college and who can act as a catalyst for change, the change agent, can begin to implement a program to address cultural and ethnic disparities among stakeholders.

The second stage, *Creating a Guiding Coalition*, entails the formation of a team of people who are committed to making the changes necessary to address the issue of a lack of diversity among administrators. The change agent will have to gather together a group of people, presumably consisting of administrators, faculty, and staff, who believe in the goal of diversity and are committed to increasing diversity and ameliorating the disparities. According to Kotter (1996), the members of this group should have the respect of their colleagues. By using well-respected people as part of the coalition of change, the change agent may generate greater buy-in from constituents.

Stage three, *Developing a Vision and Strategy*, requires that the change agent and the guiding coalition develop a clear vision and express that vision in simple terms to other stakeholders. According to Kotter's model, an important part of this process is seeking the input of stakeholders. Administrators, faculty, and staff should therefore be invited to contribute to the formation of a shared vision for diversity leadership at the institution (Kotter, 1996). In doing so, the change agent and the coalition can minimize feelings of distrust and disappointment among stakeholders. The change agent is encouraged to have an open meeting with all members of the college community and engage in a frank conversation about the direction of the institution in regards to diversity and inclusivity. The change agent should then solicit others' advice on how to achieve the goal of increased diversity in a way that works for all stakeholders. Lastly, the change agent should meet with the coalition to discuss how to put these suggestions in place. There must be ongoing dialogues among the leadership and the members, and the college's shared vision must be at the heart of all these conversations.

The fourth stage, *Communicating the Change Vision*, requires that the change agent and the coalition use every available method to communicate the shared vision and strategies for promoting diversity leadership initiatives. They should address concerns in a way that makes employees feel validated and part of the democratic process within the college. Every communication, every meeting, and every activity must be in line with the college's stated vision or mission. The leader must re-affirm stakeholders' commitment to increasing minority representation within the administrative ranks. By soliciting input from all constituents and valuing their roles in the creation and implementation of the vision, the change agent may be able to generate greater feelings of trust and comfort with the vision. If he or she fails to do so, the sustainability of the diversity initiatives is highly doubtful.

The fifth stage, *Empowering Employees for Broad-Based Action*, involves removing obstacles that can impede the change process. This stage is designed to provide encouragement to the faculty and staff by acknowledging their commitment to the shared vision, diversity leadership. The achievement of short-term goals should be recognized by the change agent and the coalition. This is necessary because short-term goals allow people to experience growth throughout the change process, versus encountering constant obstacles without recognition of their overcoming those challenges. Rewarding the participants assisting in reaching the organization's ultimate goals will strengthen the institution and develop confidence among its members. Often, change managers fail to acknowledge members' modest advancements, preferring instead to wait for prodigious successes.

Kotter's sixth stage, *Generating Short-term Wins*, is to create opportunities for an organization and its members to obtain multiple victories throughout the application of the new direction outlined by the organization. This step allows employees and leaders to celebrate the success of benchmarks, while working towards the ultimate goals in changing the organization's direction or implementing a new vision for the organization. Creating wins also gains the support of disbelievers and other people who are not fully bought into the new vision. Failure to consider this step can result in distrust within the organization. The members may not trust the vision and leadership, the members may not trust one another, and the new members may not trust the structure of the organization.

In Kotter's (1996) eight-step model for organizational change, he addresses stage seven, *Consolidating Gains and Producing More Change*, by stating that leaders should create continuous improvements to strengthen organizational change. Kotter (1996) suggests that organizational leaders should avoid contentment and should constantly seek improvement in all areas of the organization. This will not only strengthen the organization; it will prevent complacency among its members. Change will become the foundation of the organization, and there will be less risk of members fearing change. Most people inherently resist change, but through Kotter's model, leaders can implement protocols to promote continuous improvement and a lack of complacency. An organization must evolve as time goes on. If organizations fail to constantly improve their policies and procedures, they will cease to be relevant and will ultimately be unsuccessful in maintaining the organizations' growth and members' satisfaction. It is necessary for all organizations to analyze their strengths and accomplishments, as well as their shortcomings, and to avoid complacency (Kotter, 1996). They must set goals and continue to incorporate new ideas and fresh people with new perspectives who can enhance the organization.

The eighth and last stage of Kotter's (1996) organizational change process, *Anchoring New Approaches in the Culture*, requires that change be maintained by having visible change agents in the organization, using every opportunity to reflect on the successes of the vision. Until new behaviors and attitudes are rooted in social norms and shared values, they are subject to degradation as soon as the pressure for change is removed (Kotter, 1996). When members of the college community feel that they are succeeded in improving the diversity among the college's leadership, they may believe that diversity efforts no longer need to be sustained. However, this is not the case. New members must be orienting and the original leaders of the change process should be recognized when embedding change into an organization's culture.

Organizations should avoid using traditions as handicaps; in order for the organization to thrive, members must not remain stagnant. Recognition is necessary, but complacency is unacceptable. Change and the vision it creates must circulate the inner mechanisms of the college. Anchoring a commitment to diversity leadership into the culture of a college can be a difficult task, but it is necessary to successfully fulfill the college's vision for change.

Using Technology to Support Discourse on Diversity Issues

Increases in diversity among college students, greater competition for students, and restricted financial resources have significantly impacted the way that IHEs function (Davidson-Shivers, 2002; Robinson-Neal, 2009). Because this is the case, administrators are increasingly relying on technology to improve productivity and to achieve their colleges' missions (Duderstadt, Atkins, & Van Houweling, 2002; Sterling, 2011). Technology

offers new, more innovative ways for community colleges to connect with students, attract faculty who are committed to their vision, and remain proactive in a changing educational landscape (Duderstadt, et al., 2002; Robinson-Neal, 2009; Sterling, 2011).

In the market-driven system that higher education has become, students have certain expectations from the college they choose to attend. Because students have grown accustomed to the convenience that information and communications technologies afford them, many now expect that same level of convenience in all aspects of their lives, including their choice of educational institution (Duderstadt, et al., 2002). When their expectations are not realized, students could search for alternatives that will meet their view of what their college experience should entail. For some students, those expectations may include attending a college that is as diverse as the students' experiences (Frost, 2007; Richardson, 1991). The lack of diversity or a lack of sensitivity to diversity issues may cause students to look elsewhere to fulfill their goal of a postsecondary education (Frost, 2007).

Due to changes in the market and student perceptions, community colleges have had to adjust their methods and their instructional strategies to suit students (Crozier, et al., 2008; Duderstadt, et al., 2002). To that end, IHEs have been compelled to repackage and promote themselves, especially in regards to issues of diversity and inclusivity (Crozier, et al., 2008). A strong Internet presence is critically important, as more students, prospective students, and prospective employees rely on the Internet to learn about college services, compare educational commodities, and gather information. A website that does not highlight a college's commitment to diversity may cause students to forego one institution for another that offers more inclusivity and connectedness (Meyer, 2008). Students may perceive schools that do not appear diverse as places where the students will not be welcomed into the college community.

Because educational institutions are now required to negotiate between traditional brick-and-mortar classrooms and online educational settings, asynchronous learning and distance education are approaches that have expanded significantly (Duderstadt, et al., 2002). In addition to providing opportunities to enhance student achievement and engender feelings of inclusivity among students, community colleges can use Web-based programs to implement diversity awareness initiatives for all stakeholders (Smith & Ayers, 2006). For example, instead of presenting diversity training sessions that are delivered in a face-to-face setting, online, modularized instruction may allow colleges to provide the same content at a lower cost, thus sharing their change vision with more faculty and staff, and doing so in a more efficient way (McKimm & Swanwick, 2010). Faculty and staff benefit because such courses are more convenient (Kasworm, Sandmann, & Sissel, 2000); this is particularly true for support staff who may be unable to attend lengthy training sessions.

Creating an environment where the values of faculty and staff are welcomed is one factor in generating greater buy-in for diversity initiatives. Web 2.0 tools may be able to play a role in sharing the change vision for diversity leadership. Wikis are tools that can be used to change a college's culture by allowing the democratic sharing of thoughts (Chawner & Lewis, 2006; Windley, 2007). They provide an opportunity for users to construct a forum for collaborative communication and shared content authoring (Sauer, et al., 2005). Instead of merely being consumers of knowledge, wiki users can become producers of it. With wikis, colleagues may work independently or in cohorts to discuss their shared vision of diversity at their institution (Achterman, 2006). Not only that, but both synchronous and asynchronous collaboration can be accomplished with the aid of a wiki (Achterman, 2006). In fact, wikis lend themselves to asynchronous group interactions.

Wikis promote social democracy in education (Hauser, 2007; Lamont, 2007; Sarrel, 2007). At a college that is committed to improving its representation of minority leaders, the change agent/leader could serve as the moderator of a campus-wide employee wiki, and faculty and staff could be the authors/editors. Thus, the leader's role becomes that of a facilitator, instead of a dictator (Engstrom & Jewett, 2005). This approach is less hands-on, allowing the change agent to play a more limited, less authoritative role in discussing the college's diversity initiatives (Engstrom & Jewett, 2005).

Increasingly, professional organizations are using wikis to disseminate information and create a shared body of knowledge. In fields from software development, to journalism, to law, people are developing wikis to speed the process of sharing information and communicating (Dorroh, 2005; Gibson, 2006; Sarrel, 2007). At this time, science and technology disciplines appear to be more likely to utilize wikis than other disciplines (Sauer, et al., 2005; Skiba, 2005); however, this fact is rapidly changing as other fields see the apparent advantages of wikis.

To illustrate how other organizations are using wikis: Libraries and librarians are utilizing wiki technology to encourage interest in library science, discuss best practices in the field, and communicate with library patrons (Achterman, 2006; "ALSC Wiki Introduced," 2007; Gordon & Stephen, 2007; Hauser, 2007; Kajewski, 2006). University libraries at schools like the University of Houston and Stony Brook University have adopted wikis as communication tools as well (Chase, 2007; Coombs, 2007). Even the U.S. Department of Defense's Defense Intelligence Agency (DIA) is using wikis to coordinate and manage its military intelligence-gathering missions (Havenstein, 2007). More widespread use of wikis in both the private and public sectors is likely to follow.

Openness and transparency are encouraged by the use of wikis (Chase, 2007). In order to ensure that these characteristics add to the organization, each member of a group project should have an individual page on the wiki (Sarrel, 2007). This lets everyone see what everyone else is working on and could eliminate the duplication of services. When everyone's work and responsibilities are on display, members of the college may feel a greater sense of accountability to the organization (Sarrel, 2007).

More and more organizations are adopting wikis to speed their communication processes and to encourage open collaboration among work groups, departments, and other stakeholders. This can be particularly beneficial to a community college that is engaged in the process of promoting diversity and inclusivity and in creating an environment that fosters these goals. Wikis have the potential to revolutionize the way colleges work, as they are often low-cost methods of connecting and staying in touch with the people who matter to the organization, both internally (within the college) and externally (with current students, prospective students, prospective employees, community members, etc.).

Because of their communal nature, Skiba (2005) refers to wikis as social software. As such, wikis promote social interaction and discourse among users, which some researchers believe is one of the most notable advantages of wikis (Engstrom & Jewett, 2005). Indeed, wikis create a sense of community. In educational settings, students, faculty, and staff can become part of a community of learners, sharing ideas, facts, and information (Engstrom & Jewett, 2005). Further, they can discuss their ideas and perceptions about the college's diversity initiatives. Users of wikis may believe that their contribution to the wiki is just as important as others,' resulting in greater feelings of connectedness to the college. Stakeholders experience the power of having a voice, of having control, and of having the opportunity to share their experiences.

Another benefit of wikis is that they decentralize the creation and transmission of knowledge (Coombs, 2007). At a community college, presidents and executive-level administrators are typically the chief decision-makers (Eddy, 2005).

Yet, by using a college-wide wiki, others may have a greater voice. Administrators are no longer viewed as having all the power; through the use of wikis, they are managers and overseers of the wiki's content. The users of wikis—faculty, staff, and students—are the creators of wikis (Coombs, 2007). This is analogous to a magazine subscriber becoming a contributing editor with just a few keystrokes and mouse clicks. The result is that wikis can create a sense of ownership and pride throughout the college community (Chase, 2007).

Yet another boon of wikis is that, while highly changeable, most wiki software has built-in measures to keep users from inadvertently, or perhaps purposely, deleting or permanently altering the site. Other features include the inability of users to edit the same page at the same time (Chawner & Lewis, 2006). In addition, wikis allow users to create and modify pages without the users having to know a great deal about coding or computer languages; with a little practice, changes can be made simply using a browser interface (Chawner & Lewis, 2006). These design aspects improve the ease-of-use of wikis, and thereby increase the likelihood of college-wide participation.

By establishing wikis, members of the college community can observe what areas generate the most user interest. Content that attracts a great deal of attention from members of a wiki can be highlighted and expanded upon, while less-desirable content can be eliminated or improved (Lamont, 2007). In this way, wikis can serve as databases or repositories of information that is most helpful to its users, and wikis can include built-in search engines that expedite data searches.

By creating a college-wide wiki, administrators, faculty, staff, and students at community colleges can build a culture that demonstrates their shared vision for plurality of thought, diversity, and inclusivity. In doing so, they can lay the groundwork for greater minority representation at the administrative level because, in order to have more minority leaders, a college must first show that they are committed to diversity (Bumphus & Roueche, 2007). Through the use of technology and an ongoing dialogue about diversity issues, community colleges can improve minority participation in leadership and the decision-making process.

DIRECTIONS FOR FUTURE RESEARCH

Community colleges must continue their efforts to increase the number of minority administrators (Bumphus & Roueche, 2007). While they have made strides, their work is not complete. Potential avenues for further research include the need for greater understanding of what specific factors may act as barriers for minorities seeking executive-level positions at IHEs. In addition, the hiring practices for administration jobs at community colleges may be examined, with a focus on search committees' judgments of fitness to lead and how these judgments affect who becomes a finalist for the job. Yet another research area would be how community colleges create an environment where diversity is truly fostered, encouraged, and appreciated. Too often, institutions appear to value diversity, yet their demographics and other external measures show otherwise (Robinson-Neal, 2009). By examining these issues, researchers may develop a better understanding of the factors that affect minority participation in community college administration.

CONCLUSION

In conclusion, leadership in higher education is changing. The shift from an Anglo American, male-dominated hierarchy to a more pluralistic, inclusive structure translates into a more equal playing field for all. The responsibility of leadership should be egalitarian; restrictions to leadership opportunities based on race or gender will ultimately need to be eradicated in order to improve governance for an increasingly diverse student population. As minorities have more opportunities to move their careers to an executive path, they will likely have more chances to demonstrate effective leadership.

Kotter (1996) recommends that an organization's leadership should generate a sense of urgency, form a guided coalition, collectively create a vision, communicate that vision, and remove obstacles to the completion of the vision. Using Kotter's method and educational technology tools such as online diversity training and wikis, community colleges can capitalize on their fundamental principles of educational opportunities, equity, access, equality, and social justice. Community college administrators and educators must develop a national agenda that can support efforts to produce more minority leaders, leaders who may uniquely understand the experiences of the minority students that community colleges serve. It is only through a sustained, concerted effort, one rooted in the belief in the value of diversity, that the number of minority leaders at IHEs in this country will significantly increase.

REFERENCES

Achieving the Dream. (2005, August). *Achieving the dream state policy newsletter*. Retrieved from http://www.achievingthedream.org/_images/_index03/Policy_Newsletter_Aug05.pdf

Achterman, D. (2006). Making connections with blogs and wikis. *CSLA Journal, 30*(1), 29–31.

American Association of Community Colleges. (2009). *Fast facts*. Retrieved from http://www.aacc.nche.edu/AboutCC/Pages/fastfacts.aspx

Andreescu, V., & Vito, G. F. (2010). An exploratory study on ideal leadership behaviour: The opinions of American police managers. *International Journal of Police Science & Management, 12*(4), 567–583. doi:10.1350/ijps.2010.12.4.207

Astin, A. W. (1993). *What matters in college: Four critical years revisited*. San Francisco, CA: Jossey-Bass.

Barnes, R. A., & Piland, W. E. (2010). Impact of learning communities in developmental English on community college student retention and persistence. *Journal of College Student Retention: Research. Theory into Practice, 12*(1), 7–24.

Bentley, W. (2007). A Christian philosophy of leadership: The servant model. *The National Black Evangelical Association.* Retrieved from http://www.The-NBEA.org

Betts, K. S., Urias, D., Betts, K., & Chavez, J. (2009). Higher education and shifting U.S. demographics: Need for visible career paths, professional development, succession planning & commitment to diversity. *Academic Leadership On-Line Journal, 7*(2). Retrieved from http://www.academicleadership.org/emprical_research/623.shtml

Bumphus, W. G., & Roueche, J. E. (2007). Community colleges often lead the way in diversity efforts. *Diverse Issues in Higher Education, 24*(11), 82.

Chase, D. (2007). Transformative sharing with instant messaging, wikis, interactive maps, and Flickr. *Computers in Libraries, 27*(1), 7–56.

Chawner, B., & Lewis, P. H. (2006). WikiWiki-Webs: New ways to communicate in a web environment. *Information Technology & Libraries, 25*(1), 33–43.

Coombs, K. A. (2007). Building a library web site on the pillars of web 2.0. *Computers in Libraries, 27*(1), 16–19.

Crews, D. M., & Aragon, S. R. (2004). Influence of a community college developmental education writing course on academic performance. *Community College Review, 32*(2), 1–18. doi:10.1177/009155210403200201

Crozier, G., Reay, D., Clayton, J., Colliander, L., & Grinstead, J. (2008). Different strokes for different folks: Diverse students in diverse institutions—Experiences of higher education. *Research Papers in Education, 23*(2), 167–177. doi:10.1080/02671520802048703

Davidson-Shivers, G. V. (2002). IT in higher education. In Reiser, R. A., & Dempsey, J. V. (Eds.), *Trends & Issues in Instructional Design & Technology* (pp. 256–268). Columbus, OH: Merrill-Prentice Hall.

Dorroh, J. (2005). Wiki: Don't lose that number. *American Journalism Review, 27*(4), 50–51.

Duderstadt, J. J., Atkins, D. E., & Van Houweling, D. (2002). The impact of information technology on the higher education enterprise. In *Higher Education in the Digital Age: Technology Issues and Strategies for American Colleges and Universities* (pp. 117–148). Westport, CT: Praeger Publishers.

Dunning, J. (2009). African-American students in remedial English and reading at a community college: Their experiences and perspectives. *New York University.* Retrieved from http://ezproxy.pvamu.edu/login?url=http://search.proquest.com/docview/304949232?accountid=7062

Eddy, P. L. (2005). Framing the role of leader: How community college presidents construct their leadership. *Community College Journal of Research and Practice, 29*(9/10), 705–727. doi:10.1080/10668920591006557

Engstrom, M., & Jewett, D. (2005). Collaborative learning the wiki way. *TechTrends: Linking Research & Practice to Improve Learning, 49*(6), 12–68.

Frost, M. (2007). Texas students' college expectations: Does high school racial composition matter? *Sociology of Education, 80*(1), 43–65. doi:10.1177/003804070708000103

Gibson, S. (2006). Veni, vidi, wiki. *eWeek, 23*(46), 22-28.

Gordon, R. S., & Stephen, M. (2007). Putting wikis into play. *Computers in Libraries, 27*(2), 42–43.

Gregory-Mina, H. J. (2009). Four leadership theories addressing contemporary leadership issues as the theories relate to the scholarship, practice, and leadership model. *Academic Leadership On-Line Journal, 7*(3). Retrieved from http://www.academicleadership.org/349/four_leadership_theories_addressing_contemporary_leadership_issues_as_the_theories_relate_to_the_scholarship_practice_and_leadership_model/

Hauser, J. (2007). Media specialists can learn web 2.0 tools to make schools more cool. *Computers in Libraries, 27*, 6–48.

Havenstein, H. (2007). Companies may face lawsuits if employees abuse web 2.0 tools. *Computerworld, 41*, 36.

Kaba, A. (2011). Black American females as geniuses. *Journal of African American Studies, 15*(1), 120–124. doi:10.1007/s12111-010-9134-1

Kajewski, M. A. (2006). Emerging technologies changing public library service delivery models. *APLIS, 19*(4), 157–163.

Kasworm, C. E., Sandmann, L. R., & Sissel, P. A. (2000). Adult learners in higher education. In Wilson, A. L., & Hayes, E. R. (Eds.), *Handbook of Adult and Continuing Education* (pp. 449–463). San Francisco, CA: Jossey-Bass.

Kotter, J. P. (1996). *Leading change*. Boston, MA: Harvard Business School Press.

Lamont, J. (2007). Blogs and wikis: Ready for prime time? *KM World, 16*(1), 14–26.

McKimm, J., & Swanwick, T. (2010). Web-based faculty development: E-learning for clinical teachers in the London deanery. *The Clinical Teacher, 7*(1), 58–62. doi:10.1111/j.1743-498X.2009.00344.x

Meyer, K. (2008). The "virtual face" of institutions: What do home pages reveal about higher education? *Innovative Higher Education, 33*(3), 141–157. doi:10.1007/s10755-008-9071-2

Nikaien, Z., Ganjouie, F., Tondnevis, F., & Kamkari, K. (2012). Effects of leadership styles on coaches of Iran's national teams' success and athletes' perception of success. *Annals of Biological Research, 3*(1), 677–683.

Northouse, P. G. (2010). *Leadership: Theory and practice*. Thousand Oaks, CA: Sage.

Pascarella, E. T., & Terenzini, P. T. (1991). *How college affects students: Findings from twenty years of research*. San Francisco, CA: Jossey-Bass.

Portugal, L. M. (2006). Diversity leadership in higher education. *Advancing Women in Leadership Online Journal, 21*. Retrieved from http://www.advancingwomen.com/awl/summer2007/portugal.htm

Reed, L., & Evans, A. E. (2008). What you see is [not always] what you get! Dispelling race and gender leadership assumptions. *International Journal of Qualitative Studies in Education, 21*(5), 487–499. doi:10.1080/09518390802297797

Richardson, R. C. Jr. (1991). 6 ways universities can maintain quality and diversity. *Education Digest, 56*(5), 22–25.

Robinson-Neal, A. (2009). Exploring diversity in higher education management: History, trends, and implications for community colleges. *International Journal for Leadership in Learning, 13*(4). Retrieved from http://iejll.synergiesprairies.ca/iejll/index.php/iejll/article/view/690

Sarrel, M. D. (2007). Wicked productive wikis. *PC Magazine, 26*(4), 88.

Sauer, I., Bialek, D., Efimova, E., Schwartlander, R., Pless, G., & Neuhaus, P. (2005). "Blogs" and "wikis" are valuable software tools for communication within research groups. *Artificial Organs, 29*(1), 82–89. doi:10.1111/j.1525-1594.2004.29005.x

Smith, D. R., & Ayers, D. F. (2006). Culturally responsive pedagogy and online learning: Implications for the globalized community college. *Community College Journal of Research and Practice, 30*(5/6), 401–415. doi:10.1080/10668920500442125

Smith, M. L., & Roysircar, G. (2010). African American male leaders in counseling: Interviews with five AMCD past presidents. *Journal of Multicultural Counseling and Development, 38*(4), 242–255. doi:10.1002/j.2161-1912.2010.tb00134.x

Sterling, R. V. (2011). The effect of metacognitive strategy instruction on student achievement in a hybrid developmental English course. *University of South Alabama*. Retrieved from http://ezproxy.pvamu.edu/login?url=http://search.proquest.com/docview/868853212?accountid=7062

United States Census Bureau. (2010). Educational attainment in the United States: 2009. *Statistical Abstract of the United States*. Retrieved from http://www.census.gov/population/www/socdemo/education/cps2009.html

Wiki Introduced, A. L. S. C. (2007). ALSC wiki introduced. *American Libraries, 38*(2), 11.

Windley, P. J. (2007). Capitalize on emerging collaboration options. *InfoWorld, 29*, 26.

ADDITIONAL READING

Brown, A. L. (2009). Brothers gonna work it out: Understanding the pedagogic performance of African American male teachers working with African American male students. *The Urban Review, 41*, 416–435. doi:10.1007/s11256-008-0116-8

Brown, A. L. (2009). O brotha where art thou? Examining the ideological discourses of African American male teachers working with African American male students. *Race, Ethnicity and Education, 12*(4), 473–493. doi:10.1080/13613320903364432

Clapp, J. R. Jr. (2010). Diversity leadership: The rush university medical center experience. *Hospital Topics, 88*(2), 61–66. doi:10.1080/00185861003768993

Hopkins, W. E., & Hopkins, S. A. (1999). Diversity leadership: A mandate for the 21st century workforce. *Journal of Leadership & Organizational Studies, 55*(3), 129–140. doi:10.1177/107179199900500311

Kezar, A., & Eckel, P. (2008). Advancing diversity agendas on campus: Examining transactional and transformational presidential leadership styles. *International Journal of Leadership in Education: Theory and Practice, 11*(4), 379–405. doi:10.1080/13603120802317891

Knoell, D. M. (1994). California community college faculty from historically underrepresented racial and ethnic groups. *New Directions for Community Colleges, 87*, 27–33. doi:10.1002/cc.36819948705

León, D. J., & Nevarez, C. (2007). Models of leadership institutes for increasing the number of top Latino administrators in higher education. *Journal of Hispanic Higher Education, 6*(4), 356–377.

Lumby, J., & Morrison, M. (2010). Leadership and diversity: Theory and research. *School Leadership & Management: Formerly School Organisation, 30*(1), 3–17.

Lynn, M. (2002). Critical race theory and the perspectives of Black men teachers in the Los Angeles public schools. *Equity & Excellence in Education, 35*, 119–130. doi:10.1080/713845287

Martinez, R. O. (2005). Latino demographic and institutional issues in higher education: Implications for leadership development. In Leon, D. (Ed.), *Lessons in Leadership* (pp. 17–55). London, UK: Emerald Group Publishing. doi:10.1108/S1479-3644(2005)0000005004

Overstreet, M., Okiror, L., Weber, M. J., & McCray, J. (1998). Multicultural leadership development through experiential learning. *Journal of Family and Consumer Sciences: From Research to Practice, 90*(3), 42–46.

Owen, D. S. (2009). Privileged social identities and diversity leadership in higher education. *Review of Higher Education, 32*(2), 185–207. doi:10.1353/rhe.0.0048

Perkins, B. (2011, February 17). Critical shortage of Black male teachers. *New York Amsterdam News*, pp. 13-36.

Robinson, B. B., & Albert, A. C. (2009). HBCU's institutional advantage: Returns to teacher education. In Gasman, M., Baez, B., & Sotello-Viernes, C. (Eds.), *Understanding Minority-Serving Institutions* (pp. 183–202). Albany, NY: State University of New York Press.

Skiba, D. J. (2005). Do your students wiki? *Nursing Education Perspectives, 26*(2), 120–121.

Smith, D. G., & Parker, S. (2005). Organizational learning: A tool for diversity and institutional effectiveness. *New Directions for Higher Education, 131*.

Sullivan, P. (2006). Diversity, leadership, and the community college: A case study. *Community College Journal of Research and Practice, 30*(5-6), 383–400. doi:10.1080/10668920500208096

Whiting, G. (2009). Gifted Black males: Understanding and decreasing barriers to achievement and identity. *Roeper Review, 31*(4), 224–233. doi:10.1080/02783190903177598

Williams, D. A. (2007). Achieving inclusive excellence: Strategies for creating real and sustainable change in quality and diversity. *About Campus, 12*(1), 8–14. doi:10.1002/abc.198

Williams, D. A., & Clowney, C. (2007). Strategic planning for diversity and organizational change: A primer for higher-education leadership. *Effective Practices for Academic Leaders, 2*(3), 1–16.

Wilson, A. B. (2012). Redefining the role and practices of leadership educators: The relationship between multicultural competence and the use of the social change model of leadership development. *CSPA-NYS Journal of Student Affairs, 12*(1). Retrieved from http://www.libraryinnovation.org/index.php/CSPANY/article/view/220

Young, M., Mountford, M., & Skrla, L. (2006). Infusing gender and diversity issues into educational leadership programs: Transformational learning and resistance. *Journal of Educational Administration, 44*(3), 264–277. doi:10.1108/09578230610664850

KEY TERMS AND DEFINITIONS

Diversity: Diversity can be defined as the individual differences within a given population, including but not limited to class, age, gender, race, ethnicity, national origin, religion, sexual orientation, and physical handicap and other disabilities. Organizations that are committed to diversity encourage all stakeholders to maximize their full potential, regardless of these differences.

Diversity Leadership: Diversity leadership is the way in which leaders within an organization leverage the individual differences of stakeholders to implement policies and procedures that achieve the common good. Effective diversity leadership allows for plurality of thought, views, and opinions, and welcomes the voices of others in decision-making processes. Further, diversity leadership efforts involve the recruitment, retention, and promotion of minorities to administrative roles.

Inclusivity: Inclusivity is the policy or practice of not excluding persons based upon their diversity. In an organization that values inclusivity, people are able to participate fully, regardless of their individual differences or their possible status as members of a minority group.

Institutions of Higher Education (IHEs): IHEs are post-secondary schools that award degrees and/or certificates to persons who are older than the age of compulsory school attendance in the U.S. IHEs may be public or private, and most are accredited by a regional or national accrediting body.

Leadership: Leadership refers to the ways in which a person in a position of authority influences others to achieve a shared objective within an organization. Leadership involves meeting the demands of change, being innovative, establishing a shared vision, motivating others, and creating an environment that fosters communication and collaboration.

Minority: Minorities are persons who, as a sub-group of a larger demographic, have been historically disenfranchised and/or marginalized due to the inequitable distribution of power by the larger group. Minority groups in the U.S. include, but are not limited to, women, African Americans, Hispanics, Asians, and persons with disabilities.

Technology: Technology is the use of advanced knowledge and tools, often electronic tools (e.g., computers, Internet, software programs, etc.), to achieve a specified goal.

Wikis: Wikis are hypertext documents that, in theory, allow anyone to alter the documents' content. The word *wiki* can refer to both the document and the software used to create it. They provide a method by which a shared body of information can be collected, distributed, analyzed, arranged, and rearranged.

Compilation of References

Abdallah-Pretceille, M. (2006). Interculturalism as a paradigm for thinking about diversity. *Intercultural Education, 17*(5), 475–483. doi:10.1080/14675980601065764

Abdellaoui, M., Bleichrodt, H., & L'Haridon, O. (2008). A tractable method to measure utility and loss aversion under prospect theory. *Journal of Risk and Uncertainty, 36*(3), 245–266. doi:10.1007/s11166-008-9039-8

Acar, F. P. (2010). Analyzing the effects of diversity perceptions and shared leadershiop on emotional conflict: A dyanmic approach. *International Journal of Human Resource Management, 21*(10), 1733–1753. doi:10.1080/09585192.2010.500492

Achieving the Dream. (2005, August). *Achieving the dream state policy newsletter*. Retrieved from http://www.achievingthedream.org/_images/_index03/Policy_Newsletter_Aug05.pdf

Achterman, D. (2006). Making connections with blogs and wikis. *CSLA Journal, 30*(1), 29–31.

Adegbuyi, P., & Uhomoibhi, J. (2008). Trends in the development of technology and engineering education in emerging economies. *Multicultural Education & Technology Journal, 2*(3), 132–139. doi:10.1108/17504970810900432

Adobor, H., & McMullen, R. (2007). Supplier diversity and supply chain management: A strategic approach. *Business Horizons, 50*(3), 219–229. doi:10.1016/j.bushor.2006.10.003

Agarwal, R., Animesh, A., & Prasad, K. (2009). Social interactions and the "digital divide": Explaining variations in Internet use. *Information Systems Research, 20*(2), 277–294. doi:10.1287/isre.1080.0194

Aguirre, A., Martinez, R. O., & Association for the Study of Higher Education. (2006). *Diversity leadership in higher education*. San Francisco, CA: Jossey-Bass.

Aguirre, A. Jr, & Martinez, R. O. (2002). Leadership practices and diversity in higher education: Transitional and transformational frameworks. *The Journal of Leadership Studies, 8*, 53–62. doi:10.1177/107179190200800305

Airasian, P., & Walsh, M. (1997). Constructivist cautions. *Phi Delta Kappan, 78*(6), 444–449.

Akyuz, G., & Rehan, M. (2009). Requirements for forming an e-supply chain. *International Journal of Production Research, 47*(12), 3265–3287. doi:10.1080/00207540701802460

Allen, B. (2009, April 6). Top army chaplain raises Jewish ire with call for fasting during Passover. *Associated Baptist Press*. Retrieved from http://www.abpnews.com/content/view/3977/53/

Allen, P., Strathern, M., & Varga, L. (2010). Complexity: The evolution of identity and diversity. *Complexity, Difference and Identity. Issues in Business Ethics, 26*(2), 41–60. doi:10.1007/978-90-481-9187-1_3

American Association of Community Colleges. (2009). *Fast facts*. Retrieved from http://www.aacc.nche.edu/AboutCC/Pages/fastfacts.aspx

Anderson, L. W., & Krathwohl, D. R. (Eds.). (2001). *A taxonomy for learning, teaching, and assessing: A revision of Bloom's taxonomy of educational objectives*. Boston, MA: Allyn & Bacon.

Andreescu, V., & Vito, G. F. (2010). An exploratory study on ideal leadership behaviour: The opinions of American police managers. *International Journal of Police Science & Management*, *12*(4), 567–583. doi:10.1350/ijps.2010.12.4.207

Applebee, A., Langer, J., Nystrand, M., & Gamoran, A. (2003). Discussion based approaches to developing understanding: Classroom instruction and student performance in middle and high school English. *American Educational Research Journal*, *40*(3), 685–730. doi:10.3102/00028312040003685

Applebee, A., Langer, J., & Purves, A. (1991). *Final report*. Alexandria, VA: Center for the Learning and Teaching of Literature.

Archer, C. M. (1996). *A qualitative study of the communicative experience of a Venezuelan and a North American.* (Unpublished Doctoral Dissertation). University of Houston. Houston, TX.

Archer, C. M. (2001). *Training for effective cross-cultural communication.* Retrieved from http://culturebump.com/relatedmaterials.htm

Archer, C. M. (l991). *Living with strangers in the USA: Communicating beyond culture.* Englewood Cliffs, NJ: Prentice-Hall.

Archer, C. M. (2004). *Toolkit for culture and communication.* Houston, TX: University of Houston.

Archer, C. M., & Nickson, S. C. (2012). Culture-bump: An instructional process for cultural insight. In Grocci, J., Alsudairi, M., & Buskist, B. (Eds.), *Handbook of College and University Teaching: Global Perspectives.* Thousand Oaks, CA: Sage Publications. doi:10.4135/9781412996891.n26

Archer, C. M., & Nickson, S. C. (2012). The role of culture bump in developing intercultural communication competency. *Psychology Learning & Teaching*, *11*(3). doi:10.2304/plat.2012.11.3.335

Arend, B. (2009). Encouraging critical thinking in online threaded discussions. *The Journal of Educators Online*, *6*(1), 1–23.

ASHE. (2006). Diversity, leadership, and organizational culture in higher education. *ASHE Higher Education Report*, *32*(3), 23–45.

Astin, A. W. (1993). *What matters in college: Four critical years revisited.* San Francisco, CA: Jossey-Bass.

Austen, P. (2010). Informal instructional teacher leaders: How principals can support their effect on instructional reform. *Academic Leadership*, *8*(3), 1–7.

Ausubel, D. P. (1960). The use of advance organizers in the learning and retention of meaningful verbal material. *Journal of Educational Psychology*, *51*, 267–272. doi:10.1037/h0046669

Avery, D. R., McKay, P. F., Wilson, D. C., & Tonidandel, S. (2007). Unequal attendance: The relationships between race, organizational diversity cues, and absenteeism. *Personnel Psychology*, *60*(4), 875–902. doi:10.1111/j.1744-6570.2007.00094.x

Bailey, J., Rehmat, A. P., Lombardi, D., & Keppelman, E. (2012). *Developing science teacher leaders through long-term professional development: A cross-case analysis of four teachers.* Washington, DC: National Association for Research in Science.

Baker, S. (2008). *The numerati.* New York, NY: Houghton Mifflin Harcourt.

Balkin, R. S., Schlosser, L. Z., & Heller Levitt, D. (2009). Religious identity and cultural diversity: Exploring the relationships between religious identity, sexism, homophobia, and multicultural competence. *Journal of Counseling and Development*, *87*(4), 420–427. doi:10.1002/j.1556-6678.2009.tb00126.x

Bambrick-Santoyo, P. (2010). *Driven by data: A practical guide to improve instruction.* San Francisco, CA: Jossey-Bass.

Bandura, A. (1997). *Self-efficacy: The exercise of control.* New York, NY: W.H. Freeman.

Banks, J. A., Cookson, P., Gay, G., Hawley, W. D., Irvine, J. J., & Nieto, S. (2001). Diversity within unity: Essential principles for teaching and learning in a multicultural society. *Phi Delta Kappan*, *83*(3), 196–203.

Barabasi, A. (2003). *Linked: How everything is connected to everything else and what it means.* New York, NY: Plume Publishing.

Barabasi, A. (2010). *Bursts: The hidden pattern behind everything we do.* New York, NY: Dutton. doi:10.1063/1.3431332

Barberis, N., Huang, M., & Santos, T. (2001). Prospect theory and asset prices. *The Quarterly Journal of Economics, 116*(1), 1–53. doi:10.1162/003355301556310

Barkley, S. (2007). *Tapping student effort: Increasing student achievement.* Cadiz, KY: Performance Learning Systems, Inc.

Barna Group. (2006). *Barna update: House church involvement is growing.* Retrieved from http://www.barna.org/

Barnes, R. A., & Piland, W. E. (2010). Impact of learning communities in developmental English on community college student retention and persistence. *Journal of College Student Retention: Research. Theory into Practice, 12*(1), 7–24.

Barney, J. (1991). Firm resources and sustained competitive advantage. *Journal of Management, 17*(1), 99–120. doi:10.1177/014920639101700108

Barney, J. (1999). How a firm's capabilities affect boundary decisions. *Sloan Management Review, 40,* 137–145.

Barney, J. (2001). Resource-based theories of competitive advantage: A ten-year perspective on the resource-based view. *Journal of Management, 27,* 643–650. doi:10.1177/014920630102700602

Barney, J., Wright, M., & Ketchen, D. (2001). The resource-based view of the firm: ten years after 1991. *Journal of Management, 27*(6), 625–641. doi:10.1177/014920630102700601

Barzilai-Nahon, K. (2006). Gaps and bits: Conceptualizing measurement for digital divides. *The Information Society, 22*(5), 269–278. doi:10.1080/01972240600903953

Barzilai-Nahon, K., Gomez, R., & Ambikar, R. (2008). Conceptualizing a contextual measurement for digital divides: Using an intergrated narrative. In Ferro, E., Dwivedi, Y. K., & Williams, R. G. (Eds.), *Overcoming Digital Divides: Constructing an Equitable and Competitive Information Society.* Seattle, WA: University of Washington.

Bass, B. M. (1994). *Bass and Stogdill's handbook of leadership: Theory, research, and managerial applications* (3rd ed.). New York, NY: Free Press.

Bass, B. M., & Avolio, B. J. (1994). *Improving organizational effectiveness through transformational leadership.* Thousand Oaks, CA: Sage.

Bates, R. J. (1982). Towards critical practice of educational administration. *Studies in Educational Administration, 27,* 1–21.

Beachum, F., & Dentith, A. (2004). Teacher leaders creating cultures of school renewal and transformation. *The Educational Forum, 68,* 276–286. doi:10.1080/00131720408984639

Belanger, F., & Carter, L. (2009). The Impact on the digital divide on e-government use. *Communications of the ACM, 52*(4), 132–135. doi:10.1145/1498765.1498801

Bellah, R. N., & Tipton, S. M. (2006). *The Robert Bellah reader.* Durham, NC: Duke University Press.

Bell, M. P., & Berry, D. P. (2007). Viewing diversity through different lenses: Avoiding a few blind spots. *The Academy of Management Perspectives, 21*(4), 21–25. doi:10.5465/AMP.2007.27895336

Benimoff, R. (2009). *Faith under fire: An army chaplain's memoir.* New York, NY: Crown.

Benishek, L. A., Bieschke, K. J., Park, J., & Slattery, S. M. (2004). A multicultural feminist model of mentoring. *Journal of Multicultural Counseling and Development, 32,* 428–442.

Benjamin, M. J. (1998). Justice, justice shall you pursue: Legal analysis of religious issues in the army. *The Army Lawyer, 1,* 1–18.

Benmamoun, M., Kalliny, M., & Cropf, R. (2012). The Arab spring, MNEs, and virtual public spheres. *Multinational Business Review, 20*(1), 26–43. doi:10.1108/15253831211217189

Bentley, W. (2007). A Christian philosophy of leadership: The servant model. *The National Black Evangelical Association.* Retrieved from http://www.The-NBEA.org

Berkley University. (2011). *Digital youth research: Kids' informal learning via digital media.* Retrieved October 12, 2011 from http://digitalyouth.ischool.berkeley.edu/

Berkman Center for Internet and Society. (2010). *Next generation connectivity: A review of broadband, internet, transitions and policy from around the world.* Retrieved from http://cyber.law.harvard.edu

Berkovich, I. (2011). No we won't! Teachers' resistance to educational reform. *Journal of Educational Administration, 49*(5), 563–578. doi:10.1108/09578231111159548

Berlak, J., & Weber, V. (2004). How to make e-procurement viable for SME suppliers. *Production Planning and Control, 15*(7), 671–677. doi:10.1080/0953728041 2331298139

Berry, B., Barnett, J., Betlach, K., C'de Baca, S., Highley, S., & Holland, J. M. … Wasserman, L. (2011). *Teaching 2030: What we must do for our students and for our public schools… now and in the future.* New York, NY: Teacher's College Press.

Berry, B., Daughtrey, A., & Wieder, A. (2010). *Teacher leadership: Leading the way to effective teaching and learning.* Washington, DC: Center for Teaching Quality.

Bertot, J. (2009). Public access technologies in public libraries: Effects and implications. *Information Technology & Libraries, 28*(2), 81–92.

Bess, M. (2006). *Choices under fire: Moral dimensions of World War II.* New York, NY: Knopf.

Betances, S. (2001). *Ten steps to the head of the class: A challenge to students.* Chicago, IL: New Century Forum.

Betts, K. S., Urias, D., Betts, K., & Chavez, J. (2009). Higher education and shifting U.S. demographics: Need for visible career paths, professional development, succession planning & commitment to diversity. *Academic Leadership On-Line Journal, 7*(2). Retrieved from http://www.academicleadership.org/emprical_research/623.shtml

Birbeck, M. (2005). *Xform and Internet applications.* Retrieved February 27, 2007 from http://internet-apps.blogspot.com/2005/08/delicious-link-manager-written-in.html

Birrell, S. (2011). The use of blogs to prompt learner reflection during first co-operative education work terms. In *Proceedings of the International Conference on e-Learning Mexico,* (vol. 3, pp. 423 – 430). IEEE.

Blackboard. (2012). *Blackboard.* Retrieved March 1, 2012, from http://www.blackboard.com

Blascovich, J. J., & Hartel, C. R. (2007). *Human behavior in military contexts.* Washington, DC: The National Academies Press.

Blase, J., & Blase, J. (1996). Micro-political strategies used by administrators and teachers in instructional conferences. *The Alberta Journal of Educational Research, 42,* 345–360.

Blau, S. (2003). *The literature workshop: Teaching texts and their readers.* Portsmouth, NH: Heinemann.

Bliss, J. P., Tidwell, P. D., & Guest, M. A. (1997). The effectiveness of virtual reality for administering spatial navigation training to firefighters. *Presence (Cambridge, Mass.), 6*(1), 73–86.

Bloom, B. S. (1956). *Taxonomy of educational objectives, handbook I: The cognitive domain.* New York, NY: David McKay Co Inc.

Blumner, R. E. (2008, May 4). This atheist finds he needs a foxhole. *St. Petersburg Times.* Retrieved from http://www.tampabay.com/opinion/columns/article483665.ece

Bonvillain, D. G., & McGuire, W. G. (2009). *Cultural DNA.* Washington, DC: American University.

Bonvillain, D., & McGuire, W. G. (2009). *Cultural DNA.* Washington, DC: American University.

Borders, L. D., Young, J. S., Wester, K. L., Murray, C. E., Villalba, J. A., Lewis, T. F., & Mobley, A. K. (2011). Mentoring promotion/tenure-seeking faculty: Principles of good practice within a counselor education program. *Counselor Education and Supervision, 50,* 171–188. doi:10.1002/j.1556-6978.2011.tb00118.x

Boyd-Dimock, V., & McGree, K. (1995). Leading change from the classroom: Teachers as leaders. *Issues about. Change, 4*(4), 1–10.

Boyer, E. L. (1995). *The basic school: A community for learning.* San Francisco, CA: Jossey-Bass Inc.

Brayboy, B. M. J. (2003). The implementation of diversity in predominantly white colleges and universities. *Journal of Black Studies, 34*, 72–86. doi:10.1177/0021934703253679

Brodahl, C., Hadjerrouit, S., & Hansen, N. (2011). Collaborative writing with web 2.0 technologies: Education students' perceptions. *Journal of Information Technology Education, 10*(2), 73–103.

Bromiley, P. (2010). Looking at prospect theory. *Strategic Management Journal, 31*(12), 1357–1370. doi:10.1002/smj.885

Brosnan, M. J. (1998). The impact of computer anxiety and self-efficacy upon performance. *Journal of Computer Assisted Learning, 14*, 223–234. doi:10.1046/j.1365-2729.1998.143059.x

Brown, L. (2004). Diversity: The challenge for higher education. *Race, Ethnicity and Education, 7*(1), 22–34.

Brown, T. (1996). Prospect theory. In Kiel, L. D., & Elliott, E. (Eds.), *Chaos Theory in the Social Sciences* (pp. 15–44). Ann Arbor, MI: University of Michigan Press.

Bruffee, K. (2009). Collaborative learning and the "conversation of mankind". In Miller, S. (Ed.), *The Norton Book of Composition Studies*. New York, NY: W.W. Norton & Company.

Bruner, J. (2004). Life as narrative. *Social Research, 71*(3), 691–710.

Bryant, S., & Terborg, J. (2008). The impact of peer mentor training on creating and sharing organizational knowledge. *Journal of Managerial Issues, 20*, 11–29.

Bumphus, W. G., & Roueche, J. E. (2007). Community colleges often lead the way in diversity efforts. *Diverse Issues in Higher Education, 24*(11), 82.

Burdette, A. M., Wang, V., Elder, G. H., Hill, T. D., & Benson, J. (2009). Serving god and country? Religious involvement and military service among young adult men. *Journal for the Scientific Study of Religion, 48*(4), 794–804. doi:10.1111/j.1468-5906.2009.01481.x

Bush, G. W. (2003). Address to the nation on Iraq from the U.S.S. Abraham Lincoln. *Weekly Compilation of Presidential Documents, 39*, 516-518. Retrieved from http://frwebgate2.access.gpo.gov/cgi-bin/TEXTgate.cgi?WAISdocID=ij6veJ/22/1/0&WAISaction=retrieve

Butler, J. W., Chavez, J., & Corbeil, J. R. (2007). The effect of one-day traning in digital storytelling on inservice teachers' anxiety toward computers. *TCEA Educational Technology Research Symposium, 1*, 8-15.

Caligiuri, P., Lepak, D., & Bonache, J. (2010). *Managing the global workforce*. West Sussex, UK: John Wiley & Sons.

Capra, F. (2002). *The hidden connections: A science for sustainable living*. New York, NY: HarperCollins.

Carr, J. F., Herman, N., & Harris, D. E. (2005). *Creating dynamic schools through mentoring, coaching, and collaboration*. Alexandria, VA: ASCD.

Carroll, J. B. (1963). *A model of school learning*. New York, NY: McGraw-Hill.

Carroll, J. M., & Bishop, A. P. (2005). Special section on learning in communities. *The Journal of Community Informatics, 1*(2), 116–133. Retrieved from http://ci-journal.net/index.php/ciej/article/view/335/243

Carr-Ruffino, N. (1996). *Managing diversity: People skills for a multicultural workplace*. Cincinnati, OH: International Thompson.

Carruthers, J. (1993). The principles and practice of mentoring. In Caldwell, B. J., & Carter, E. M. A. (Eds.), *The Return of the Mentor: Strategies for Workplace Learning*. London, UK: The Falmer Press.

Carter, C., & Jennings, M. (2000). *Purchasing's contribution to the socially responsible management of the supply chain*. Phoenix, AZ: CAPS Research.

Cave, D. (2011, September 27). Mexico turns to social media for information and survival. *The New York Times*. Retrieved November 1, 2011, from http://www.nytimes.com/2011/09/25/world/americas/mexico-turns-to-twitter-and-facebook-for-information-and-survival.html?r=2&scp=2&sq=crowd%20sourcing%20political%20global&st=cse

Chakravarthy, B., & Coughlan, S. (2011). Emerging market strategy: Innovating both products and delivery systems. *Strategy and Leadership, 40*(1), 27–32. doi:10.1108/10878571211191675

Chandler, C. (1996). Mentoring and women in academia: Reevaluating the traditional model. *NWSA Journal, 3*(8), 79–100. doi:10.2979/NWS.1996.8.3.79

Chase, D. (2007). Transformative sharing with instant messaging, wikis, interactive maps, and Flickr. *Computers in Libraries*, *27*(1), 7–56.

Chawner, B., & Lewis, P. H. (2006). WikiWikiWebs: New ways to communicate in a web environment. *Information Technology & Libraries*, *25*(1), 33–43.

Chetty, R., Friedman, J. N., & Rockoff, J. E. (2011). The long-term impacts of teachers: Teacher value-added and student outcomes in adulthood. *Executive Summary of National Bureau of Economic Research Working Paper No. 17699*. Retrieved April 1, 2012 from http://obs.rc.fas.harvard.edu/chetty/value_added.html

Cheyne, J. A. (2010). The rise of the nones and the growth of religious indifference. *Skeptic*, *15*(4), 56–60.

Chin, J. L. (2010). Introduction to the special issue on leadership and diversity. *The American Psychologist*, *65*(3), 150–156. doi:10.1037/a0018716

Christensen, C., Horn, M., & Johnson, W. (2008). *Disrupting class*. New York, NY: McGraw Hill.

Chua, S. L., Chen, D.-T., & Wong, A. F. L. (1999). Computer anxiety and its correlates: a meta-analysis. *Computers in Human Behavior*, *15*(5), 609–623. doi:10.1016/S0747-5632(99)00039-4

Church, Maria. J. (2011). *Three strategies for team success*. Retrieved from http://www.lovebasedleadership.com

Cilliers, P. (1998). *Complexity and postmodernism: Understanding complex systems*. New York, NY: Routledge.

Clairborne, S. (2005). On evangelicals and interfaith cooperation: An interview with Tony Campolo. *Cross Currents*, *55*(1), 54–65.

Clair, J. A., Beatty, J. E., & Maclean, T. L. (2005). Out of sight but not out of mind: Managing invisible social identities in the workplace. *Academy of Management Review*, *30*(1), 78–95. doi:10.5465/AMR.2005.15281431

Clark, D. R. (2004). *The art and science of leadership*. Retrieved December 17, 2011 from http://nwlink.com/~donclark/leader/diverse.html

Clark, R. E. (1994). Media will never influence learning. *Educational Technology Research and Development*, *42*(2), 21–29. doi:10.1007/BF02299088

Clegg, S., Harris, M., & Hopfl, H. (2011). *Managing modernity*. Oxford, UK: Oxford University Press.

Collay, M. (2006). Discerning professional identity and becoming bold, socially responsible teacher-leaders. *Educational Leadership and Administration*, *18*, 131–146.

Collins, C. J., & Smith, K. G. (2006). Knowledge exchange and combination: The role of human resource practices in the performance of high-technology firms. *Academy of Management Journal*, *49*, 544–560. doi:10.5465/AMJ.2006.21794671

Common Core State Standards Initiative. (2010). *Common core state standards for mathematics*. Retrieved from http://www.corestandards.org/the-standards

Congress (2009, August 18). *Letter to the honorable Robert M. Gates*. Retrieved from https://salsa.wiredforchange.com/o/1607/images/House%20Letter%20Final.pdf

Connerly, M. L., & Pedersen, P. B. (2005). *Leadership in a diverse and multicultural environment*. Thousand Oaks, CA: Sage Publications.

Cook, H. (2007). Service before self? Evangelicals flying high at the U.S. air force academy. *Journal of Law and Education*, *36*(1), 1–33.

Cook, R. J. (2008). Embracing diversity at Allegheny College: Signs of success at a residential college of the liberal arts and sciences. *Journal of Diversity in Higher Education*, *1*(1), 1–7. doi:10.1037/1938-8926.1.1.1

Coombs, K. A. (2007). Building a library web site on the pillars of web 2.0. *Computers in Libraries*, *27*(1), 16–19.

Cooper, J. J. (2006). The digital divide: The special case of gender. *Journal of Computer Assisted Learning*, *22*(5), 320–334. doi:10.1111/j.1365-2729.2006.00185.x

Cox, T. (1993). *Diversity in organizations: Theory, research, and practice*. San Francisco, CA: Berrett-Koehler.

Cox, T. (2001). *Creating the multicultural organization: A strategy for capturing the power of diversity*. San Francisco, CA: Jossey Bass.

Crang, M., Crosbie, T., & Graham, S. (2006). Variable geometries of connection: Urban digital divides and the uses of information technology. *Urban Studies (Edinburgh, Scotland)*, *43*(13), 2551–2570. doi:10.1080/00420980600970664

Crews, D. M., & Aragon, S. R. (2004). Influence of a community college developmental education writing course on academic performance. *Community College Review*, *32*(2), 1–18. doi:10.1177/009155210403200201

Crozier, G., Reay, D., Clayton, J., Colliander, L., & Grinstead, J. (2008). Different strokes for different folks: Diverse students in diverse institutions—Experiences of higher education. *Research Papers in Education*, *23*(2), 167–177. doi:10.1080/02671520802048703

Cuban, L. (2011). Teacher, superintendent, scholar: The gift of multiple careers. *Leaders in Educational Studies*, *3*, 45–54. doi:10.1007/978-94-6091-755-4_5

Cummins, J., Brown, K., & Sayers, D. (2007). *Literacy, technology, and diversity: Teaching for success in changing times.* Boston, MA: Allyn and Bacon.

Cunningham, G. B. (2010). The influence of religious personal identity on the relationships among religious dissimilarity, value dissimilarity, and job satisfaction. *Social Justice Research*, *23*(1), 60–76. doi:10.1007/s11211-010-0109-0

Daniels, H. (2007). Pedagogy. In Daniels, H., Cole, M., & Wertsch, J. V. (Eds.), *The Cambridge Companion to Vygotsky* (pp. 307–331). Cambridge, UK: Cambridge University Press.

Danielson, C. (2007). The many faces of leadership. *Educational Leadership*, *65*(1), 14–19.

Daniels, P. (2005). Technology revolutions and social development: Prospects for a green technoeconomic paradigm in lower income countries. *International Journal of Social Economics*, *32*(5), 454–482. doi:10.1108/03068290510591290

Dao, J. (2011, April 26). Atheists seek chaplain role in the military. *The New York Times.* Retrieved from http://www.nytimes.com/2011/04/27/us/27atheists.html?_r=1&scp=1&sq=Atheists%20seek%20chaplain%20role%20in%20the%20military&st=cse

Darden, C. (2003). *Delivering on diversity: A walk in the other guy's shoes.* Retrieved from http://www.ohio.edu/orgs/one/dd.html

Darling-Hammond, L. (2003). Keeping good teachers: Why it matters what leaders can do. *Educational Leadership*, *60*(8), 6–13.

Darling-Hammond, L., & Falk, B. (1997). Supporting teaching and learning for all students: Policies for authentic assessment systems. In Goodwin, A. L. (Ed.), *Assessment for Equity and Inclusion: Embracing All Our Children* (pp. 51–75). New York, NY: Routledge.

Davidson, S. (2009). Communities of inquiry. In Davidson & Carber (Eds.), *Taking the PYP Forward: The Future of the IB Primary Years Programme,* (pp. 27–42). Melton, UK: John Catt Educational Ltd.

Davidson, M. N., & Foster-Johnson, L. (2001). Mentoring in the preparation of graduate researchers of color. *Review of Educational Research*, *71*, 549–574. doi:10.3102/00346543071004549

Davidson-Shivers, G. V. (2002). IT in higher education. In Reiser, R. A., & Dempsey, J. V. (Eds.), *Trends & Issues in Instructional Design & Technology* (pp. 256–268). Columbus, OH: Merrill-Prentice Hall.

Davis, B. (2005). Teacher as consciousness of the collective. *Complicity: An International Journal of Complexity and Education*, *2*(1), 86–88.

Davis, B., & Sumara, D. (2006). *Complexity and education.* New York, NY: Lawrence Erlbaum.

Davis, B., Sumara, D., & Kapler, R. (2008). *Engaging minds* (2nd ed.). New York, NY: Routledge.

Davis, N. M. (2010, February). The great recession's lasting legacy. *HRMagazine.*

de Janasz, S. C., & Sullivan, S. E. (2004). Multiple mentoring in academe: Developing the professional network. *Journal of Vocational Behavior*, *64*, 263–283. doi:10.1016/j.jvb.2002.07.001

Department of Defense. (2001). *MIL-HDBK-29612, part 2A: Department of defense handbook, instructional systems development/systems approach to training and education (part 2 of 5 parts).* Washington, DC: Department of Defense.

Derry, S. J. (2007). *Guidlelines for video research in education.* Retrieved March 5, 2012, from http://drdc.uchicago.edu/what/video-research-guidelines.pdf

Devaraj, S., & Kohli, R. (2003). Performance impacts of information technology: Is actual usage the missing link. *Management Science, 49*(3), 273–289. doi:10.1287/mnsc.49.3.273.12736

Dewan, S., & Riggins, F. J. (2005). The digital divide: Current and future research directions. *Journal of the Association for Information Systems, 6*(12), 298–337.

Dick, W., & Carey, L. (1996). *The systematic design of instruction* (4th ed.). New York, NY: Harper Collins.

Digital Youth Network. (2011). *Digital youth network organization.* Retrieved November 1, 2011 from http://www.digitalyouthnetwork.org/

Dlab, M., & Hoic-Bozic, N. (2011). An approach to adaptivity and collaboration support in a web-based learning environment. *International Journal of Emerging Technologies in Learning, 3,* 28–30.

DoD Instruction 1304.28. (2004). *Guidance for the appoitment of chaplains for the military departments.* Washington, DC: DOD.

DOD Report No. H06L102270308. (2007, July 20). *Alleged misconduct by DOD officials concerning Christian embassy.* Washington, DC: DOD.

DODD. 1344.10. (2008). *Political activities by members of the armed forces.* Washington, DC: DOD.

DODI. 1300.06. (2007). *Conscientious objectors.* Washington, DC: DOD.

DODI. 1300.17. (2009). *Accommodation of religious practices within the military services.* Washington, DC: DOD.

Dorroh, J. (2005). Wiki: Don't lose that number. *American Journalism Review, 27*(4), 50–51.

Drake, W. (2000). *Carnegie endowment for international peace: Impact on global economic structures and processes.* Retrieved November 12, 2007 from http://www.carnegieendowment.org/events/index.cfm?fa=eventDetail&id=11&

Dreher, G. F., & Ash, R. A. (1990). A comparative study of mentoring among men and women in managerial, professional, and technical positions. *The Journal of Applied Psychology, 75*(5), 539–546. doi:10.1037/0021-9010.75.5.539

Drescher, K. C., Smith, M. W., & Foy, D. W. (2007). Spirituality and readjustment following war-zone experiences. In Figley, C. R., & Nash, W. P. (Eds.), *Combat Stress Injury: Theory, Research, and Management.* New York, NY: Routledge.

Drucker, P. (1996). *The leader of the future.* San Francisco, CA: Jossey-Bass.

Drucker, S., & Gumpert, G. (2007). Through the looking glass: Illusions of transparency and the cult of information. *Journal of Management Development, 26*(5), 493–498. doi:10.1108/02621710710748329

Drumheller, K., & Lawler, G. (2011). Capture their attention: Capturing lessons using screen capture software. *College Teaching, 59*(2), 93. doi:10.1080/87567550903252793

Dubrow, R. T. (2009). *The female advantage.* Retrieved from http://www.boston.com/bostonglobe/ideas/articles/2009/05/03/the_female_advantage/?page=1

Duderstadt, J. J., Atkins, D. E., & Van Houweling, D. (2002). The impact of information technology on the higher education enterprise. In *Higher Education in the Digital Age: Technology Issues and Strategies for American Colleges and Universities* (pp. 117–148). Westport, CT: Praeger Publishers.

Dudley-Nicholson, J. (2011, June 22). The internet's silent sentinel. *Herald Sun.* Retrieved from http://www.heraldsun.com.au/ipad/the-internets-silent-sentinel/story-fn6bn9st-1226079510340

Duffy, R. (2005). *Supply base rationalization.* Phoenix, AZ: CAPS Research.

DuFour, R., & Eaker, R. (2005). *On common grounds.* Bloomington, IL: Solution Tree.

Dunning, J. (2009). African-American students in remedial English and reading at a community college: Their experiences and perspectives. *New York University.* Retrieved from http://ezproxy.pvamu.edu/login?url=http://search.proquest.com/docview/304949232?accountid=7062

Durbin, A. J. (2007). *Leadership: Research findings, practice and skills* (5th ed.). New York, NY: Houghton Mifflin.

Eberle, C. (2007). God, war, and conscience. *The Journal of Religious Ethics, 35*(3), 479–507. doi:10.1111/j.1467-9795.2007.00316.x

Eck, D. L. (2002). *A new religious America: How a "Christian country" has become the world's most religiously diverse nation*. New York, NY: HarperOne.

Eco, U. (1980). *The name of the rose*. Snzogno, Spain: Gruppo Editorial-Fabbri-Bompiani.

Eddy, P. L. (2005). Framing the role of leader: How community college presidents construct their leadership. *Community College Journal of Research and Practice, 29*(9/10), 705–727. doi:10.1080/10668920591006557

Edgell, P., Gerteis, J., & Hartmann, D. (2006). Atheists as 'other': Moral boundaries and cultural membership in American society. *American Sociological Review, 71*(2), 211–234. doi:10.1177/000312240607100203

Edgell, P., & Tranby, E. (2007). Religious influences on understandings of racial inequality in the United States. *Social Problems, 54*(2), 263–288. doi:10.1525/sp.2007.54.2.263

Education Resource Information Center. (2012). *Website*. Retrieved from http://www.eric.ed.gov/ERICWebPortal/resources/html/collection/about_collection.html

Edutopia.org. (2012). *The George Lucas educational foundation*. Retrieved from http://www.edutopia.org

Egge, S. A. M. (1999). Creating an environment of mutual respect within the multicultural workplace both at home and globally. *Management Decision, 37*(1), 24–28. doi:10.1108/00251749910251996

Eisman, D. (2008, December 28). Military aims to muzzle evangelizing at recruiting sites. *The Virginia Pilot*. Retrieved from http://hamptonroads.com/2008/12/military-aims-muzzle-evangelizing-recruiting-sites

Eley, P. M. (2008). *Does using computer software make a difference in learning geometric and probability concepts?* Retrieved March 5, 2012, from repository.lib.ncsu.edu/ir/bitstream/1840.16/2652/1/etd.pdf

Eley, P. M., & Moffett, N. (2012). *Framing techological teaching from a leadership diversity point of view*. Unpublished.

Eley, P. M., & Hines, K. W. (2011). Students tell the story best: Creative mathematics storytelling using narrative software. *Centroid, 37*(2), 9–13.

Ely, R. J., & Rhode, D. L. (2010). Women and leadership: Defining the challenges. In Nohria, N., & Khurana, R. (Eds.), *Handbook of Leadership Theory and Practice* (pp. 377–410). Boston, MA: Harvard Business Press.

Engstrom, M., & Jewett, D. (2005). Collaborative learning the wiki way. *TechTrends: Linking Research & Practice to Improve Learning, 49*(6), 12–68.

Eurostat. (2012). *Indicators, households which have broadband access*. Retrieved from http://epp.eurostat.ec.europa.eu/portal/page/portal/information_society/data/main_tables

Evans, G. L., & Cokley, K. O. (2008). African American women and the academy: Using career mentoring to increase research productivity. *Training and Education in Professional Psychology, 2*, 50–57. doi:10.1037/1931-3918.2.1.50

Evers, C., & Lakomski, G. (Eds.). (1996). *Exploring educational administration: Coherentist applications and critical debates*. New York, NY: Pergamon.

Fahey, J. J. (2005). *War and the Christian conscience: Where do you stand?* Maryknoll, NY: Orbis.

Fay, K., & Whaley, S. (2004). *Becoming one community: Reading and writing with English language learners*. Portland, OR: Stenhouse.

Field, A. (2009). *Discovering statistics using SPSS* (3rd ed.). London, UK: Sage Publication.

Fischer, G., Rohde, M., & Wulf, V. (2007). Community-based learning: The core competency of residential, research-based universities. *International Journal of Computer-Supported Collaborative Learning, 2*(1), 9–40. Retrieved from http://www.springerlink.com.libdata.lib.ua.edu/content/x7m1270830277315/doi:10.1007/s11412-007-9009-1

Flanagan, B., & Calandra, B. (2005). Podcasting in the classroom. *Learning and Leading with Technology*, *33*(3), 20–25.

Fonseca, C. (2010). The digital divide and the cognitive divide: Reflections on the challenge of human development in the digital age. *Information Technologies & International Development*, *6*, 25–30.

Forno, A., & Merlone, U. (2007). The emergence of effective leaders: An experimental approach and computational approach. In Hazy, J., Goldstein, J., & Lichtenstein, B. (Eds.), *Complex Systems Leadership Theory* (pp. 205–227). Mansfield, MA: ISCE Publishing.

Fowler, S. M., & Pusch, M. D. (2010). *Intercultural simulation games: A review of the United States and beyond*. Retrieved from http://sag.sagepub.com/content/41/1/94.refs.html

Fowler, S. M., & Blohm, J. M. (2004). An analysis of methods for intercultural training. In Landis, D., Bennett, J. M., & Bennett, M. J. (Eds.), *Handbook of Intercultural Training* (pp. 37–84). Thousand Oaks, CA: Sage Publications. doi:10.4135/9781452231129.n3

Freeman, Y. S., & Freeman, D. (2006). *Teaching reading and writing in Spanish and English in bilingual and dual language classrooms*. Portsmouth, UK: Heinemann.

Friday, E., & Friday, S. S. (2003). Managing diversity using a strategic planned change approach. *Journal of Management Development*, *22*, 863–880. doi:10.1108/02621710310505467

Friedman, T. (2005). *The world is flat: A brief history of the twenty-first century*. New York, NY: Farrar, Straus, and Giroux.

Froese, P., Bader, C., & Smith, B. (2008). Political tolerance and God's wrath in the United States. *Sociology of Religion*, *69*(1), 29–44. doi:10.1093/socrel/69.1.29

Frost, M. (2007). Texas students' college expectations: Does high school racial composition matter? *Sociology of Education*, *80*(1), 43–65. doi:10.1177/003804070708000103

Fullan, M. (2002, May). The change. *Educational Leadership*, 16–20.

Fuller, R. M., Vician, C., & Brown, S. A. (2006). E-learning and individual characteristics: The role of computer anxiety and communication apprehension. *Journal of Computer Information Systems*, *46*(4), 103–115.

Gagne, R. M., Briggs, L. J., & Wager, W. W. (1988). *Principles of instructional design* (3rd ed.). New York, NY: Holt, Rinehart, Winston.

Garcia, M., Hudgins, C., Musil, C. M., Nettles, M. T., Sedlacek, W. E., & Smith, D. G. (2001). Assessing campus diversity initiatives: A guide for campus practitioners. In *Understanding the Difference Diversity Makes: Assessing Campus Diversity Initiatives*. Washington, DC: Association of American Colleges and Universities.

Garrity, R. (2010). Future leaders: Putting learning and knowledge to work. *Horizon*, *18*(3), 266–278. doi:10.1108/10748121011072717

Gaziolglu, S., & Caliskan, N. (2011). Cummulative prospect theory challenges traditional expected utility theory. *Applied Financial Economics*, *21*(21), 1581–1586. doi:10.1080/09603107.2011.583393

Geertz, C. (1973). *The interpretation of cultures: Selected essays*. New York, NY: Basic Books.

Gibbons, P. (2002). *Scaffolding language, scaffolding learning: Teaching second language learners in the mainstream classroom*. Portsmouth, UK: Heinemann.

Gibson, S. (2006). Veni, vidi, wiki. *eWeek*, *23*(46), 22-28.

Gingrich, N. (2012). *Interview*. Retrieved from http://www.mediaite.com/tv/gingrich-contrasts-inclusion-and-outreach-outreach-is-when-5-white-guys-have-a-meeting-and-call-you/

Ginsberg, B. (2011). *The fall of the faculty*. Oxford, UK: Oxford University Press.

Giovannini, M. (2004). What gets measured gets done: Achieving results through diversity and inclusion. *Journal for Quality and Participation*, *27*(4), 21–27.

Girod, S., & Bellin, J. (2011). Revisiting the "modern" multinational enterprise theory: An emerging-market multinational perspective. *Research in Global Strategic Management*, *15*, 167–210. doi:10.1108/S1064-4857(2011)0000015013

Glastra, F., Meerman, M., Schedler, P., & de Vries, S. (2000). Broadening the scope of diversity management. *Industrial Relations*, *55*(4), 698–721.

Goldstein, J. (2007). A new model for emergence and its leadership implications. In Hazy, J., Goldstein, J., & Lichtenstein, B. (Eds.), *Complex Systems Leadership Theory* (pp. 62–91). Mansfield, MA: ISCE Publishing.

Goldstein, J., Hazy, J. K., & Lichtenstein, B. B. (2010). *Complexity and the nexus of leadership: Leveraging nonlinear science to create ecologies of innovation*. New York, NY: Palgrave Macmillan.

Goleman, D. (1995). *Emotional intelligence*. New York, NY: Bantam.

Gonzalez, J. A., & DeNisi, A. S. (2009). Cross-level effects of demography and diversity climate on organizational attachment and firm effectiveness. *Journal of Organizational Behavior*, *30*, 21–40. doi:10.1002/job.498

Goodstein, L. (2005, June 23). Air force academy staff found promoting religion. *The New York Times*. Retrieved from http://www.nytimes.com/2005/06/23/politics/23academy.html?scp=1&sq=Air%20Force%20academy%20staff%20found%20promoting%20religion&st=cse

Gordon, R. S., & Stephen, M. (2007). Putting wikis into play. *Computers in Libraries*, *27*(2), 42–43.

Gore, A. (2000). *Best practices in achieving workforce diversity*. Washington, DC: U.S. Department of Commerce and Vice President Al Gore's National Partnership for Reinventing Government Benchmark Study.

Gouseti, A. (2010). Web 2.0 and education: Not just another case of hype, hope and disappointment? *Learning, Media and Technology*, *35*(3), 351–356. doi:10.1080/17439884.2010.509353

Graesser, A. C., & King, B. (2007). Technology-based training. In Blascovich, J. J., & Hartel, C. R. (Eds.), *Human Behavior in Military Contexts* (pp. 1–22). Washington, DC: The National Academies Press.

Graham, S. (2011). *A diversity leadership program*. Retrieved from http://www.stedmangraham.com/

Graham, S. (2002). Bridging urban digital divides? Urban polarisation and information and communications technologies (ICTs). *Urban Studies (Edinburgh, Scotland)*, *39*(1), 33–56. doi:10.1080/00420980220099050

Grammich, C. (2004). Many faiths of many regions: Continuities and changes among religious adherents across U.S. counties. *RAND Labor and Population Report WR-211*. Retrieved from http://www.rand.org

Granka, L. A. (2010). The politics of search: A decade retrospective. *The Information Society*, *26*(5), 364–374. doi:10.1080/01972243.2010.511560

Granovetter, M. (1973). The strength of weak ties. *American Journal of Sociology*, *6*, 1360–1380. doi:10.1086/225469

Gray, L., Thomas, N., Lewis, L., & National Center for Education Statistics. (2010). Educational technology in U.S. public schools: Fall 2008. In *Teaching as Leadership: The Highly Effective Teacher's Guide to Closing the Achievement Gap*. San Francisco, CA: Jossey-Bass.

Greenfield, T. (1984). The decline and fall of science in educational administration. *Interchange*, *17*, 57–80. doi:10.1007/BF01807469

Greenhalgh, L. (2008). *Increasing MBE competitiveness through strategic alliances*. Washington, DC: U.S. Department of Commerce.

Greenleaf, R. (1998). *The power of servant leadership*. San Francisco, CA: Berrett-Kohler Publishers, Inc.

Gregory-Mina, H. J. (2009). Four leadership theories addressing contemporary leadership issues as the theories relate to the scholarship, practice, and leadership model. *Academic Leadership On-Line Journal, 7*(3). Retrieved from http://www.academicleadership.org/349/four_leadership_theories_addressing_contemporary_leadership_issues_as_the_theories_relate_to_the_scholarship_practice_and_leadership_model/

Griffiths, D. E. (1964). The nature and meaning of theory. In Griffiths, D. E. (Ed.), *Behavioral Science and Educational Administration*. Chicago, IL: University of Chicago Press.

Gronn, P. (2002). Distributed leadership. In Leithwood, K., & Hallinger, P. (Eds.), *Second International Handbook of Educational Leadership Administration* (pp. 653–697). Boston, MA: Kluwer. doi:10.1007/978-94-010-0375-9_23

Gruys, M. L., & Sackett, P. R. (2003). Investigating the dimensionality of counterproductive work behavior. *Journal of Selection and Assessment, 11*, 30–42. doi:10.1111/1468-2389.00224

Gunkel, D. (2003). Second thoughts: Toward a critique of the digital divide. *New Media & Society, 5*(4), 499–522. doi:10.1177/146144480354003

Gurin, P., Day, E. L., Hurtado, S., & Gurin, G. (2002). Diversity and higher education: Theory and impact on educational outcomes. *Harvard Educational Review, 72*(3), 330–366.

Gurstein, M. (2003). Effective use: A community informatics strategy beyond the digital divide. *First Monday, 8*(12).

Hajjar, R. M. (2010). A new angle on the U.S. military's emphasis on developing cross-cultural competence: Connecting in ranks' cultural diversity to cross-cultural competence. *Armed Forces and Society, 36*(2), 247–263. doi:10.1177/0095327X09339898

Hallinger, P. (Ed.). (2002). *Second international handbook of educational leadership and administration*. London, UK: Kluwer.

Hamilton, R. (2011, October 6). Out of the smoke-filled room and onto the internet. *The New York Times*. Retrieved from http://www.nytimes.com/2011/10/07/us/for-public-input-crowdsourcing-online.html

Hammond, T. C. (2007). A task-oriented framework for stand-alone technology intergration classes. *Journal of Computing in Teacher Education, 23*(4), 119–124.

Hamston, J. (2006). Bakhtin's theory of dialogue: A construct for pedagogy, methodology and analysis. *Australian Educational Researcher, 33*(1), 55–74. doi:10.1007/BF03246281

Hanna, J. (2008, September 26). Second soldier sues over religious freedom issues. *Associated Press*. Retrieved from http://www.militaryreligiousfreedom.org/press-releases/complaint_sept.html

Hannigan, T. P. (1990). Traits, attitudes, and skills that are related to intercultural effectiveness and their implications for cross-cultural training: A review of the literature. *International Journal of Intercultural Relations, 14*(1), 89–111. doi:10.1016/0147-1767(90)90049-3

Hansen, F. (2003). Diversity's business case: Doesn't add up. *Workforce, 82*(4), 28–32.

Hargittai, E. (2002). The second-level digital divide: Differences in people's online skills. *First Monday, 7*(4), 1–20.

Hargittai, E. (2003). The digital divide and what to do about it. In *New Economy Handbook* (pp. 821–839). New York, NY: Elsevier Science.

Hargittai, E. (2010). Digital natives? Variation in internet skills and uses among members of the "net generation". *Sociological Inquiry, 80*(1), 92–113. doi:10.1111/j.1475-682X.2009.00317.x

Hargreaves, A., & Fink, D. (2006). *Sustainable leadership*. San Francisco, CA: Jossey-Bass.

Harper, M. (2007). The stereotyping of nonreligious people by religious students: Contents and subtypes. *Journal for the Scientific Study of Religion, 46*(4), 539–552. doi:10.1111/j.1468-5906.2007.00376.x

Harris, A. (2008). *Distributed school leadership*. London, UK: Routledge.

Harrison, C., & Killion, J. (2007). Ten roles for teacher leaders. *Educational Leadership, 65*(1), 74–77.

Hatch Act (5 U.S.C. 7323) (1993).

Haury, D. L. (2001). *Cultivating leadership among science and mathematics teachers*. Columbus, OH: Eric Database.

Hauser, J. (2007). Media specialists can learn web 2.0 tools to make schools more cool. *Computers in Libraries, 27*, 6–48.

Havenstein, H. (2007). Companies may face lawsuits if employees abuse web 2.0 tools. *Computerworld, 41*, 36.

Hays-Thomas, R. (2004). Why now? The contemporary focus on managing diversity. In Stockdale, M. S., & Crosby, F. J. (Eds.), *The Psychology and Management of Workplace Diversity* (pp. 3–30). Malden, MA: Blackwell.

Hazy, K. (2007). *Complex systems leadership theory.* Mansfield, MA: ISCE Publishing.

Heafner, T., & Friedman, A. (2008). Wikis and constructivism in secondary social studies: Fostering a deeper understanding. *Computers in the Schools, 25*(3-4), 288–302. doi:10.1080/07380560802371003

Heffes, E. (2006, November 1). Diversifying suppliers isn't costly. *Financial Executive.*

He, J., & Freeman, L. A. (2010). Understanding the formation of general computer self-efficacy. *Communications of AIS, 26*(12), 225–244.

Held, D. (1999). *Global transformations.* Stanford, CA: Stanford University Press.

Helsper, E., & Eynon, R. (2010). Digital natives: Where is the evidence? *British Educational Research Journal, 36*(3), 503–520. doi:10.1080/01411920902989227

Henschen, D., Stodder, D., Crosman, P., Mcciellan, M., Mcwhorter, N., & Patterson, D. (2007). Seven business and tech trends for '07. *Intelligent Enterprise.* Retrieved January 2, 2007, from http://www.crn.com/sections/breakingnews/breakingnews.jhtml?articleId=196800329

Hens, T., & Vlcek, M. (2011). Does prospect theory explain the dispostion effect? *Journal of Behavioral Finance, 12*(3), 141–157. doi:10.1080/15427560.2011.601976

Herek, G. M. (1987). Religious orientation and prejudice: A comparison of racial and sexual attitudes. *Personality and Social Psychology Bulletin, 13*(1), 34–44. doi:10.1177/0146167287131003

Herring, C. (2009). Does diversity pay? Race, gender, and the business case for diversity. *American Sociological Review, 74,* 208–224. doi:10.1177/000312240907400203

Hertz, M. B. (2011, October 24). A new understanding of the digital divide. *Edutopia.* Retrieved on November 2, 2011 from http://www.edutopia.org/blog/digital-divide-technology-internet-access-mary-beth-hertz

Hesselbein, F., Goldsmith, M., & Beckhard, R. (1996). *The Drucker foundation: The leader of the future.* San Francisco, CA: Jossey-Bass.

Hezlett, S. A. (2005). Proteges' learning in mentoring relationships: A review of the literature and an exploratory case study. *Advances in Developing Human Resources, 7*(4), 505–526. doi:10.1177/1523422305279686

Hicks-Clarke, D., & Iles, P. (2000). Climate for diversity and its effects on career and organizational attitudes and perceptions. *Personnel Review, 29*(3), 324–345. doi:10.1108/00483480010324689

Hoffman, D. L., & Novak, T. P. (Producer). (1998). *Bridging the digital divide: The impact of race on computer access and internet use.* Retrieved from elab.vanderbilt.edu

Holden, J. (1995). *Mentoring frameworks for Texas teachers.* East Lansing, MI: National Center for Research on Teacher Learning.

Hollein, M. N. (2011). Making the business case for diversity. *Financial Executive, 27*(5), 6.

Hornsby, J. S., Kuratko, D. F., & Zahra, S. A. (2002). Middle managers' perception of the internal environment for corporate entrepreneurship: assessing a measurement scale. *Journal of Business Venturing, 17,* 253–273. doi:10.1016/S0883-9026(00)00059-8

House, E., Glass, G., Mclean, L., & Walker, F. (1978). No simple answer- Critique of the "follow through" evaluation. *Educational Leadership, 35*(6), 462–464.

Hout, M., & Fischer, C. S. (2002). Why more Americans have no religious preference: Politics and generations. *American Sociological Review, 67*(2), 165–190. doi:10.2307/3088891

Hsieh, J. J. P.-A., Rai, A., & Keil, M. (2008). Understanding digital inequality: Comparing continued use behavioral models of the soci-economically advantaged and disadvantaged. *Management Information Systems Quarterly, 32*(1), 97–126.

Huffaker, D. (2010). Dimensions of leadership and social influence in online communities. *Human Communication Research, 36,* 593–617. doi:10.1111/j.1468-2958.2010.01390.x

Humphreys, D. (2000). Diversity plan trends aim to meet 21st century challenges. *Black Issues in Higher Education, 16,* 34–36.

Humpreys, D. (2000). National survey finds diversity requirements common around the country. *Diversity Digest, 5*(1), 1–2.

Humrickson, E. (2011). *Information literacy instruction in the Web 2.0 library.*

Hunter, C. E., & Smith, L. M. (2011). Exploring the management of religious diversity within the US military. In McDonald, D. P., & Parks, K. M. (Eds.), *Managing Diversity in the Military: The Value of Inclusion in a Culture of Uniformity* (pp. 311–368). New York, NY: Routledge.

Hunzicker, J., Lukowiak, T., Huffman, V., & Johnson, C. (2009). Tomorrow's teacher leaders: Nurturing a disposition of leadership. *Academic Leadership Live: The Online Journal, 9*(2). Retrieved December 13, 2011, from http://www.academicleadership.org/article/Tomorrow_s_Teacher_Leaders_Nurturing_a_Disposition_of_Leadership

Hurtado, S., Milem, J., Clayton-Pedersen, A., & Allen, W. (1998). Enhancing campus climates for racial/ethnic diversity: Educational policy and practice. *The Review of Higher Education, 21*(3), 279–302. doi:10.1353/rhe.1998.0003

Hurtado, S., Milem, J., Clayton-Pedersen, A., & Allen, W. (1999). Enacting diverse learning environments: Improving the climate for racial/ethnic diversity in higher education. *ASHE-ERIC Higher Education Report, 26*(8).

Ingersoll, R., & Kralik, J. (2004). *The impact of mentoring on teacher retention: What the research says.* Denver, CO: Education Commission of the States.

Introna, L., & Nissenbaum, H. (2000). Shaping the web: Why the politics of search engines matters. *The Information Society, 16*(3), 1–17.

Irizarry, C., & Gallant, L. (2006). Managing diversity: Interpretation and enactment in a healthcare setting. *Qualitative Research Reports in Communication, 7*(1), 43–50. doi:10.1080/17459430600964901

Irvine, J. (2002). *In search of wholeness: African American teachers and their culturally specific classroom practices.* New York, NY: Palgrave Macmillan.

Jashapara, A., & Tai, W.-C. (2011). Knowledge mobilization through e-learning systems: Understanding the mediating roles of self-efficacy and anxiety on perceptions of ease of use. *Information Systems Management, 28*(1), 71–83. doi:10.1080/10580530.2011.536115

Johnson, N. (2008). Online reviews second only to word of mouth in purchase decisions. *Small Business Network.* Retrieved from http://searchenginewatch.com/article/2053296/Online-Reviews-Second-Only-to-Word-of-Mouth-in-Purchase-Decisions

Johnson, L., Smith, R., Willis, H., Levine, A., & Haywood, K. (2011). *The 2011 horizon report.* Austin, TX: The New Media Consortium.

Johnson, W. B. (2002). The intentional mentor: Strategies and guidelines for the practice of mentoring. *Professional Psychology, Research and Practice, 33*, 88–96. doi:10.1037/0735-7028.33.1.88

Jolly, R. S. (2007). The application of the religious freedom restoration act to appearance regulations that presumptively prohibit observant Sikh lawyers from joining the U.S. army judge advocate general corps. *Chapman Law Review, 11*(1), 155–182.

Jonassen, D. H. (2005). *Modeling with technology: Mindtools for contemporary change* (3rd ed.). Englewood Cliffs, NJ: Prentice Hall.

Jones, S., Johnson-Yale, C., Millermaier, S., & Perez, F. (2009). U.S. college students' Internet use: Race, gender and digital divides. *Journal of Computer-Mediated Communication, 14*(2), 244–264. doi:10.1111/j.1083-6101.2009.01439.x

Jonsson, P. (2010, January 22). Trijicon sights: How the 'Jesus gun' misfired. *Christian Science Monitor.* Retrieved from http://www.csmonitor.com/USA/Military/2010/0122/Trijicon-sights-How-the-Jesus-gun-misfired

Jordan, B. (2008, February 26). Flag ritual returns to Annapolis chapel. *Military.com.* Retrieved from http://militaryreligiousfreedom.org/press-releases/fowler.html

Jordan, B. (2009, April 15). Sikhs want DOD turban, hair bans lifted. *Military.com.* Retrieved from http://www.military.com/news/article/sikhs-want-dod-turban-hair-bans-lifted.html?ESRC=eb.nl

Joyce, B., Weil, M., & Calhoun, E. (2004). *Models of teaching*. Boston, MA: Pearson Education, Inc.

Jstor. (2011). *Books at JSTOR: Leading university presses announce plan to publish books online at JSTOR*. Retrieved October 12, 2011, from http://about.jstor.org/news-events/news/books-jstor-leading-university-presses-announce-plan-publish-books-online-jstor

Jukes, I., McCain, T., & Crockett, L. (2011). Education and the role of the educator in the future. *Phi Delta Kappan*, *92*(4), 8–14.

Jung, J. Y., Qui, J. L., & Kim, Y. C. (2001). Internet connectedness and inequality. *Communication Research*, *28*(4), 507–535. doi:10.1177/009365001028004006

Kaba, A. (2011). Black American females as geniuses. *Journal of African American Studies*, *15*(1), 120–124. doi:10.1007/s12111-010-9134-1

Kahneman, D., & Tversky, A. (1979). Prospect theory: An analysis of decision under risk. *Econometrica*, *47*(2), 263–291. doi:10.2307/1914185

Kajewski, M. A. (2006). Emerging technologies changing public library service delivery models. *APLIS*, *19*(4), 157–163.

Kalev, A., Dobbin, F., & Kelly, E. (2006). Best practices or best guesses? Assessing the efficacy of corporate affirmative action and diversity policies. *American Sociological Review*, *71*, 589–617. doi:10.1177/000312240607100404

Karsten, M. F. (2006). *Management, gender, and race in the 21st century*. New York, NY: University Press of America.

Kasworm, C. E., Sandmann, L. R., & Sissel, P. A. (2000). Adult learners in higher education. In Wilson, A. L., & Hayes, E. R. (Eds.), *Handbook of Adult and Continuing Education* (pp. 449–463). San Francisco, CA: Jossey-Bass.

Katz, J. E., & Rice, R. E. (2002). *Social consequences of Internet use, access, involvement and interaction*. Cambridge, MA: MIT Press.

Kaye, R. (2008, July 8). Atheist soldier sues army for 'unconstitutional' discrimination. *CNN*. Retrieved from http://articles.cnn.com/2008-07-08/us/atheist.soldier_1_tours-discrimination-bible?_s=PM:US

Keil, M., Amershi, B., Holmes, S., Jablonski, H., Luthi, E., & Matoba, K. … von Unruh, K. (2007). *Training manual for diversity management*. Washington, DC: International Society for Diversity Management.

Kelleher, C., Whalley, A., & Helkkula, A. (2011). Collaborative value co-creation in crowd-sourced online communities: Acknowledging and resolving competing commercial and communal orientations. *Research in Consumer Behavior*, *13*, 1–18. doi:10.1108/S0885-2111(2011)0000013004

Keller, J. M. (1983). Motivational design of instruction. In Reigeluth, C. M. (Ed.), *Instructional-Design Theories and Models: An Overview of their Current Status*. Hillsdale, NJ: Lawrence Erlbaum Associates.

Kerr, R., Garvin, J., Heaton, N., & Boyle, E. (2006). Emotional intelligence and leadership effectiveness. *Leadership and Organization Development Journal*, *27*(4), 265–279. doi:10.1108/01437730610666028

Ketterer, J., & Marsh, G. (2006). Re-conceptualizing intimacy and distance in instructional models. *Online Journal of Distance Learning Administration*. Retrieved from http://www.westga.edu/%7Edistance/ojdla/spring91/ketterer91.pdf

Ketterer, J. J. (2008). Zone of proximal development. In Salkind, N. J. (Ed.), *Encyclopedia of Educational Psychology*. Thousand Oaks, CA: Sage Publications.

Kezar, A. (2008). Understanding leadership strategies for addressing the politics of diversity. *The Journal of Higher Education*, *79*(4), 406–441. doi:10.1353/jhe.0.0009

Kezar, A. J. (2007). Tools for a time and place: Phased leadership strategies to institutionalize a diversity agenda. *The Review of Higher Education*, *30*(4), 413–439. doi:10.1353/rhe.2007.0025

Kirkpatrick, J., & Kirkpatrick, W. (2009). *Kirkpatrick then and now: A strong foundation for the future*. New York, NY: Kirkpatrick Publishing.

Korstanje, M. (2011). Swine flu in Buenos Aires: Beyond the principle of resilience. *International Journal of Disaster Resilience in the Built Environment*, *2*(1), 59–73. doi:10.1108/17595901111108371

Korupp, S. E., & Szydlik, M. (2005). Causes and trends of the digital divide. *European Sociological Review*, *21*(4), 409–422. doi:10.1093/esr/jci030

Kosmin, B. A., & Keysar, A. (2008). *American religious identification survey (ARIS) 2008*. Hartford, CT: Institute for the Study of Secularism in Society & Culture.

Kosmin, B. A., & Mayer, E. (2001). *American religious identification survey*. New York, NY: The Graduate Center of the City University of New York.

Kossek, E. E., & Zonia, S. C. (1993). Assessing diversity climate: A field study of reactions to employer efforts to promote diversity. *Journal of Organizational Behavior*, *14*, 61–81. doi:10.1002/job.4030140107

Kotter, J. P. (1996). *Leading change*. Boston, MA: Harvard Business School Press.

Kowch, E. G. (2003). *Policy networks and policy communities in three western Canadian universities and two provinces: A neo-institutional approach to a pan-institutional issue*. (Unpublished Doctoral Dissertation). University of Saskatchewan. Saskatoon, Canada.

Kowch, E. G. (2008). *Characteristics of high capacity, semi-autonomous teams – Are you ready for this?* Paper presented at the meeting of the Association of Education Communications and Technology Annual Conference. Orlando, FL.

Kowch, E. (2005). The knowledge network: A fundamentally new (relational) approach to knowledge management & the study of dependent organizations. *Journal of Knowledge Management Practice*, *6*, 13–37.

Kowch, E. (2007). *Alberta central server/thin client shared services: System leadership study 2*. Edmonton, Canada: Alberta Education Publication.

Kowch, E. (2009). New capabilities for cyber charter school leadership: An emerging imperative for integrating educational technology and educational leadership knowledge. *TechTrends*, *53*(1), 40–49.

Kozma, R. B. (1994). A reply: Media and methods. *Educational Technology Research and Development*, *42*(3), 11–14. doi:10.1007/BF02298091

Kram, K. E. (1983). Phases of the mentor relationship. *Academy of Management Journal*, *26*, 608–625. doi:10.2307/255910

Kreitz, P. A. (2008). Best practices for managing organizational diversity. *Journal of Academic Librarianship*, *34*(2), 101–120. doi:10.1016/j.acalib.2007.12.001

Kuflik, T. (2011). A visitor's guide in an active museum: Presentations, communications and reflection. *Journal on Computing and Cultural Heritage*, *3*(3). doi:10.1145/1921614.1921618

Kuhberger, A., & Tanner, C. (2010). Risky choice framing: Task versions and a comparison of prospect theory and fuzzy-trace theory. *Journal of Behavioral Decision Making*, *23*(3), 314–329. doi:10.1002/bdm.656

Kuhn, T. S. (1977). *The essential tension*. Chicago, IL: University of Chicago Press.

Kumar, S., & Chang, C. (2007). Reverse auctions: How much total supply chain cost savings are there? A conceptual overview. *Journal of Revenue and Pricing Management*, *6*(2), 77–85. doi:10.1057/palgrave.rpm.5160077

Kurien, P. (2004). Multiculturalism, immigrant religion, and diasporic nationalism: The development of an American Hinduism. *Social Problems*, *51*(3), 362–385. doi:10.1525/sp.2004.51.3.362

Kvasny, L., & Keil, M. (2006). The challenges of redressing the digital divide: A tale of two U.S. cities. *Information Systems Journal*, *16*, 23–53. doi:10.1111/j.1365-2575.2006.00207.x

Ladson-Billings, G. (1994). *The dreamkeepers: Successful teachers of African American children*. San Francisco, CA: Jossey-Bass.

Ladson-Billings, G. (2001). *Crossing over to Canaan*. San Francisco, CA: Jossey-Bass.

LaFraniere, S., & Barboza, D. (2011, March 21). China tightens censorship of electronic communications. *The New York Times*. Retrieved November 2, 2011, from http://www.nytimes.com/2011/03/22/world/asia/22china.html?_r=1&ref=internetcensorship

Lambert, L. (2003). Leadership redefined: An evocative context for teacher leadership. *School Leadership & Management, 23*(4), 421–430. doi:10.1080/136324303 2000150953

Lamont, J. (2007). Blogs and wikis: Ready for prime time? *KM World, 16*(1), 14–26.

Lancaster, A. R., Klein, R. M., & Wetzel, E. S. (2004). *U.S. department of defense retention trends*. Arlington, VA: Defense Manpower and Data Center.

Langer, J. (1991). *Literary understanding and literature instruction: Report series 2.11*. Albany, NY: Center for the Learning and Teaching of Literature.

Langer, J. (2001). Beating the odds: Teaching middle and high school students to read and write well. *American Educational Research Journal, 38*(4), 837–880. doi:10.3102/00028312038004837

Langer, J. (2011a). *Envisioning literature: Literary understanding and literature instruction* (2nd ed.). New York, NY: Teachers College Press.

Langer, J. (2011b). *Envisioning knowledge: Building literacy in the academic disciplines*. New York, NY: Teachers College Press.

Lankau, M. J., & Scandura, T. A. (2002). An investigation of personal learning in mentoring relationships: Content, antecedents, and consequences. *Academy of Management Journal, 45*(4), 779–790. doi:10.2307/3069311

Lankau, M., & Thomas, C. (2009). Preventing burnout: The effects of LMX and mentoring on socialization, role stress, and burnout. *Human Resource Management, 48*(3), 417–432. doi:10.1002/hrm.20288

Lankes, D. (2006). *The social internet: A new community role for libraries?* Retrieved March 3, 2007 from http://quartz.syr.edu/rdlankes/blog/?p=156http://quartz.syr.edu/rdlankes/blog/?p=156

Lawrence, L. (2007, November 20). Military chaplains: Being a cog of conscience in the military killing machine. *Christian Science Monitor*. Retrieved from http://www.csmonitor.com/2007/1120/p20s01-usmi.html

Lawrence, S., & Giles, C. L. (2000). Accessibility of Information on the web. *Intelligence, 11*(1). doi:10.1145/333175.333181

Leavitt, C. C. (2011). *Developing leaders through mentoring: A brief literature review*. Columbus, OH: ERIC.

LeBaron, M. (2003). *Bridging cultural conflicts: A new approach for a changing world*. San Francisco, CA: Jossey-Bass Publishing.

Leigh, A., & Atkinson, R. D. (2001). *Clear thinking on the digital divide*. New York, NY: Progressive Policy Institute.

Leithwood, K., & Jantzi, D. (2005). A review of transformational school leadership research: 1996-2005. *Leadership and Policy in Schools, 4*(3), 177–199. doi:10.1080/15700760500244769

Lemov, D. (2010). *Teach like a champion: 49 techniques that put students on the path to college*. San Francisco, CA: Jossey-Bass.

Lenhart, A., Horrigan, J., Rainie, L., Allen, K., Boyce, A., & Madden, M. (2003). *The ever-shifting internet population: A new look at internet access and the digital divide*. Washington, DC: Pew Internet and American Life Project.

Lentz, B., & Oden, M. (2001). Digital divide or digital opportunity in the Mississippi delta region of the US. *Telecommunications Policy, 25*(5), 291–313. doi:10.1016/S0308-5961(01)00006-4

Leopold, J. (2009, April 6). Army faces backlash for scheduling 'day of fast' on feast of Passover. *The Public Record*. Retrieved from http://pubrecord.org/religion/845/army-faces-backlash-for-scheduling-day-of-fast-on-feast-of-passover/

Levin, B., & Fullan, M. (2008). Learning about system renewal. *Educational Management and Leadership, 36*, 289–304. doi:10.1177/1741143207087778

Levine, J. (2006). *The shifted librarian*. Retrieved March 26, 2007 from http://www.theshiftedlibrarian.com/archives/2005/11/07/digital_utes.html

Levy, J. S. (1997). Prospect theory, rational choice, and international relations. *International Studies Quarterly, 41*(1), 87–112. doi:10.1111/0020-8833.00034

Lewin, K. (1944). A research approach to leadership problems. *The Journal of Applied Psychology, 17*(7), 392–398.

Libecap, G. (2011). Introduction - Entrepreneurship and global competitiveness in regional economies: Determinants and policy implications. *Advances in the Study of Entrepreneurship. Innovation & Economic Growth*, *22*, ix–xii.

Lieberman, A., Saxl, E., & Miles, M. (1988). Teacher leadership: ideology and practice. In Lieberman, A. (Ed.), *Building a Professional Culture in Schools*. New York, NY: Teachers College Press.

Lim, N., Cho, M., & Curry, K. (2008). *Planning for diversity: Options and recommendations for DoD leaders*. Santa Monica, CA: RAND Corporation.

Lim, W., So, H., & Tan, S. (2010). eLearning 2.0 and new literacies: Are social practices lagging behind? *Interactive Learning Environments*, *18*(3), 203–218. doi:10.1080/10494820.2010.500507

Lin, C., & Ha, L. (2009). Subcultures and use of communication information technology in higher education institutions. *The Journal of Higher Education*, *80*(5), 564–590. doi:10.1353/jhe.0.0064

Lindsey, R. B., Robins, K. N., & Terrell, R. D. (2003). *Cultural proficiency: A manual for school leaders* (2nd ed.). Thousand Oaks, CA: Corwin Press.

Loden, M. (1995). *Implementing diversity*. New York, NY: McGraw-Hill.

Loden, M., & Rosener, J. (1991). *Workforce America! Managing employee diversity as a vital resource*. Homewood, IL: Irwin.

Lowe, E. (1999). Promise and dilemma: Perspectives on racial diversity and higher education. In Lowe, E. (Ed.), *Promise and Dilemma* (pp. 3–43). Princeton, NJ: Princeton University Press.

Lumby, J., & Coleman, M. (2007). *Leadership and diversity: Challenging theory and practice in education*. London, UK: Sage Publications, Ltd.

Lumpkin, A. (2011). A model for mentoring university faculty. *The Educational Forum*, *75*, 357–368. doi:10.1080/00131725.2011.602466

Lustig, M. W. (2009). *Intercultural competence: Interpersonal communications across cultures* (6th ed.). Reading, MA: Allyn & Bacon.

Lynne, S., & Solomon, G. (2010). *Web 2.0: New tools, new school*. Eugene, OR: International Society for Technology Education.

Mager, R. F. (1997). *Measuring instructional results: Or got a match?* Atlanta, GA: CEP Press.

Magnuson, S. (2002). New assistant professors of counselor education: Their 1st year. *Counselor Education and Supervision*, *41*, 306–320. doi:10.1002/j.1556-6978.2002.tb01293.x

Malan, R. (2011). *Immersive virtual workspaces for collaboration*. Paper presented at the Defense GameTech User Conference. Orlando, FL.

Mannix, E., & Neale, M. A. (2006). What differences make a difference? *Psychological Science in the Public Interest*, *6*, 31–55. doi:10.1111/j.1529-1006.2005.00022.x

Mansour, E. (2012). The role of social networking sites (SNSs) in the January 25th revolution in Egypt. *Library Review*, *61*(2), 128–159. doi:10.1108/00242531211220753

Marin, P. (1981, November 14). Living in moral pain. *Psychology Today*, 71–80.

Marion, R., & Uhl-Bien, M. (2001). Leadership in complex organizations. *The Leadership Quarterly*, *12*(4), 381–556. doi:10.1016/S1048-9843(01)00092-3

Marzano, R. (2007). *The art and science of teaching: A comprehensive framework for effective instruction*. Alexandria, VA: The Association for Supervision and Curriculum Development.

Marzano, R. J. (2009). Teaching with interactive whiteboards. *Multiple Measures*, *67*(3), 80–82.

Mathews, J. (2003). Constructivism in the classroom: Epistemology, history and empirical evidence. *Teacher Education Quarterly*, *30*(3), 51–64.

Mathtype. (2012). *Mathtype*. Retrieved March 5, 2012, from http://www.chartwellyorke.com/mathtype.html

Matusov, E. (2007). Applying Bakhtin scholarship on discourse in education: A critical review of essay. *Educational Theory*, *57*(2), 215–237. doi:10.1111/j.1741-5446.2007.00253.x

McClellan, J. L. (2010). Leadership and complexity: Implications for practiced within the advisement leadership bodies at colleges and universities. *Complicity: An International Journal of Complexity and Education, 7*, 32–51.

McDonald, D. P., & Parks, K. M. (2008). *3C identifying, applying & assessing. DEOMI Technical Presentation.* Washington, DC: DEOMI.

McDonald, D., & Parks, K. (2012). *Managing diversity in the military: The value of inclusion in a culture of uniformity.* New York, NY: Routledge.

McFadden, A. C. (2008). Podcasting and RSS. In Kelsey, S., & St. Armant, K. (Eds.), *The Handbook on Research on Computer-Mediated Communications.* Hershey, PA: IGI Global.

McKay, P. F., Avery, D. R., Tonidandel, S., Morris, M. A., Hernandez, M., & Hebl, M. R. (2007). Racial differences in employee retention: Are diversity climate perceptions the key? *Personnel Psychology, 60*, 35–62. doi:10.1111/j.1744-6570.2007.00064.x

McKelvey, B., & Lichtenstein, B. (2007). Leadership in the four stages of emergence. In Hazy, J., Goldstein, J., & Lichtenstein, B. (Eds.), *Complex Systems Leadership Theory.* Mansfield, MA: ISCE Publishing.

McKimm, J., & Swanwick, T. (2010). Web-based faculty development: E-learning for clinical teachers in the London deanery. *The Clinical Teacher, 7*(1), 58–62. doi:10.1111/j.1743-498X.2009.00344.x

McLuhan, M. (1994). *Understanding media: The extensions of man.* Cambridge, MA: MIT Press.

Melton, J. G. (1995). The changing scene of new religious movements: Observations from a generation of research. *Social Compass, 42*(2), 265–276. doi:10.1177/003776895042002009

Meyer, K. (2008). The "virtual face" of institutions: What do home pages reveal about higher education? *Innovative Higher Education, 33*(3), 141–157. doi:10.1007/s10755-008-9071-2

Military Leadership Diversity Commission. (2010). *Business-case arguments for diversity and diversity programs and their impact in the work-place.* Retrieved from http://diversity.defense.gov/Resources/Commission/docs/Issue%20Papers/Paper%2014%20%20Business%20Case%20Arguments%20for%20Diversity%20and%20Programs.pdf

Miller, S. (2008, September 15). Workforce diversity. *Broadcasting & Cable*, 19-20.

Miller, J. H., & Page, S. E. (2007). *Complex adaptive systems.* Princeton, NJ: Princeton University Press.

Miller, S. M. (2003). How literature discussion shapes thinking: ZPD's for teaching/learning habits of the heart and mind. In Kozulin, A., Gindis, B., Ageyev, V. S., & Miller, S. M. (Eds.), *Vygotsky's Educational Theory in Cultural Context* (pp. 289–316). Cambridge, UK: Cambridge University Press. doi:10.1017/CBO9780511840975.016

Millership, P. (2011, October 11). World intrigued by "occupy wall street" movement. *Reuters.* Retrieved November 5, 2011, from http://www.reuters.com/article/2011/10/11/us-usa-wallstreet-world-idUSTRE79A3OB20111011

Mills, J. (2011). *Open sim for wounded warriors.* Paper presented at the 2011 Advanced Distributed Learning iFest Conference. Orlando, FL.

Minority Business Development Agency. (2012). *Minority-owned business growth and global reach.* Retrieved from http://www.mbda.gov/sites/default/files/Minority-OwnedBusinessGrowthandGlobalReach_Final.pdf

Mintzberg, H., Ahlstrand, B., & Lampel, J. (1998). *Strategy safari: A guided tour through the wilds of strategic management.* New York, NY: Simon & Schuster.

Mital, M., Israel, D., & Agarwal, S. (2010). Information exchange and information disclosure in social networking web sites: Mediating role of trust. *The Learning Organization, 17*(6), 479–490. doi:10.1108/09696471011082349

Mitchell, C., & Sackney, L. (2011). *Profound improvement* (2nd ed.). New York, NY: Routledge.

MMR. (2011). How to advance women, build diversity and grow your business. *MMR, 24.*

Mockabee, S. T. (2007). A question of authority: Religion and cultural conflict in the 2004 election. *Political Behavior, 29*(2), 221–248. doi:10.1007/s11109-006-9023-4

Molenda, M., Pershing, J. A., & Reigeluth, C. M. (1996). Designing instructional systems. In Craig, R. L. (Ed.), *The ASTD Training and Development Handbook* (4th ed., pp. 266–293). New York, NY: McGraw-Hill.

Monczka, R., Handfield, R., Giunipero, L., & Patterson, J. (2011). *Purchasing & supply chain management* (5th ed.). Mason, OH: South-Western/Cengage Learning.

Moodle.org. (2011). *Website.* Retrieved November 1, 2011 from http://www.moodle.org

Mor Barak, M. E., Cherin, D. A., & Berkman, S. (1998). Organizational and personal dimensions in diversity climate: Ethnic and gender differences in employee perceptions. *The Journal of Applied Behavioral Science, 34*, 82–104. doi:10.1177/0021886398341006

Moran, R. T. (2007). *Managing cultural differences* (7th ed.). Burlington, MA: Butterworth-Heinemann.

Mount, M. (2009, May 22). Military burns unsolicited bibles sent to Afghanistan. *CNN.* Retrieved from http://edition.cnn.com/2009/WORLD/asiapcf/05/20/us.military.bibles.burned/

Mullen, C. A., & Hutinger, J. L. (2008). At the upping point: Role of formal faculty mentoring in changing university research cultures. *Journal of In-service Education, 34*, 181–204. doi:10.1080/13674580801951012

Muller, C. B. (2009). Understanding e-mentoring in organizations. *Adult Learning, 20*(1), 25–30.

Muse, J. (2009). How to win the diversity battle. *Advertising Age, 80*(7), 8.

Nagel, D. (2011, February 2). Will smartphones eliminate the digital divide? *The Journal.* Retrieved November 1, 2011, from http://thejournal.com/Articles/2011/02/01/Will-Smart-Phones-Eliminate-the-Digital-Divide.aspx?Page=1

National Council of Teachers of Mathematics. (1989). *Curriculum and evaluation standards for school mathematics.* Reston, VA: NCTM.

National Research Council. (2008). Human behavior in military contexts. In Blascovich, J. J., & Hartel, C. R. (Eds.), *Committee on Opportunities in Basic Research in the Behavioral and Social Sciences for the U.S. Military.* Washington, DC: National Academies Press.

National Teachers of Mathematics. (1994). Board approves statement on algebra. *NCTM News Bulletin, 6*(1).

Naumann, S. E., & Bennett, N. (2000). A case for procedural justice climate: Development and test of a multilevel model. *Academy of Management Journal, 43*, 881–889. doi:10.2307/1556416

NCTM. (2000). *National council of teachers of mathematics.* Retrieved February 8, 2010, from my.nctm.org/standards/document/chapter3/index.htm

NCTM. (2008). *The role of technology in the teaching and learning of mathematics.* Retrieved October 17, 2011, from www.nctm.org/uploadedFiles/About_NCTM/Position_Statements/Technology%20final.pdf

Nelson, B. (2011, April 1). The role of social media in the Middle East uprising. *Ahramonline.* Retrieved from http://english.ahram.org.eg/NewsContentP/4/9021/Opinion/The-Role-of-Social-Media-in-the-Middle-East-Uprisi.aspx

Nielsen Company. (2008). *Three screen report: Television, internet and mobile usage in the U.S.* New York, NY: The Nielsen Company.

Niemann, Y., & Maruyama, G. (2005). Inequities in higher education: Issues and promising practices in a world ambivalent about affirmative action. *The Journal of Social Issues, 61*, 407–426. doi:10.1111/j.1540-4560.2005.00414.x

Nikaien, Z., Ganjouie, F., Tondnevis, F., & Kamkari, K. (2012). Effects of leadership styles on coaches of Iran's national teams' success and athletes' perception of success. *Annals of Biological Research, 3*(1), 677–683.

Noah, M. (2011, May 23). Gays in military: 'Conscience protections' needed for chaplains, 21 entity leaders say. *Baptist Press.* Retrieved from http://www.bpnews.net/printerfriendly.asp?ID=35362

North Carolina State University College of Education. (2002). *GIS is an interdisciplinary technology tool.* Retrieved March 5, 2012, from http://www.ncsu.edu/gisined/text-why.html

Northouse, P. G. (2010). *Leadership: Theory and practice.* Thousand Oaks, CA: Sage.

Norum, P. S., & Weagley, R. O. (2006). College students, internet use, and protection from online identity theft. *Journal of Educational Technology Systems, 35,* 45–59. doi:10.2190/VL64-1N22-J537-R368

Notten, N., Peter, J., Kraaykamp, G., & Valkenbury, P. M. (2008). Research note: Digital divide across borders – A cross-national study of adolescents' use of digital technologies. *European Sociological Review, 25*(5), 551–560. doi:10.1093/esr/jcn071

November, A. (2010). *Empowering students with technology* (2nd ed.). Thousand Oaks, CA: Sage.

NTIA. (1995). *Falling through the net: A survey of the "have nots" in rural and urban America.* Retrieved from http://www.ntia.doc.gov/ntiahome

NTIA. (1998). *Falling through the net II: New data on the digital divide.* Retrieved from http://www.ntia.doc.gov.ntiahome

NTIA. (1999). *Falling through the net: Defining the digital divide.* Retrieved from http://www.ntia.doc.gov/ntiahome

NTIA. (2000). *Falling through the net: Toward digital inclusion.* Retrieved from http://www.ntia.doc.gov/ntiahome

NTIA. (2002). *A nation online: How Americans are expanding their use of the internet.* Retrieved from http://www.ntia.doc.gov/ntiahome

NTIA. (2011a). *Broadband adoption report.* Retrieved from http://www.ntia.doc.gov/report/2011/exploring-digital-nation-computer-and-internet-use-home

NTIA. (2011b). *New commerce department report shows broadband adoption rises but digital divide Persists.* Retrieved from http://www.ntia.doc.gov

O'Reilley, C., Williams, K., & Barsade, S. (1997). Group demography and innovation: Does diversity help? In Huber, G., & Glick, W. (Eds.), *Organizational Change and Redesign.* Oxford, UK: Oxford University Press.

Oblensky, N. (2010). *Complex adaptive leadership: Embracing paradox and uncertainty.* Burlington, VT: MPG Books.

OECD. (2010). *Economic outlook interim projections.* Paris, France: OECD.

Ogle, D. (2009). Creating contexts for inquiry: From KWL to PRC2. *Knowledge Quest, 38*(1), 56–61.

Oliha, H., & Collier, M. J. (2010). Bridging divergent diversity standpoints & ideologies: Organizational initiatives and trainings. *The International Journal of Diversity in Organisations. Communities and Nations, 10*(4), 61–73.

Otto, R. (1923). *The idea of the holy.* London, UK: Oxford University Press.

Owen, D. E., Walk, K. D., & Hill, S. S. (1991). Authoritarian or authority-minded? The cognitive commitments of fundamentalists and the Christian right. *Religion and American Culture, 1*(1), 73–100. doi:10.2307/1123907

Owen, D. S. (2009). Privileged social identities and diversity leadership in higher education. *The Review of Higher Education, 32*(2), 185–207. doi:10.1353/rhe.0.0048

Owens, R. G., & Valesky, T. C. (2007). *Organizational behavior in education: Adaptive leadership and school reform* (9th ed.). Boston, MA: Pearson.

Packer-Williams, C., & Evans, K. (2011). Retaining and reclaiming ourselves: Perspectives on a peer mentoring group experience for new African American women professors. *Perspectives in Peer Programs, 23*(1), 9–23.

Page, S. (2007). *The difference: How the power of diversity creates better groups, firms, schools and societies.* Princeton, NJ: Princeton University Press.

Paley, A. R. (2008, May 29). Marine in Iraq suspended over coins quoting gospel. *Washington Post.* Retrieved from http://www.washingtonpost.com/wp-dyn/content/article/2008/05/29/AR2008052903683.html?sid=ST2008053001342

Palfrey, J., & Gasser, U. (2008). *Born digital: Understanding the first generation of digital natives.* New York, NY: Basic Books.

Parco, J. E., & Fagin, B. S. (2007). The one true religion in the military. *The Humanist, 67*(5), 11–17.

Parks, K. Crepeau, L., & McDonald, D. (2008). *Psychometric properties for the DEOMI diversity climate scale (DDCS): Overview and final scale*. DEOMI Technical Report. DEOMI.

Parks, K. M. (2008). *Diversity management solutions and the DoD: For defense equal parks, opportunity management institute (DEOMI)*. DEOMI Technical Report. DEOMI.

Parmara, D., Wu, T., Callarman, T., Fowler, J., & Wolfe, P. (2010). A clustering algorithm for supplier base management. *International Journal of Production Research, 48*(13), 3803–3821. doi:10.1080/00207540902942891

Partridge, B., Pitcher, P., Cullen, J., & Wilson, J. (1980). The three dimensional structure of fish schools. *Behavioral Ecology and Sociobiology, 6*(4), 277–288. doi:10.1007/BF00292770

Pascarella, E. T., & Terenzini, P. T. (1991). *How college affects students: Findings from twenty years of research*. San Francisco, CA: Jossey-Bass.

Payne, C. M., Payne, J. S., & Craig. (2011). *A comparative study of face-to-face and online Iraqi culture training and the development of cross-cultural competence: Studies 4 and 5*. ISLET (Integrated System for Learning Education and Training).

Pearcy, D., Giunipero, L., & Wilson, A. (2007, Winter). A model of relational governance in reverse auctions. *Journal of Supply Chain Management*, 4-15.

Peelen, E., Kees, V., Beltman, R., & Klerkxc, A. (2009). An empirical study into the foundations of CRM success. *Journal of Strategic Marketing, 17*(6), 453–471. doi:10.1080/09652540903371695

Peng, G. (2010). Critical mass, diffusion channels and digital divide. *Journal of Computer Information Systems, 50*(3), 63–71.

Pew Forum on Religion in Public Life. (2008). *U.S. religious landscape survey*. Washington, DC: Pew Research Center. Retrieved from http://religions.pewforum.org/

Phillips, J. (1996). Measuring the results of training. In Craig, R. (Ed.), *The ASTD Training — Development Handbook*. New York, NY: McGraw-Hill.

Pinder-Grover, T., & Groscurth, C. (2009). *Prinicples for teaching the millenial generation: Innovative practices of U-M faculty*. Center For Research and Teaching Learning Occasional Papers.

Pink, D. (2011). *Forget shareholders, maximise consumer value instead*. Retrieved November 9, 2011 from http://www.telegraph.co.uk/finance/comment/8583476/Forget-shareholders-maximise-consumer-value-instead.html

Pinkard, N. (2005). How the perceived masculinity and/or femininity of software applications influences students' software preferences. *Journal of Educational Computing Research, 32*, 57–78. doi:10.2190/3LEE-MLCE-NK0Y-RUEP

Pope, P. (2002). *Relationship mapping: A tool for diagnosing relationships*. West Chester, OH: M.A.P. Publishing, Inc.

Porter, A. (1997). Supply-base 'optimization' stokes market competition. *Purchasing, 123*(6), 18–21.

Portugal, L. M. (2006). Diversity leadership in higher education. *Advancing Women in Leadership Online Journal, 21*. Retrieved from http://www.advancingwomen.com/awl/summer2007/portugal.htm

Pounder, J. S. (2008). Transformational classroom leadership: A novel approach to evaluating classroom performance. *Assessment & Evaluation in Higher Education, 33*(3), 233–243. doi:10.1080/02602930701292621

Prensky, M. (2001b). Digital natives, digital immigrants, part II: Do they really think differently? *On the Horizon, 9*(6), 1-6. Retrieved November 1, 2011, from http://www.marcprensky.com/writing/Prensky%20-%20Digital%20Natives,%20Digital%20Immigrants%20-%20Part2.pdf

Prensky, M. (2001). Digital natives, digital immigrants. *Horizon, 9*(5), 1–6. doi:10.1108/10748120110424816

Presser, S., & Chaves, M. (2007). Is religious service attendance declining? *Journal for the Scientific Study of Religion, 46*(3), 417–423. doi:10.1111/j.1468-5906.2007.00367.x

Price, B. J. (2008). Computer-mediated collaboration. In Kelsey, S., & St. Armant, K. (Eds.), *The Handbook on Research on Computer-Mediated Communications*. Hershey, PA: IGI Global. doi:10.4018/978-1-59904-863-5.ch037

Priego, E. (2011). *How Twitter will revolutionise academic research and teaching*. Retrieved March 3, 2012, from http://www.guardian.co.uk/higher-education-network/blog/2011/sep/12/twitter-revolutionise-academia-research

Pugalee, D. K., Frykholm, J., & Shaka, F. (2001). Diversity, technology, and policy: Key considerations in the development of teacher leadership. In Nesbit, C. R., Wallace, J. D., Pugalee, D. K., Miller, A. C., & DiBiase, W. J. (Eds.), *Developing Teacher Leaders: Professional Development in Science and Mathematics* (pp. 289–307). Columbus, OH: ERIC Publications.

Pugh, S. D., Dietz, J., Brief, A. P., & Wiley, J. W. (2008). Looking inside and out: The impact of employee and community demographic composition on organizational diversity climate. *The Journal of Applied Psychology, 93*, 1422–1428. doi:10.1037/a0012696

Pullins, E. B., & Fine, L. M. (2002). How the performance of mentoring activities affects the mentor's job outcomes. *Journal of Personal Selling & Sales Management, 22*(4), 259–271.

Putler, D. S. (1992). Incorporating reference price effects into a theory of consumer choice. *Marketing Science, 11*(3), 287–309. doi:10.1287/mksc.11.3.287

Quezada, R., & Louque, A. (2002). Developing diverse faculty in culturally proficient education programs. *Multicultural Education, 9*, 10–14.

Rachlin, H. (1990). Why do people gamble and keep gambling despite heavy losses. *Psychological Science, 1*(5), 294–297. doi:10.1111/j.1467-9280.1990.tb00220.x

Ragins, B. R., & Kram, K. E. (2007). *The roots and meaning of mentoring*. Thousand Oaks, CA: Sage.

Ragusa, J. M. (2004, June). Improving integrated project team interaction through virtual (3D) collaboration. *Engineering Management Journal*.

Rainey, M. (2012). The first annual higher education excellence in diversity award. *Insight into Diversity*. Retrieved from http://www.insightintodiversity.com/aarjobs/index.php?option=com_content&view=article&id=39:virginia-state-university&catid=20:aar-closer-look

Rainie, L. (2006). How the internet is changing consumer behavior and expectations. *Pew Internet and American Life Project*. Retrieved from http://www.pewtrusts.org/uploadedFiles/wwwpewtrustsorg/Fact_Sheets/Society_and_the_Internet/PewInternetSOCAP050906.pdf

Rajala, J. (2003). Wireless technology in education. *The Journal*. Retrieved November 10, 2011 from http://thejournal.com/articles/16482

Redden, E. (2007, December 18). More spiritual, but not in church. *Inside Higher Education*. Retrieved from http://www.insidehighered.com/news/2007/12/18/spirituality

Reed, L., & Evans, A. E. (2008). What you see is [not always] what you get! Dispelling race and gender leadership assumptions. *International Journal of Qualitative Studies in Education, 21*(5), 487–499. doi:10.1080/09518390802297797

Reese, A. (2001, August 1). Supplier diversity and e-procurement: Why your initiatives are not at odds. *Supply & Demand Chain Executive*.

Reichers, A. E., & Schneider, B. (1990). Climate and culture: An evolution of constructs. In Schneider, B. (Ed.), *Organizational Climate and Culture* (pp. 5–39). San Francisco, CA: Jossey-Bass.

Reigeluth, C. M. (1999). *Instructional-design theories and models*. London, UK: Routledge.

Reigeluth, C. M., & Garfinkle, R. J. (1994). Envisioning a new system of education. In Reigeluth, C. M., & Garfinkle, R. J. (Eds.), *Systemic Change in Education*. Englewood Cliffs, NJ: Educational Technology Publications.

Reigeluth, C., & Duffy, F. (2008, May). The AECT futureminds initiative: Transforming America's school systems. *Educational Technology*.

Reinhart, W., & Rogoff, J. K. (2009). *This time is different: Eight centuries of financial folly*. Princeton, NJ: Princeton University Press.

Religious Freedom Restoration Act (RFRA) (2006), 42 U.S.C. 2000bb-1.

Relly, J. (2011). Corruption, secrecy, and access-to-information legislation in Africa: A cross-national study of political institutions. *Research in Social Problems and Public Policy, 19*.

Rice, T. W. (2003). Believe it or not: Religious and other paranormal beliefs in the United States. *Journal for the Scientific Study of Religion*, *42*(1), 95–106. doi:10.1111/1468-5906.00163

Richard, O. C. (2000). Racial diversity, business strategy, and firm performance: A resource-based view. *Academy of Management Journal*, *43*(2), 164–177. doi:10.2307/1556374

Richardson, R. C. Jr. (1991). 6 ways universities can maintain quality and diversity. *Education Digest*, *56*(5), 22–25.

Riche, M. F., & Kraus, A. (2009). *Approaches to and tools for successful diversity management: Results from 360-degree diversity management case studies*. CNA searchMemorandum D00203153.A2. Retrieved from http://diversity.defense.gov/Resources/Commission/docs/Business%20Case/Approaches%20To%20and%20Tools%20for%20Successful%20Diversity%20Management.pdf

Rieber, L. P. (1996). Seriously considering play: Designing interactive learning environments based on the blending of microworlds, simulations, and games. *Educational Technology Research and Development*, *44*(2), 43–58. doi:10.1007/BF02300540

Riel, M., & Becker, H. J. (2008). Characteristics of teacher leaders for information and communication technology. In Voogt, J., & Knezek, G. (Eds.), *International Handbook of Information Technology in Primary and Secondary Education* (pp. 397–417). New York, NY: Springer. doi:10.1007/978-0-387-73315-9_24

Ringdal, G. I., & Ringdal, K. (2010). Does religiosity protect against war-related distress? Evidence from Bosnia and Herzegovina. *Politics and Religion*, *3*(2), 389–405. doi:10.1017/S175504831000009X

Rittgers, D. (2007). These dishonored dead: Veteran memorials and religious preferences. *First Amendment Law Review*, *5*, 400–433.

Robinson, J. M. (2011). Leadership makes the difference for EEO and diversity effectiveness. *State Magazine*. Retrieved from http://digitaledition.state.gov/publication/index.php?i=57364&m=&l=&p=11&pre=&ver=swf

Robinson, J. P., Dimaggio, P., & Hargittai, E. (2003). New social survey perspectives on the digital divide. *IT & Society*, *1*(5), 1–22.

Robinson-Neal, A. (2009). Exploring diversity in higher education management: History, trends, and implications for community colleges. *International Journal for Leadership in Learning*, *13*(4). Retrieved from http://iejll.synergiesprairies.ca/iejll/index.php/iejll/article/view/690

Roby, D. (2011). Teacher leaders impacting school culture. *Education*, *131*(4), 782–790.

Roegiers, X. (2007). Curricular reforms guide schools: But, where? *Prospects*, *37*(2), 155–186. doi:10.1007/s11125-007-9024-z

Rogers, E. M. (1995). *Diffusions of innovations*. New York, NY: Collier Macmillan.

Rorty, R. (1989). *Contingency, irony and solidarity*. Cambridge, UK: Cambridge University Press. doi:10.1017/CBO9780511804397

Rosenblatt, L. (2005). The transactional theory of reading and writing. In Rosenblatt, L. (Ed.), *Making Meaning with Texts* (pp. 1–37). Portsmouth, UK: Heinemann.

Rosenzweig, S. A. (1996). Restoring religious freedom to the workplace: Title VII, RFRA, and religious accommodation. *University of Pennsylvania Law Review*, *144*(6), 2513–2536. doi:10.2307/3312675

Ross, J. A., & Gray, P. (2006). Transformational leadership and teacher commitment to organizational values: The mediating effects of collective teacher efficacy. *School Effectiveness and School Improvement*, *17*(2), 179–199. doi:10.1080/09243450600565795

Rost, J. C. (1991). *Leadership for the twenty-first century*. New York, NY: Praeger.

Rudenstine, N. (1996). Why a diverse student body is so important. *The Chronicle of Higher Education*, *42*, B1–B2.

Ryan, K., & Cooper, J. (2010). Those who can, teach. In Ryan, K., & Cooper, J. (Eds.), *Those Who Can, Teach* (pp. 197–234). Boston, MA: Wadsworth Cengage Lerning.

Samover, L. A., & Porter, R. E. (1976). *Intercultural communication: A reader* (2nd ed.). Belmont, CA: Wadsworth Publishing Company.

Sandoval, B. A., & Yuengling, R. (2011). Getting to "ground truth" in the military: Conducing diversity assessments. In D. P. McDonald & K. P. Parks (Eds.), *Managing Diversity in the Military: The Value of Inclusion in a Culture of Uniformity.* Abingdon, UK: Routledge Taylor and Francis Group.

Sarrel, M. D. (2007). Wicked productive wikis. *PC Magazine, 26*(4), 88.

SAS. (2012). *SAS.* Retrieved March 5, 2012, from http://www.sas.com/govedu/edu/curriculum/index.html

Sauer, I., Bialek, D., Efimova, E., Schwartlander, R., Pless, G., & Neuhaus, P. (2005). "Blogs" and "wikis" are valuable software tools for communication within research groups. *Artificial Organs, 29*(1), 82–89. doi:10.1111/j.1525-1594.2004.29005.x

Scandura, T. A. (1992). Mentorship and career mobility: An empirical investigation. *Journal of Organizational Behavior, 13*(2), 169–174. doi:10.1002/job.4030130206

Schecter, S. R., & Cummins, J. (2003). *Multilingual education in practice: Using diversity as a resource.* Portsmouth, UK: Heinemann.

Scherer, M. (2007). Playing to strengths. *Educational Leadership, 65*(1), 7.

Schiffer, S. (2002). A normative theory of meaning. *Philosophy and Phenomenological Research, 65*(1), 186–192. doi:10.1111/j.1933-1592.2002.tb00194.x

Schlechty, P. (2009). *Leading for learning.* San Francisco, CA: Jossey-Bass. doi:10.1002/9781118269497

Schllinger, R. (2011, September 20). Social media and the Arab spring: What have we learned? *The Huffington Post.* Retrieved October 10, 2011 from http://www.huffingtonpost.com/raymond-schillinger/arab-spring-social-media_b_970165.html

Schneider, B. (1975). Organizational climates: An essay. *Personnel Psychology, 28,* 447–479. doi:10.1111/j.1744-6570.1975.tb01386.x

Schneider, B., Gunnarson, S. K., & Niles-Jolly, K. (1994). Creating the climate and culture of success. *Organizational Dynamics, 23*(1), 17–29. doi:10.1016/0090-2616(94)90085-X

Schneider, B., & Reichers, A. E. (1983). On the etiology of climates. *Personnel Psychology, 36,* 19–39. doi:10.1111/j.1744-6570.1983.tb00500.x

Schultz, K. M. (2006). Religion as identity in postwar America: The last serious attempt to put a question on religion in the United States census. *The Journal of American History, 93*(2), 359–384. doi:10.2307/4486234

Schwandt, D. R., & Szabla, D. (2007). Systems leadership: Co evolution or mutual evolution towards complexity? In Hazy, J., Goldstein, J., & Lichtenstein, B. (Eds.), *Complex Systems Leadership Theory* (pp. 35–59). Mansfield, MA: ISCE Publishing.

Scott, J. (2000). *Social network analysis: A handbook.* London, UK: Sage.

Searby, L., & Shaddix, L. (2008). Growing teacher leaders in a culture of excellence. *Professional Educator, 32*(1), 1–6.

Segal, D. R., & Segal, M. W. (2004). America's military population. *Population Bulletin, 59*(4), 3–40.

Segev, E., & Ahituv, N. (2010). Popular searches in Google and Yahoo!: A "digital divide" in information uses? *The Information Society, 26,* 17–37. doi:10.1080/01972240903423477

Selwyn, N. (2003). ICT access for all? Access and use of pubic ICT sites in the UK. *Communicatio Socialis, 6*(3), 350–375.

Sergiovanni, T. (1989). The leadership needed for quality schooling. In Sergiovanni, T., & Moore, J. (Eds.), *Schooling for Tomorrow.* Boston, MA: Allyn and Bacon.

Shane, L., III. (2008, November 12). Military atheists want new rules on prayer. *Stars and Stripes.* Retrieved from http://www.stripes.com/news/military-atheists-want-new-rules-on-prayer-1.85154

Sharlet, J. (2009, May). Jesus killed Mohammed: The crusade for a Christian military. *Harper's Magazine.* Retrieved from http://www.harpers.org/archive/2009/05/0082488

Shay, J. (2002). *Odysseus in America.* New York, NY: Scribner.

Shin, D., Shin, Y., Choo, H., & Beom, K. (2011). Smartphones and smart pedagogical tools: Implications of smartphones as u-learning devices. *Computers in Human Behavior*, *27*(6), 2207–2214. doi:10.1016/j.chb.2011.06.017

Shirky, C. (2011, January/February). The political power of social media. *Foreign Affairs*. Retrieved November 5, 2011, from http://www.foreignaffairs.com/articles/67038/clay-shirky/the-political-power-of-social-media

Siegel, D. J. (2006). Organizational response to the demand and expectation for diversity. *Higher Education*, *52*(3), 465–486. doi:10.1007/s10734-006-0001-x

Singer, M. J., Kring, J. P., & Hamilton, R. M. (2006). *Instructional features for training in virtual environments*. Technical Report A103554. Orlando, FL: Army Research Institute.

Singh, A., & Kaur, H. (2009, January 26). *Re: Captain K. S. Kalsi & Second Lieutenant T. S. Rattan (Sikh health professionals)*. [PDF document]. Letter to Secretary of Defense Robert M. Gates. Retrieved from www.sikhcoalition.org/documents/SikhCoalitionLettertoRobertGates.pdf

SMART. (2012). *SMART*. Retrieved March 5, 2012, from http://smarttech.com/us/Solutions/Higher+Education+Solutions/Products+for+higher+education/Complementary+hardware+products/SMART+Response

Smidt, C. (2005). Religion and American attitudes toward Islam and an invasion of Iraq. *Sociology of Religion*, *66*(3), 243–261. doi:10.2307/4153098

Smith, A. (2010). The internet and campaign 2010. *Pew Internet & American Life Project*. Retrieved November 4, 2011, from http://www.pewinternet.org/Reports/2011/The-Internet-and-Campaign-2010/Summary.aspx

Smith, A. (2010). *Mobile access 2010*. Washington, DC: Pew Internet & American Life Project.

Smith, D. R., & Ayers, D. F. (2006). Culturally responsive pedagogy and online learning: Implications for the globalized community college. *Community College Journal of Research and Practice*, *30*(5/6), 401–415. doi:10.1080/10668920500442125

Smith, L. E. (2008). What's in a name? Scholarship and the pathology of conservative Protestantism. *Method and Theory in the Study of Religion*, *20*(3), 191–211. doi:10.1163/157006808X317446

Smith, M. L., & Roysircar, G. (2010). African American male leaders in counseling: Interviews with five AMCD past presidents. *Journal of Multicultural Counseling and Development*, *38*(4), 242–255. doi:10.1002/j.2161-1912.2010.tb00134.x

Smith, W. J., Howard, J. T., & Harrington, K. V. (2005). Essential formal mentor characteristics and functions in governmental and non-governmental organizations from the program administrator's and the mentor's perspective. *Public Personnel Management*, *34*(1), 31–58.

Solomon, G., & Schrum, L. (2007). *Web 2.0: New tools, new schools*. Eugene, OR: International Society for Technology in Education.

Sorkin, A. R. (2009). *Too big to fail*. New York, NY: Penguin Group.

Sproull, L., & Kiesler, S. (1991). *Connections: New ways of working in the networked organization*. Cambridge, MA: MIT Press.

Steele, J. (2011). Tunisia's clean elections lead the way. *The Guardian*. Retrieved October 25, 2011 from http://www.guardian.co.uk/commentisfree/2011/oct/25/tunisia-election-middle-east?intcmp=239

Steele, C. M. (2010). *Whistling Vivaldi: And other clues to how stereotypes affect us*. New York, NY: W. W. Norton and Company, Inc.

Steensland, B., Park, J. Z., Regnerus, M. D., Robinson, L. D., Wilcox, W. B., & Woodberry, R. D. (2000). The measure of American religion: Toward improving the state of the art. *Social Forces*, *79*(1), 291–318.

Stefani. (2006, May 18). Religion in the military. *Pacifism Blogspot*. Retrieved from http://verbal-pacifism.blogspot.com/2006/05/religion-in-military.html

Steiner, L., & Kowal, L. (2009). *Instructional coaching*. Retrieved April 1, 2012 from http://www.readingrockets.org/article/25980/

Stelter, B. (2011). F.C.C. push to expand net access gains help. *The New York Times*. Retrieved November 9, 2011 from http://www.nytimes.com/2011/11/09/business/media/fcc-and-cable-companies-push-to-close-digital-divide.html

Sterling, R. V. (2011). The effect of metacognitive strategy instruction on student achievement in a hybrid developmental English course. *University of South Alabama*. Retrieved from http://ezproxy.pvamu.edu/login?url=http://search.proquest.com/docview/868853212?accountid=7062

Stevens, F. G., Plaut, V. C., & Sanchez-Burke, J. (2008). Unlocking the benefits of diversity: All-inclusive multiculturalism and positive organizational change. *The Journal of Applied Behavioral Science*, *44*, 116–133. doi:10.1177/0021886308314460

Stevens-Roseman, E. S. (2009). Older mentors for newer workers: Impact of a worker-driven intervention on later life satisfaction. *Journal of Workplace Behavioral Health*, *24*(4). doi:10.1080/15555240903358652

Steyaert, J. (2000). *Digital skills: Literacy in the information society*. The Hague, The Netherlands: Rathenau Instituut.

Stogdill, R. M. (1950). Leadership, membership, and organization. *Psychological Bulletin*, *47*(1), 1–14. doi:10.1037/h0053857

Study Island. (2012). *Study island*. Retrieved March 5, 2012, from http://www.studyisland.com/

Subban, P. (2006). Differentiated instruction: A research basis. *International Education Journal*, *7*(7), 935–947.

Sugarman, L. (1985). Kolb's model of experiential learning: Touchstone for trainers, students, counselors, and clients. *Journal of Counseling and Development*, *64*(4), 264–268. doi:10.1002/j.1556-6676.1985.tb01097.x

Sullo, B. (2004). *Activating the desire to learn*. Alexandria, VA: Association for Supervision and Curriculum Development.

Surin, J. A. (2010). Occupying the internet: Responding to the shifting power balance. *The Round Table*, *99*(407), 195–209. doi:10.1080/00358531003656388

Suzuki, D., & McConnell, A. (1997). *The sacred balance: Rediscovering our place in nature*. Vancouver, Canada: Greystone Books.

Szekely, L., & Nagy, A. (2011). Online youth work and eYouth - A guide to the world of digital natives. *Children and Youth Services Review*, *33*(11), 2186–2197. doi:10.1016/j.childyouth.2011.07.002

Sztajn, P., Marrongelle, K., & Smith, P. (2011). *Supporting implementation of the common core state standards for mathematics*. Raleigh, NC: William & Ida Friday Institue.

Tamin, R., Bernard, R., Borokhovski, E., Abrami, P., & Schmid, R. (2011). What forty years of research says about the impact of technology on learning: A second-order meta-analysis and validation study. *Review of Educational Research*, *81*, 4-28. Retrieved October 12, 2011 from http://rer.sagepub.com/cgi/content/long/81/1/4

Tatum, B. D. (1992). Talking about race, learning about racism: The application of racial identity development theory in the classroom. *Harvard Educational Review*, *62*(1), 1–24.

Tatum, B. D. (1997). *Why are all the black kids sitting together in the cafeteria? And other conversations about race*. New York, NY: Basic Books.

Tatum, B. D. (2002). Choosing to be black: The ultimate white privilege? In Singley, B. (Ed.), *When Race becomes Real: Black and White Writers confront their Personal Histories* (pp. 215–224). Chicago, IL: Lawrence Hill Books.

Taylor, K. (2011). Arab spring was really a social media revolution. *TG Daily*. Retrieved October 12, 2011 from http://www.tgdaily.com/software-features/58426-arab-spring-really-was-social-media-revolution

Taylor, P., & Cohn, D. (2012). A milestone en route to a majority minority nation. *Report of Pew Social & Demographic Trends*. Retrieved from http://www.pewsocialtrends.org/2012/11/07/a-milestone-en-route-to-a-majority-minority-nation/

Teacher Leadership Exploratory Consortium. (2010). *Model teacher leader standards*. Retrieved December 13, 2011, from http://tlstandards.weebly.com/index.html

Teachertube. (2012). *Teachertube*. Retrieved March 2012, from http://www.teachertube.com

Teo, T., & Lai, K. (2009). Usage and performance impact of electronic procurement. *Journal of Business Logistics*, *30*(2), 125–139. doi:10.1002/j.2158-1592.2009.tb00115.x

Tesh, G., & Archer, C. M. (2012). *Culture bump guides: Culture bump kids*. Retrieved from http://textesoliv.org/culture-bump-guides-culture-bump-kids/

Tessmer, M., & Wedman, J. F. (1990). A layers-of-necessity instructional development model. *Educational Technology Research and Development*, *38*(2), 77–85. doi:10.1007/BF02298271

Texas Instruments. (2011). *Education technology*. Retrieved March 5, 2012, from http://education.ti.com/educationportal/sites/US/productDetail/us_cbl_2.html

Thaler, R. (1980). Toward a positive theory of consumer choice. *Journal of Economic Behavior & Organization*, *1*(1), 39–60. doi:10.1016/0167-2681(80)90051-7

Thatcher, J. B., & Perrewe, P. L. (2002). An empirical examination of individual traits as antecedents to computer anxiety and computer self-efficacy. *Management Information Systems Quarterly*, *26*(4), 381–396. doi:10.2307/4132314

Thiederman, S. (2003). *Making diversity work: Seven steps for defeating bias in the workplace*. Chicago, IL: Dearborn Publishing Co.

Thomas, D. A., & Ely, R. J. (2007). Making differences matter. In *The Jossey-Bass Reader on Educational Leadership* (2nd ed.). San Francisco, CA: Jossey-Bass.

Thomas, D. C., & Inkson, K. (2003). Does your CQ measure up? In Thomas, D. C., & Inkson, K. (Eds.), *Cultural Intelligence: People Skills for Global Business*. New York, NY: Berrett-Koehler Publishers.

Thomas, K. M. (2005). *Diversity dynamics in the workplace*. Belmont, CA: Thomson Wadsworth.

Thomas, K. M., Mack, D. A., & Montagliani, A. (2004). The arguments against diversity: Are they valid? In Stockdale, M. S., & Crosby, F. J. (Eds.), *The Psychology and Management of Workplace Diversity* (pp. 31–52). Malden, MA: Blackwell.

Thomas, R. (1999). *Building a house for diversity: A fable about a giraffe & an elephant offers new strategies for today's workforce*. New York, NY: AMACOM.

Thomas, R. (2001). *Harvard business review on managing diversity*. Boston, MA: Harvard Business School Publishing. doi:10.1007/978-3-322-84445-3

Thomas, R. R. (1996). *Redefining diversity*. New York, NY: American Management Association.

Thompson-Klein, J. (2010). *Creating interdisciplinary campus cultures: A model for strength and sustainability*. San Francisco, CA: Jossey-Bass.

Time Magazine. (2009). *The future of work*. Retrieved November 10, 2011 from http://www.time.com/time/covers/0,16641,20090525,00.html

Tomlinson, C., Brighton, C., Hertberg, H., Callahan, C. M., Moon, T. R., Brimijoin, K., & Reynolds, T. (2003). Differentiating instruction in response to student readiness, interest, and learning profile in academically diverse classrooms: A review of literature. *Journal for the Education of the Gifted*, *27*(2-3), 119–145.

Tomlinson, S. (1997). Edward Lee Thorndike and John Dewey on the science of education. *Oxford Review of Education*, *23*(3), 365–383. doi:10.1080/0305498970230307

Trepel, C., Fox, C. R., & Poldrack, R. A. (2005). Prospect theory on the brain? Toward a cognitive neuroscience of decision under risk. *Brain Research. Cognitive Brain Research*, *23*(1), 34–50. doi:10.1016/j.cogbrainres.2005.01.016

Tripp, S., & Bichelmeyer, B. (1990). Rapid prototyping: An alternative instructional design strategy. *Educational Technology Research and Development*, *38*(1), 31–44. doi:10.1007/BF02298246

Tuggle, C. S., Sirmon, D. G., Reutzel, C., & Bierman, L. (2010). Commanding board of director attention: Investigating how organizational performance and CEO duality affect board members' attention to monitoring. *Strategic Management Journal*, *31*, 946–968.

Tversky, A., & Kahneman, D. (1992). Advances in prospect theory: Cumulative representation of uncertainty. *Journal of Risk and Uncertainty*, *5*, 297–323. doi:10.1007/BF00122574

Tyler, C. (2010). *Australian internet censorship: Necessary evil or nanny state gone mad?* Retrieved November 7, 2011, from http://www.associatedcontent.com/article/2749033/australian_internet_censorship.html?cat=25

Tyler, J., & Pillers, R. (2011). Unsustainability in today's international development. *USA Today Magazine, 139*(I2788), 26-28.

U.S. Census Bureau. (2010). *U.S. census bureau, current population survey: Computer and internet use.* Washington, DC: U.S. Department of Commerce.

U.S. Department of Commerce. (2006). *A nation online: Entering the broadband age.* Retrieved November 2, 2011, from http://www.ntia.doc.gov/reports/anol/NationOnlineBroadband04.pdf

UCLA. (2003). *The UCLA internet report: Surveying the digital future, year three.* Los Angeles, CA: University of California.

Uhl-Bein, M., Marion, R., & McElvey, B. (2007). Complexity leadership theory: Shifting leadership from the industrial age to the knowledge era. *The Leadership Quarterly, 18*(4), 298–318. doi:10.1016/j.leaqua.2007.04.002

Ulrich, D., & Smallwood, N. (2012). What is Leadership? In Mobley, W. H., Wang, Y., & Li, M. (Eds.), *Advances in Global Leadership* (pp. 9–36). London, UK: Emerald Group Publishing Limited. doi:10.1108/S1535-1203(2012)0000007005

United Nations. (2004). *Report of United Nations populations division.* Retrieved from http://www.un.org/esa/population/publications/longrange2/WorldPop2300final.pdf

United States Census Bureau. (2010). Educational attainment in the United States: 2009. *Statistical Abstract of the United States.* Retrieved from http://www.census.gov/population/www/socdemo/education/cps2009.html

United States Government Accountability Office. (2005). *Report to the ranking minority member, committee on homeland security and government affairs, U.S. senate.* Retrieved from http://www.gao.gov/new.items/d0590.pdf

Vajoczki, S., Watt, S., Marquis, N., Liao, R., & Vine, M. (2011). Students approach to learning and their use of lecture capture. *Journal of Educational Multimedia and Hypermedia, 20*(2), 195–214.

van Dijk, J., & Hacker, K. (2000). *The digital divide as a complex and dynamic phenomenon.* Paper presented at the International Communication Association. Acapulco, Mexico.

van Dijk, J. (1999). *The network society, social aspects of new media.* Thousand Oaks, CA: Sage.

van Dijk, J. (2006). Digital divide research, achievements and shortcomings. *Poetics, 34,* 221–235. doi:10.1016/j.poetic.2006.05.004

van Knippenberg, D., De Dreu, C. K. W., & Homan, A. C. (2004). Work group diversity and group performance: An integrative model and research agenda. *The Journal of Applied Psychology, 89*(6), 1008–1022. doi:10.1037/0021-9010.89.6.1008

van Knippenberg, D., Haslam, S. A., & Platow, J. (2007). Unity through diversity: Value in diversity beliefs, work group diversity, and group identification. *Group Dynamics, 11*(3), 207–222. doi:10.1037/1089-2699.11.3.207

Van Knippenberg, D., & Schippers, M. C. (2007). Work group diversity. *Annual Review of Psychology, 58,* 1–27. doi:10.1146/annurev.psych.58.110405.085546

Vara, V. (2006). *Offices co-op consumer web tools like "wikis" and social networking.* Retrieved October 17, 2011, from http://online.wsj.com/article/SB115802778487360244.html

Vehovar, V., Sicherl, P., Husing, T., & Dolnicar, V. (2006). Methodological challenges of digital divide measurements. *The Information Society, 22,* 279–290. doi:10.1080/01972240600904076

Venkatesh, V., & Davis, F. D. (2000). A theoretical extension of the technology acceptance model: Four longitudinal field studies. *Management Science, 46,* 186–204. doi:10.1287/mnsc.46.2.186.11926

Venkatesh, V., & Goyal, S. (2010). Expectation disconfirmation and technology adoption: Polynomial modeling and response surface analysis. *Management Information Systems Quarterly, 34*(2), 281–303.

Verkamp, B. J. (1988). The moral treatment of warriors in the early middle ages. *The Journal of Religious Ethics, 16*(2), 223–249.

von Bertalanffy, L. (1969). *General system theory.* New York, NY: George Braziller.

Wald, J. (Producer). (2011, November 10). *Piers Morgan Tonight* [Television broadcast]. Los Angeles, CA: Cable News Network. Retrieved from http://piersmorgan.blogs.cnn.com/2011/11/10/gen-colin-powells-advice-for-america-i-think-our-system-needs-to-take-a-deep-breath/

Wald, K. D., Owen, D. E., & Hill, S. S. (1989). Habits of the mind? The problem of authority in the new Christian right. In Jelen, T. G. (Ed.), *Religion and Political Behavior in the United States* (pp. 93–108). New York, NY: Praeger.

Waldrop, M. (1992). *Complexity*. New York, NY: Simon and Schuster.

Wallsten, S. (2009). *Understanding international broadband comparisons*. Washington, DC: Technology Policy Institute.

Wang, H., & Hong, Y. (2009). China: Technology development and management in the context of economic reform and opening. *Journal of Technology Management in China*, *4*(1), 4–25. doi:10.1108/17468770910942816

Warschauer, M., & Matuchniak, T. (2010). New technology and digital worlds: Analyzing evidence of equity in access, use, and outcomes. *Review of Research in Education*, *34*(1), 179–225. doi:10.3102/0091732X09349791

Waters, J. K. (2009). The kids are all right. *The Journal*, *36*(3), 38–42.

Watras, J. (2009). Academic studies, science, and democracy: Conceptions of subject matter from Harris to Thorndike. *Philosophical Studies in Education*, *40*, 113–124.

Wattal, S., Hong, Y., Mandviwalla, M., & Jain, A. (2011). *Technology diffusion in the society: Analyzing digital divide in the context of social class*. Paper presented at the Hawaii International Conference on System Sciences. Maui, HI.

Whittaker, Z. (2011). London's met police uses 'blanket tracking system' to intercept, remotely shut down mobile phones. *ZDNet.com*. Retrieved November 2, 2011, from http://www.zdnet.com/blog/london/londons-met-police-uses-8216blanket-tracking-system-to-intercept-remotely-shut-down-mobile-phones/422?tag=search-results-rivers;item1

Wiengarten, F., Fynes, B., Humphreys, P., Chavez, R., & McKittrick, A. (2011). Assessing the value creation process of e-business along the supply chain. *Supply Chain Management. International Journal (Toronto, Ont.)*, *16*(4), 207–219.

Wiki Introduced, A. L. S. C. (2007). ALSC wiki introduced. *American Libraries*, *38*(2), 11.

Wilcox, C., & Jelen, T. (1990). Evangelicals and political tolerance. *American Politics Research*, *18*(1), 25–46. doi:10.1177/1532673X9001800102

Williams, D. A., & Wade-Golden, K. C. (2008). The complex mandate of a chief diversity officer. *The Chronicle of Higher Education*, *55*(5), B44.

Williams, R., Karousou, R., & Mackness, J. (2011). Emergent learning and learning ecologies in web 2.0. *International Review of Research in Open and Distance Learning*, *12*(3), 39–59.

Willower, D. J., & Forsythe, B. (1999). A brief history of scholarship on educational administration. In Murphy, J., & Louis, K. (Eds.), *Handbook of Research on Educational Administration* (pp. 1–25). San Francisco, CA: Jossey-Bass.

Wilson, T. (2004). *Strangers to ourselves*. Boston, MA: Harvard University Press.

Windley, P. J. (2007). Capitalize on emerging collaboration options. *InfoWorld*, *29*, 26.

Wisner, J., Tan, K., & Leong, G. (2012). *Principles of supply chain management: A balanced approach* (3rd ed.). Mason, OH: South-Western/Cengage Learning.

Wood, S. (2010). Technology for teaching and learning: Moodle as a tool for higher education. *International Journal of Teaching and Learning in Higher Education*, *22*(3), 299–307.

Worden, S. (2005). Religion in strategic leadership: A positivistic, normative/theological, and strategic analysis. *Journal of Business Ethics*, *57*(3), 221–239. doi:10.1007/s10551-004-6943-y

Worthington, I. (2009). Corporate perceptions of the business case for supplier diversity: How socially responsible purchasing can pay. *Journal of Business Ethics*, *90*, 47–60. doi:10.1007/s10551-008-0025-5

Worthington, I., Ram, M., Boyal, H., & Shah, M. (2008). Researching the drivers of socially responsible purchasing: A cross-national study of supplier diversity initiatives. *Journal of Business Ethics*, *79*, 319–331. doi:10.1007/s10551-007-9400-x

Wuthnow, R., & Hackett, C. (2003). The social integration of practitioners of non-western religions in the United States. *Journal for the Scientific Study of Religion*, *42*(4), 651–667. doi:10.1046/j.1468-5906.2003.00209.x

Yager, M., Ruark, G., & Metcalf, K. (2010). *A comparison of instructor-led and computer-based delivery methods for a curriculum to interpret nonverbal behavior in cross-cultural interactions*. White Paper. Unpublished.

Yagil, D., & Luria, G. (2010). Friends in need: The protective effect of social relationships under low-safety climate. *Group & Organization Management*, *35*, 727–750. doi:10.1177/1059601110390936

Yammer.com. (2011). *Website*. Retrieved December 13, 2011 from https://www.yammer.com/

Yang, J., Chen, C., & Jeng, M. (2010). Integrating video-capture virtual reality technology into a physically interactive learning environment for English learning. *Computers & Education*, *55*(3), 1346–1356. doi:10.1016/j.compedu.2010.06.005

Yee, N. (2006). The labor of fun: How video games blur the boundaries of work and play. *Games and Culture*, *1*(1), 68–71. doi:10.1177/1555412005281819

Yong, A. (2007). The future of evangelical theology: Asian and Asian American interrogations. *Asia Journal of Theology*, *21*(2), 371–397.

Young, D. (2001, Winter). Categorizing corporate web-based supplier diversity initiatives. *Journal of Computer Information Systems*, 57–68.

Young, P. A. (2008). Integrating culture in the design of ICTs. *British Journal of Educational Technology*, *39*(1), 6–17.

Youtube. (2012). *Youtube*. Retrieved March 5, 2012, from http://www.youtube.com

Yuengling, R. (2002). *The 2003 annual: Consulting*. New York, NY: Wiley.

Yunus Center. (2012). *The Muhammad Yunus center*. Retrieved from http://www.muhammadyunus.org

Yu, P. (2001). Bridging the digital divide: Equality in the information age. *Cardoza & Entertainment*, *20*(1), 1–52.

Zellers, D. F., Howard, V. M., & Barcic, M. A. (2008). Faculty mentoring programs: Envisioning rather than reinventing the wheel. *Review of Educational Research*, *78*(3), 552–588. doi:10.3102/0034654308320966

Zickuhr, K. (2010). [*Major trends in online activities*. Washington, DC: Pew Internet & American Life Project.]. *Generations (San Francisco, Calif.)*, 2010.

Zuboff, S. (1988). *In the age of the smart machine*. New York, NY: Basic Books.

About the Contributors

Joél Lewis received a Bachelor of Science in Human Resource Management, Master of Science and Ph.D. in Instructional Design and Development from the University of South Alabama. Joél is currently an Associate Professor at the University of South Alabama, College of Education in Instructional Design and Development. She is a Co-Director of the Center for Design and Performance Improvement, Co-Chair of the College of Education Diversity Committee, and is sponsor of the IDD Graduate Student Association. She has received awards such as the Lisa Mitchell Bukstein Foundation Scholarship for Developing Faculty in Education, Pillans Middle School Leadership and Service Award, Mortar Board: National College Senior Honor Society Top Professor Award, Leadership Alabama Initiative Participant, and Mobile Bay Monthly's Forty under Forty Inaugural Class. Her research interests include diversity, leadership development, and technology integration.

André Green, an Associate Professor of Science Education in the College of Education at the University of South Alabama, earned his B.S. and M.S. degrees in Chemistry from Alabama State University (1995) and Hampton University (1998), respectively, and an Ed.S (2001) and Ph.D. (2006) in Science Education from Virginia Tech. Dr. Green also holds an appointment in the Department of Chemistry at USA. He is an experienced Principal Investigator with who has received approximately $5M in grants management from the National Science Foundation (#09344829 and #1135621), Alabama State Department of Education, and various foundations and other governmental agencies since his arrival at the university in 2006. His research interests focus on minority access to the STEM disciplines, the training of STEM teachers, STEM teacher leadership, mentoring, and the induction of educators into the profession. He has extensive experience in working with minority students from urban environments and has developed educational programs of community outreach to improve the academic achievement of economically challenged students.

Daniel Surry is a Professor in the Instructional Design and Development program at the University of South Alabama in Mobile, Alabama. He teaches courses in Instructional Design, Performance Technology, Educational Psychology, and Educational Research. He has also been on the faculty at the University of Southern Mississippi and the University of Alabama and served as Instructional Technologist at California State University, Fresno. He holds a Doctor of Education in Instructional Technology from the University of Georgia, a Master's of Science in Instructional Design from the University of South Alabama, and a Bachelor's of Arts in Mass Communication from the University of Alabama. His research and consulting interests focus on how technology, organizations, and social systems influence each other. He currently serves as the Editor-in-Chief of the journal *TechTrends* and was previously the North American Corresponding Editor for the *British Journal of Educational Technology*. He has written numerous articles and book chapters and presented his research at local, regional, national, and international conferences.

* * *

Carol M. Archer is the creator of the Culture Bump communication system (theory, methodology, and approach). For the past 32 years, Dr. Archer has taught ESL and cross-culture communication at the Language and Culture Center at the University of Houston. Dr. Archer has consulted with multi-national corporations, universities, and governments worldwide. Dr. Archer has conducted extensive ethnographic research into inter-personal, intercultural communication, resulting in publications and video productions.

Dorothy Guy Bonvillain, Educator, Business Coach, Consultant, and Facilitator, earned a PhD in Educational Administration and International Education from American University in Washington, DC. A writer, speaker, and facilitator, she specializes in transformational leadership, personal growth and development, and Cross-Cultural Competence (3C). Her experience crosses a global spectrum—from high school principal in Arizona to leading an international research team as Special Consultant to the Minister of Education in the Sultanate of Oman. She managed programs in Washington, DC, for the Royal Embassy of Saudi Arabia, the National Council on US-Arab Relations, and lectured at Foreign Service Institute. Before co-founding LBL Consultants, she was trainer/curriculum developer for General Dynamics Information Technology and Chief of Partnership for the TRADOC Culture Center, U.S. Army. Her published works include *Traditional Handicrafts of Oman* as well as several published articles in professional journals.

Butler Cain is an Assistant Professor in the Department of Communication at West Texas A&M University and advises the student newspaper. He received his Ph.D. in Media History from The University of Alabama. Before coming to WTAMU, Butler spent a decade as News Director of Alabama Public Radio in Tuscaloosa, Alabama. He then moved to South Korea, where he taught English language writing and literary analysis. Butler is a member of the Society of Professional Journalists and serves on SPJ's Journalism Education and International Journalism committees. He is also a founding member of SPJ's Texas Panhandle Professional chapter.

Lemuria Carter is an Assistant Professor at North Carolina Agricultural and Technical State University. Her research interests include technology adoption, e-government, and online trust. She has published in several top-tier information journals, including the *Journal of Strategic Information Systems, Information Systems Journal, Communications of the ACM*, and *Information Systems Frontiers*. She has served as track and mini-track chair for the Americas Conference on Information Systems and the Hawaii International Conference on System Sciences. In addition, Dr. Carter's initial study on e-government adoption published in *Information Systems Journal* (ISJ) in 2005 is one of the most cited papers on the topic, with more than 263 Google citations and 75 ISJ citations. It was reported as the most cited paper in the history of ISJ as of January 2008 (in 2009 the journal stopped reporting this information).

S. Raj Chaudhury joined the Biggio Center at Auburn University as Associate Director in February 2009. His interests are in the Scholarship of Teaching and Learning and the application of advanced learning technologies in the teaching of science. He holds a B.A. in Physics from Vassar College and received both his M.S. and his Ph.D., also in Physics, from the University of California, Los Angeles.

Elizabeth Culhane, PhD, is the Senior Research Psychologist at DEOMI for the Dr. Richard Oliver Hope Research Center for Human Relations. Dr. Culhane received her PhD and M.S. degree in Industrial/Organizational Psychology from Florida Institute of Technology and her B.S. degree in Psychology from the University of Toledo. Dr. Culhane primarily works in simulation and technology at DEOMI and focuses her research efforts on equal opportunity, employment equal opportunity, training, and cross-cultural competence.

Peter M. Eley is an Assistant Professor of Mathematics Education at Fayetteville State University (FSU) with a specialty in middle school mathematics. Prior to joining the faculty at FSU, Dr. Eley worked at Winston-Salem State University and Saint Augustine's College. He holds North Carolina teacher certifications in middle grades and high school mathematics and taught public school at Eaton Johnson Middle (Henderson, NC) and South Granville High (Creedmoor, NC). Dr. Eley holds 4 degrees, a Bachelor's of Science in Pure Math (Elizabeth City State University), Master's of Science in Applied Math, Master's of Science in Math Education, and Doctorate of Philosophy in Math Education (North Carolina State University). Dr. Eley's current research interests are in equity/policy and using technology to teach mathematics. He is currently conducting research projects that provide professional development utilizing the Common Core Standards. In these workshops teachers learn how to utilizing real world problems to engage students. He can be reached at http://www.drpeterEley.com and via Twitter @drpetereley.

Kathy Evans is an Associate Professor and Program Coordinator of the Counselor Education Program at the University of South Carolina. She teaches for both the entry level and doctoral level counseling degree programs where she emphasizes the acquisition of social justice skills and multicultural competence in counseling and supervision. She has held numerous leadership positions at the local, regional, and national levels. Dr. Evans' research interests and presentations focus on multicultural, career, and feminist issues. She has authored/co-authored four books, the latest of which is *Experiential Approach for Developing Multicultural Competence.*

David Russell Faulkner was born in Baton Rouge, Louisiana, but spent most of his life in the Mobile, Alabama, area. After graduating from W.P. Davidson High School in Mobile, he completed a B.S. in Biology at the University of Mobile and a M.S. in Zoology from the University of Southern Mississippi. While running a diagnostic lab the University of South Alabama (USA), he earned an M.S. in Instructional Design. While at USA, he taught Media at the University of Mobile, and then moved to serve as a Media Specialist and Instructor at Mary Holmes College in West Point, Mississippi. After a semester-long visit to the doctoral program at the University of Alabama, David entered the doctoral program in Instructional Design and Development (ID&D) at the University of South Alabama, completing his Ph.D. in 1999. In 1998, while working on his dissertation, David began work as an instructional systems designer at Lockheed Martin in Pensacola. Since then, he has worked for several notable organizations, the most recent being JHT, Inc. David has been a Designer, Evaluator, Analyst, Program/Project Manager, and Consultant. He is also an accomplished violinist, fiddler, guitarist, mandolinist, and composer.

Mike Guest is currently the Chief Research Scientist for the Dr. Richard O. Hope Human Relations Research Center at the Defense Equal Opportunity Management Institute. Dr. Guest received a Ph.D. in Applied Experimental and Human Factors Psychology from the University of Central Florida in Orlando. Additionally, he holds a M.A. degree in Experimental Psychology (Human Factors) from the University of Alabama in Huntsville, and a B.S. degree in Psychology from Auburn University at Montgomery. He has previously worked at the Army Research Institute, investigating virtual reality training applications and cognitive modeling for simulated environments. Dr. Guest has an extensive user research and usability engineering background, including positions with companies such as Microsoft, IBM, Siebel, and eBay/PayPal. More recently, Dr. Guest was a Research Psychologist at the Naval Aerospace Medical Research Lab in Pensacola, FL, focusing on selection and training program development for Unmanned Aircraft Systems (UAS).

Michelle Hale holds an MS in human environmental sciences, interactive technology emphasis, and is an adjunct instructor with the University of Alabama, College of Human Environmental Sciences Programs. She is currently pursuing her PhD in instructional leadership, instructional technology emphasis, at the University of Alabama. Ms. Hale's research interests include all facets of cognition as it relates to computer-mediated learning, distance/asynchronous learning, generational differences in the use of technology, as well as social media as an element of a classroom or business plan. Ms. Hale serves as consultant to various businesses and schools, providing guidance and direction toward integrating technology into their existing educational, communication, and marketing plans.

Charlotte Hunter, a retired Navy veteran, serves as a Senior Research Analyst with the Defense Equal Opportunity Management Institute (DEOMI), where she studies cultural issues within the Department of Defense, with particular attention given to policy issues regarding religious accommodation and discrimination in the military and federal workplaces.

Andrea M. Kent is an Associate Professor of Literacy Education in the Department of Leadership and Teacher Education, and the Director of Field Services in the College of Education at the University of South Alabama. As a former elementary education teacher and reading coach, she enjoys working with preservice and inservice teachers, mentoring and developing best practices in teaching. She is an experienced staff developer with the Alabama State Department of Education, and local school districts. She spends much of her time in schools, recognizing that they are her laboratories. Her research interests include literacy development in all content areas, teacher leadership, mentoring and induction, and meaningful technology integration.

Eugene G. Kowch is an Associate Professor of education in the leadership and technology group at the University of Calgary. His interdisciplinary professional work includes senior level experience as a corporate development engineer for major international energy companies, K-12 teaching and principalships, and service as the deputy superintendent of a school district. With a Doctorate in Educational Administration (Policy), Dr. Kowch and his graduate students research organization, leader, and system development for the knowledge era by considering the people, institutions, and macro environments who work to lead technologically engaged organizations. He advises several university and public corporate boards and editorial boards, including the *British Journal of Educational Technology*, the *European Society for Systemic Innovation*, the *Canadian Journal of Learning and Technology*, and the *Canadian Journal of Educational Policy*. He has published over 100 articles on education policy, leadership, change, and innovation around the world.

Susan Ferguson Martin is Assistant Professor of Education at the University of South Alabama in Mobile, Alabama, where she is the advisor for English Education, English as a Second Language Education, and Foreign Language Education. She also teaches basic grammar and oral communication skills to international undergraduate and graduate students. Dr. Ferguson's graduate program in ESOL education is fully online, serving students across the United States and in multiple countries. Her focus is in training content area classroom teachers and preservice teachers to better serve the needs of English language learners, as well as preparing educators for teaching English abroad.

Daniel P. McDonald is the Executive Director of Research, Development, and Strategic Initiatives for the Defense Equal Opportunity Management Institute (DEOMI). Under his leadership, the research and development functions at DEOMI have expanded tremendously in depth and scope, which now include vital work in the areas of cultural capabilities, diversity management, and strategic planning. He has authored over one hundred reports, articles, or book chapters that examine equal opportunity, diversity, human, team, or organizational performance topics. He has worked nearly 20 years in support of the U.S. DoD, including being Research Fellow for the Army Research Institute, a Research Psychologist for the Naval Aviation Enterprise, and in his current capacity as a Senior Social Scientist at DEOMI in support of the U.S. Office of the Secretary of Defense.

Anna C. McFadden is a partner in emTech Consulting and holds the position of Associate Professor at the University of Alabama, College of Human Environmental Science, in the Institute for Interactive Technology. Dr. McFadden's research areas include the use of mobile technologies, online media, evaluation of student appliances, and faculty integration of technology in higher education. She has co-authored textbooks, chapters in textbooks, and numerous articles for professional journals, including a recent chapter on podcasting and RSS, appearing in *The Handbook on Research on Computer-Mediated Communications*. She has also served as a consultant for The U.S. Department of State, Office of Overseas Schools, the U.N., and a range of other international organizations, working extensively overseas since 1980. She was nominated as part of a for the 2010 Blackmon-Moody Outstanding Professor Award.

William Gary McGuire is currently employed as a Department of Air Force Civilian working at the Defense Equal Opportunity Management Institute (DEOMI) as the Deputy Dean of Education and Training. Dr McGuire was born in Mobile, Alabama, and after graduating from C.F. Vigor High School, he joined the Army, retiring after 29 years of service. He is a graduate of the University of South Alabama (Undergraduate), SD Bishop State (HBCU), the University of Maryland (Masters Degree in Clinical Psychology with emphasis on Child Behavior), and the University of Florida in Gainesville, Florida (PhD in Clinical Psychology). Since joining the Civil Service, he has been a Senior Fellow, Researcher, and Educator representing the Department of Defense on several working groups including the Comprehensive Review Working Group (CRWG) and the Repeal Implementation Team (RIT) on the removal of Public Law 10-654 to change the Don't Ask, Don't Tell, Don't Harass, Don't Pursue to open service to the country for all. Dr. McGuire has published several papers and book chapters on such topics as: "Cultural DNA: A Metaphoric discussion on American Culture," a chapter titled "Diversity 2K10 and Beyond," and a guide book on *EO Language for Senior Leaders*.

Juanita McMath holds an MA in Higher Education Administration and is a Faculty Instructor with the University of Alabama, College of Human Environmental Sciences Programs. Her areas of research are computer-mediated learning communities and cultural diversity addressed by technology. In 2008, she won the Outstanding New Advisor Award from the National Academic Advising Association. She serves on the Public Relations Committee and Student Affairs Committee for the college.

Porche Millington is a full-time student studying Economics at North Carolina Agricultural and Technical State University in Greensboro, North Carolina. Her expected graduation date is May 2012. Ms. Millington works closely with Dr. Lemuria Carter as a Student Research Assistant. Her research interests include Information Technology (IT) in improving healthcare and government services. She has published in the *Journal of Organizational and End User Computing*. She is a novice to research but looks forward to her continuing growth and future research.

Felicia Mokuolu is a Doctoral student in Industrial/Organizational Psychology, at Florida Institute of Technology in Melbourne, Florida. In addition to her role as a Graduate Research Fellow at the Defense Equal Opportunity Management Institute (DEOMI) at Patrick Air Force Base, Ms. Mokuolu serves as a Senior Consultant at Worthings Consulting in Melbourne, Florida. She partners with a variety of clients in non-profit, government, and the private sector to achieve multi-level business goals. As a Graduate Research Fellow at DEOMI, her research predominantly lies within the areas of Cross-Cultural Competence (3C), Equal Opportunity (EO), and emotions in organizations. In the capacity of Compensation Consultant for Sacred Heart Health Systems in Pensacola, FL, she partnered with senior managers, and top management executives, to test and implement a broad range of system-wide organizational development and change initiatives. She possesses considerable expertise in the areas of training, executive coaching, talent management, and organizational development. Ms. Mokuolu holds a Masters degree in Industrial/Organizational Psychology from the University of Oklahoma, in Norman, Oklahoma. She graduated magna cum laude from Georgia State University, in Atlanta, Georgia, with Advanced Honors in Psychology and a minor in Biology.

Mark Mouck completed a Bachelor of Arts in English Literature and a Bachelor of Science in Education at Ohio University. He completed a Masters degree at Endicott College in 2012 and was honored to be the commencement speaker at graduation. He has been teaching high school literature, speech, debate, and theater for 14 years. He has taught on the west side of Chicago, where he was awarded the Phi Beta Kappa Chicago Debate League Coach of the Year; at an international school in Warsaw, where he taught International Baccalaureate English and International Baccalaureate Theatre; and at an international school in Tunis, where he learned about revolutions first hand and now teaches the Humanities to 8th graders. He swam in a Tsunami in Thailand, hiked the Tatra Mountains of Europe, and took a motorcycle across the U.S. as well as the Alps.

Stacey C. Nickson is the Assistant Director of the Biggio Center at Auburn University and Founder of their Cultural Insight Program. Dr. Nickson's recent publications reflect her research interests, including human communication systems and global initiatives to prepare future academics. Dr. Nickson is a graduate of Indiana University Bloomington and earned a Doctorate from the University of Southern California in Los Angeles.

Catherine Packer-Williams is an Assistant Professor in the Counselor Education Program in the Department of Professional Studies in the College of Education and an Affiliate Professor in the Psychology Department in the College of Arts and Sciences at the University of South Alabama. She teaches and supervises students in the Professional School Counseling and Clinical Mental Health Counseling Master's Programs and the Clinical/Counseling Psychology Doctoral Program. Dr. Packer-Williams' scholarly activities focus on the intersections of race, gender, education, and counseling/counseling psychology. She has contributed to the growing body of literature that better illuminates the experiences of African American women in the academy, particularly in regards to mentoring, professional identity, and psychological well-being.

Kizzy M. Parks is President of K. Parks Consulting, Inc., an 8(a) Certified woman-minority owned/operated small business providing full-service analytics and metrics services, recruiting, training and development, and workforce consulting. The firm is a Minority Business Enterprise registered with the State of Florida specializing in helping organizations create a high-performance workforce, providing customized business solutions based upon business management principles as well as practical knowledge and experience. The firm brings both consulting experiences and research-based problem solving to assist in developing human resources solutions for diverse organizations. The firm's areas of expertise include diversity and inclusion solutions; organizational assessments and metrics development; talent and performance management, training, and development; and data analysis. The firm has provided services to the Department of Defense, the Defense Equal Opportunity Management Institute, and several Fortune 500 companies. Dr. Kizzy M. Parks is also an Adjunct Professor at Brevard Community College and Walden University. She received her Doctor of Philosophy in Industrial/Organizational Psychology and Master of Science in Industrial Organizational Psychology degrees from the Florida Institute of Technology, and her Bachelor of Arts in Psychology degree from Alfred University. She focuses on research in diversity and inclusion management, work-life balance, and organizational wellness and effectiveness. Her published work includes recent articles in the *Journal of Occupational Health Psychology* and the *Business Journal of Hispanic Research*. She has an edited book titled *Managing Diversity in the Military: The Value of Inclusion in a Culture of Uniformity*. Dr. Parks has facilitated and/or presented her work at numerous professional conferences, a commission meeting, and at organizations such as the American Psychological Association, the Association for Psychological Science, the American Society for Training and Development, the Air National Guard, the Army National Guard, the Florida National Guard, the US Army Reserve, Federally Employed Women, the Military Leadership Diversity Commission, the National Guard Bureau, NASA-Goddard Space Flight Center, the Naval Air Systems Command, the Society for Industrial and Organizational Psychology, and the Southern Management Association. She is a member of the American Psychological Association, the Joint Diversity Executive Council-National Guard Bureau, the Society for Human Resource Management, the Society for Industrial and Organizational Psychology, the Society for Military Psychology, and the Society for Occupational Health Psychology.

Barrie Jo Price, Ed.D, partner in emTech Consulting, Professor, the University of Alabama, Institute for Interactive Technology, College of Human Environmental Sciences, is a Consultant for U.S. Department of State and corporations. She served on the George Lucas Educational Foundation Board, National Board of Professional Teaching Standards, Association for Advancement of International Education, and other groups. She received the 2008 Paul Orr Award for Central America, MAIS Leadership

Award, and was selected for AAIE Hall of Fame. She has co-authored numerous books and chapters and teaches online classes at Alabama, where she was nominated as part of a for the 2010 Blackmon-Moody Outstanding Professor Award.

Patricia F. Sanders is a faculty member at the University of North Alabama where she is an Assistant Professor in Communications. She teaches in the areas of Radio-TV-Electronic Media and Broadcast Journalism. Her research interests include women and minorities in media, radio broadcasting and multimedia, in particular its impact on traditional and contemporary journalism. Prior to her work in higher education, Dr. Sanders worked in commercial radio news for almost 20 years, including being a news director, and in the public radio sector as a network bureau director and anchor for 10 years. Dr. Sanders has also won numerous awards for her journalistic work. She is very active in her campus community and also does public speaking and professional voice-over work. Dr. Sanders obtained her Bachelor's and Master's degrees from the University of North Alabama and her Ph.D. in Communication from Regent University. Her personal interests include community volunteerism, traveling, reading, writing, and meeting new people. She is married to Lintord Sanders. They have two children, Patrick and Erica, both engineers in the oil/petroleum industry.

Lyman M. Smith, Captain, CHC, USN, Retired, is a PhD candidate (ABD) at the University of Florida. His principle area of study is religion and politics, and he is currently pursuing research on the influence of religious institutions on DOD policy regarding homosexual service in the military. Chaplain Smith served as a Navy chaplain for 23 years. He is an ordained minister of the Presbyterian Church (USA). In addition to his current academic pursuit, Chaplain Smith also holds degrees in strategy and national security studies, divinity, religious education, public administration, and civil engineering.

RaShaunda V. Sterling, is a Department Chair and a Professor of Developmental Writing at San Jacinto College in Houston, Texas. She received her Doctorate in Instructional Design and Development from the University of South Alabama, her Master's degree in Curriculum and Instruction from Baylor University, and her Bachelor's degree in English from Prairie View A&M University. She has worked as an English Professor for nearly a decade. In addition to teaching, Dr. Sterling is also an Instructional Designer. Her primary research interests include developmental education, technology integration, and metacognitive strategy instruction to enhance teaching and learning.

Alvin J. Williams is Distinguished Professor of Marketing, Mitchell College of Business, University of South Alabama. Prior to this time, he was Interim Dean, College of Business, and Professor of Marketing, University of Southern Mississippi, Hattiesburg, where he worked from 1980-2008. Williams served as Department Chair from 1988-2005. He is past President and Co-Chair of the Board of Governors, Society for Marketing Advances, and past Editor of the *Journal of Supply Chain Management.* Williams has conducted over 350 presentations and seminars for supply management and marketing professionals in the USA, Europe, South Africa, India, and China. He has published in various academic and professional journals in marketing and supply management. He has twice been awarded outstanding teaching award. Williams earned a BS degree at the University of Southern Mississippi, MA degree from the University of Alabama, and a Ph.D. from the University of Arkansas.

James Williams has served Prairie View A&M University since 2001, first as a Developmental Mathematics Instructor and more recently as an Instructor of Principles of Effective Learning (Learning Frameworks Course). He has worked as a GED instructor at Houston Community College and an Adjunct Developmental Mathematics Instructor at Lone Star College – CyFair. He has conducted workshops on student success program enhancements, curriculum design and revision, and best practices for Developmental Mathematics Instruction. He is passionate about embedding an interactive learning structure for student success and excellence at every level of the institution. Mr. Williams holds a M.Ed. in Curriculum and Instruction and a B.S. in Interdisciplinary Studies, and he is currently pursuing his Doctorate in Educational Leadership.

Index

U

usage access divide 52

V

virtual collaboration tools 136, 138, 146
Virtual Learning Environment (VLE) 42
Voice-Over-Internet Protocol (VOIP) 136
Vygotskian idea 198
Vygotsky's theory 198, 207

W

Web 2.0 tools 209, 223
workforce demographics 122
workforce inclusion 140

Z

Zone of Proximal Development (ZPD) 198